The Shore Whalers of Western Australia

Historical Archaeology of a Maritime Frontier

Martin Gibbs

Studies in Australasian Historical Archaeology
Volume 2

Australasian Society for Historical Archaeology

SYDNEY UNIVERSITY PRESS

Published 2010 by SYDNEY UNIVERSITY PRESS
University of Sydney Library
sydney.edu.au/sup
In association with the Australasian Society for Historical Archaeology

© Martin Gibbs 2010
© Sydney University Press 2010

Reproduction and Communication for other purposes

Except as permitted under the Act, no part of this edition may be reproduced, stored in a retrieval system, or communicated in any form or by any means without prior written permission. All requests for reproduction or communication should be made to Sydney University Press at the address below:

Sydney University Press, Fisher Library F03, University of Sydney
NSW 2006 AUSTRALIA

Email: sup.info@sydney.edu.au

National Library of Australia Cataloguing-in-Publication entry
Author: Gibbs, Martin, 1966-
Title: The shore whalers of Western Australia : historical archaeology of a maritime frontier / by Martin Gibbs.
ISBN: 9781920899622 (pbk.)
Series: Studies in Australasian historical archaeology ; v.2.
Notes: Interim CIP record (NLApp11633)
Includes bibliographical references.
Subjects: Offshore whaling--Western Australia--History.
Whaling--Western Australia--History.
Navigation--History--19th century.
Western Australia--Antiquities.
Dewey Number:
639.2809941

Australasian Society for Historical Archaeology Editorial Board

Dr Eleanor Casella, Senior Lecturer, University of Manchester, United Kingdom.
Dr Sarah Colley, Senior Lecturer, University of Sydney, Sydney, New South Wales.
Emeritus Professor Graham Connah, Australian National University.
Dr Clayton Fredericksen, Heritage Division, Dept of the Environment & Water Resources, Canberra, ACT.
Dr Susan Lawrence, Senior Lecturer, Latrobe University, Melbourne, Victoria.
Professor Tim Murray, Latrobe University, Melbourne, Victoria.
Dr Neville Ritchie, Waikato Conservancy, Dept of Conservation, Hamilton, New Zealand.
Dr Martin Gibbs, Senior Lecturer, University of Sydney, Sydney, New South Wales.

General Editor

Dr Mary Casey

Monograph Editors

Dr Martin Gibbs
Dr Peter Davies

Volume Editor

Dr Peter Davies

Cover Illustration

William Duke (1815-1853) '*The Rounding*'. Published by R.V. Hood, Hobart, 1848. Reproduced by permission of the W L Crowther Library, Tasmanian Archive and Heritage Office.
*Note – In the absence of any historical images of Western Australian shore whaling, this contemporary Tasmanian drawing presents a scene which would have been almost identical to those seen on the southwest coast.

CONTENTS

CONTENTS iii
ABOUT THE SERIES v
FOREWORD v
ACKNOWLEDGEMENTS vi

CHAPTER 1 INTRODUCTION 1
    RESEARCH OBJECTIVES 2
        Maritime Industrial Frontiers 2
        Whaling in the 19th Century 4
    DOCUMENTARY RESEARCH 6
        Whaling station records 6
        Government records 6
        Newspaper reports 7
        Personal records 7
        Maps, plans and images 7
        Memoirs and oral histories 8
        Previous Archaeological Research 8
    CONCLUSION 8
    HISTORICAL WEIGHTS & MEASURES 9

CHAPTER 2 HISTORY OF SHORE WHALING 10
        Pre–settlement (1616–1826) 11
        Early Settlement (1826–1842) 11
        Consolidation (1843–1869) 21
        Decline (1870–1879) 25
    ABORIGINAL WHALERS 27
        Nyungar Traditional Life 27
        Contact with Whalers and Whaling 27
        Aboriginal Whalers 28
        Whaling and Aboriginal Spiritual Life 30
        Whaling in Aboriginal Performance 30
        Whaling as Opportunity 31

CHAPTER 3 PROCESS AND PRODUCTION 32
    EMPLOYMENT CONDITIONS 32
        Employment Structure and Payment
        systems 32
        Worker Experience and Involvement
        Patterns 33
        Ethnicity 36
        Development of Labour Legislation 36
        Development of Labour Legislation 37
        Ownership and Management 37
    WHALING PARTIES & STATIONS 38
        Number and Size of Whaling Parties 38
        Number of Workers 40
        Whaling Stations 41
    WHALING TECHNOLOGY 42
        Equipment supply 42
        Diffusion of Technology 44
        Local Manufacture 44
    PRODUCTION AND EFFICIENCY 45
        The Whaling Season 45
        Catch efficiency 46
        Species of catch and catch strategy 47

**CHAPTER 4 LOCATION AND
          ORGANISATION** 55
    SITE SELECTION 55
        Lease Agreements 60
    ARCHAEOLOGICAL SURVEY 61
        Environmental background 61
        Archaeological Survey 61
        Location - Bays and Headlands 62
        Look–outs 62
        Flensing areas 64
        Carcass Disposal 64
        Processing Area and Tryworks 65
        Oil Storage 67
        Boat ramps & launching areas 67
        Whalecraft storage and work areas 67
        Barracks and Domestic Buildings 67
        Other Structures 68
        Water Supply 68
        Gardens 69
        Burials 69
        Aboriginal Sites 69
    DISCUSSION 69

**CHAPTER 5 EXCAVATION OF CHEYNE
          BEACH** 71
    SITE DESCRIPTION 71
        Environment 71
    EXCAVATION METHOD 73
    STRATIGRAPHY 74
        Structure One 74
        Structure Two 76
        Midden Area 76
        Summary of Stratigraphic Units 77
    BUILDINGS AND STRUCTURES 77

CHAPTER 6 ARTEFACT ANALYSIS 80
    HOUSEHOLD/STRUCTURAL 80
        Architectural/Construction artefacts 80
        Hardware 82
        Furnishings/Accessories 82
        Distributions in the Structural Category ... 82
    FOODWAYS 83
        Procurement 83
        Preparation 84
        Service 84
        Storage 87
        Distribution of ceramic and glass vessels .. 89
        Faunal Remains 89
        Distributions in the Foodways Category ... 95
    CLOTHING 96
        Fasteners 96
        Manufacture 97
        Other 97
        Distribution in the Clothing Category 97

PERSONAL 98
    Medicinal and Toiletries 98
    Cosmetic 99
    Recreational 99
    Monetary 100
    Decorative - jewelry, hairpins, hatpins.... 101
    Other 101
LABOUR 102
    Whalecraft and Boating equipment 102
ABORIGINAL ARTEFACTS 102
ARTEFACT DISTRIBUTION 102

CHAPTER 7 LIFE AT CHEYNE BEACH 104
THE ALBANY SETTLEMENT 104
    Cheyne Beach 105
INTERPRETATION OF THE
ARCHAEOLOGICAL EVIDENCE 106
    Domestic Life 107
    Import Patterns and Local Manufacture .. 112
    Aboriginal Contact 113
CONCLUSIONS 113

**CHAPTER 8 LIFE ON THE MARITIME
               INDUSTRIAL FRONTIER 115**
THE MARITIME INDUSTRIAL
FRONTIER 116
    Whaling as Industrial Process 118
    Life on the Maritime Frontier 120
CONCLUSIONS 121
ADDENDA 122

**APPENDIX A SITE HISTORIES AND
               SURVEYS 123**
    Survey Method 123
NORTHWEST COAST 123
    Malus Island 123
LOWER WEST COAST 124
    Marmion/Sorrento 126

    North Fremantle 127
    Bathers Bay / Fremantle 127
    Carnac Island 129
    Rottnest Island 129
    Safety Bay 130
    Bunbury Whaling Station 130
    Mininup 131
    Toby Inlet 132
    Castle Rock 133
SOUTH COAST 134
    Torbay/ Migo Island 134
    Barker Bay/ Whaling Cove 135
    Two Peoples Bay 137
    Cheyne Beach 138
    Cape Riche 139
    Doubtful Island Bay 140
EAST COAST 141
    Middle Island 141
    Barrier Anchorage 142
    Thomas's Fishery 143
ADDITIONAL SITES 143
    Colonial Stations 143
    Single–Use sites 144
    Foreign shore stations 144
    Sealers Camps 145

APPENDIX B HISTORICAL DATA 146
B.1 Whaling Stations and Owners 146
B.2 Whaling parties, boats, whalers. 148
B.3 Biographical and Ownership Data 149
B.4 Reported Oil and Bone Production 150
B.5 Exports of oil and bone, ... 151
B.6 Destinations of Oil and Bone Exports 152
B.7 Cheyne Beach and Castle Rock, ... 153
B.8 Oil yields from individual whales 153

BIBLIOGRAPHY 154

ABOUT THE SERIES

The *Studies in Australasian Historical Archaeology* series is designed to make the results of high–quality research in historical archaeology available to archaeologists, other researchers, students and the public. A particular aim of the series is to ensure that the data from these studies are also made available, either within the volumes or in associated websites, to facilitate opportunities for inter–site comparison and critical evaluation of analytical methods and interpretations. Future releases in the series will include edited and revised versions of Australasian higher–degree theses, major pieces of consultancy and academic research, and commissioned studies on other topics of interest.

FOREWORD

This monograph has been a long time coming, but it has benefited significantly from the intellectual distance Martin has been able to put between himself and the PhD dissertation on which the present volume is based. Thankfully he has also translated it from "thesis–ese", which he may not have done so thoroughly had he rushed into print right after gaining his doctorate. The result of his rumination and editing is a scholarly but highly readable treatise on a fascinating aspect of colonial history.

Martin set himself a ambitious task when he began this project. After working through a variety of trials and tribulations of the sort familiar to many doctoral candidates, he focussed his attention on Cheyne Beach and what was a small but very nicely–formed shore whaling site nestled in the dunes about 50 km northeast of Albany in the far southwest of the continent. I visited the site while Martin and his crew were excavating, and was struck not only by the quality of the site and Martin's work on it, but also the stark beauty of the wider location. The many tiger snakes that infested the place just made it all the more, um…interesting to be there. Although Cheyne Beach seems atypical in some ways, being associated with a domestic residence in a way other shore whaling stations weren't, Martin's careful attention to the global historical context of the Australian whaling industry and his detailed analysis of the varied artefacts he recovered has allowed him to fit the site firmly into the greater scheme of things at the time.

It is this last that I find most astonishing. Here was a place that was at the utter ends of the earth when it was in use, but which saw its occupants steadfastly maintaining their connections with the wider world, and Britain in particular, when we might have expected them to adapt much more to local conditions, given the effort it must have taken to "remain respectable". Martin is not the first to reveal such behaviours on colonial frontiers, but his lucid exposition of this particular case adds usefully to our understanding of how ordinary people manage in the trying circumstances into which they can be thrust by the dynamics of world affairs. That the site of their labours and his is now largely gone is a poignant reminder of why we do what we do as archaeologists.

Prof. IAN LILLEY
Aboriginal and Torres Strait Islander Studies Unit
The University of Queensland

ACKNOWLEDGEMENTS

This volume is dedicated to my wife Melissa for indulging me while I finally got this whale off my back, and to my parents John and Rosemary Gibbs and my siblings Steve, Russ, Jenni and their partners and children for ensuring my survival the first time around.

For their intellectual and/or practical support and encouragement in the revision into this current volume I would particularly like to thank David Roe, Rodney Harrison, Brad Duncan, Kathryn Przywolnik, Shane Burke, Annie Clarke, Sarah Colley, Mary Casey, Denis Gojak, Eleanor Casella, Judy Birmingham, Susan Lawrence and Peter Davies who also proof read the volume.

I will not repeat the original acknowledgements in full, in part because of their size, but also because this was the only part of the original dissertation which attracted the ire of the examiners. In retrospect I might have been a bit more formal and restrained in my fulsome explanations of peoples' contributions, although it still seems to me that in the marathon that is a PhD there isn't necessarily a huge gap between the intellectual and personal wellbeing of the student. That said, this time for the sake of brevity I will simply list them.

Previous researchers: The late Ian Heppingstone of the Royal Western Australian Historical Society and National Trust of Australia (W.A.) who wrote the original history of shore whaling in Western Australia was kind enough to discuss his work several times. Dr Michael Pearson and Mr Jack MacIlroy also generously discussed their previous archaeological research on the whaling sites of Western Australia and Mr MacIlroy also kindly provided permission to use his site plan of the Bathers Beach tryworks excavation.

Supervisors: Thanks to Prof. Sandra Bowdler (who did two stints separated by 6 years), Prof. Ian Lilley and Dr David Bulbeck for their advice and support before, during and after the process.

Field and laboratory assistants: Special thanks to Donald Lantzke who was my main assistant for most of my fieldwork and Fiona, Conner and Mark Bush for undertaking the huge task of sorting the ceramics. My apologies to anyone I have forgotten:

Ryan Hovingh	Kevin Edwards
Robin Stevens	Wendy Bradshaw
Angela Murphy	Darren Cooper
Lynley Wallis	Jemma Pope
Ben Zuvella	Carol Prince
Ursula Frederick	Sarah Grimes
Veronica Carr	Natasha Mutch
Robin Gregory	Karyn McCloud
Julie Cooper	Cathy Morgan
Sally Stewart	Lyle Palmer
Sam Sweeney	Theo Amesz
Mark Waiters	Lewis Adie
Nicky Martin	Nikky Lewis

and UWA students Emma, Justine, Jenny, Kerri, Graeme and Rachel (whose surnames I neglected to record).

Fellow postgraduate students and colleagues: (Centre for Archaeology, University of Western Australia) for sharing the experience in what was sometimes an exciting and eventually a challenging period.

Cathy Stokes	Celmara Pocock
Lynda Strawbridge	Gaye Nayton
Bruce Veitch	Peter Veth
Sue O'Connor	Jenny Smith
Madge Schwede	Kate Morse
Alison Clarke	Elizabeth Bradshaw

Professional colleagues who provided advice or kindly sent copies of documents and sources. I have listed their associations at the time of the original research:
Dr Moya Smith & Alex Baynes (WA Museum)
Dr Mike McCarthy (WA Maritime Museum)
Dr Lenore Layman (Murdoch University)
Denis Gojak (National Parks and Wildlife, NS.W.)
Iain Stuart (Victoria Archaeological Survey)
Dr Peter Bell (Sth Aust. Dept of Environment)
Dr Michael Pearson (Aust. Heritage Commission)
Dr Nigel Prickett (Auckland Institute and Museum)
Mike Nash & Kathy Evans (Tas. Parks and Wildlife)
Justin McCarthy & Diana Coultas (Austral Archaeology)

Funding: I received a three year Australian Postgraduate Award and a small National Estate grant via the National Trust of Australia (WA). The National Trust of Australia (W.A.) and its C.E.O. Tom Perrigo also allowed me study time on the project while in their employ.

Site access: The Shire of Albany kindly permitted me to excavate at Cheyne Beach and Whaling Cove (Barker Bay), while the Dept. of Conservation and Land Management (WA) gave permission to survey several sites under their control.

CHAPTER 1
INTRODUCTION

It would be difficult to claim that the shore–based whaling industry which operated in Western Australia in the 19th century was a commercial success. If later conventional histories are to be believed, the whaling companies established with a flourish on the west and south coasts in the late 1830s lasted only several years into the early 1840s. In that time the industry provided limited financial returns, after which it apparently faded into obscurity with just the occasional hint of inconsequential activity on the economic and geographic margins of the colony. Similarly, for those years when hopes were high the written record of the industry is robust. Once the prospects of whaling being the economic saviour of the colony had receded the documentary evidence diminishes to the blandest and briefest of government and newspaper recordings. Despite this, many coastal communities continued to engage in whaling as an important part of their local seasonal economies, with the industry surviving over 40 years until the late 1870s and possibly beyond.

As with other colonies, later successes with pastoralism, timber and mining washed away both interest in and understanding of the early significance of whaling. In Western Australia particularly, any memory of 19th century shore whaling is overshadowed by its 20th century descendant. With the Cheyne Beach Whaling Company operating near Albany until 1978, popular images of whaling are of motorized chase vessels, explosive harpoons and massive mechanised processing plants processing a catch of hundreds of animals per year. Any notion of the earlier industry is ambiguously associated with sealers, runaway convicts and assorted other ruffians operating at the physical, social and legal edges of European settlement.

This volume explores the historical and archaeological evidence of the 19th century shore whalers of Western Australia. Although it constructs a narrative of the history of the fishery and its operations, the central concern is to understand the processes by which the industry and its participants progressively transformed to meet and survive the changing economic, social, technological and environmental conditions. It considers the social aspects of the participants in whaling and those living on the margins of European settlement, as well as cross–cultural contacts within the context of whaling. In this respect it addresses a broader concern with the nature of adaptation by the non–Aboriginal colonists of Western Australia.

During the 1980s and early 1990s when this research was originally undertaken a broad reconsideration was being made of the role of whaling and other early maritime industries in the economic and social development of colonial Australia. This combined with a renewed interest in cross–cultural 'contact'. The coastal zone plays a critical role in such studies as the area where incoming groups first experience and respond to new terrestrial environments and where initial encounters between cultural groups are most likely to take place. Colonization, or invasion from the perspective of indigenous inhabitants, generally proceeded fastest along the coastal margins with their more familiar resources and easier transport by boat or ship. In contrast, infiltration into the interior progressed at a much slower rate and demanded a much greater degree of engagement, if not understanding, of the new environments encountered.

In many instances the official attempts to formally explore, claim lands or establish colonies along these coastal fringes were preceded by years or even decades of visitation, activity and sometimes settlement by persons and groups engaged in harvesting the products of the sea. Whalers, sealers, trepangers, pearlers, fishers and other maritime industries often operated on the geographical frontiers of the European expansion into the Australia–Pacific region, as well as on the fringes of the social and economic systems which drove it.

The potential for archaeology to make significant contributions was obvious, and in this period most States of Australia and New Zealand commenced historical and archaeological studies of whaling. What emerged was a story which contrasted to the traditional image of whalers as marginal men operating in a lawless manner. While this portrayal may on occasion have been close to the truth, the majority of these maritime industrial groups were clearly far more complex entities than previously recognised. They were often communities of men, women and children, frequently multi–racial in nature, and often with complex relationships with local indigenous populations. Grounded in a melange of maritime and other cultural traditions, they seem to have been accepting of cultural difference and practices. The locations of many of these groups on the frontier, away from ready sources of supply, also made them innovators. They were forced to engage with the environment and to adapt or invent technologies and processes which would bring them successful yields and allow them to sell their goods into the World Systems from which they were isolated physically. However, their experiences obviously varied from region to region, suggesting intensive research and comparison is vital for understanding the diversity of life on these maritime industrial frontiers.

This volume is in large part an edited version of the author's PhD dissertation, submitted to the University of Western Australia in 1995 (Gibbs 1996). Much of the core substantive material remains the same, although the discussions have been revised in the light of comparative data which has subsequently emerged from elsewhere in Australasia. In the interests of brevity many of the more detailed discussions of theory, method and artefact identification have been summarised or omitted, especially where those aspects are now commonplace or outdated. Where further detail is available in the original thesis or subsequent publications, the reader will be directed to these.

RESEARCH OBJECTIVES

The research on which volume is based had four major aims by which to explore the whaling industry of Western Australia as an example of settlement and adaptation on a maritime industrial frontier (Gibbs 1998:36).

The first objective was to examine the origin, development and decline of the shore whaling industry in Western Australia, with particular attention towards the internal economic and social factors which both encouraged its establishment and limited its growth. This included investigation of the impact and consequences of uncontrolled American whaling activity in the region. Because of the early period and the remote location of many of the stations, it was also considered important to determine the nature of interactions between Aboriginal people and whalers, including the eventual incorporation of Aboriginal men into the whaling industry.

The second objective was to determine the nature and extent of shore whaling as carried out in Western Australia. The first part of this was to explore the scale of the industry as it changed over time, including the number and size of whaling parties, the composition of the owners and workforce, and the conditions which bound the latter to service. The second part was to investigate infrastructure and techniques, and determine possible responses to local social, economic, environmental or other conditions. This included an analysis of catch strategies, effectiveness and changes in the output and value of oil and bone production and exports.

The third objective was to examine the historical and archaeological evidence for the selection and use of particular locations for whaling, with particular attention to common environmental elements. This included analysing the nature and layout of industrial and domestic components to determine commonalities and variations, as well as evidence of change over time.

The fourth objective was to explore the living and working conditions of the whalers and others who occupied these frontier maritime industrial communities. The first part was to determine how the whalers lived, the circumstances in which they were housed and their diet and material culture. The possibility was held open for comparing assemblages from different groups within the site; the manager, headsmen, boat crews, Aboriginal workers and/or other inhabitants. The second part was to examine the economies of the stations as examples of frontier settlements, considering aspects of supply and how they compared to contemporary urban settlements. Finally, investigation of the social, economic and other relationships with local indigenous communities was also considered a vital part of understanding the nature and impact of whaling activities upon the frontier.

MARITIME INDUSTRIAL FRONTIERS

The concept of the frontier has a long pedigree in historical and archaeological literature, with an equally long critique on its failings or problems (c.f. Russell 2001:1; McCarthy 2008). Despite this, it remains useful as a framework for archaeologists and has been defined as follows:

> First, the frontier is the area in which the outer edge of an expanding society adapts to the conditions of attenuated contact with the homeland and the physical conditions of a new environment. Second, because of the nature of expansion, the frontier is both spatially and temporally impermanent. It is the zone of transition within which the "wilderness" is occupied and "civilised". Third, because the process of colonisation is repetitive in nature, it is also evolutionary in the sense that the sequential change that once occurred in the centre of a newly settled frontier region tends to be repeated along its periphery as settlement within the region expands (Lewis 1977:153).

The frontier is therefore simultaneously a geographical area and a set of processes of colonisation and adaptation (Billington 1967:7). Kirch (1980:125) describes the processes of adaptation when colonizing a new or radically different habitat as 'revolutionary', with selective pressures at their highest and likely to induce the greatest range of variability in a cultural system. These stress situations lead to rapid increases in experimentation and innovation, which might include testing and implementation of 'previously maladaptive or detrimental behaviours' (Kirch 1980:116). These sometimes rapid changes in behaviour are also potentially detectable within the archaeological record through variations in the structure of sites and the activities within, including abandonment.

Although writing about pre–historic contexts, Kirch's (1980) essay on the theoretical and methodological issues in the archaeological study of adaptation provides valuable insights into the processes which might underlie cultural change in historical contexts as well. In this instance the simultaneous access to diverse documentary, oral and archaeological datasets turns the apparent limitations of a 'short' historical period into an opportunity to examine these processes at close range and from multiple perspectives, with access to emic insights into decisions and motivations (Green *et al.* 1985a).

The frontier framework also places the study of individual sites and areas within a wider regional, national and international context. For instance, the European settlement of Australia is often linked to the spread of the capitalist World System. This involved the expansion of western European socio–economic structures into new territories and the incorporation of resources and (as far as possible) the original inhabitants into that network (Wallerstein 1974; Jeans 1988; Peregrine 1990).

Individual sites are therefore viewed as part of the wider socio–cultural system changing to cope with the environment and achieve the aims of its expansion. Both local and regional adaptive strategies should therefore be reflected differentially within the archaeological record. So too should information on the nature of economic core–periphery relationships between the site, local towns or supply points and ultimately the homeland centers of production (Cressey *et al.* 1982; Hall 1990). This meshes with wider discussions of historical archaeology as the study of the emergence of capitalism (Leone and Potter 1988b, Paynter 1988, Little 1994; Johnson 1996; Orser 1996) and the material nature of colonialism (Lawrence and Shepherd 2006:71). It also links with considerations of archaeological approaches to cross–cultural engagements with indigenous peoples, arising as the capitalist system expanded into these new areas (Murray 2004).

A common device in frontier studies has been the characterization of different types of frontier, such as *insular* (agrarian, pastoral), *cosmopolitan* (industrial, camp) and so on under the premise that similarities in the intentions and functions of each settlement type will result in similarities in process (activity) and pattern (observable outcomes) (Green and Perlman 1985b). Following Steffen (1980), Hardesty (1985:213) identifies that unlike other frontiers *industrial frontiers* are specialized in nature, short term in occupancy and have a lack of interest in wider development. Their industrial purpose, usually geared towards extraction of specific resources, means they are closely linked to national and international markets and economies, making them susceptible to external forces.

Regardless of varied natural environments, particular industries also tend to attempt the same adaptive solutions, changing through 'correlated episodes' caused by newer technologies or innovations in technique sweeping through and replacing older forms (Hardesty 1985:215). Site abandonment is usually linked to resource depletion or the financial return on the resource falling below marginal value. However, there may be variations in the nature of operations and site structure, technology uptake, or other adaptive behaviours resulting from diverse factors such as local social and economic circumstances, or ethnic groups applying different cultural traditions, etc.

Frontier types also have a chronological aspect, with different frontiers succeeding one another. In this respect some American historians have specifically identified a *whaling frontier* in the Pacific, pre–dating most missionary and other commercial activities. The American whalers 'operated as the front edge of American expansionism, pushing out the boundaries of US influence' (Weeks 2006:73). Or as another writer put it, their activities expanded the sphere of US social and economic influence and served to 'Americanize' much of the Pacific during the 19th century, in advance of other developments (Gibson & Whitehead 1993: x).

The investigation of adaptation processes, usually in the guise of studies of colonization and technological innovation, has been one of the earliest and most enduring themes for Australasian historical archaeological research. The first PhD in Australian historical archaeology, undertaken by Jim Allen in the 1960s, investigated the failed military settlement at Port Essington and explored the archaeology of life on the frontier, including cross–cultural contact (Allen 2008). From the late 1960s onwards, Birmingham, Jack and Jeans (1979; 1983) recorded the remains of 19th century Australian industrial sites, looking for evidence of transference, adaptation and innovation. The *Swiss Family Robinson* model which emerged from this was an attempt to represent the processes by which industries were established and subsequent shifts occurred (Birmingham and Jeans 1983). This model suggested that initially there is an *exploratory phase* where colonists enter the new environment with their existing socio–economic structures, technologies, skills and material culture. In this period there is reliance upon imported stores of food and equipment while the colonists make a preliminary assessment of the environment and resources and select a possible *production system* (Birmingham and Jeans 1983:6). Next comes a *learning phase,* where the production system is implemented. If unsuccessful, the technologies or processes are either rejected or revised and tried again. If successful, the colonists pass into a *developmental phase*, where 'further operational reinforcements' and refinements are made, influenced by arrivals of new technology, local innovations, changes in the commercial environment, or changes in and/or increased knowledge of the biophysical environment (Birmingham and Jeans 1983:6).

Critics of the *Swiss Family Robinson* framework highlighted its simplistic nature, including the failure to account for the impact of external factors such as decisions by remote administrators and shareholders (Bairstow 1984). Similarly, it was noted that the critical role of Aboriginal people as information and labour sources was overlooked (Egloff 1994). However, other researchers were already engaging with these factors, such as Pearson's (1981) archaeological study of settlement in the Macquarie River region of New South Wales exploring the concept of frontier, environmental perceptions by settlers, continuities with Aboriginal occupations, acclimatization of pastoral practice and the impact of both local and remote decision makers.

Not surprisingly, both the *Swiss Family Robinson* model and Pearson's work aligned with contemporary historical geographical studies of colonization, presenting many of the same elements of environmental perception, information collection, decision–making, experimentation and learning processes. Cameron's (1974a; 1974b; 1977; 1981) research on the European colonization of Western Australia, which is of particular relevance to this volume, also explored the notion that colonization and adaptation processes began before immigrants left England. Intending colonists actively collected information from government and private sources, developed expectations of the natural, social and economic environments they were entering and selected what they felt or had been advised were appropriate supplies and materials (Cameron 1981). These efforts were further influenced or constrained by factors such as the veracity of the information and advice they received and the conditions or restraints imposed by government, sponsors, employers or others who they felt provided authoritative opinions.

More recent studies of the archaeology of colonization have reiterated this relationship between environmental knowledge and perception, cumulative experience or learning and progressive adaptation, although with greater emphasis on the wider landscape perspective consistent with current interests. Rockman (2003:4) defines the three basic forms of information a human group requires about an environment as:
- *locational* (locations and physical characteristics of necessary resources),
- *limitational* (boundaries and costs of resources, such as seasonality availability or variation), and
- *social* (attribution of names, meanings and patterns to natural features and the transformation of environment into a human landscape).

As proposed by earlier writers, these types of knowledge are seen as being in a dynamic feedback loop. Rockman (2003:9) notes how such information contributes to the 'push' factors (conditions encouraging movement to a new environment) versus 'pull' factors (conditions making colonization attractive) in decisions to migrate and colonize, stay or abandon.

Since the 1980s the renewed interest in cross–cultural contact and the nature of colonialism has seen increasing exploration of early encounters and negotiations from both indigenous and non–indigenous perspectives (e.g. Harrison & Williamson 2002; Murray 2004). Many of these studies have considered indigenous participation in relation to frontier settlement and industry (e.g. Harrison 2002; McNiven 2001), addressing earlier concerns over the lack of recognition of indigenous agency.

Writing of the early European presence in Torres Strait and in the context of cross–cultural contact and negotiations, McNiven (2001:178) distinguishes *coastal frontiers* as areas 'where outsiders arrive from the sea and/or inland for permanent settlement along the coast'. In contrast, *maritime frontiers* are where non–indigenous visitors such as whalers, sealers or pearlers set up short–term camps, usually for the singular purpose of exploiting marine resources although this category might also include explorers, shipwreck survivors and others. Maritime industrial sites were generally impermanent although occupation might be repeated on a seasonal basis or continuous over a period of years. McNiven (2001) also raises the significance of beaches as a locale for contact and exchange between cultures (c.f. Dening 1980). These distinctions are of direct relevance to the current study, leading to the use of the term *maritime industrial frontier* to describe the context of the 19th century shore whalers.

WHALING IN THE 19TH CENTURY

By the early 19th century the processes of whaling were part of a well–established international tradition, operating at one of three levels (Little 1969; Chamberlain 1988).

1. *Pelagic or Open sea whaling*: the most expensive but most lucrative form of the industry, employing whaleships of between 150 to 400 tons primarily to follow the global deep–sea migrations of the sperm whale (*Physeter macrocephalus*). Several smaller whaleboats would be launched from each ship to chase and kill whales, with the carcass returned to the larger vessel for processing. These whaleships were self–contained whaling stations, fully equipped to spend three or even four years at sea, resorting to land only to take on supplies of wood, water and fresh food. Pelagic whaling produced most of the whale oil traded in the 19th century.

2. *Bay whaling*: involving whaleships stationed in bays frequented by coastal migrating species such as right whales (*Eubalaena glacialis*) and humpback whales (*Megaptera novaeangliae*). These vessels might work in conjunction with a shore party, but were usually independent, moving out to their prey and often progressively tracing the whale migrations along the coasts. Pelagic whaleships would sometimes alternate their open sea operations by spending several months 'wintering' near shore and carrying out bay whaling.

3. *Shore–based whaling*: the least capital–intensive method, where a station or fishery was established in a bay or inlet, with whaleboats rowing out from shore to intercept coastal migrating whale species. Consequently, the scope of operations was restricted to areas within easy rowing or sailing distance of the fishery and limited to the 4–5 months of the year in which the whales passed by. A slightly more sophisticated version which extended the range of the shore station was to use a small vessel of cutter or schooner size as a launching platform for the boats and to assist in 'cutting–in' the whale (Little 1969:116). However, most of the infrastructure, in particular the living areas and the main industrial component, remained on land and as such is archaeologically detectable.

The processes of Australasian shore–based whaling have been seen as a re–invention (Dakin 1933) or 're–introduction of an ancient whaling technique' (Pearson 1983:40), exhibiting continuity from Basque operations of the 13th century or earlier. The establishment of shore stations in Australasia may well have come from persons familiar with existing shore–based traditions in Britain, America or elsewhere, although it is possible that it occurred through the medium of pelagic whaling, adapting the techniques used aboard ship. The relationship between shore–based and ship–based whaling is obvious from the shared pool of equipment, techniques and terminology, while as this study will show there was obviously a flow of workers between the different forms of whaling. The general industrial processes involved in shore whaling in Australasia have been described in detail by a variety of writers (Dakin 1938; Colwell 1969; Morton 1982; Nash 2003; Pearson 1983), although the following summary is provided as background to the historical discussion and to introduce relevant terminology.

Migrating humpback and right whale populations pass along the Australian coasts between June and November. Prior to their appearance a suitable site along the migration route would be selected at which to establish the *station* or *fishery*. Industrial and domestic facilities were constructed or refurbished, whaleboats and whaling equipment (referred to as *whalecraft*) purchased or serviced and oil casks coopered so that the station could commence operation immediately upon sighting whales. The crews might also engage in boat races to bring them up to the necessary peak of fitness. A look-out was maintained on a nearby headland or vantage point, watching for signs of the migrating whales and signaling sightings by voice, horn, flags or other means. Once alerted the whaleboats were launched, or alternatively might already be cruising adjacent waters in readiness, hoping to gain some advantage in time.

Whaleboats were 28–30 feet (8.5–9 m) long, double ended with a six foot (1.8 m) beam, shallow draft, weighing only 1000 pounds (454 kg) to increase speed and manoeuvrability and steered by a long sweep oar (Mawer 1999:240). Each boat was stocked with an assortment of equipment including several hundred fathoms of tarred 2 inch (5 cm) hemp line coiled into tubs, harpoons, lances, water kegs, food, buckets, oars, sails and other paraphernalia. The six man crew would row or sail out to the whales as quietly as possible so that the animals would not be startled into flight. The *harpooner* (also known as the *boat–steerer*) would initially work one of the front oars, while the *headsman* who was in charge of the vessel worked the steering oar. The oarsmen were referred to as *pulling hands*.

Once the boat was close to the whale, the harpooner would stand, take up the *iron* (harpoon) and throw or preferably stab (*place*) it into the whale, fixing a line between whale and boat. Because it was crucial to remain secured to the whale, many variations to the barbed harpoon head were designed. By the 1850s gun–harpoons had also come into use as a means of launching irons, despite the difficulties of use on the small boats.

If struck, the whale would normally attempt to flee by swimming away or sounding (diving), often pulling the whaleboat in its wake in what was referred to as the Nantucket sleigh ride. At this point the harpooner and headsman swapped places, with the latter taking up the steering oar to become the boat steerer, and the former moving into the bow to ready the lance. Despite the risk and seeming lack of logic to this awkward manoeuvre, it is well recorded in many accounts, including in *Moby Dick* (Melville 1851: Chapter 62).

Buckets or wooden boards called *drogues* were attached to the line to increase the drag and tire the whale sooner, although on occasion the boats were pulled for hours and many miles out to sea. Once exhausted the whale would surface and the crew would row or pull on the line to draw the whaleboat close. The headsman would then use the long killing *lance* to stab and probe within the whale's body, hoping to puncture the heart, vital organs or arteries. There are a number of references to whales 'spouting blood' prior to their final demise, which could take several hours or more. At any point during this procedure the line might break or run to its full extent, the iron *pull* from the blubber, or the whale turn and smash the boat and occupants. If so, the second or third (*pick–up*) boats of the same party would move in with their own harpoons and again attempt to secure the prize. There were also rules that governed when other whaling parties might take their own opportunity to chase the whale (Mawer 1999:97).

After the whale was dead, the flukes were cut away to reduce drag and lines attached from the whale to one or more boats for the long haul home. For pelagic or bay whalers the ship could move into position, but for shore whalers the return to the fishery could take all day and extend far into the night, with the crew attempting to guide themselves back by means of landmarks or beacons. In extreme conditions the whale was cut free and an attempt made to retrieve it the next day. On other occasions the whale might sink, although after a few days the gases from decomposition would raise it again, as long as sharks, killer whales or other predators had not consumed it.

The whale carcass was eventually brought into the waters near the fishery and secured by ropes and chains adjacent to a granite shelf, jetty or a floating deck known as a *stage*. The whale was then *cut–in* or *flensed* by the crew, standing on the body or an adjacent platform and using razor sharp blades on poles known as *flensing knives* or *spades* to slice the blubber away from the body. Ten by one foot (3 x 1 m) strips of blubber known as *blanket pieces* were peeled from the whale by a strong rope passing over a set of upright shearlegs and connected to a large winch or capstan fixed on shore and turned by half a dozen men. The blanket pieces would be further reduced into approximately 15 inch by four inch (37 x 10 cm) *horse pieces* and then minced on a table (horse) into *sliver pieces, bible leaves* or *books*. A mechanical cutter could also be used at this stage. Prickett (2002:11) suggests that in New Zealand the person in charge of the flensing was known as the *tonguer* and was paid in part for his duties with the tongue oil. It is unclear if this usage also applied to Australian stations.

The process of extracting the oil from the blubber was known as *trying–out*:

> The sliver pieces were thrown into a large iron cauldron called a 'trypot', set up in a brickwork furnace, and there the blubber was heated and stirred until all the oil had been removed, at which time the solid blubber residue [*scrap*] was scooped off and used to feed the furnace fire, while the oil was bailed out, usually into large copper coolers. Once cool the oil could then be casked up for storage or shipment to market (Pearson 1983:41).

The furnace into which the trypots were built was called a *tryworks*, normally situated not far above the high tide mark to reduce the distance which the blubber had to be carried or hauled. Tryworks were often roofed over to protect the oil from rain. The filled oil barrels would be stored away from the tryworks and in such a way as to prevent shrinkage resulting in loss of oil.

Several other parts of the whale were also utilized, especially the baleen referred to as *whalebone* (or simply *bone*) from the mouths of the humpback and right whales, and the *ambergris* from sperm whales (Cousteau and Paccalet 1986). The use of whale products will be discussed in more detail below. Once stripped of all usable elements the remains of the whale carcass would be discarded, presumably by towing the remains back out into the ocean, or at least away from the station, and allowing them to sink.

A final important aspect common to all forms of 19th century whaling was the method of payment for workers, usually referred to as a *lay*. This was a fixed percentage share of the total catch value, determined at the commencement of the season or cruise and based upon the individual's experience and position in the whaling party. Payment therefore depended directly upon the success of the whaling party.

DOCUMENTARY AND ARCHAEOLOGICAL RESEARCH

Prior to this study a brief outline of the history of shore whaling in Western Australia had already been written by Heppingstone (1966), with further site specific information available in the 1987 National Trust survey of whaling sites (MacIlroy 1987). While this material was a valuable starting point, a comprehensive re-investigation of the original sources was necessary. It soon became obvious that contemporary references to whaling were thinly spread through a wide range of published and unpublished government and unofficial sources. It was also clear that the range of information likely to be provided by these documentary sources was extremely limited and that archaeological research would play a vital role in providing data about the operation of whaling in Western Australia. Because of this situation, the nature of the major documentary and other non-archaeological sources utilized within this project is described below and some of the organizational behaviours inherent in their origins and uses are considered (Potter 1992:92; Wilkie 2006).

Whaling station records

Other than several brief and relatively uninformative letters, only one major document originating from a whaling station was located during this study. This journal, written by William Frederick Seymour (a.k.a. Frederick William Palmer) the manager and headsman of the Castle Rock Whaling Company, covers the years 1846–50 and 1852–53 (BL 2838A). The types of information recorded suggest that the journal was a record for, or the basis for a report to, the absentee owners of the station. In most instances it documents the major activities and production during each 24 hour period, or disruptions to the same. It records in brief entries any whale sightings, chases, strikes, kills and the times taken for processing. Maintenance activities such as boat repairs and coopering are noted, as are some domestic arrangements including the killing of bullocks for food. On several occasions problems with the men are reported. There are also margin notes which appear in some cases to be station accounts, although these consist of brief jottings, rather than comprehensive budgets. A copy of the 1850 crew agreement for Castle Rock station also survives (BL MN470).

A second document is the ledger of Albany Merchant Thomas Brooker Sherratt, relating to the establishment and costs of his 1836 Doubtful Island Bay station (Sherratt 1836). Although less coherent than the Seymour diary, the ledger provides insights into the financial arrangements behind establishing and supplying the first Western Australian whaling station.

The almost complete absence of documents from other whaling stations may be the result of a variety of factors, including the destruction of what may have been a limited body of material to begin with, or widespread illiteracy of workers and even managers. It may also be the result of the limited scale of the industry not requiring or generating an appreciable number of records or encouraging their survival.

Government Records

Government functions in the Western Australian colonies were centralized under the Colonial Secretary's Office (CSO) in Perth. Until the 1850s the different administrative duties such as Government Surveyor, Harbour Master, etc, were often performed by individuals or very small groups. Because of minimal staff and the distance between settlements, minor or routine affairs in each region were handled by the Resident Magistrate (Government Resident), who was normally a wealthy settler appointed by the Governor. For matters beyond the Resident's capacity or authority a letter would be sent, usually with any original correspondence from the settlers, to Perth for opinion or direction. Responses were then returned, with copies held by the CSO.

Correspondence relating to whaling can be grouped into two main subjects; requests for the lease of land on which to operate a whaling station, and complaints about foreign intrusions upon local whaling parties. In the former instance these documents range from descriptions of the area required, to negotiations about the fees (see Chapter Four). It is probable that a larger body of mundane matters associated with whaling were simply dealt with by the Resident Magistrate at a local level without records being preserved. The most serious matters might require correspondence with the Colonial Office, Admiralty or other authorities in Britain, leading to further records in other series.

There are several problems associated with using the CSO records. As whaling was not treated as a distinct industry or subheading in the records, the relevant documents are spread under a large number of regional, subject and individual settler correspondence categories, with some eccentricities in original and current organization of records. Consequently, there is the possibility that further documents will emerge, especially those concerning specific stations.

Two other bodies of government records provided useful information. The first is the Blue Books (BB), the annual statistical report of the colony submitted to the Colonial Office in England. The 'Fisheries' section recorded in varying detail the returns of the whaling stations, normally consisting of the total oil and bone taken in each region, and the estimated value. Sometimes the number of whales caught and the number of whaleboats in each area was also recorded, although in other instances some or all of the regions would be grouped together into a single total. Blue Book reports occasionally omit returns from more distant stations, or show figures which appear inconsistent with other contemporary reports. In the latter case it may be that oil was sold directly from the stations including illegally to foreign whalers, before the final declaration was made.

The Blue Books also include export records for the colony, which also vary in detail between years. Sometimes a full report is made exports of oil and bone from the ports of Fremantle and Albany including the destinations of these items. However, sometimes returns are incomplete, are combined between ports and across years, or are completely omitted.

The second body of official reports is the *Government Gazette* (GG) which recorded government notices and after 1847 included listings of whaleboat crews registered with particular parties under the *Ordinance to provide a summary remedy for Breach of Contracts connected with the fisheries of the Colony* (*Statutes of Western Australia*, 10 Victoria, No.16, 1847). This statute provided means for the owners or managers to severely prosecute any crewman deserting during the season, and while not all parties consistently registered under it, the lists in the Government Gazette provide one of the few insights into the employment histories on men in the industry.

Newspaper reports

Contemporary newspapers provide the main sources of historical information; in particular the government–run *Perth Gazette* (PG) and the privately owned *Inquirer* (Inq). Reports on whaling activity were frequent until the late 1840s, possibly as a result of a shortage of other reportable news. In this period the editors of the pro–government *Perth Gazette* and the blatantly anti–establishment *Inquirer* took opposing stands on many matters. This often appeared as the former publication 'boosting' the doings and prospects of the settlement, and the latter published several days later impugning the original reports or exposing (with varying levels of objectivity) misconduct on the part of the government and major settlers. This provides interesting contrasts and perspectives on the progress of the industry and its role in the local economy.

As the settlements spread along the west coast and the contribution of whaling to the local export market diminished, the level of reporting dropped. Items on whaling became shorter and limited to a 'filler' role, except in the case of exceptional events such as conflicts with foreign whalers or reports on a good season's catch. As all the journals produced during the study period originated from the Swan River colony, reports from the distant settlements, particularly Albany and the other south coast areas, were often scant and in many cases second hand.

All issues of the *Perth Gazette* released (weekly) from 1833 to 1865 were reviewed, with the following 15 years until 1880 being sampled. Similarly, all editions of the *Inquirer* were read from 1842 to 1874 and then selectively to 1880. Other shorter–lived papers both pre–dating and contemporary with these journals were also read.

Personal records and contemporary commentaries

Very few individuals – owners, managers, or participants in whaling on either coast – appear to have left records of any kind in either local or State archives. However, several contemporary diarists (e.g. Moore 1884; Wollaston 1991) refer to whaling activity, as do several visitors to the colony, including whalers (e.g. Whitecar 1860; Gatchell 1844; Haley 1948). There are also various promotional pamphlets, settler guides and commentaries on the Western Australian settlements which various described, encouraged or criticized whaling efforts (e.g. Ogle 1839; Anon 1842; Anon 1843; Knight 1870; Andrews n.d.).

Maps, plans and images

One of the most surprising aspects of the historical research was the almost complete absence of maps, plans or images (photographic or artistic) of shore whaling stations in Western Australia. The only exception to this is the Bathers Beach station. Due to its proximity to Fremantle the site has various surveys and plans which show buildings and major features, as well as several drawn and photographic images from the period after its closure (Reece and Pascoe 1983:36; MacIlroy 1986). However, as will be shown, in many respects this station was atypical of sites elsewhere in the colony.

The simplest explanation to account for these omissions is the isolated situation of most of the whaling stations. The Survey Department of Western Australia was a very small group responsible for mapping an area of 2,525,500 km^2. The continual opening of new regions ensured that except for location boundaries and some town surveys, only major landscape features were initially plotted. The whaling stations were only seasonal fishing camps on annual leases and therefore not of great concern in the recording process. In most instances only one survey, if any, passed through a region during the period the industry was active. In some instances current maps do have indicative names (e.g. Whaling Cove in Barker Bay, Whalebone Point in Doubtful Island Bay, Whalers Bay at Malus Island), although their dates of origin are unknown. There are a greater number of 'whale' place–names which have no apparent association with the 19th century industry. The absence of artwork is harder to explain, although it may be that local artists did not find whaling a suitable subject or simply that there were no artists living or working near any of the stations.

Memoirs and oral histories

During the early 20th century and particularly at the time of the Western Australian centenary in 1929 memoirs of 'pioneers' were published in various newspapers. Several recalled participating in or observing whaling activities, especially on the south coast (Chester 1924; McKail 1927; Mitchell 1927; Keyser 1929; Sale 1936). It is in this collection that the handful of anecdotal or oral accounts about the Western Australian whaling stations and their workers are recorded.

During the project a number of long–term residents of areas near whaling sites, particularly retired fishermen and mariners on the south coast, were interviewed to determine whether a body of information relating to the 19th century whaling still survived. In many instances knowledge of the early whalers has been obscured by the subsequent episodes of mechanized whaling after 1912. However, several persons were aware that certain bays or locations were used shore whalers and in some instances specific archaeological features were identified. These features often turned out to be associated with early 20th century salmon fishing camps, although thanks to the same need for a sheltered bay, in several instances these features were indeed established on or near the sites of the earlier whaling stations.

The information collected from Charles 'Snapper' Westerberg at Cheyne Beach turned out to be extraordinary as the only instance where the informant was aware of the location and significance of the whaling station and was also able to provide several small items of anecdotal oral information. Mr. Westerberg, a descendant of an early fishing family, had originally been shown the site as a child in the 1920s and even without visible surface evidence was able to show the 1987 National Trust survey the location of at least of one of the whaling station structures (MacIlroy 1987).

Previous Archaeological Surveys and Excavations

During the late 1970s and 1980s several archaeological surveys recorded the remains of 19th century whaling activity in the Dampier Archipelago (MacIlroy 1979), Fremantle region (Pearson 1984; MacIlroy 1986) and Cape Arid–Middle Island area (Pearson 1988). In the face of new urban development encroaching upon coastal areas, the National Trust of Australia (W.A.) commissioned MacIlroy (1987) to locate and assess the significance of surviving sites, based on historical research undertaken by Trust member Ian Heppingstone. MacIlroy also subsequently undertook excavations at the Bathers Beach (Fremantle) station prior to a proposed development (MacIlroy 1986).

Subsequent to the original dissertation research further historical and archaeological research has been undertaken of whaling sites in the Albany region (Wolfe 1994; 2003). A further survey has also been made of features at Port Gregory newly exposed by storm action and erosion of shorefront dunes (Rodrigues and Anderson 2006).

CONCLUSION

One of the abiding concerns of historical archaeology continues to be the relationships between the documentary, archaeological and other data sets including oral history. This is less to reassure ourselves of the validity of archaeological research in periods where these other data sources are available than to ensure that we remain focused on investigating the ambiguities between them (Deetz 1977; Schuyler 1977; Deagan 1982; Beaudry *et al.* 1991:165). The preceding review is important as it establishes that the documentary record of shore whaling in Western Australia is quite limited in scope, a fact which has important implications for the research design and the significance of the archaeological research. This historical information can all be placed into three major categories.

1. Reports of major events and trends,
2. Records of production and exports,
3. General details of station location, ownership and management.

Consequently, there is a sharp boundary between what can be described by documentary (or non–archaeological) sources and what can only be described through archaeological investigation.

In brief, the main progress of the industry as a component of the Western Australian economy can be charted (Chapter Two). Aspects of the industrial process and the success in production can also be contrasted with what is known for other parts of Australasia (Chapter Three). However, in dealing with individual stations it is only possible to identify their locations broadly, usually to the point of knowing that a certain bay (or sometimes a certain portion of a bay) was used in particular years. With the exception of Bathers Beach (Fremantle), there are no indications of the precise locations of stations, or descriptions of their original organization or character. Aside from several anecdotal accounts and the few notes contained in Seymour's Castle Rock diary, there is no knowledge of the life or conditions on the stations.

In essence, the point at which the historical record is unable to provide any further information is also the boundary at which the archaeological record becomes most effective as a source of insight. This dichotomy in terms of what each data source was able to provide clarified the design of the archaeological component of this study. Three stages were identified.

1. A survey of locations described in the historical record to identify any surviving physical remains of the whaling industry, and to determine the common topographic characteristics in which these sites were situated. From this location model the probable positions of other sites without visible surface expressions could be identified.

2. Recording of structural and artefact evidence at these sites to determine if there were common characteristics in the organization and nature of both industrial and habitation areas.

3. Excavation to investigate the lifeways of the occupants through detailed analysis of structural and artefact evidence.

HISTORICAL WEIGHTS & MEASURES

For the sake of continuity, all quotations retain their archaic, vernacular, or incorrect spellings, although where necessary a modern equivalent is provided. The original non–metric measures cited in the historical sources have also been retained in the text. Metric conversions have been made where appropriate or necessary, particularly in reference to the site survey or excavation and analysis components of the research.

Imperial	Imperial	Metric
Distances		
1 foot =	12 inches =	0.30 m
1 yard =	3 feet =	0.91 m
1 chain =	22 yards =	20.11 m
1 mile =	80 chains	
=	1760 yards =	1.61 km
Area		
1 acre =	4840 sq. yards =	0.40 hectares
Weight		
1 pound =	16 ounces =	453.59 gm
1 stone =	14 pound =	6.35 kg
1 cwt =	112 pound =	50.80 kg
1 ton =	20 cwt	
=	2240 lb =	1016.00 kg
Volume		
1 gallon =	4 quarts =	4.55 litres
1 barrel =	36 gallons =	163.66 litres
1 tun =	7 barrels	
=	252 gallons	= 1146.00 litres

Table 1.1 Non–metric measures referred to in the text.

CHAPTER 2
HISTORY OF SHORE WHALING IN WESTERN AUSTRALIA

The factors that encouraged the British colonies in Australasia to pursue whaling were clearly embedded in social and economic circumstances of the 18th and 19th century (Pearson 1983). The massive changes in technology and demography that formed the industrial revolution had resulted in a vastly expanded market for whale oil, primarily as a lighting fuel in fluid and wax (candle) form, and as a high quality lubricant for machines and precision instruments. In addition, whale oil and waxes were required for a variety of other manufacturing processes such as wool and fiber cloth production, leather treatment and manufacture of toilet soaps and perfumes (Chamberlain 1988). The flexible baleen from the mouths of humpback and right whales had a variety of uses in the manufacture of clothing, furniture and a diversity of other items including springs and umbrella ribs (Cousteau and Paccalet 1986).

The dynamic expansion of whaling through the later part of the 18th century had initially seen French, British, American (and to a lesser extent Dutch and German) pelagic whaling fleets competing in the Atlantic. During the last quarter of the 18th century the British whalers were able to gain supremacy, in the first instance through the crippling of the American whaling fleet as part of the English offensive during the revolution of 1775. This was followed by the 1784 passing of an Act by the British Parliament that placed a massive £18 per tun duty on foreign oil entering England, effectively closing off American access to what was then the major market (Mawer 1999:44). Finally, American whalers and vessels were being encouraged to desert to British ports such as Milford Haven or the French port of Dunkirk.

As a result of this virtual monopoly the British whaling fleet was able to expand rapidly during the late 18th century, although the flourishing international market for sperm oil was such that the Americans were still able to find markets and rebuild their fleet. However, the increasingly over–fished Atlantic waters forced attention towards untried regions and in 1789 the British whaler *Emilia* became the first vessel to round Cape Horn and test the Pacific whaling grounds. As this ship returned with its full cargo of oil, news of the potential of the new grounds was hastily transmitted throughout the industry. This heralded a boom period of several decades, with British, French but particularly American whaling fleets rapidly spreading through the Pacific and Indian oceans (Churchward 1949; Colwell 1969; Mawer 1999).

The origins of whaling in Australasian waters and the development of a colonial industry has already been discussed in some detail by other writers (Morton 1982; Chamberlain 1988) and need only be summarised briefly here. Initial British efforts to penetrate the new whaling grounds were severely hampered by the existing trade monopolies on the Indian and Pacific Oceans, held by the East India Company and to a lesser extent the South Sea Company. These prevented access to the region and curtailed early plans to establish a new southern fishery based in the Australasian colonies. Various concessions and relaxations were made over time to allow whalers into these areas, although it was not until 1819 that all restrictions were lifted (Morton 1982: 121). By this time the American fleet was well established in the Pacific, while the British fleet was edging towards its decline.

Surrounded by the successes of the pelagic whaling fleets and the flourishing oil market, the administrators and major capitalists of the Australasian colonies quickly came to view whaling as a potential staple industry that would provide a lucrative product for export. By 1805 the first shore station had been established in the Derwent River in Tasmania, while a number of vessels based in or visiting Australia had begun operations in adjacent seas (Nash 2003). The possibility of a colonial whaling industry independent of and in competition with the British fishery produced a strong reaction in England. In an unsuccessful attempt to control or curtail this development, the British government in 1809 imposed severe duties on colonial oil imported to Britain. Colonial produce attracted duties of approximately 29 times higher for sperm oil and 16 times higher for black (right and humpback whale) oil as for that from English whalers (Morton 1982:121). These duties remained in place until 1823, when a change in policy abolished the excise.

The growth of Australasian whaling therefore really dates from the mid–1820s, encouraged by the removal of the tariffs on colonial oil, the withdrawal of the British whalers from the Pacific and the growing domestic market (Chamberlain 1988). Close proximity to the resource meant that operating costs were reduced compared to UK–based whalers, increasing the profit margin and assisting in the development of pelagic, bay and shore whaling ventures. Shore whaling parties from Sydney and Hobart soon spread along the coasts of eastern Australia and Tasmania and across the Tasman Sea to New Zealand.

The scale of the shore whaling industry in each area varied from two boat fisheries to as many as 11 boats or more at some New Zealand stations (Morton 1982:228). In some instances shore whaling comprised 'only one strand of a diverse land–based interest' for settlers and was combined with grazing, timber–getting and other maritime interests (Pearson 1985:5). Until as late as 1834 whale products provided the major export income for New South Wales, although by 1850 wool, timber and coal production had increased to the point where the fishery contributed only one percent of total earnings (Little 1969).

In virtually all regions the shore whaling industry appears to have peaked in the late 1830s, followed by a rapid decline during the 1840s. The closure of many Australasian shore stations in the late 1840s has not been clearly explained, although in part it has been linked with a decline in whale stocks and resulting fall in production (Pearson 1985; Campbell 1992). With agricultural, pastoral and other interests now well established, investors' capital could be directed towards more profitable ventures, including pelagic whaling. The economic depression during that decade created further financial difficulties for station owners, resulting in either abandonment or re–organisation on a more modest scale (Little 1969). Shore whaling continued in various parts of eastern Australia and New Zealand on a greatly reduced scale for several more decades, with a handful of stations and individuals operating sporadically even into the 20th century. By 1910 modern forms of shore whaling with powered chase boats, explosive harpoons and large–scale processing infrastructure had almost completely replaced the older, open boat forms of the industry.

PRE–SETTLEMENT (1616–1826)

Faced with a buoyant oil market and successes in other parts of Australasia, it is surprising that it took so long for the Western Australian colonists to engage in whaling. However, while not independent of developments in the rest of Australasia, the whaling industry that emerged was neither closely related to or the product of the pelagic or shore whalers of either Tasmania or New South Wales.

Since the early 17th century a succession of Dutch, French and English commercial and exploratory vessels had observed the western Australian coast, reporting scientific curiosities but finding little of potential commercial value. The exception was that in almost all cases comment was made on the number of whales seen. When British explorer George Vancouver arrived in King George Sound in September of 1791 in the midst of the whale season, he noted that 'The little trouble these animals took to avoid us, indicated their not being accustomed to... visitors' (Vancouver 1984: 353). Only five months later, in April of 1792, the whalers *Asia* and *Alliance* of Nantucket made an exploratory visit to Shark Bay, although being in the wrong season for either humpback or right whales the vessels quickly departed northward. In the three years since *Emilia*'s successful voyage into the Pacific the spread of the American whaling fleet had been swift, often preceding government sponsored explorations. Between August and December of 1800 the British whalers *Elligood* and *Kingston* also cruised the western Australian coast, but with more success (Richards 1991).

In the opening years of the 19th century a new series of intensive French and British explorations of the Australian coasts began, all making frequent sightings of whales. French Captain Nicolas Baudin suggested in his published journals that if whaling vessels were to visit the west coast in the right period, they would '...obtain their cargo very promptly and successfully' (Cornell 1974:512). In particular Baudin was attracted to Shark Bay, which had been a focal point of their investigations and offered a protected anchorage for vessels, stating:

> This place would be worth settling, if one considered it a suitable area for whaling; the only commercial activity on this coast presenting advantages that should not be overlooked. I am convinced that the Dutch had their reasons for not giving us a more accurate plan of it than the one on their charts (Cornell 1974:512).

In February of 1803, Baudin's vessels encountered the American sealing ship *Union* in the harbour now known as Two People Bay. The sealer was visiting the area on the strength of the information in Vancouver's published journal, hoping to obtain a full cargo of skins before proceeding to China. In the following year at least one other American sealer visited King George Sound (Fanning 1924), suggesting that private interests were effectively utilising the information about the Australian coast generated by the official expeditions, in addition to amassing intelligence through their own explorations and other sources. By 1818 when the French and British dispatched the Freycinet and King expeditions respectively there was clear evidence of increasing European activity along the south and west coasts, quite probably related to whaling and sealing (Marchant 1982). When Dumont d'Urville visited King George Sound in October 1826, sealing parties from the eastern Australian colonies were clearly well established on the offshore islands of the south coast (Lockyer 1826).

EARLY SETTLEMENT (1826–1842)

In December 1826 a small detachment of soldiers and convicts under the command of Major Edmund Lockyer arrived at King George Sound on the south coast to establish a military outpost known as Fredrickstown and later Albany. Its purpose was partially to forestall any remaining French colonial ambitions, but also to determine the suitability of the area for a new penal colony (Garden 1977). Lockyer was directed to investigate and report on the natural assets of the area, making his own observations about the immediate vicinity but also interviewing the several gangs of eastern Australian sealers already living and operating in and about King George Sound. The sealers claimed to have hunted on the islands of the southwest coast from as early as 1820 and had penetrated as far north as the Swan River. As well as describing rivers, islands and natural features, the sealers also recalled encounters with Aboriginal groups (HRA III (6):490, 2/4/1827).

Based on these interviews, Lockyer reported to Governor Darling his concern that unless sealing was regulated almost immediately, a valuable resource would be 'irreparably injured if nor destroyed altogether' (HRA III (6):471, 22/1/1827). He suggested the Government lay claim to the coastal islands, prohibit private sealing and farm the seal populations every three years, while placing restrictions upon activities during the breeding season. Lockyer extended this note of urgency to the large numbers of sperm whales in the adjacent waters, although he recorded that the sealers said these were as yet unexploited because 'the whale ships' (of unstated origin) would not approach too close for fear of the coast (HRA III (6):490, 2/4/1827). However, his reports were largely ignored, with Governor Darling stating in a letter to Earl Bathurst that he had 'in fact given no attention to the subject, being without means of carrying into effect any measures which might be deemed expedient to adopt' (HRA I (13):273, 3/5/1827).

In 1829 a new British settlement was established at the Swan River on the west coast, based on the 1827 reports by a young naval officer named James Stirling. In contrast to earlier explorers who had disparaged the potential of a west coast colony, Stirling extolled the virtues of the region, arguing that its position in relation to the prevailing winds meant that military and naval forces stationed there could be easily dispatched to either the eastern Australian colonies or India (Statham–Drew 2003). He also suggested that the location was ideal for China traders to call in for refreshments before proceeding northwards. As the Chinese were generally not interested in European goods, Stirling proposed that the normally light outward cargoes of British vessels could be supplemented with articles to supply the Swan River Colony. Once there they could obtain refreshments and ship a new full cargo of local produce such as timber, trepang, sealskins and whale oil, which were of greater interest to the Asian merchants (HRA III (6): 585, 20/7/1828).

The motivations behind Stirling's enthusiasm for a new colony have been the subject of some discussion, with the point raised that his uncle happened to be a director of the East India Company which still controlled British trade in the Indian Ocean (Cameron 1975, 1981; Appleyard and Manford 1979). In summarising the main advantages of the proposed settlement, Stirling recognised the potential for a whale and seal fishery, although it was simply one of a large number of possible industries suggested as a means making the submission more attractive (HRA III (6): 577, 18/4/1827). His main thrust was that this was an extremely fertile region ideally suited for an agricultural settlement and that he should be given the role of Governor of the new colony.

Although the Colonial Office initially rejected his proposals, Stirling personally petitioned for support upon his return to England. A timely change in government administration placed several sympathisers for the scheme in senior positions, with further encouragement possibly provided by renewed French and American activity in the area (Cameron 1978).

The key was to be land apportionment based upon capital investment. For every £3 worth of equipment which could be used to improve land or was applicable to farm production, the settler would be entitled to a grant of 40 acres (16.2 hectares). Cash did not entitle a settler to land, although as a means of inducing settlers to provide their own labourers, any servants and their families brought over were given a value, resulting in an indenture system. Stirling was also allowed to head the settlement, being given the title of Lt. Governor.

Although there was initially an unprecedented enthusiasm for the new settlement, several factors soon emerged which immediately endangered the colony's existence. First was that the rush of arrivals completely overwhelming the planned processes of exploration, land division and apportionment. This situation was exacerbated by the realization that the fertile area had been grossly over–estimated, in reality being limited to narrow strips along the rivers. Many of the arrivals lacked suitable skills for colonising and had over–invested in agricultural equipment as a means of maximising their land grant. They had often chosen inadequate or inappropriate gear, sometimes based on poor or incorrect advice. Insufficient food supplies and the difficult conditions in the tent settlement at Fremantle caused many settlers to continue on to the eastern colonies or immediately return to England to spread their tales of woe. When news of this state of affairs filtered back to England emigration rapidly slowed and then halted, leaving the Swan River Colony with a black reputation for many years to come (Cameron 1978).

For the settlers who remained the first several years were marked by poor crop yields and high stock losses as they experimented with the unfamiliar seasons and conditions. Their early over–expenditure on capital purchases had left them with limited cash reserves, making it difficult to import further equipment or diversify their activities away from agricultural production.

Among the settlers were also persons originally from eastern Australia who had established small service and trading enterprises at the Swan River Colony. Their departure removed much of the liquid capital, leaving the settlement in a precarious economic position that would last for the better part of a decade (Statham 1981a).

Faced with a range of other difficulties, it is not surprising that Stirling's initial attitude towards fostering a whale fishery was relatively cautious. In a despatch to the Colonial Secretary in January 1830, only six months after settlement, he reported as follows.

> The facilities which are offered for carrying on a whale fishery have not escaped the attention of some of the settlers even this early. I have had applications from several parties but judging the time not arrived I have not hastened by particular encouragement such establishments. It is believed

that there is an abundance of fish to make such a fishery possible and the coast is visited between the months of May and November by a multitude of whales; it will be my object to foster these fisheries and boats and small vessels drawing their maintenance from these shores (cited in Heppingstone 1966:30).

Over the next several years there were numerous proposals, prospectuses and submissions to establish whaling parties, most requesting government support (e.g. CSR 10/62, 18/11/1830; SRP 18/27, 7/8/1832; SRP 6/95, 24/12/1830; PG 23/3/1833; PG 5/11/1834). In many instances Stirling offered various kinds of assistance including land grants or leases, while colonists recorded in their diaries and letters their hopes that eventually one of these ventures would be successful, as it would 'be a chief means of giving stability to the colony' (Moore 1884a:167). However, all of these schemes failed, mostly from being unable to raise the capital to purchase the necessary equipment.

In August 1833 the *Perth Gazette* noted large numbers of whales along the coast adjacent to Fremantle, bemoaning the lack of equipment to pursue and capture them (PG 17/8/1833). Despite this, in the same issue there was a report of a five–week old whale calf being caught by two men fishing between Carnac and Garden Islands. The blubber, which they flensed off at Carnac Island, was taken back to Fremantle and tryed out to give 45 gallons (170 L) of oil (PG 17/8/1833). The following week's issue also recorded that a whale had been thrown ashore at North Fremantle, with the finder trying out over 100 gallons (378 L) of oil (PG 24/8/1833).

By the end of 1833 the initial economic crisis in the Swan River colony had passed and in her analysis of the early economy of the settlement Statham (1980) has identified the years between 1834 and 1837 as a period of consolidation. The settlement became self–sufficient in basic foodstuffs, the first products of the pastoral industry were exported and immigration recommenced on a small scale. There was also limited development of the non–rural sector, mainly based upon military and public works contracts, although some small industries such as boat building were also established (Ewers 1971).

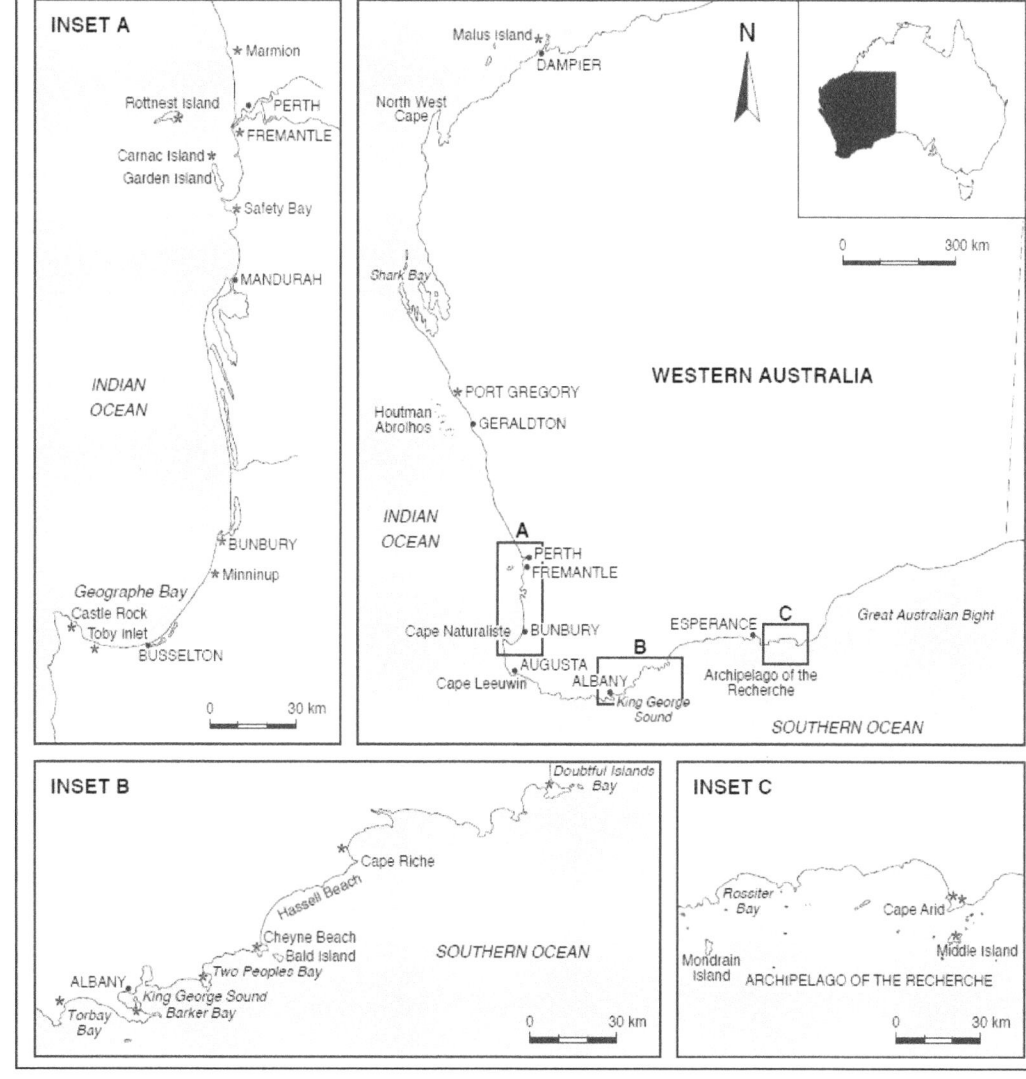

Figure 2.1 Main settlements and shore whaling stations. (Drawing – Wei Ming)

While most local transactions were still undertaken through a barter system, a cash economy was finally starting to emerge and small reserves of liquid capital were accumulating (Statham 1981a). Many of the workers in the colony remained indentured as servants to the major settlers, although a labour market had begun to develop where free men could sell their services for relatively high wages, especially in contract seasonal labour.

In addition to the increased range of economic activity, official and private explorations once again began to range through the southwest, examining the potential for pastoral and agricultural settlement (Jarvis 1979). Administrative responsibility for the King George Sound outpost was transferred to Swan River and the southern settlement began a slow expansion as a free colony (Garden 1977). The general impression is one of growing confidence amongst settlers and government that the colony would finally prove to be viable.

Colonial attentions were also turning towards finding resources with export potential. The booming oil market and the successes of the other Australasian colonies clearly made whaling an attractive proposition in both official and private eyes. The *Perth Gazette*, generally considered the mouthpiece of the Government, ran a series of articles presenting whaling as an easily pursued and remunerative industry (PG 24/8/1833; PG 3/5/1834; PG 13/8/1836). Exploration parties reported sightings of large numbers of whales along the southwest coast and as far north as Shark Bay (PG 8/11/1834; PG 16/7/1836; PG 3/9/1836; SRG 29/12/36). A report on the potential for a fishery at the Swan River estimated that from 10–40 whales were sighted annually between the mainland, Rottnest Island and Garden Islands, and that if a look–out was kept at least five times that many would be seen (PG 16/7/1836).

Despite being surrounded by this bounty, whaling still required specialised equipment that had to be made or imported and paid for. Although Blainey (1966:111) states that in eastern Australia a whaling station could be established 'for a mere £300', a situation which may have been true of Western Australia a decade later, in this initial phase there were neither local manufacturing industries nor an existing body of cheap or second–hand whalecraft which could be drawn upon. Governor Stirling estimated that capital of £1000 would be necessary to establish a four boat shore fishery, with a further £1105 for annual costs (1837a:260; Figure 2.4). Morton's (1982:225) research suggests that even this figure may have been optimistic and that £1500 to £2000 in capital would have been required.

Although the colonial economy was now stable, this did not mean that it was affluent. Promotional pamphlets distributed in England during this period described the prospects for a whale fishery at some length (Irwin 1835; Anon 1836), starting again the long and ultimately unsuccessful attempt to attract investors or new colonists with an ambition to go whaling.

Several further local efforts were made towards forming whaling companies, most of which either failed to become established (PG 7/5/1836; PG 3/9/1836; CSR 46/20), or had to be modified into less capital intensive activities such as sealing (PG 8/11/1836). The exception was in May 1836 when Thomas Booker Sherratt, an Albany merchant, informed the Colonial Secretary that he and William Lovett of Van Diemen's Land were preparing a whaling party at King George Sound (PG 7/5/1836; Garden 1978:64). A later set of reminiscences state that Lovett arrived from Hobart Town in 1835 in the barque *Jess* 'with extensive whaling equipment' to join Sherratt and Mr. Dring of Perth in whaling and sealing about Albany (Keyser 1929). Sherratt's ledger (Sherratt 1836) records the name of John W. Lovitt, presumably a member of the well known Tasmania maritime family who owned several whaling vessels during this period (Lawson 1949). If so, this is the only known instance of eastern Australian investment in a Western Australian whaling party. From Sherratt's ledger it appears that the partnership provided Sherratt with equipment, experience and additional capital to overcome the prohibitive establishment costs.

Although nothing more is mentioned through the year, a late report confirmed that a fishery had been formed and even achieved a moderate success.

> The whaling party... is on a small scale... 15 whales were struck during last season and 7 were taken, but whether from the insufficiency of means or the want of experience on the part of those employed remains to be determined, not more than 15 tons of oil and about 2 tons of whalebone were obtained. (PG 24/12/1836)

It would appear that this station was located in Doubtful Island Bay, 160km north–east of Albany (SDUR S3/271: 6/12/1836). From the perspective of later whaling operations, the catch by this first station was average, although the yield of oil was remarkably low. The export return of the 13 tuns of oil was reported as £520, with the total value of whalebone and sealskins cleared through the port listed as £630 (BB 1836).

By 1837 the economic environment of the Western Australian colonies had improved to the extent that the settlers had accumulated sufficient capital to make several major developments possible. The first of these was the establishment of the Bank of Western Australia, presenting many colonists with their first opportunity for making short–term loans with which to buy stock and equipment or attempt new ventures (Ogle 1839). The second was a growing import market that, together with the rise in exports, resulted in the expansion of businesses, fortunes and influence of merchants resident in the colony (Statham 1981a). The third was the establishment of two whaling companies at Fremantle, financed through a broad joint–stock investment involving a number of the major settlers and merchants in the Swan River colony.

In contrast with most of the whaling parties subsequently formed, both of these companies were based on a relatively elaborate formal investment structure. The Fremantle Whaling Company, whose station was on Bathers Beach in Fremantle, had an initial capital of £400 from shares of £20 each (SRG 11/5/1837). It was later necessary to raise a further £300 with a release of £10 shares (PG 19/8/1837). The Northern Whaling Company based on Carnac Island (also referred to as the Carnac or Perth Whaling Company) operated with capital of £600, raised from shares of £10 each (SRG 4/5/1837). Further details of the companies and their main investors are provided in reports from the *Swan River Guardian* (SRG 4/5/1837; SRG 11/5/1837), while Statham (1980; 1981a) has discussed their financial structures in some detail. The history of the 1837 season has already been described on a number of occasions (Kimberley 1897; Battye 1912; Heppingstone 1966; Statham 1980; Statham–Drew 2003) and will only be briefly reviewed.

The establishment and operation of the two Fremantle whaling parties became closely associated with the various political factions and disputes within the colony. The Fremantle Company in particular benefited from two major public works performed on their grant using prison labour; the construction of a stone jetty and the quarrying of a tunnel through the adjacent hillside to simplify access from Bathers Beach. In addition, each group attempted to gain advantage through dealings with the several American whaling vessels that put into Fremantle during the year. Daniel Scott, a major investor in the Fremantle Company, was accused of using his position as Harbour Master to purchase whaling equipment from the American whaler *Cambrian* to the exclusion of the Northern Company (SRG 16/3/1837). On the other hand, the Northern Company convinced several crew members from the same vessel to join their party (PG 15/4/1837). When formed, both parties were comprised of three boats, totalling about 20 men per station.

The 1837 season was characterised by an obvious lack of skill in both of the whaling parties, severe damage or loss of equipment and a disastrously high loss of life, totalling seven dead and several other serious injuries by the end of the season. Although it is probable that the headsmen and boat steerers had some prior experience, most of the boat hands were inexperienced boys aged 21 years or less (PG 8/7/1837). The fishing did not proceed as successfully as predicted, with the two parties frequently competing but often forced to cooperate to achieve any result at all. By August it was decided to unite the two stations for the remainder of the season, with operations ceasing in mid–October (PG 19/8/1837; PG 14/10/1837).

Parallel developments were occurring on the south coast in 1837, with two whaling stations established at Doubtful Island Bay (Wolfe 2003). Information on these parties, remote from the settlement and the eyes of newspaper correspondents is sparse. Thomas Booker Sherratt continued his partnership with William Lovett (CSR 53/45: 14/4/1837), while George Cheyne, another Albany merchant, also decided to enter the industry (Garden 1977). During the early stages of the season, Sherratt wrote a series of letters complaining of the presence of American whaling vessels along the south coast (CSR 55/14: 5/5/1837). Although initially appealing to the captain of a visiting British man–of–war to drive the foreigners off the coast (CSR 53/43: 14/4/1837), Sherratt was quickly pacified by entering into a relationship with the master of the American whaler *Charles Wright* (CSR 55/29, 9/8/1837). The terms of this situation were partly reported in a letter to the *Swan River Guardian*:

> we are to have all of the bone of the whales caught by us. For the first 30 tuns of oil, Captain Coffin to have [one quarter]. After 30 tuns one half. We are to have no other troubles with whales but catch them. Captain Coffin to cooper all our casks for £5. Captain C to have the oil after the last 30, at a fixed price. These are better terms than the first we offered to join upon. (SRG 29/6/1837).

There are no other details of the nature of the agreement, particularly whether any other equipment or assistance was provided. Cheyne had also formed an association with an American vessel, although details are similarly obscure. From indirect evidence, it appears that Cheyne's whaling crew actually embarked on the foreign vessel and joined with the American crew in bay whaling operations, receiving a share of the catch at a fixed rate (CSR 55/29: 9/8/1837).

Although the total catch record and gross value of the 1837 season's production is not recorded, the combined result of the west coast stations saw the export of 71 tuns of oil worth £1420 and 4.5 tons of whale bone worth £360. From the south coast the export amounted to £900 worth of oil and £180 worth of bone (BB 1837). This was a far cry from the 250 to 300 tuns of oil per station confidently estimated earlier in the season (SRG 29/6/1837), and still lower than the estimated value of £4200 that had been suggested at a later point in the year (Stirling 1837a). However, in the context of the Western Australian economy the £2860 of whale products immediately formed the state's major export; exceeding the previous year's total export of £2700 and bringing the 1837 total to £6906 (Figure 2.2, Figure 2.3).

Aside from an increase in export earnings, the economic and social consequences of the foundation of the whaling industry were felt throughout the colony. The contracts and orders to supply the stations with food and equipment, as well as to construct buildings and other works, further helped to stimulate local economic growth and development. It is, however, significant that the principal investors in both the south and west coast parties were merchants or persons with strong maritime interests (SRG 4/5/1837; SRG 11/5/1837). By supplying capital with which to establish whaling operations, these individuals could expect returns not only from the sale of oil, but also from receiving preference in servicing the needs of the parties. The controlling influence and involvement of merchant groups was to remain a dominant factor throughout the history of the whaling industry in Western Australia.

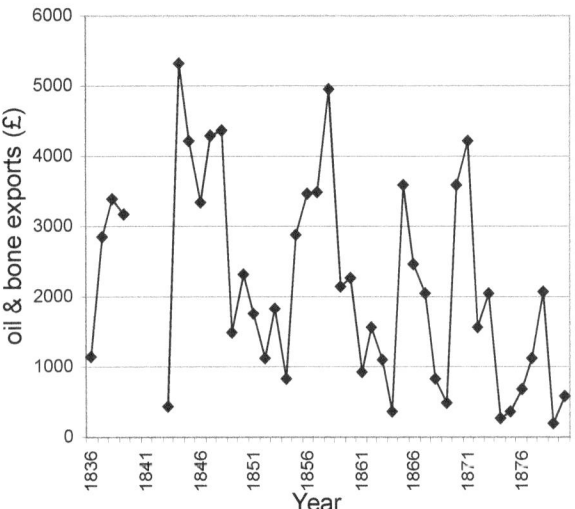

Figure 2.2 Reported returns from whale products exported from Western Australia 1836–1880.

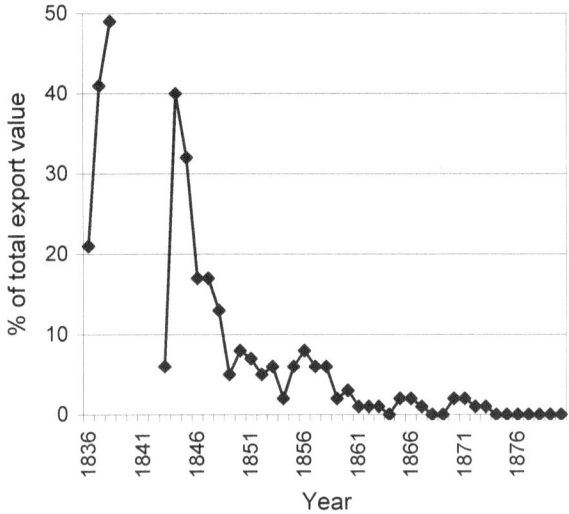

Figure 2.3 Whale products as a percentage of total value of exports from Western Australia 1836–1880.

An immediate consequence of whaling was the major drain on the colony's labour market. As already described, the low population and indenture system still placed free labour at a premium, so that the loss of 40 or more men to exclusive employment in the whaling parties near Fremantle was sorely felt (Moore 1884:307). As one newspaper reporter commented;

> you will meet with few labourers, no matter what description, but follow the hue and cry "in for spouting!" This sound is not most agreeable to those who are following different pursuits and require labourers. It is an idle infatuation, for nine-tenths are not fit to pull an oar (PG 22/4/1837).

Experienced boatmen were the most sought after and there were complaints about the scarcity of fish at the markets as a consequence of nearly all of the fishermen having been employed by the whaling parties (PG 15/7/1837). Although the labour shortage at the Swan River obviously caused some inconvenience, this should be seen from the perspective of the south coast situation, where the 24 or more men engaged in whaling represented at least 20% of the total male (not necessarily adult) population.

The social consequence of whaling that is the hardest to define but perhaps was the most significant at the time is the sense of excitement that the new industry obviously produced in the settlers. Life in the Western Australian colonies was difficult, often disappointing and despite occasional organised events which were not necessarily accessible to all classes, quite dull. As a result, the spectacle of whale hunting immediately became a favourite entertainment, with lengthy accounts of proceedings appearing in the colonial papers throughout 1837. In addition there was the psychological effect of seeing a colonial industry achieving 'instant' success, without the slow, difficult and often uncertain processes involved in agriculture or pastoralism. Amongst the settlers there was 'no talk now but of 'lays' and 'spouting', and other technical whaling terms' (Moore 1884:307). Another report stated that the whole of Western Australia had gone 'mad for whaling', it being 'the chief topic of discourse of all classes, sexes and ages' (PG 6/5/1837). Even though the season itself was only partially successful, the achievements of the whaling industry effectively raised the morale amongst the European population.

The arrival of foreign whaling vessels at both Albany and Fremantle during 1837 heralded the emergence of an external but highly significant influence upon the colonial whaling industry. American whaling ships had been present in the region for several years, mostly trading with the small and isolated outpost at Augusta (Molloy 1834), although there is little evidence that they had engaged in industrial activity prior to 1836. The 1837 season appears to have been aimed at testing the viability of the region, with the American captains intending to send for other ships should they prove successful (CSR 52/142: 24/3/1837).

The threat to the local whaling industry offered by these foreign whaling vessels, as they 'swarmed' about the coast (PG 15/4/1837) was immediately obvious to the settlers and calls for protection were soon made (CSR 53/43: 14/4/1837). The situation was defused temporarily during 1837 by the American captains entering into arrangements with or providing equipment to all of the south and west coast parties, as described above. However, the local authorities began their first tentative enquires of the Colonial Office and Admiralty in England to define the rights of American and French vessels to fish along the coasts (CO 18/198: 4/7/1837).

Rather than the expansion that might have been expected from the partial success of the 1837 season, the years between 1838 and 1842 saw a rapid decline of the colonial whaling industry. While there had been four parties operating during 1837, the following season saw a reduction to three stations and one 'tonguing party' that salvaged blubber from the whale carcasses discarded by pelagic whaling vessels. This decreased to two parties in 1839, with the fall continuing over the next three years (Figure 3.7) until in 1842 there was only one unconfirmed report of a station in Two People Bay (CSR 112/145: 29/11/1842).

On first examination the failure to develop the whaling industry is difficult to understand, given that in 1838 and 1839 whale products still formed the major export item of the colony, surpassing even the 1837 returns (Figure 2.2). The potential for fishing was still readily visible in the number of whales passing along the coast, and accentuated by the continuing successes of the rapidly growing foreign fleet in the region. However, several factors can be seen as restricting growth during the period prior to 1843.

The first limiting factor was that while the 1837 whaling season had been successful in the broader context of the colony's economy, the individual parties did not return dividends to investors. Despite being formed with far less capital than that projected as required for a four boat fishery, both of the Fremantle parties, inexperienced and beset by problems during 1837, had failed to return their establishment costs. The Northern Company, which also appears to have suffered from poor management (PG 5/8/1837), was forced to discontinue operations and liquidate its assets (PG 17/2/1837; PG 3/3/1838), dissolving soon afterwards (PG 26/5/1838). The Fremantle Company had been more successful and had also attempted to diversify by sealing after the whaling season (SRG 7/12/1837; SRG 21/12/1837). This group was obviously still hopeful of achieving success at whaling, making improvements to the station and calling tenders for supplies in anticipation of the coming year (PG 21/4/1838; PG 12/5/1838). However, it is not surprising that while the settlers could see the potential benefits of a fishery, on an individual level they became reluctant to risk their own money in the pursuit.

Governor Stirling's (1837a) analysis of the future prospects of the whaling industry had revealed this problem, even before the close of the 1837 season (Stirling 1837a: 250, 258). His table (reproduced here as Figure 2.4) projecting the land, capital and labour which would be required for expansion envisaged three levels of operation, the least expensive or *submedial* level consisting of seasonal shore whaling by the settlers within each region. The *medial* category required a small vessel to engage in bay whaling, while the most expensive or *supermedial* category was comprised of fitting out a full sized vessel for pelagic whaling within the region. It is interesting that these levels correspond quite closely with Little's (1969) categories of whaling.

While Stirling portrayed the future of the local whaling industry as very positive, it was only at the point where the colonists engaged in bay or pelagic whaling that appreciable dividends could be expected. At least some of the colonists recognised from an early stage that without a further injection of capital and an expansion of operations there would not be significant profits from whaling, and even before the conclusion of the 1837 season there had been plans for creating a pelagic whaling industry.

As described earlier, the figures presented in Stirling's table, based on the 'present circumstances' of the colony (Stirling 1837a:260), proposed a minimal establishment of four boats, requiring an initial capital outlay of at least £1000 and annual expenses of £1105. However, even with reasonable success the expected clear profit, at least in the first year of operation, would be only about £50, or 5% of the total investment.

> In these cases the amount of capital, in proportion to the number of persons, is small, and although the gross returns are great, the net profit remaining is less than any other vocation.

The initial meeting resolved that the capital would be £5000 in shares of £25 (to be paid in instalments), with the aim of purchasing and equipping a ship in England (PG 15/7/1837). One feature of its prospectus was reported to be a rule forbidding any foreigner from holding an interest in the company, an obvious reproach to the other Fremantle parties (SRG 27/7/1837). Despite grand intentions, by the opening of the 1838 season the company was unable to raise the desired capital and scaled down its plans to opening a small shore station (PG 5/5/1838; PG 21/4/1838).

It is clear that while the colony's economy was steadily growing, there were still only limited reserves of liquid capital with which to invest in an expanded venture. The formation of the original two Fremantle whaling companies, both of which were based on far less capital than the £1000 suggested in Stirling's (1837) *submedial* category, had required a broad joint-stock investment from a number of major settlers. There simply was not the cash to raise the £2500 required of Stirling's *medial* (bay whaling) level, or the £5000 proposed in the Western Australian Whaling Company's scheme, a situation which Stirling was forced to admit at the end of the 1838 season

> It is now perceived that in a small community like this where wages are high and provisions dear, and where the proper description of vessel cannot at present be procured, the bay fishing labours under great disadvantages, and will not yield to those who undertake it a large profit (Stirling 1838).

Stirling and other agents began a more active campaign to promote the colonial fishery in the hope of attracting English investment. The main argument was that if British whaleships based themselves in the colony, the time and expense saved in not having to refit and undertake the lengthy voyage south would make them directly competitive with the American and French fleets (Stirling 1837a, 1838; PG 20/10/1838). This overture was in most respects a reiteration of the proposals generated by the eastern Australian colonies a decade or two earlier (Morton 1982; Chamberlain 1988), receiving new vigour when combined with growing colonial resentment against foreign whalers.

The theme of presenting the whaling potential of the Western Australian coast as a significant British resource being lost to foreign powers was to become a familiar part of colonial promotions (Buckton 1840; Anon 1843; Andrews n.d.). In later years, almost until the close of the industry in the 1870s, this would expand into a discussion of the failure of the British Southern Fishery to take advantage of the situation (Inq 20/7/1870; Knight 1870). Despite the obvious potential of such a move, by the 1830s the British whaling industry was in decline (Jackson 1978) and neither these nor similar proposals from New Zealand (Enderby 1847; Morton 1982) inspired renewed interest.

The reluctance of both colonial and British capitalists to invest in whaling might also be traced to the massive fluctuations in the oil market during this period. As a result of existing surplus and continuing competition between British and American suppliers, the price of black oil on the London market had dropped from above £45 per tun in 1837, down to only £20 per tun in 1838 (Chamberlain 1988:48). It was not until 1843 that prices returned to their former level, and this in part can be seen as a factor in the recovery, or at least re–establishment, of the Western Australian whaling industry after this date.

The continued inability of the colonists to engage effectively in the whale fishery, while watching the rising numbers and continuing successes of the foreign whaling vessels along their coasts, resulted in a growing frustration during the late 1830s and early 1840s. Several contemporary writers attempted to estimate the size of the foreign fleet in the region, the first being a report of May 1838 stating that up to that time 40 American whaling ships had touched on the coast for provisions (Buckton 1840).

1. OCCUPATIONS. Class	2. Order	3. Description and Extent of the Land or Station required in each Occupation. (Acres)	4. Description, Quantity, and Value of the Capital or Stock required. (Value)	5. Description, Number, and Customary Wages of the Persons required. (Amount)	6. Description and Amount of Annual Expenses. (Amount)	7. Description, Quantity, and estimated Value of the Gross Returns. (Value)	8. Amount of Net Return before Payment of customary Wages, constituting the Fund applicable to Wages, Rent, Taxes, and Profit (£. s.)	9. Amount and Rate of Net Profit in each Occupation, after Payment of customary Wages and Annual Expenses	10. Surplus, after Payment of Annual Expenses, customary Wages and Colonial Profit, forming the Fund for Rent or Fiscal Charges. (£. s.)
STOCK KEEPING.	Submedial	Natural pasture, probably . . 2,000	Breeding cattle, about 50 head, and provisions . £.500	Herdsmen, 1 in number . . £.30	Wages, provisions, and casualties, at 10 per cent . £115	Increase of stock . . £240	155 0	125*l.*, or 25 per cent.	..
	Medial	Natural pasture, suitable to sheep . 3,000	Sheep, about 600 in number, and provisions for 12 months . 1,500	Herdsman's family, three in number . 50 / 30 / 20	Wages, provisions, & casualties, at 7½ per cent 300	Increase, and wool . . 900	700 0	600*l.*, or 40 per cent.	225 0
	Supermedial	Arable land, a small part, and the rest good sheep-pasture . 7,500	Sheep, horses, and cattle . 6,500 Buildings, implements, & provisions . 1,000	Superintendent 150 3 shepherds . 100 3 ploughmen . 100 8 boys and women . . 250	Wages, provisions, casualties, at 5 per ct.; wear and tear, and seed . . 2,000	Increase, wool, produce of tillage . . 5,375	3,875 0	3,375*l.*, or 45 per cent.	1,500 0
TILLAGE.	Submedial	Superior arable land, 25 acres, selected out of . 125	Buildings, clearing, fencing, seed, provisions . 125	Cultivator, 1 in number . 30	Ploughing, assistance at harvest-time, wages, provisions, seed, &c. . 118 15	Produce in wheat, estimated at 375 bushels; potatoes, at 25*l.* 150	61 5	31*l.* 5*s.*, or 25 per cent.	..
	Medial	Superior arable land, 50 acres, selected out of . 250	Team, implements, small stock, buildings, seed, &c. . 625	One family, of 1 at 50*l.*, 1 at 30*l.*, 2 at 15*l.*, and 1 at 10*l.* . 120	Wages, provisions, casualties, seed, wear & tear 350	Produce in general . 600	370 0	250*l.*, or 40 per cent.	93 15
	Supermedial	Arable and pasture land, in proper proportions, 5,000	Live-stock . 3,750 Buildings, teams, provisions, &c. 3,750	Superintendent, at . . 200 Ploughmen, shepherds, women, boys, 29 in number . 650	Wages, provisions, seed, wear & tear, casualties, &c. . . 2,900	Various sorts of produce from stock and tillage 6,650	4,600 0	3,750*l.*, or 50 per cent.	1,875 0
WHALING.	Submedial	Suitable bays for whaling stations.	Boats, gear, casks, provisions, advances to men . . 1,000	4 headsmen 20 boatmen coopers & labourers — onlays at 50 per cent.	Wear and tear, casks, provisions . . 705 Lays to boatmen . . 400	Oil and bone, estimated at 1,155	400 0	50*l.*, or 5 per cent.	..
	Medial	Bays and coasts suitable to whaling.	A small vessel, boats, gear, casks, provisions, &c. . . 2,500	Same number of persons as above . — onlays at 40 per cent.	Wear and tear, casks, provisions, insurance, &c. . 1,525 Lays . . 600	Ditto, at . 2,500	975 0	375*l.*, or 15 per cent.	..
	Supermedial	Whaling grounds, whether within or beyond the precincts of the settlement.	A ship, boats, gear, casks, provisions, &c.; advances to men, and other expenses . 7,500	Same number of persons as above mentioned — onlays at 33⅓ per ct. on the amount taken.	Wear and tear, casks, provisions, insurance, &c. . 2,500 Lays . . 1,200	Ditto, at . 5,575	3,075 0	1,875*l.*, or 25 per cent.	..

Figure 2.4 '*Table illustrative of the Combinations which take place in respect of Land, Capital, and Labour, in Colonial Pursuits*' (reproduced from Stirling 1837a).

In 1841 William Nairn Clarke, editor of the *Inquirer*, reckoned that 150 American whaling vessels appeared annually in Western Australian waters (Inq 1/9/1841). Another commentator suggested there were between 200 and 300 foreign vessels in the 1840 or 1841 season (Anon 1842). As a means of independently assessing the extent of this foreign activity and the probable impact upon the local whaling industry, a database of all whaleship sightings along the Western Australian coast was compiled. Although the large amount of foreign whaling in areas away from the settlements prevents a complete listing of vessels in the region, the trends revealed in Figure 2.5 show that the years between 1840 and 1842 certainly represented a peak of foreign activity. From this evidence, it is conceivable that Nairn Clarke's estimate of 150 ships (Inq 1/9/1841) may have closer to accurate than previously thought. The database of foreign whaling vessels, primarily consisting of American (U.S.) ships, is available (Gibbs 1995) with an analysis of the American whaling activity provided in another paper (Gibbs 2000).

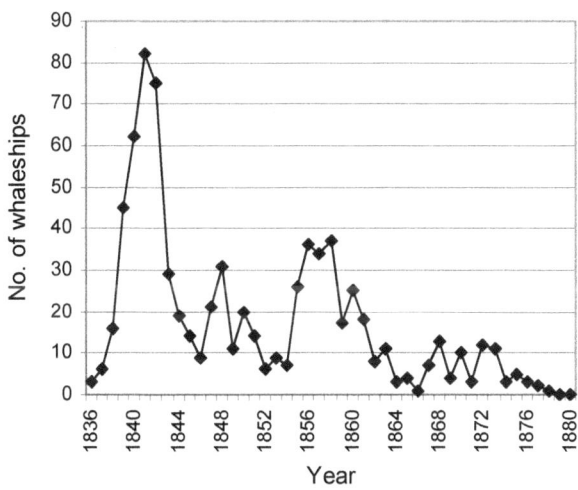

Figure 2.5 Foreign Whaleships reported in Western Australian Waters 1835–1880.

It was not possible to determine the number of whales killed or the quantity of oil removed from the coast by foreign whalers (although see Bannister *et al.* 1981). Despite the lack of statistical data, the constant stream of reports in the colonial press clearly suggests that the ocean about Western Australian, also known as the New Holland Ground, was a highly productive area. The pelagic whalers would hunt the sperm whales offshore during the appropriate season, then retire to the coast to bay–whale while 'wintering' (Gibbs 2000). One frequently cited example was that two American and one French ship stationed at Two People Bay had taken catches worth nearly £27,000, almost wholly from the W.A. coast, in a period of less than two years (PG 1/12/1838; Buckton 1840). Other reports gave similarly impressive figures (Inq 3/8/1842; CO 18/20:41 3/12/1838; CO 18/26:281, 30/6/1840).

It was usually while they were wintering along the coast that the foreign vessels came into conflict with local whaling parties (Gibbs 2000). In the direct competition of chasing the same whale, the colonials stood little chance against the experienced and well–equipped American boats. Vessels anchored in adjacent bays could also compete indirectly, either by catching the whales before they passed through to the bays where the colonial parties were resident, or by *galleying* (frightening) the whales through chasing them, making them wary of other boats (CSR 189/254: 13/8/1849). This situation was exacerbated by the colonial strategy of establishing shore stations in locations previously used by the foreign vessels (see Chapter 4).

Repeated calls were made by the colony for the British government to provide some form of protection for the fishery. These were usually combined with attempts to generate interest amongst British investors. In 1837 Stirling sent a detailed dispatch to England, requesting action to restrict foreign whaling (CO 18/18:198, 4/7/1837), although it was to be several years before a response was received. Meanwhile, tensions rose and rumours circulated, with one eagerly received report being that Lord Glenelg had intimated that a man–of–war would be sent to patrol the Western Australian coasts in the following season (PG 8/12/1839).

Colonial Office correspondence (CO 18/23–30) reveals the lengthy discussions between various individuals and committees in England, weighing the situation and possible responses or actions. However, the uncertainty as to the rights of the American whalers, as well as the difficulties which might arise from any attempt to remove them, resulted in guarded responses such as that from the Board of Trade.

> By the Law of Nations the inhabitants of every country have the exclusive rights of fishing within three miles of low water mark, upon the coast and harbours thereof, unless the subjects of other states have, by treaty or immemorial usage acquired the right to fish therein... I can not, however, undertake to advise that Great Britain has any just right to exclude foreigners from fishing on such parts of the coast of Western Australia as are not in British occupation. (CO 18/29: 54, 25/1/1841)

There also appears to have been a body of opinion, revealed in margin notes and memoranda, that it was not necessarily beneficial to the Western Australian colony to have the foreigners driven away (CO 18/25: 54, 15/2/1841; CO 18/29: 24, 29/1/1841). As the colonists were unable to engage in the fishery themselves, it was felt that the Americans were not depriving them of any advantage. Instead, the Americans resorting there and providing 'a large... and reliable market for various commodities produced there' was promoting the international interests of the settlements.

The belated response of the Queen's Advocate followed these opinions, stating that the American whalers should be informed that Great Britain denied their right to fish within three miles of the shore of bays and harbours occupied 'bona–fide' by British subjects (CO 18/25:54, 15/2/1841). However, force would not be resorted to, except if especially directed by the Secretary of State should 'some aggravated case warranted remonstrance' (HRA I (21): 268–69, 9/3/1841; PG 30/1/41). New Zealand, which was also complaining of foreign whaling encroachments, received a similar response to their requests for assistance (HRA I (21): 270, 26/2/1841).

Despite their obvious inability to enforce any directives, the colonial authorities attempted to apply the three–mile limit on the settled bays of the colony, including the bays in which local whalers had established themselves. In 1843 the Government Magistrate of Albany posted a notice stating that foreign ships interfering with bay whaling establishments risked seizure of their vessels (CSR 119/99, 22/6/1843). On the west coast foreign vessels were also advised of the three mile limit and told that as Geographe Bay was considered a settled bay they were not to fish beyond a line drawn due east from the head of Cape Naturaliste to the opposite coast (Heppingstone 1969). While the American whalers generally abided by these conditions, they were well aware of their role in the coastal exploration of the region and responded accordingly.

> I hereby acknowledge receipt of a copy of a letter from the Colonial Government in which they say we have no right to whale in this bay, but at the same time do not intend to interfere with us so long as there are no English whalers at the same place. This act of courtesy I consider our due for having found and proved the best anchorages on this coast such as Doubtful Island, Cape Riche and Two People Bay, Geographe, Leschenault and Safety Bay all of which have been proven by Yankee enterprise. (CSR 85/82, 24/1/1840)

Although the American whalers normally avoided confrontations, possibly for the sake of continuing trade relations, there are numerous references to foreign ships fishing adjacent to settled areas and even in close proximity of Fremantle. Whitecar's comments during a visit to King George Sound in 1856 may well sum up the American attitude.

> It is the law of the English Coast, that no fishing should be carried on within three miles of the coast of colonies. This law is a dead letter in the Indian Ocean, excepting where their fisheries exist; and I am sure that, had whales made their presence in this bay whilst we were present, our boats would have been down among them. (Whitecar 1860: 219)

This situation lasted until at least 1860, when it finally became possible to pass and enforce legislation preventing foreign whaling.

Beyond the cautious and sometimes strained relationship with the colonial whalers, the trade activities of the foreign whalers became a major factor in the early survival of most of the coastal settlements outside Fremantle. Despite Churchward's (1949; 1979) claims to the contrary, the commercial interaction was clearly two–way, with the American whaleships forming both a significant export market and an important source of imported goods. For the foreign whalers the small settlements provided a valuable opportunity for obtaining wood, water and food supplies without having to return to Batavia, Sydney or New Zealand. As suggested by the Colonial Office, for the colonists the pelagic whalers became consumers for produce that would not otherwise have had a market.

The initial appearance of American whalers at the main ports had been heralded with high expectations of developing a profitable commerce in supplying them with produce (PG 18/2/1837). Unfortunately, greed and poor judgment on the part of the colonial merchants and administration appears to have impeded the opportunity for developing the market to its full potential. Complaints from the American captains with regard to the prices of produce and the port fees at the major harbours emerged in early 1839 (PG 23/2/1839). These were not taken seriously until 1842 when, after several unheeded warnings about the slack attitude towards providing reasonable services, the Americans stopped calling at Fremantle and Albany (PG 5/3/42). It was not until 1846 and the repeal of the harbour fees that American ships returned to those ports (Inq 29/4/1846).

In contrast to the main settlements healthy commerce continued at the more isolated harbours, particularly Augusta, with the increasing demands for produce amounting to thousands of pounds of income (e.g. Inq 3/8/1842; Inq 26/4/1843). In an admirable feat of entrepreneurship, in 1842 George Cheyne established a private anchorage and supply base for the whalers at his Cape Riche property, 90 kilometres east of Albany (PG 18/11/1843). It was reputed to afford a high standard of service and not only could vessels be provisioned there without having to pay port fees, but the captains also did not have the worries of desertion or drunkenness that usually attended visits to the larger settlements.

In addition to the sale of provisions, the inhabitants of the smaller ports (and to a lesser extent Fremantle) were also able to purchase from the Americans a range of commodities that were often in short supply by normal means. This included smuggling of spirits and other items to avoid payment of duty and taxes; a relatively easy process given the vast and largely unpoliced coastline. Both sides were also willing to engage in barter; a situation that gave the Americans increased purchasing power and allowed the colonists to preserve their limited supply of currency. In the early years of the settlement this helped fill the gap created by irregular supply from England and uncertain distribution through the coastal trade.

Whaling vessels, particularly those which made repeated visits to the same ports, also provided an important social outlet for the remote settlements, with this contact obviously valued by the whalers as well (Shann 1926; Hasluck 1955; Gatchell 1844; Jennings 1983). Detailed examination of relationships with foreign whalers is provided in Gibbs (2000).

CONSOLIDATION (1843–1869)

The years between 1843 and 1869 represent the main period of shore whaling in Western Australia. Whereas the preceding phase might be seen as one of experimentation, it was during this phase that the patterns of station organisation and operation by which the industry can be characterised were established. Although there is no clear dividing event, two main stages can be distinguished. From the re–commencement of whaling in 1843 until the mid–1850s was a time of expansion, with new operators entering the industry and new locations and modes of organisation being tested. This gave way to a period of stability that saw little change within the industry, lasting until a decline in activity in the late 1860s. While the broad historical development of the industry is documented here, specific aspects of the organisation and operation of the whaling in Western Australia are examined in Chapters 3 and 4.

Re–establishment of the colonial whaling industry occurred amidst a variety of forces that both encouraged and limited its potential scope. The first several years of the 1840s had seen Western Australia experience buoyant economic activity which included an increase in immigration. However, this changed during 1843 when a dramatic drop in new settler arrivals, increased government expenditure and falling livestock and grain prices combined to throw the colony back into an economic recession. An unfavourable balance of trade also developed, once again reducing liquidity as capital was lost through high import payments (Statham 1981a). It is probable that part of this decline can be attributed to the recently lost trade with the American whaleships.

The Governor appealed to the settlers for help in redressing this situation, urging them to reduce their imports while exporting as much colonial produce as possible (Inq 8/5/1844; Statham 1981a). It was in this period of searching for potential export items that attention was once again drawn to whaling. The recovery of international oil prices to the pre–1838 high of £45 per tun (Chamberlain 1988), combined with the still obvious potential for a successful fishery along the coast, provided further incentive for local merchants. One south and one west coast party had started operation by mid–1843, and in the following year that number had doubled (Figure 3.7). By late 1844 the export earnings of the new whaling ventures and other industries fostered under the Governor's campaign had successfully reduced the effects of the recession (Statham 1981a).

The relative ease with which the settlers were able to re–commence shore whaling despite the surrounding economic difficulties might be traced to the unexpected increase in availability of cheap whaling equipment in the colony. During the first half of the 1840s over half a dozen American and French whaling vessels were wrecked along the south and west coasts of Western Australia. Rather than attempt to repair and refloat their vessels, the captains chose to dispose of the hulls and all of the whalecraft on board (Table 2.1).

These pelagic whaleships carried enough whalecraft for their three to four year cruise, which was sufficient to completely equip two or more shore stations. Most notable was the fact that the prices received at auction for these cargoes was usually under £400, significantly less than the costs of purchasing and importing equipment from England, and without the prolonged delays in transport. In particular, if the vessel was at the end of its voyage and had a full cargo of oil, the master would quickly dispose of all of the whalecraft as a means of maximising profits from the cruise (Whitecar 1860). The body of cheap whalecraft now amassed in the colony, together with further development of associated manufacturing and service industries, markedly reduced the establishment costs that had bedevilled the local industry.

The labour market had also been slowly growing and there was now a body of men with prior whaling experience, including a fluctuating population of deserters from foreign vessels. There rapidly evolved a situation where a relatively small amount of capital, maybe even the £300 mentioned by Blainey (1966:111), was sufficient for a colonist to form a small whaling party. In addition to the cargoes from the wrecks, visiting American whalers were often willing to sell surplus equipment to local fisheries and merchants. The whaling parties that emerged during this phase of re–establishment were more modest than those seen prior to 1843. Whereas the Fremantle and Northern whaling companies were large stations that had expended much of their capital and effort in developing fixed assets, the new parties appear to have opted for a smaller and simpler scale of operation (Chapters 4 and 5).

Although there is little historical evidence on the nature of the stations, they were generally only two or three boat fisheries, with facilities limited to basic processing plant and huts for between 13 and 21 hands. It is possible that this reflected the nature of the leases, which were annual and saw all improvements revert to the government at the end of the term.

It was this clause which had sealed the fate of the Northern Company, only emerging when the company had tried to save itself by attempting to sell the Carnac Island station back to the government 'for a reasonable consideration' (PG 24/3/38). However, as the industry stabilised the continuing associations of particular parties with particular station sites created a security of tenure that allowed them to develop their facilities with only a limited risk of removal or resumption.

Name	Wrecked	Location	Equipment sold or auctioned	References
Samuel Wright	8/7/1840	Bunbury	Wreck plus whaleboats, gear, rigging etc for £300 to Captain Coffin, the former captain. 400 fathoms whale line.	PG 1/8/1840 PG 8/8/40
North America (1)	8/7/1840	Bunbury	Wreck plus whaleboats, gear, rigging etc for £400 to J.R. Phillips	PG 1/8/1840
Governor Endicott	8/7/1840	Toby's Inlet	hull for £400 and all material connected with vessel for £300 to Captain Coffin	PG 1/8/1840
Avis	28/8/1842	Two People Bay	Sale of hull, oil, cargo and materials at Albany.	Inq 21/9/1842
North America (2)	15/4/1843	Bunbury	Hull to D. Scott. Whaling gear possibly sold to J.K. Child	PG 22/4/1843 Henderson 1980
Cervantes	20/6/1844	Jurien Bay	Wreck and all stores, whaling gear, cutting in falls, whale boats, anchors, chain cables, kedge anchor, spare planks oars and casks sold to Mr. Wickstead for £155	PG 13/7/1844 PG 27/7/1844
Halcyon	5/8/1844	Toby's Inlet	'Hull with masts, rigging, sails, tryworks, gear...'. Hull sold to J. Molloy for £60. Whaleboats sold to T. Habgood	PG 24/8/1844, PG 21/9/1844
Merope	28/2/1844	Fremantle	'Hull to Mr. Jecks for £100'. 'Hull & whaling gear re-sold to D. Scott for £150	PG 26/4/1845 PG 2/5/1845
Iris	29/6/1855	Port Gregory	'... bread, slops, clothing, casks, trypots, copper cooler, sails, spars, rigging... superior whaling gear, comprising everything fit for a season'	Inq 31/10/1855

Table 2.1 Whalecraft sold from wrecked American whaleships 1840–1855.

The simpler operation and decreased overheads of the whaling stations also saw the emergence of less elaborate financial structures. Ownership of most of the stations can be traced to a single investor, or small partnerships of several local merchants and landowners. The Fremantle Whaling Company still existed, although the directors increasingly chose to lease the station to individuals in return for a fixed rent or a percentage of the catch, rather than engage in organising a whaling party themselves (PG 3/5/1848).

While various arrangements were still being made between American and colonial whalers (CSR 131/59: 31/7/1844), no evidence has been found to show that either foreign or eastern Australian interests were financing any of the Western Australian parties. Except in the broadest market-related terms, the continuing development of the colonial whaling industry apparently remained independent of the interests of other Australasian whalers. It is, however, worth reiterating that other Australasian whalers had also been adversely affected by the economic difficulties of the 1840s. Combined with diminishing whale stocks and reduced returns, a similar pattern of closure or simplified operations obtained and is often taken to mark the 'end' of shore whaling (Dakin 1938; Morton 1982; Campbell 1992; Nash 2003).

The 1840s and early 1850s saw the formation of a succession of small whaling parties on both the south and west coasts of Western Australia. Many of these groups were short-lived, surviving no more than one or two seasons before being sold or disbanded (Chapter 3). It is difficult to determine the cause of this high turnover, although it is probable that inexperience still played a large part in local difficulties.

The total annual number of whaling operations across both coasts remained at half a dozen parties or less, usually with a higher concentration on the west coast. Although analysis of historical sources suggests that all whaling parties have been accounted for, the poor communications of the period, particularly between the south and west coasts, allows the possibility that there may have been other small or short-lived stations which have not been identified.

Several new locations were tested, including some of those used in the first years of the whaling industry (see Figures 4.1 and 4.2). Possibly as a result of the limited number of suitable bays, the west coast fisheries were generally situated in or adjacent to the harbours in which settlements were or soon would be located. This created an association between whaling and hinterland development, although not necessarily with the direct links to pastoralism seen in Eastern Australia (Little 1969).

In contrast, the greater range of suitable locations along the south coast saw shore parties rapidly spread beyond King George Sound, even though settlement was to remain focused around Albany. The process of selecting suitable locations and the histories of individual stations are discussed in detail in Chapter 4.

Two brief sorties into bay whaling occurred during the 1840s. The first began in 1841, with the purchase of the barque *Napoleon* by Daniel Scott and a Liverpool syndicate (Heppingstone 1973; Inq 21/7/41; PG 16/7/41). Although there were several brief periods of whaling along the Western Australian coast, the ship's log shows that most of the time she was engaged northwards between the Timor Sea and the Sulu Sea (BL 239A/1). In late 1844 she was loaded with cargo and set sail for England, but did not return to Western Australia.

The second episode was with the English barque *Merope*, which had been driven ashore at Woodman's Point during a gale and then was also sold with all of her whalecraft to Captain Scott (PG 1/3/1845, Inq 5/4/1845, PG 3/5/1845). Once re-floated, *Merope* remained a more consistent presence along the Western Australian coast. In late April of 1846 *Merope* under Captain Harding sailed for the sperm whaling grounds (PG 25/4/46) but at a later date also bay whaled at Augusta and assisted the Castle Rock shore station. After being given English registry *Merope* was then sent to England with a cargo (CO 18/47:25, 17/2/1848) and is not thought to have returned to Western Australia. In both the cases of *Merope* and *Napoleon* it is hard to determine if whaling was ever the primary purpose of the vessels, and if it was, why they failed to pursue it more vigorously.

Between 1843 and 1846 various stations reported disruptions or desertions by whaling hands, sometimes impeding operations and resulting in the loss of whales. Although the offenders in at least two of these incidents were sentenced to imprisonment with hard labour (Inq 3/9/1845), there were calls for a revision to the law of engagement to provide better regulation of whalers' conduct (Inq 10/9/1846). The potential of continued disturbances to damage the success of the fishery was obviously considered serious enough to result in the passing of an act to allow articles of agreement to be drawn between whalers and their employers (*Statutes of Western Australia*, 10th Victoria, No.16, 1847). The contracts worked in favour of the station owners, allowing them to punish breaches of contract with a range of penalties from fines to imprisonment. It is not known if anyone was prosecuted under these regulations, although analysis of known whalers and their positions within the parties provides an important insight into both the nature of the parties and the men who worked in the whaling industry.

From the mid–1840s the Blue Books (government statistical reports) provide a regular annual record of oil and bone returns from each region, together with the estimated value of the catch and export returns from oil and bone during that year. Although not complete, these figures reveal that the industry as a whole was achieving reasonable catch success (Figure 3.22) and until the early 1850s producing a moderate export income (Figure 2.2). Unfortunately, the peak in oil prices after this time (Chamberlain 1988) was not met with a corresponding increase in colonial production or export returns. In the context of the rest of the colonial economy, wool and sandalwood had significantly overtaken whale products as the major export income earners. The contribution of whale products fell below eight percent by 1849, and by 1861 it had dropped below two percent (Butlin *et al.* 1987: 122).

The presence of, and occasional direct competition with, American whalers continued to be a factor in the fortunes of the local shore stations, with several incidents and complaints reported during 1844 (PG 11/5/1844; Inq 16/10/1844). Undoubtedly, the intensive fishing which had taken place since 1837 had also considerably reduced the coastal whale stocks of the region, seriously decreasing the opportunities for the colonial stations. The repeal of port fees (Inq 29/4/46) saw a slow return by foreign vessels to the major ports, although by this time Western Australia had lost the opportunity of becoming a major supply base for the American fleet. Figure 2.3 shows that after the peak of the early 1840s the number of American vessels in the region declined rapidly, hastened in the late 1840s by the loss of ships and men to the Californian gold rush (Gibbs 2000).

An important aspect of the Western Australian whaling industry that becomes evident during the 1840s is the complete separation of both management and activity between the west and south coasts. Although officially part of the same colony, the settlements at Albany and the Swan River were for many years divided by a sea voyage that lasted a week or more. While joined in the broader administrative and economic sense, they were in most respects separate colonies, pursuing their own patterns of development.

With regard to the whaling industry, no evidence has been found to suggest interaction between merchants, investors, or even workers in the south coast parties with their counterparts along the west coast. This separation also extended to physical boundaries, with the difficulties of rounding Cape Leeuwin and Cape Naturaliste creating a formidable natural barrier against movement between the two regions. Such a voyage was well beyond the capabilities of the small colonial whaling parties, resulting in south coast shore whaling activities only extending east of Torbay, while the west coast parties did not pass south beyond Cape Naturaliste.

This dichotomy in the colonial whaling activity, which lasted until the close of operations in the late 1870s, meant that Western Australia effectively had two whaling industries. This presents possibilities for comparison between the two regions, some of which will be explored in later sections. However, the remainder of this narrative will continue to follow broad developments and influences within the colony as a whole, and treat the whaling activity on both coasts as a single entity.

June 1850 marked a major turning point in the social and economic development of the Western Australian colonies, being the point when that the first shipload of convicts arrived from England. Although many sectors of the Western Australian community retained the anti–transportation stance that had predominated since colonisation, a concerted campaign by the powerful pastoralist body known as the York Agricultural Society forced the change in policy.

By the mid–1840s, the further development of the agricultural, timber and pastoral industries had once again created a shortage of free labourers in the colony. As a result, these men were able to demand extremely high wages and conditions for their seasonal or contract employment, causing discontent among the employers. It was the pastoralists, wealthy, well organised and politically connected in both the colony and England, who led the push for convict labour. Their ostensible motive was that the introduction of convicts would have wide reaching benefits for the colony through the completion of public works, the introduction of Imperial expenditure to support the system, increased land values and the lowering of food and other prices. However, their actual purpose was clearly to break the labour situation by introducing a flood of cheap and controllable workers (Statham 1981b).

The arrival of the convicts, their guards and the Imperial funding that sustained the system certainly did produce some of the effects predicted by the York Agricultural Society, although an economic boom period did not result (Statham 1981a; Gibbs 2001). With respect to the whaling industry, it can be supposed that the change in the labour market did have a flow–on effect in making men available for employment. Convicts themselves were not allowed to be engaged on boats for the obvious reason of the escape opportunities so offered, although some stations did try to obtain permission to use ticket–of–leave men (convicts allowed to seek employment from free settlers) in their parties.

The second important change in the early 1850s was the spread of European settlement beyond the original boundaries of the southwest. The colonial administration had previously been loath to stretch its limited resources and consequently had restricted any expansion of settlement above the Swan River. However, the discovery of minerals in the lower Murchison region in the late 1840s, together with pressure from the York Agricultural Society to open new pastoral runs, resulted in the 1850 decision to establish new outposts at Port Gregory and Champion Bay (Geraldton), some 450 km north of Fremantle (Bain 1975). By 1854 one of the major settlers at Port Gregory, Captain Henry Sanford, had established his own whaling party. Two years later he had gone into partnership with Fremantle whaler Joshua Harwood, while John Bateman had also sent crews into the area.

By the mid–1850s the whaling industry on both coasts had entered a period of stability. Out of the many owners and operators seen during the preceding phase a number had survived and were now joined by several new figures to become a consistent presence until at least the end of the 1860s. On the west coast there were Bateman, Harwood and Heppingstone, with the latter's son–in–law George Layman inheriting the Castle Rock operation after his death in 1858. On the south coast there were Thomas, Sherratt and McKenzie. Many of these men were the second generation to be involved in whaling in Western Australia, had worked their way through the local industry and were now taking an active part in the operation of their own parties, usually as headsmen.

Although most of the whaling parties remained closely associated with particular stations, there was an increasing trend towards using more than one station during a season, following the whale migrations. On the west coast this had come into practice with the occupation of Port Gregory, with both Bateman's and Harwood's groups starting in the north before moving southward to Fremantle or Bunbury to catch the later season. As this system developed, it appears that parties were sometimes maintained at both a northern and southern location, with the former group later returning to strengthen the Fremantle operation, or passing directly southward to a new position.

Similar developments were to occur on the south coast, although at a slightly later date. Albany had remained a small and depressed village, servicing American whaleships and the occasional P&O Company steamer, with shore whaling still forming an important component of the local income. There had been some hinterland development, but it was not until the 1860s and 1870s that small pastoral communities began to develop along the coast to the east of Albany at Bremer Bay, Esperance and later at Eucla (Garden 1977:135). After a slump in the 1850s, the south coast whaling industry had managed to revive to three small parties operating in and around King George Sound. There are a few reports from this time which suggest that the whaling parties had begun to split their seasons, spending the later half at stations around Cape Arid and Middle Island, about 550km east from Albany (Inq 12/11/1862; Sale n.d.). Although there was trade between the whalers and the few European settlers of these remote areas (Erikson 1978), it is hard to demonstrate a direct association between the opening of the pastoral frontier and the eastward movement of the whalers.

Despite this increased effort, the individual stations on both coasts were no longer making the sorts of catches seen in the 1840s. The estimated value of the annual yield fluctuated between £1000 and £4000 per season (Figure 3.25). Export earnings also averaged close to several thousand pounds per year (Figure 2.1), which was now a negligible component of the total colonial economy (Figure 2.2). A rise in local consumption of oil resulting from increases in population and public amenities must also have reduced the availability of oil for export. Another major influence was the discovery of petroleum in Pennsylvania in 1859, although it was to be another decade before the sale of kerosene would begin to have a serious impact upon the local and international whaling community (Whipple 1979).

In 1858 an incident occurred near Fremantle where it was claimed that the boats of the American whaler *Lapwing* had deliberately 'galleyed' or frightened a whale as one of the local whaling parties attempted to harpoon it. Joshua Harwood, the owner of the shore station, attempted to sue Captain Cumiskey for £600 damages and is reported in contemporary papers as settling out of court for £300 (Inq 23/2/1859; Inq 6/4/1859). However, Heppingstone (1969) suggests that this amount was awarded by a jury, followed by a successful appeal which resulted in the judge ruling that Americans were friendly aliens with acknowledged rights to fish in British waters (Inq 23/2/1859; BL Acc. 991).

The case of Harwood vs. Cumiskey appears to have stirred up many of the old resentments regarding foreign whaling in the region. On the advice of English legal authorities (Heppingstone 1966), the Legislative Council passed an Act in December 1860 entitled 'An Ordinance to prohibit Aliens and Foreigners taking whales and other fish in the Waters of Western Australia' (*Statutes of Western Australia* 24th Victoria, No. 12., 1860). The preamble states that the act was formed to prevent aliens and foreigners in foreign ships and vessels from taking whales on the coast of Western Australia to the prejudice of British subjects and in breach of sovereign rights. Foreigners caught taking whales, or persons aiding such actions, would be liable to fines between £5 and £20, a strangely ineffectual sort of penalty given that each whale yielded many times that value.

Although clearly establishing the legal means of preventing or at least rapidly resolving further situations of conflict, it is hard to determine what real effects the act had on whaling in the area. A fraction of the American vessels seen in previous years now visited the region and in the following year these were still being regularly reported at the outports (PG 1/3/1861). The advent of the American Civil War in the same year effected a further reduction in the number of vessels soon after (Figure 2.3). Between 1861 and 1865 Confederate attacks on Yankee whaleships and re–deployment or sinking of vessels as a defensive measure reduced the size of the American whaling fleet by nearly 50 per cent (Whipple 1979:156). When hostilities ceased there was a return by American whalers to the New Holland Grounds off the Western Australian coast, but with numbers tailing off during the 1870s and 1880s.

In general, the 1860s was a decade of economic growth in Western Australia. The public works undertaken by or as a result of convicts facilitated communications and movement through the colony, while the extra labour supply and demand for goods and services resulting from their presence made a variety of formerly marginal industries viable (Appleyard 1981:214). Although the early sandalwood trade had declined sharply, the export of other forms of timber was steadily rising. Returns from the mineral industries increased with the new copper and lead discoveries around Northampton and the Murchison River, although wool showed the sharpest increase in export revenues.

Despite up to eight stations operating in the opening years of the decade, the reported total return of whale oil fell below sixty tuns between 1860 and 1864, with a correspondingly steep drop in export returns (Figure 2.1). This situation is not explained in contemporary newspaper accounts, although comment was made about the continuing high prices for colonial oil (Inq 19/10/1864). A later report stated that 'the take on our shores is not sufficient for our demands, and the few tuns at King George Sound find a market in South Australia where...from £50–60 a tun is realised' (Inq 24/5/1865). If accurate, oil prices on the local market were from £10 to £20 higher per tun than those seen on the London market for the same period (Chamberlain 1988:48). Despite the potential for high returns and aside from a good season and high yields in 1865, the shore whaling industry in Western Australia continued to slump. By 1869 there was only one station on each coast.

It is possible that the neglect of the whaling industry resulted from the buoyant state of the other colonial industries described above. However, the agent that had enabled or at least encouraged these other industrial developments was soon to be removed, possibly resulting in the final revival of the shore whaling industry.

DECLINE (1870–1879)

In 1868 the transportation of British convicts to Western Australia ceased, reducing the flow of Imperial finance which had supported the system. Economic and demographic growth had also slowed, compounded by a shortage in available capital for new ventures. Finally, the droughts of 1869 and 1870 created difficulties for agriculture and resulted in a reduction in decreased wool exports, normally the colony's economic mainstay (Appleyard 1980).

It is possible that, as in the earliest years of the colony, the short–term revival of whaling on both coasts was a response to the difficulties being experienced on the land. The 1870 census report devoted a lengthy section to whaling, stating that over the last several years there had been a rapid increase in the number of whales visible along the coast, with a large fleet of Americans expected off the coast in the following season. The discussion closed with a note reminiscent of thirty years earlier, stating that the Americans continued to provide a salutary example to the local capitalists, 'for here, outside the threshold of our door, is unlimited, unbounded wealth, taken annually away by a strange nation, thousands of miles away' (Knight 1870: 16).

Although the renewed whaling activity took slightly different forms on both coasts, the focus appears to have been on areas at some distance from the main settlements. Along the west coast the revival was encouraged by the opening on the new northwest settlements at Roebourne and Cossack. The neighbouring Dampier Archipelago had long been known as a highly productive region for whaling, and had been heavily exploited by Americans vessels in previous decades (Wace and Lovett 1973:13). The colonial interest in its potential was more recently inspired by reports of successful cruises by the eastern Australian whaler *Emily Smith* in 1868 (Inq 30/9/1868; Her 3/10/68; Heppingstone 1966). Possibly faced with the opportunity to combine trading activities in the region with an income derived from whaling, a station was established on Malus Island by merchants W. and S. Pearse in partnership with William Marmion (Inq 20/7/1870). Two years later John Bateman, in partnership with a local merchant, also commenced operations in the area (Inq 30/11/1872).

While the 1870 and 1871 seasons were very successful, 1872 progressed badly for both northwest stations as a result of rough weather (Herald 21/9/1872). Both of these parties relied upon their respective vessels to cruise the archipelago for whales, possibly making them more susceptible to these sorts of poor weather conditions. In the following year neither group sent a party to Malus Island, focusing instead on Port Gregory and their more southerly stations. After this point the decline on the west coast was rapid, with only one unidentified station operating in 1874 and 1875. In 1877 John Bateman's schooner *Star*, under command of his son Francis, went on a whaling cruise about the Dampier Archipelago, leasing Malus Island as a shore–station (SDUR B10/1144C/, 12/1/1877). The vessel later returned to Fremantle with 147 casks of oil, although for an unknown reason these are not entered in the Blue Book report (PG 23/11/1877).

The situation on the south coast during this final phase was somewhat more complex, with several new operators, most with previous associations with the Albany whaling industry, emerging as owners or managers (Appendix B.1). The pattern of moving between stations appears to have held for at least the first half of the decade, with the Barker Bay, Cheyne Beach and Cape Riche stations still being mentioned. However, much of the activity of the later part of the decade is obscured as a result of the cancellation of all whaling leases on the south coast in 1873. In 1872, Hugh McKenzie had challenged Thomas Sherratt's use of his whaling leases to exclude other parties from certain bays (BL Acc. 346, 16/1/1873). Early in the following year the Commissioner for Crown Lands had decided that, rather than allow this monopoly to continue, the leases should be removed and the harbours left open 'for all comers' (BL Acc. 346, 12/2/1873). At this point the use of particular stations, especially around the remote east coast area (Cape Arid) becomes difficult to follow.

Although between one and three parties operated each year during this period, with the exception of 1875 which had a return of 40 tuns of oil (BB 1875), the total annual yield was usually less than 20 tuns (Figure 3.25). In 1879 three two–boat parties registered for the east coast, becoming the last official shore whalers in the colony.

It was in this closing phase of whaling in Western Australia that a final belated attempt was made to enter the pelagic fishery. In 1873 a syndicate of five Albany businessmen purchased the American whaling barque *Islander*, refitting it in Hobart for a total of £4500 (Her 14/6/1873). Throughout the 1870s she cruised along the south coast and on occasion the west coast, with one unsuccessful voyage towards Timor (Chamberlain 1988:155). Shipping reports show that *Islander* called at King George's Sound every three months or so, although in most respects she was more closely allied with the Tasmanian pelagic whaling industry and had no apparent connections with local shore fisheries (O'May 1957; Chamberlain 1988).

An even more elaborate scheme for pelagic whaling was proposed in 1876, inspired by the previous season's success of five American and eastern Australian vessels, presumably including *Islander*. After a series of meetings between Albany businesspersons, provisional directors were appointed to draft a prospectus for The King George Sound Whaling Company (Inq 21/6/1876). The capital of the company was to be £12,000, increasing to £20,000 if necessary, for the purpose of purchasing and fitting two or three whalers at New Bedford. Although nothing was to come of this venture, it provides an interesting contrast between what was deemed possible in 1876 and the difficulties in raising only £400 in 1836.

The *Blue Book* reports of export returns from whale products show several peculiarities that require some explanation. The first is in 1871, when the total yield of oil is reported as 119 tuns (with an unspecified quantity of bone), which represents a good but not spectacular return. The total estimated value, however, is given as £6905, the highest recorded in the history of whaling in the colony. This is much higher than would be expected if accepting Chamberlain's (1988:48) figures of £35 to £40 per tun for black oil on the depressed London market in this period. It is also substantially more than the 1871 total export return for whale products which is reported as only £4231 (Figure 2.1). It is possible that the estimated value was misquoted or misprinted, or that a large quantity of whalebone (then commanding over £400 per ton) was collected, although in the latter case there is no evidence in the following years of large or valuable quantities of bone being exported.

After the closure of the west coast fisheries the export return from oil and bone dropped sharply, with only £258 and £357 being recorded from the south coast in 1874 and 1875 respectively. The *Blue Book* then shows an unexpected rise between 1876 and 1878 inclusive with as much as £6600 per year being returned from whale product exports, followed by a further £4238 for 1880. As it is unlikely that the few remaining shore whaling operations could suddenly generate such high returns, this can only be attributed to the production from the *Islander* being added to the total. This would also explain why most of this oil is recorded as being exported to Tasmania, where the *Islander* was most frequently based. By using the expedient of removing exports to Tasmania from the totals, the more modest oil yield of the shore whalers, peaking at £1962 in 1878, can be traced (Appendix B5 and B6). No further returns from the whale fishery were recorded after 1880.

The close of the 1879 season can therefore be seen as the end of the shore whaling industry of Western Australia. In 1880, John Bateman's schooner *Star* sailed from Fremantle for a whaling cruise south of Fremantle. Equipped with two whale boat crews and with Bateman himself (now in his late 50s) as one of the headsmen, the voyage was unsuccessful, with the ship wrecking on its return journey to Fremantle (Henderson 1988). There is no evidence that a shore station was established.

In August of 1882 several humpback whales entered Princess Royal Harbour at Albany. It was reported that:

> the old enthusiasm for whale killing seized those who had in years gone by been engaged in the business, and a boat with crew, harpoon gun, bombs and lances, soon started in pursuit of the monster from the deep. (PG 8/8/1882)

The passion for whaling continued for two days, although their chances at success were foiled by faulty equipment. After that time a look–out was kept for another several weeks, although no further report was made.

McKail (1927) also related that after the close of the industry, John Cowden of Albany 'often made up a crew to give me a chance to see a whale fastened to and killed'. However, he suggested that this diversion finally ended after an episode where a female whale repeatedly attempted to rescue her dead calf, despite being lanced several times as she came close to the boats. While acknowledging the excitement of the hunt, McKail (1927) stated that 'very few, after witnessing that special cow and her love for her offspring, would care to make a sport of it'. Wolfe (2003) has argued that these late episodes of shore whaling throughout the late 19th century and early 20th century constitute a continuation of the industry.

However, since these events seem to have been sporadic, they are perhaps better seen as a continuation of what by then was a form of traditional practice amongst the Albany maritime community

Although the era of the traditional open–boat shore whaler eventually ended in Western Australia, it was not the end of whaling itself. In 1912 a new and more deadly phase began with the arrival of the Norwegian whalers. Using powered whale chasers, explosive harpoons and modern industrial shore stations, the hunt for humpback and then sperm whales began again and was not to end until 1978.

ABORIGINAL WHALERS

One of the most important elements of the maritime industrial frontier is that sites such as whaling stations were often the points of first contact between Aboriginal and non–Aboriginal groups. Even where there had been prior contact, the shore whaling camps were usually a far more sustained presence than the fleeting encounters with explorers or other transients.

This section explores the nature and impact of the interaction between Aboriginals and shore whalers in the various regions of Western Australia. A different approach to this data is also provided in a separate paper (Gibbs 2003a).

Nyungar Traditional Life

As for other areas of the continent, the Aboriginal inhabitants of southwest Western Australia (usually referred to by the portfolio name of *Nyungar*) did not traditionally hunt for whale, locally known as *mimanga* (Moore 1884). The animals did, however, strand frequently enough that whale blubber and meat were considered a preferred or luxury food, with the occasion becoming an excuse for an impromptu gathering of nearby local groups.

The ethnohistorical literature of the region is studded with accounts of Aboriginal people coming together to spend several days feasting (Meagher 1973:23; Gibbs 1987:47). The flesh would be cut off and either eaten raw or roasted over a fire, while the blubber was rubbed onto the bodies of the participants (Grey 1841:277; Shann 1926:96; WA 9/10/1937). These positive associations with whale meat consumption may have contributed to relations between Aboriginal groups and with shore whaling parties (Gibbs 1987:47).

Contact with Whalers and Whaling

The colonial shore whalers were far from the being the first Europeans encountered by coastal Aboriginal groups in Western Australia, with intermittent contacts from the 17th century onwards. However, opportunities for contact intensified dramatically after the 1790s with the settlement of the eastern Australian colonies, the entry of commercial whalers and sealers into the Pacific, and the series of scientific expeditions already described. It is some measure of the level of European activity that by the first years of the 1820s the *Mineng* peoples of what would several years later become the site of Albany were almost completely indifferent to the appearance and activities of Europeans (King 1827; Fanning 1832).

Reynolds (1982:175) has already noted that frontier maritime industries such as whaling were 'probably less disruptive of Aboriginal life than either mining or pastoralism' and fitted easily into the accustomed pattern of coastal use. The whaling stations only required a small plot of land and as Aboriginal use of the whales had been opportunistic, their capture did not impinge negatively upon the traditional subsistence resource base. As the whaling process at this time only required the blubber, baleen and several other minor body parts, this left the bulk of the animal unused. While it is possible that a small portion of the whale beef was taken for use at the station, the rest of the carcass seems to have been made available for consumption by the Aboriginal population. Suddenly there was the opportunity to indulge regularly in what formerly had been a sporadically available, but favoured, food source.

Throughout the southwest large groups of Aboriginal people were reported as spending the several months of the whaling season camped by the stations, feasting on whale meat (Hitchcock 1927; Burton 1954; Haley 1948; Stokes 1848). It is unclear exactly how this arrangement proceeded, although presumably they were allowed access to the whale for the several days while it was flensed and the oil was tried out, after which the carcass was pulled back out to sea for disposal. Aboriginal owners of these areas may also have perceived this as their rightful share to the resource. There is no historical record to suggest that there was any attempt to restrict or control access to the whale flesh, although economic and social reciprocity relationships almost certainly developed between the groups as a consequence.

Other types of trade for European materials and foodstuffs almost certainly also took place, although the only clear historical data are from Castle Rock near Busselton. Station manager Seymour's diary (Seymour 20/9/1852) states that the cook had been 'seen giving the natives sugar'. Similarly, the Articles of Agreement for whalers at that station in 1850 specifically contains a clause that 'Natives are on no account to be retained in the employment of individuals, a charge will be made for any provision seen or known to be distributed among them' (BL 1208A; see also Figure 3.1). What this employment by individual whalers may have consisted of is uncertain. Although the limited survey of the wider hinterland of the shore stations located no Aboriginal sites, it is probable that the camps used during the whaling season would contain European material.

Various types of relationships between whalers and indigenous women, including long–term cohabitation and marriages, are well known elsewhere in Australia and New Zealand (Staniforth *et al.* 2001; Russell 2007).

However, so far there has been no clear historical or archaeological evidence for of these associations in Western Australia.

While the nature of the whaling activities favoured good relations between the two groups, the differing extent of European settlement on each coast created differences in the texture of the engagements between the groups. The west coast bore the brunt of the settlement activities and despite a slow start the number and spread of the European population along the coastal fringe did increase rapidly. As agricultural and pastoral settlement expanded across the coastal plains and adjacent inland regions, the opportunities for Aboriginal groups to exploit their traditional resource base rapidly diminished. Communities were either forced to pursue their economy in the more marginal areas or succumb to an increasing dependence upon European food sources, either as rations or payment for labour.

In his study of Aboriginal–European relations during this period, Green (1983) suggests that the potential of the whaling stations to provide an alternative protein source became a notable factor in the changing economic and demographic patterns.

> It is important to realise that the whaling season was between May and September, the period when traditionally the Aborigines moved inland to hunt kangaroos and escape the heavy coastal rains. The whaling industry, therefore, must have had a marked effect on the economy of the Nyungar. When commercial whaling ventures failed or suffered a period of recession, the Aborigines were forced to rely upon traditional food harvests and returned inland across the areas where cattle were already replacing the kangaroo (Green 1983:184).

All of the whaling stations of the lower west coast were situated within relatively close proximity to towns or other European settlements and therefore might have been considered 'frontier' sites for only a brief time in the 1840s. The stations could be readily supplied with food from these nearby communities, suppressing the need for their inhabitants to either forage on their own accord, or engage economic arrangements with the Aboriginal population. Although there are no specific accounts of violence at whaling stations, there had also been a long history of inter–racial conflict within the region, often over diminishing resources.

The expansion of settlement northward to Port Gregory in the 1850s saw interaction with a new Aboriginal cultural bloc. Relations with settlers were strained and sometimes brutal (Bain 1975), with a visiting American whaler characterising the law as applied to Aboriginals as 'a word and a blow; the blow, which is generally fatal, coming first' (Whitecar 1860:84). This sort of violence is not completely borne out in the formal documentary record for the area, although government presence was limited and frontier reporting of such incidents was inadequate. Further north, on the Dampier Archipelago, most of the Aboriginal population who had utilised Malus Island and the rest of the area had been murdered in the Flying Foam massacre in 1868, two years prior to the arrival of the shore whalers (Gara 1983).

While the same pattern of marginalisation and violence would eventually affect the Aboriginal population on the south coast, the sluggish growth of the small and remote Albany settlement saw a different relationship develop with the shore whalers. The diplomacy of the Aboriginal peoples of King George Sound, exhibited in their earlier dealings with European visitors, was to extend to their relationship with the permanent settlers. The early period on the south coast has been described as a 'friendly frontier' (Green 1983:68), with few violent incidents and often close, co–operative relationships developing between the two groups.

Until the 1850s the European population of Albany remained at less than 300 persons, with only limited expansion in the hinterland about the town. Therefore, for most if not all of the whaling period the Aboriginal population of the south coast was able to maintain its traditional economy. Unlike on the west coast, the decision to frequent the whaling stations was an extension of the resource base, rather than a replacement as other options were removed. The distance of the stations from their source of supply meant a greater dependence upon local resources, which, as noted earlier, would have opened up the opportunity for an economic relationship with local Aboriginal groups.

It is also significant that the shore stations from Torbay to Cheyne Beach fell within the range of the Mineng Aboriginal community who owned the Albany area (Ferguson 1987). Tindale's (1974) map indicates that the 'tribal' boundary of the Mineng could even have extended as far east as Doubtful Island Bay. This would mean that it was not until the 1860s that the whalers passed beyond the wider range of the Aboriginal community with which they had already formed close and friendly relations.

Aboriginal Whalers

With the whaling stations often hard pressed to find workers in the meagre labour market, particularly on the south coast, it is not surprising that the Aboriginal men who frequented these sites were eventually introduced as workers. Although there are vague hints of Aboriginal involvement from the opening years of the industry, the first reliable reports of Aboriginal whalers on both coasts date from 1848 (Seymour n.d. 4/9/1848; Inq 29/11/1848). It is significant that at this stage, at least some of the Aboriginal workers on the south coast were receiving payments equal to that of the non–Aboriginal employees, suggesting they had well developed skills. This bounty was rapidly distributed amongst the Aboriginal community on the basis of traditional norms.

One of these had a full lay [payment] due to him. When they were settled with he distributed bags of flour, sugar, blankets, tobacco, knives... amongst his friends. The black ladies now declare they will accept no husbands except they will go whaling (Inq 29/11/1848).

Whether or not this last threat had an effect, by 1850 there were at least nine Aboriginal men employed on the south coast (Inq 4/12/1850). In that season, with two parties of two boats requiring a total complement of between 24 and 28 men, the Aboriginal labourers would have comprised 30% or more of the workforce.

Payments for Aboriginal workers appear to have varied depending upon the station involved. In some instances they were paid a full lay, equivalent to other workers (Inq 29/11/1848). This was presumably the case in 1851 when the Aboriginal whalers from the Cheyne Beach station returned to Albany with a £15 each (Inq 25/11/51). However, there were also situations where other combinations of cash and material re–imbursement were applied, such as documented at Bunbury in 1850.

Jack Crow, the native, is a pulling hand, upon a liberal allowance; he is to have three feeds a day, and the sum of 2s 6d on the capture of each whale, besides a further remuneration of 20s at the termination of the season. The natives expect an immediate reward for their work, and for that reason he receives his 2s 6d directly the whale is grounded. (Inq 29/5/1850).

While most Aboriginal men worked as 'pulling hands', (Table 2.2)., Billy Nadingbert and Jack Hansome are listed as boat steerers, the most senior position on a whaleboat, which also attracted a higher wage.

The registrations also demonstrate that some of the Aboriginal whalers worked on the south coast for nearly twenty years, with contemporary reports indicating that many were highly respected for their skills (McKail 1927). There are almost certainly other Aboriginal workers who have not been detected as a result of either not being registered, or being recorded under European names. In the off–season, Aboriginal men also manned the whaleboat that was used by the pilot service in Albany (Chapman 1979:40).

From the records available, most of the Aboriginal whalers appear to have been Nyungar, with the one exception of one man brought from Tasmania (Western Mail 10/2/1927). There is no sign of the kidnapping or coercion that characterised other maritime industries such as pearling and beche de mer (Green 1981:104; Loos 1982:126–159).

The rapid integration of Aboriginal men into the Western Australian whaling industry may well have had its roots in the high level of acceptance of racial and ethnic diversity traditionally seen in the various forms of whaling throughout the world. The whalers appear to have recognised, utilised and rewarded skill and effort wherever it was seen.

Name (and aliases)	Years	Stations	Position
WEST COAST			
Bungor	1858	Pt Gregory & Castle Rock	boat hand
Bunyart	1856	Fremantle	boat hand
Jack Crow	1850	Bunbury	boat hand
Thomas Jincup	1862	Bunbury	boat hand
Gundy?	1852	Castle Rock	boat hand
SOUTH COAST			
Bobby Candyup	1875	'East coast'	boat hand
Bumble Dicky	1874	'East coast'	hand
Cockellet	1863	Barker Bay	boat hand
Galpin, H	1849	Cheyne Bch	hand
Jack Hansome (Ansum, Handson)	1861–78	Torbay, Middle Isl., Doubtful Isl., Cheyne Bch, 'E. Coast'	boat steerer
Jack Hardy	1861–77	Barker Bay, Cheyne Bch, Doubtful Isl. Bay, 'E. Coast'	boat hand
Tommy King, (Jimmy King)	1867–72	Cheyne Bch, Cape Riche, 'East Coast'	boat hand
King, Henry	1863–67	Cheyne Bch	
Knapp C	1871–72	Cheyne Bch	
Mullipert	1878	'East Coast'	boat hand
Billy Nadingbert	1861	Cheyne Bch	boat steerer
Nebinyan (Nebin, Boney)	1862–77	Middle Isl., Doubtful Isl. Bay, Cheyne Bch, 'East Coast'	boat hand
Bobby Noneran (Nornaran)	1861–63	Torbay, Barker Bay	boat hand
Pegecan	1861	Barker Bay	boat hand
Pillar	-	Doubtful Isl. Bay	-
Rattler Nuterwert (Nutermut)	1861–75	Torbay, Middle Isl., Doubtful Isl. Bay, Cheyne Bch, 'E. Coast'	boat hand
Urecape Dicky	1865	Cheyne Beach	
Dicky Taylor, (alt. Dickey)	1861–75	Torbay, Middle Isl., Cheyne Bch, Doubtful Isl, 'E. Coast'	boat hand

Table 2.2 Aboriginal Whalers (Gibbs 1996)

Visiting American whaler William Whitecar noted:

> These people are remarkable for accuracy of vision and keen scent - for the former quality they are occasionally carried out by whale ships, for the purpose of looking out from the masthead, and I have been told by those who were shipmates with them, that they could discern a spout or sail at as great a distance with the naked eye, as a practiced hand could with a glass (Whitecar 1860: 83).

Other anecdotes support Aboriginal mens' abilities to see whales (e.g. *Western Mail* 10/2/1927). The proposition that Nyungar men sometimes were employed on foreign whaling vessels is borne up by an incident from 1848 when an exploration party investigating around Cape Riche encountered a Nyungar man who claimed to have been to Sydney and Hobart aboard a French whaler (Perth Gazette 29/7/1848). In 1890, the writer Henry Lawson passed through Albany and recorded meeting an elderly Aboriginal man, possibly the same person, who had spent two years aboard a French whaler and was fluent in the language (Lawson 1899).

John Thomas of Cheyne Beach regularly employed of Aboriginal men as whalers, and a great respecter of their abilities. One of the few surviving anecdotes of life on a Western Australian whaling station illustrates this. At Cheyne Beach, possibly around the 1860s, a newly arrived cook refused to serve an Aboriginal whaler,

> saying that he did not sign on to wait on niggers.
> *Tommy*: 'Then put up your dukes.'
> *Cook*: 'I'll knock you down with the fire bar. Do you think I'd dirty my hands fighting a blackfellow?'
> *Tommy*: 'You white–livered cow! You're afraid!'
> *Cook*: 'I'm afraid of no nigger.'
> Tommy: 'Then that's right, come out and have a few rounds for fun.'
> Captain Thomas, hearing strong language and high words, came on the scene.
> 'What's the matter, Tommy?'
> 'This white–livered cow refused to give me a cup of tea, me who went to a mission school, and is too cowardly to come out and have a few rounds even for fun: the cow.'
> Captain Thomas then told the cook that he was engaged to cook for the men, and that he was to treat the crews, white men and natives, alike, or leave the job (McKail 1927:23).

Whaling and Aboriginal Spiritual Life

In addition to the economic and social relationships with whalers, there is good evidence for Aboriginal people incorporating whaling into a broader realm of ceremonial and ritual life (dealt with in detail in Gibbs 2003a). In the first decade of the 20th century, Daisy Bates (1985:197) recorded that in the region of Geographe Bay there had once been a whale totem, although she noted that the last of the totem kin *(mammang borungur)* had disappeared forty years earlier 'with the departure of the whales'.

Of the limited information she was able to collect of this group, Bates noted with some interest that stranded whales could be freely eaten by the *mammang borungur* and others, apparently without the dire consequences normally associated with the consumption of one's totem animal. Her informant, an elderly Aboriginal woman who had grown up in the Vasse area, also described dreams in which she danced and balanced upon the back of a whale (BL 1212A: Box 748 XI, 3a, 1 'Native Songs'). It is interesting to speculate upon the correlation between the reported time of decline of the totem group, the demise of the right and humpback populations, and the known cessation of whaling activity in the region in the 1870s.

Bates also recorded a whale totem (*borlooloo galn'ga*) in the northwest of Western Australia (Bates, n.d. b). This was probably from the region of Roebourne and the Dampier Archipelago where she spent some time, and which was also an area closely associated with early foreign and colonial whaling activity (Gara 1983). However, she noted that the 'whale totem men' had 'died out' (Bates, n.d. b). Whale totems have also been reported from the regions closer to the Nullarbor Plain (Burgoyne 2000). It is possible that, as noted for some other objects and animals, whales may have in some cases been adopted as totem animals as a result of the commencement of the industry and its position in the post–contact economy of the Aboriginal population of the area.

Whaling in Aboriginal Performance

Several writers recorded Aboriginal songs and public ceremonial performances which referred directly to observations of whaling. A traveller camped near the Murchison River, 50km north–west of the Port Gregory station, recorded a dance being performed by Aboriginal men which 'imitated the killing of a whale as witnessed at Port Gregory, with an effigy made of bushes representing the whale' (Oldfield 1865: 256). Bates also recorded the details of a performance by Nyungar songman Nebinyan, who in his youth had been a whaler at the Cheyne Beach station.

> In the recitative which dealt with Nebinyan's whaling experiences, the whole gamut of native feeling appeared to be expressed: the sorrow of Nebin, as he saw his fire (home) recede further and further away; the stealthy gliding over the water towards the resting whale, the sharp look out, the growing excitement as the huge fish was approached; the great seas that threatened to swamp the whale boat; the swift and sure harpooning; the final surrender of the whale; the triumphant towing back to ship or beach, and the

great rejoicing over the whale feast - each of these formed a song in itself, and the actions peculiar to each stage were faithfully rendered (Bates 1980:35).

The overall structure of the song cycle would appear to have been a hunting narrative, emphasizing Nebinyan's prowess as a young man. The significance of this performance and Nebinyan's career as a whaler is explored in detail elsewhere (Gibbs 2003a).

Whaling as Opportunity

From a European perspective, involving Aboriginal men (and possibly women) in whaling initially offered an alternative and potentially cheaper source of workers in a environment where labour was expensive and scarce. However, the agency of the Aboriginal people interacting with the European maritime frontier must also be considered (c.f. Torrence and Clarke 2001a). The nature of the maritime frontier meant that the whaling stations were not the focus of the aggressive territorial and resource imperatives of most other European settlements. As described above, the shore whaling also offered alternative economic strategies for procurement of food and other social and economic interactions with Europeans. However, a more active engagement with the industry itself offered particular advantages to young Aboriginal men.

In contact situations, young Aboriginal men and women were quick to grasp opportunities to exploit new skills and economic resources to gain advantage within, or in some cases side–step, traditional hierarchies (Reynolds 1982:131; Sharp 1952). By participating in whaling, young Aboriginal men were able to demonstrate their skills and physical prowess, garnering recognition and respect from both cultures. European appointed leadership roles within the industry, such as being made 'boat steerer', not only potentially placed young men in command of their traditional superiors, but also reinforced by increased payments and access to consumer items. These could be distributed within communities creating even further status. Such appointments could therefore create alternative or parallel power structures within post–contact communities (Harrison 2003). In addition, regular and intensive interactions would also have enhanced language proficiency, creating a potential role as intermediaries in other cross–cultural interactions. Such translator and mediator roles also opened opportunities for personal advancement (c.f. Kaberry 1939:33; Sharp 1952; Reynolds 1982:131; Harrison 2002:365).

CHAPTER 3
PROCESS AND PRODUCTION

While the emergence of a shore whaling industry in Western Australia was part of a world–wide economic phenomenon, its pattern of development was very much a function of the emerging colonial economy. This chapter explores the nature of shore whaling in Western Australia, with an emphasis on how changes within the following four sub–systems influenced the general progress of the industry and by extension the archaeological patterns examined in later sections.

1. Employment conditions and structures within the shore whaling industry, with a profile of the workers and owners, their involvement in the industry, and the various conditions and controls under which they laboured.

2. The scale of shore whaling operations, including changes in the size and composition of the whaling parties and the number of stations used along both the south and west coasts.

3. The supply of whaling equipment to the colonial whalers, including the rate at which new technology diffused into the local industry, and evidence for local manufacture of whalecraft.

4. Local modes of whaling, including the efficiency of the shore whaling operation, and the relationship between the whale species caught and the success of the industry.

EMPLOYMENT CONDITIONS

Employment Structure and Payment systems

By the 19th century the similarities in equipment and process for pelagic, bay and shore whaling, combined with the constant flow of workers around the globe and between the various levels of the industry, had resulted in a relatively homogeneous employment structure and terminology. The basic structure and hierarchy of the six–man boat crews (boat hands, harpooner/boat–steerer, headsman) has already been described in Chapter One. However, the larger shore fisheries may also have had a look–out, a cooper, a cook and several other workers who would assist in the processing of the whale. Operations were overseen by a station manager, who in some instances was also the chief headsman. The station owners were not necessarily present at the stations and normally are not counted as a member of the party.

In the absence of mechanization, whaling during the 19th century relied upon the skills, knowledge and loyalties of its workers. Poor performance by the crews could seriously impair the ability of a boat to chase, fasten and kill whales, making seasoned hands a valuable commodity in both shore–based and pelagic whaling.

One of the central themes of this chapter is the great difficulty suffered by the colonial whaling parties in obtaining and retaining experienced workers.

Although the dependence on the abilities of the crews to obtain a reasonable result put the owners and managers of the whaling parties at the mercy of their men, this was to a large extent mitigated by the operation of the *lay* system of payment described in Chapter One. A lay was a fixed percentage share of the total catch value, which varied with an individual's experience and position in the party. In broad terms it was incentive–based, with hard work and skill potentially increasing the profit to be claimed by the men. On the other hand, a poor season could see the whalers left penniless, with the owner not obliged to pay them any wage at all, or even able to charge them for expenses. If one or more members within a whaling party withheld their services, the potential reduction in returns would come from both their and all other members' share of the value, a powerful incentive for self–regulation within the crews.

There are few documented examples of the pay scales to which the Western Australian whalers worked. The most detailed is in a report of 1838, which states that:

> the lay given to a mariner in this colony amounts to a 1–75th; the lay to the steersman to 1–45th; the lay given to the headsman, 1–17th; manager, 1–15th: amounting in all to 65 percent, besides provisions (PG 20/10/1838).

In 1838 the Western Australian Whaling Company (Safety Bay) advertised for able–bodied men to work for a lay of 1/50th, with all provisions found (PG 5/5/1838). The 1850 Castle Rock agreement (Figure 3.1) suggests a crewman would receive a 1/40th lay, less any expenses owing. Seymour's 1846 journal from the same station also shows that further incentives could also be given, such as a prize of six pounds of tobacco being offered to the first man to spot a whale which was subsequently killed (Seymour n.d. 1/8/1846). Although there is clearly variation, this scale of payments seems consistent with those known for shore fisheries in other parts of Australasia (e.g. Prickett 2002:5; Nash 2003:76).

As noted in Chapter Two, payments for Aboriginal workers appear to have varied depending upon the station involved. In some instances they were paid a full lay at the end of the season, equivalent to other workers (Inq 29/11/1848). However, in other instances they were paid immediately following each whale caught, or with food and goods (Inq 29/5/1850).

> ***Articles of Agreement*** entered into by George Chapman [merchant] of Busselton in the County of Sussex in Western Australia on the one part and undermentioned mariners and others on the other part [unto] whom the several articles have been [read] & of whom the several signatures have been offered herewith in the presence the Resident Magistrate of the District, the said mariners and others covenanting and agreeing to join in party for whaling in Geographe's Bay during the season of the year One Thousand eight hundred and fifty.
>
> The Season shall commence and terminate at such time as the Proprietor George Chapman may [-] [-] and determine. Each person in the Fishery having conducted himself with propriety and having [-] his [utmost] endeavour for the good of the concern shall receive a fortieth Lay, or such Lay as may be affixed to his name.
>
> At the close of the season the whole take of oil shall be gauged and of bone shall be weighed. The oil to be computed at two hundred and fifty two gallons (252) to the tun and the bone at two thousand and two hundred and forty pounds to the ton (2240) and the aforesaid George Chapman himself to purchase and pay in the manner following, for oil at the rate of five ten pounds and for Right whalebone at the rate of sixty pounds per Tun, reducing out of the proceeds payable to each person the amount due to the proprietor for slops and other miscellaneous articles. Requisition to be made ten days after the Gauging.
>
> Regularity and prompt obedience are required to ensure success in an undertaking of this nature. The Chief Headsman therefore for the time shall control and command the parties.
>
> All the carcasses of the whales are to be at the entire disposal of the proprietor.
>
> Natives are on no account to be retained in the employment of individuals, a charge will be made for any provision seen or known to be distributed among them.
>
> In the event of Sperm whales being taken, the oil produced therefrom is to be rated at the value of thirty pounds per tun (£30).
>
> An option is given to such parties as may desire to receive their proportion of oil and have it at their own disposal paying the mere expenses of the casks which may contain it.
>
>   Lay   Date
>   Man's Name
>   Description   *[Signatures: William Seymour, George [Chapman], William Longstaff]*

Figure 3.1 Transcript of 1850 Contract Agreement for Castle Rock whaling station (Battye Library 1208A).

The 1850 Castle Rock agreement (Figure 3.1) provides the only surviving contract for a Western Australian shore station. Although it cannot be assumed that this was a standard arrangement, it is suggestive of the range of expectations. Most if not all food, housing and other basic supplies during the season would also have been provided by the owner, although as suggested by the Castle Rock agreement some costs were also deducted from the lay at the end of the season.

Worker Experience and Involvement Patterns

As part of this study a biographical database of 575 men working in the Western Australian shore whaling industry was compiled, documenting their employment and position at particular stations in each season, their race or ethnicity and any other relevant details (see Gibbs 1996, Appendix E). While drawing from the widest possible range of government, newspaper and manuscript sources, it must be noted that it is still not a complete listing of workers, particularly for the period prior to the commencement of official registrations of whaling crews in 1849 (discussed below). This fact undoubtedly affects some of the statistical information presented below, but is unavoidable. Similarly, developing work histories of individuals was limited by the available evidence.

A 20% sample of database listings was cross-referenced against the *Bicentennial Dictionary of Western Australians* (Erikson 1988). Although the dictionary is also not meant to be an exhaustive listing of the pre–1888 colonial population, an appreciable portion is represented in some form. It is worth noting that of the stratified sample of 115 names checked (consisting of up to three randomly chosen entries on each page of the database), only 55 (48%) appeared in the Dictionary. Of these, 15 entries were of minimal detail and provided no biographical data at all. If we assume that this is representative of the whole database, it makes an interesting statement on the relative historical visibility (or invisibility) of the whaling population.

Two hypotheses were formed to account for this phenomenon. The first is that the whaling hands were primarily labourers who, by virtue of limited literacy and/or not owning land, were unlikely to be the subject of documentation. This proposition is almost impossible to address, given that it requires the very documentary material which is in such short supply. The second hypothesis is that the majority of whalers were resident in the colony for only short durations, limiting the potential for them to be recorded in either official or private documents.

As described in the Chapter Two, the historical record suggests that in its early years the whaling industry drew heavily upon the small and usually unskilled body of free labourers within the colony (Moore 1884; PG 22/4/1837). In the re–emergence of the industry during the 1840s the employment situation appears to have changed, with an increasing component of the workforce being comprised of whalers from the mainly American whaling vessels operating along the coast. Observing the Western Australian shore–whalers during the late 1850s, American whaler William Whitecar (1860:91) recorded that 'the officers, boat steerers and, if they can be procured, two–thirds of the crews are American'. While this may be an exaggeration, the biographical database provides evidence that at least from the 1840s onwards the key positions in the colonial whaling parties were commonly filled by experienced workers not of local origin.

Of the 49 men listed as boat–steerers in the database, only 17 (or 34%) had previously been registered in a Western Australian whaling party. Even more striking is that of the 48 men listed as headsmen, only 5 (or 10%) had previously been recorded as workers in the Western Australian fishery. It is possible that in part this results from the absence of pre–1849 records, so that earlier involvement is simply not recorded. However, the pattern seems to hold for the later periods, with new headsmen and boat steerers simply appearing in the parties. Although it was not usually possible to determine the nationality of these men, there is a reasonable presumption that a fair proportion of them could have been American, or at least from American whaleships.

The age structure of the Western Australian whalers appears to provide further support for the degree of involvement by experienced foreign workers. For the 40 men (from a random sample) for whom further biographical information was available, Figure 3.2 records their age in the year of the first season in which they reported as working for a Western Australian whaling party. Given the physical nature and danger of whaling, it might be expected that the majority of first–time whalers would be young men. While this may be represented on the graph by the slight concentration in the pre–25 year age group, the relatively wide spread of ages is suggestive of the arrival of older, experienced workers in the colony.

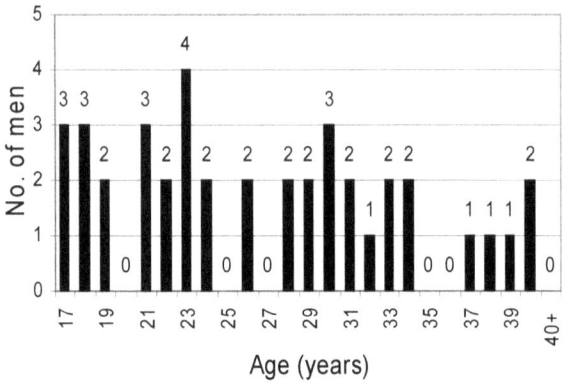

Figure 3.2 Age of whalers during first recorded season.

The recorded duration of workers' involvements in the Western Australian whaling industry was established by calculating the difference between the first and last engagements recorded in the database. Figure 3.3 clearly shows that the overwhelming majority of workers were reported for only short periods. On the west coast apparently 78% of workers participated for only one year, while 94% had departed after three years. The situation was slightly better on the south coast, with 70% apparently working only one year, and 85% gone after three years. While some proportion of this group probably comprised settlers who simply participated in the industry for a brief period before quitting, the general pattern supports the hypothesis of a short presence in the colony. The implication of this high turn–over of men is that the colonial whaling parties had difficulties in establishing a stable and experienced labour force.

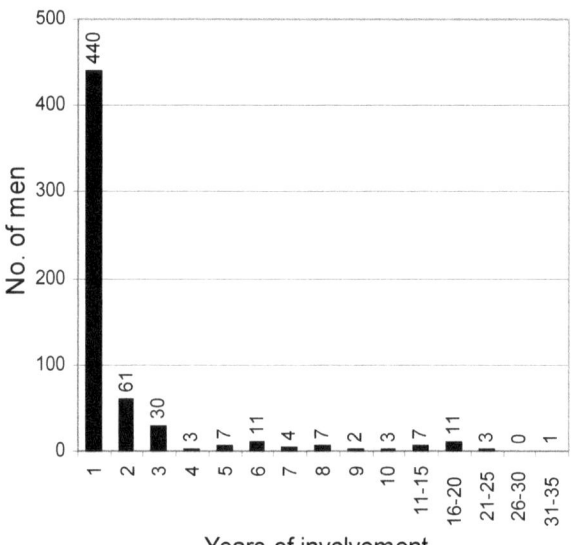

Figure 3.3 Duration of worker involvement.

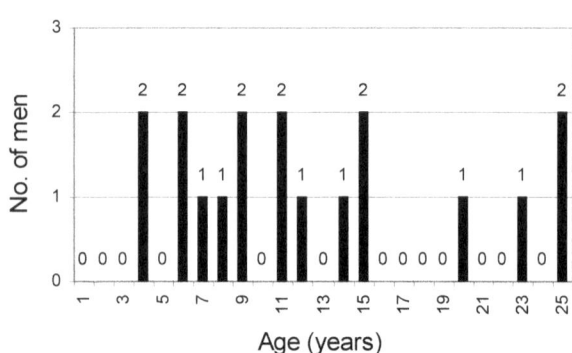

Figure 3.4 Age of headsmen in first recorded season.

To investigate this pattern further, the age of first involvement and duration of involvement in the industry by headsmen as a discrete group were also examined. Although there was only a sample of 18 ages available, Figure 3.4 shows that in comparison to the industry as a whole the headsmen formed a slightly older group. This is not surprising, as to attain the necessary level of skill would have required at least several years of experience in a whaling crew.

Figure 3.5 shows that the population of headsmen was also susceptible to a high turnover, with 48% staying only one season and 60% departing after three seasons. This is partially offset by the 20% who maintained involvement for over ten years, often managing or even owning the parties they worked in.

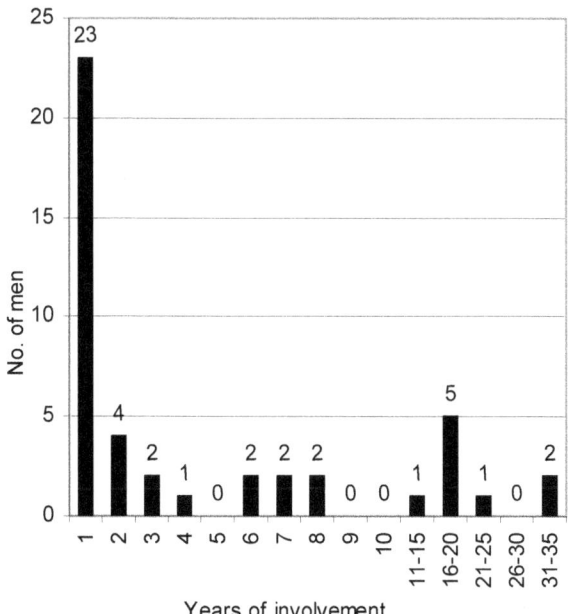

Figure 3.5 Duration of headsmen involvement.

The documentary record would strongly suggest that the supply of foreign labour and the apparent fluidity within the Western Australian whaling workforce were a function of the high level of desertion and recruitment associated with the American whaling fleet. Desertion of discontented whalers from visiting ships was frequent and geographically widespread. While it usually involved individuals, on a number of occasions large groups of half a dozen men or more were reported absent from their vessels (PG 26/5/1838; Inq 4/12/1841; Inq 9/2/1848; PG 3/1/1851; PG 26/1/1853). It is not surprising that, despite the illegality of employing deserters, the colonial whaling parties would eagerly engage experienced men. There are even a number of documented complaints by American captains that the settlers were actively attempting to entice sailors into leaving their ships and joining the shore parties (Inq 21/3/1841; Inq 17/3/1849). Conversely, the readiness of these men to leave colonial employ is also well documented (PG 23/8/1850).

The apparent inability of the colonial shore parties to stem this attrition lay in part with the seasonal nature of the industry. Unlike pelagic whaling, the shore fisheries only operated for five months per year, so that for the other seven months the men were left to find alternative employment. For many of them the most attractive proposition was to ship out on the first whaling vessel which passed by.

The problem of how to employ the whalers off–season had been recognized as early as the first season in 1836, with the Western Australian Association suggesting that suitable work could be arranged on nearby farms (Anon. 1836). These sorts of measures were only ever organized on an individual station basis, such as the Fremantle Whaling Company's attempt to keep its men (and equipment) engaged after the close of the 1837 season by forming sealing parties along the west coast (PG 13/1/1838). A number of problems were encountered and this experiment was not repeated in the following year. There is also evidence to suggest that during the summer months at least some of the south coast whaling crews were employed in sealing along the islands of the Archipelago of the Recherché (Sale n.d.; McKail 1927).

A successful but short–lived effort at arranging off–season employment for whalers was made on the south coast in 1847, when Hugh MacDonald suggested that for the remainder of the year these men could be engaged in cutting sandalwood (Garden 1977:78). For several years sandalwood exports to China boomed, until the growth of a considerable stockpile depressed the price and brought the industry to a halt. It can only be supposed that the whalers then reverted to other forms of seasonal labour such as kangaroo hunting or farm work.

A more serious problem was the mid–season desertion of hands from the shore fisheries. Quinlan's studies of labour relations in the whaling industries of Tasmania, South Australia and Western Australia suggest that this could take several forms (Quinlan 1992; Quinlan et al. 2003). Men might simply abscond from a fishery without leave, they might be deliberately lured away or 'crimped' by another party (Quinlan 1992:22), or they might join the crew of a whaleship and depart the settlement altogether. However, there are only limited historical records of Western Australian whalers being reported temporarily absent without leave (PG 13/5/1837; Seymour n.d.), while there are no known accounts of hands moving between colonial parties mid–season. This may well have been because of the relative isolation of the stations and the difficulties of moving over such distances.

Desertion as a result of recruitment by American whaleships is by far the most frequently mentioned difficulty. American whalemen who had abandoned their ships and joined the local parties were particularly susceptible to such offers. After visiting the Barker Bay station near Albany in 1857, the Whitecar (1860:219) recorded in his diary that

> amongst the men at the fishery were several Americans who had been in this part of the world for years; they did not like the country, and, if we had wanted men, would gladly have engaged and gone home with us.

The removal of key employees in mid–season could seriously endanger the success or even existence of the shore–parties, such as reported for Bunbury station in 1850 (PG 23/8/1850) and Barker Bay in 1860 (Inq 27/8/1860).

Ethnicity

The race or ethnicity of the shore whalers is difficult to determine in most cases, with their names usually anglicized in the records. However, the Western Australian whaling industry clearly shared the diverse racial background that characterized whaling enterprises around the world. William Amersely (or Hamersley) worked as headsman on various stations on the west coast between 1848 and 1862, and is recorded as being 'an African native who had had experience in American whaling ships' (Heppingstone 1966:36). William Parr, also known as 'Butty' or 'Batty' was a Maori who worked on both the west and south coasts from the mid–1850s until at least 1872 when he was in his 60s (Erikson 1988:2419). Butchart (WA 22/7/1933) described him as the champion headsman, 'a fine, big chap... his face and chest were scarred by tribal marking. His father was supposed to be a tribal chief'. Chapter Two has already discussed Aboriginal whalers working within the industry. Other names hint at non–European origins (see Gibbs 1996, Appendix E), although confirmation of a non–European background is very difficult.

Development of Labour Legislation

While desertion of crew members posed a serious threat to the success of the shore whaling parties, disruption to their operation could also come through other forms of misconduct by workers. The paucity of documentary sources means that only a few specific incidents of misconduct, used here to refer to any deliberate action by a worker which impaired the operation of the whaling party, appear in the historical record. Complaints about food appear to have been a common cause, with two of the boat hands in the 1845 Bathers Beach party refusing to attend to their duties, even after a whale had been sighted, claiming that they had been 'ill–treated on the supply of provisions' (PG 30/8/1845). Other references are vague, such as a member of the 1845 Carnac Island party declining to work as the result of 'a private broil' (PG 30/8/1845).

However, Seymour's (n.d.) diary, as the only regular record of life at a whaling station, suggests that complaints and unrest amongst boat crews was a normal part of life at the Castle Rock fishery. The following excerpts (with the original spelling and grammar left uncorrected) illustrate just some of the difficulties recorded during the 1846 season.

July 1st   All hands refused duty becose we had no sugar in our tea.
July 26th Palmers boatcrew refused to man boat to fetch some flour but at last went but not willingly Carter saying they did not ship for it.
Aug 1st   Men growling saying the headsmen eat all the fat and leave them all the lean.
Aug 2nd   Petit started for the Vasse with his boat, Liby refuses to go unless he is paid for it.
Aug 16th   Corley growling becose he culd not have as much grog as he wanted.
Aug 25th   Clement returned from the Vasse drunk and his boats crew soon put hevery thing in an uproar and comensed fighting.
Oct 9th   Clement and most of the men drunk.

In later years Seymour appears to have been less diligent in recording these sorts of events, although various other difficulties were recorded in the next several seasons.

By the mid–1840s the continued loss of men and the effects of various labour disruptions had become serious problems within the Western Australian shore whaling industry. Contemporary records suggest that the push towards developing specific legislation to regulate the conduct of whalers began in earnest in 1845, resulting from the incidents at the Carnac Island and Bathers Beach stations described above (PG 30/8/1845). The magistrate who tried the cases of the three men took into consideration not only the loss of a single whale, but also the potential effects such misconduct could have on the success of the industry. As a result, the three hands were each sentenced to three months imprisonment with hard labour as an example to the other workers (Inq 3/9/1845). Presumably the prosecutions were under the 1842 *Master and Servants Act* (*Statutes of Western Australia*, 6 Victoria No. 5) which governed the relationship between workers and employers, although as this did not really extend to maritime interests there is some uncertainty as to whether this law should (or could) have been applied in this situation (Crowley 1953).

Despite the severity of these penalties, problems with whaling hands continued during the 1846 season, prompting calls for the laws of engagement to be revised (Inq 9/9/1846; Inq 16/9/1846; Inq 23/9/1846). Agitation increased through the rest of the year, following the theme that desertions and misconduct threatened the success of the whole industry (Inq 18/11/1846, Inq 16/12/1846). The campaign was obviously successful, so that in September of 1847 *An Ordinance to provide a summary remedy for Breach of Contracts connected with the fisheries of the Colony* (*Statutes of Western Australia*, 10 Victoria, No.16) was passed to extend officially the 1842 Master and Servants Act to whalers.

Quinlan (1992) has traced the relationship between the 1847 Western Australian legislation, the 1844 South Australia Ordinance on which it was modelled, and the 1835 Tasmanian Ordinance on which this in turn was based. While the bulk of the Western Australian legislation simply copied the South Australian Ordinance, the level of negative sentiment in the colony created by the agitation described above is probably reflected in the increased severity of the penalties. Quinlan (1992:36) has summarized the legislation as follows.

Further articles of agreement had to be witnessed before a justice, then lodged with the Government Resident for the district (s2), and a notice placed in the Government Gazette within two months of their signing (s3). Those employing whalers who had already engaged to another master were liable to a fine of 50 pounds (s4)... Likewise, under s5 articled whalers who engaged elsewhere were liable to forfeit their lays, to pay a fine equal to twice any advance received and to be sentenced to three months prison with hard labour.

Not all parties signed these articles, although perhaps not surprisingly the Castle Rock crew became the first group registered under the new legislation in 1849 (CSR 190/273: 12/10/1849). As noted, their handwritten 1850 contract agreement is the only surviving example for Western Australia (Figure 3.1).

These agreements became more common over time, with the lists of owners, headsmen, boat–steers and hands providing a significant insight into both the scale of the industry and the men who worked in it. No prosecutions under this ordinance were located, although the rapid decline in the numbers and activity of the American whaleships may well have resulted in a reduction in incidents of desertion in any case.

Development of Labour Legislation

While the new ordinance increased the control of station owners and managers over their workers, it provided no new benefits or assurances of better conditions for the men. In fact, it may well have left the whalers open to abuse from the station owners. In 1856 Captain Sanford, owner of the Port Gregory station, discharged Thomas Coombs from his fishery as 'incapable of performing the duties for which he was engaged and signed articles' (CSR 367/87: 5/8/56). Sanford henceforth refused either to feed Coombs or assist him with passage southward, despite there being little or no European settlement for the 350 kilometres of desolate country between Port Gregory and Fremantle, and no other settlers in the near area from which the man could earn his way home. It was only through the nearby convict depot admitting Coombs to the hospital that he was kept from dying alone in the bush, although Sanford remained unrepentant in his refusal to assist. John Thomas at Cheyne Beach was said to have made a similar threat to a station hand; that he either did the work he was engaged for, or was to leave and walk nearly 100 kilometres overland through the bush to get back to Albany (McKail 1927). Isolation apparently made an effective disciplinary threat.

Ownership and Management

As indicated in Chapter Two, the structure of ownership of whaling parties passed through several phases during the 44 years of the Western Australian industry. Unlike the rest of the workforce, the majority of owners are relatively easy to identify and correlate with other biographical sources. As people of at least some wealth and standing this group was more likely to keep records, correspond with the government or fellow settlers, own land, or engage in other pursuits which would lead to them being historically visible. It was possible to identify 93%, or all but four of the 57, in the Bicentennial Dictionary of Western Australians (Erikson 1988).

The first several whaling parties on the west coast of Western Australia were established with formal company structures and used capital drawn from a broad joint–stock investment. For reasons outlined previously, only the Fremantle Whaling Company was to survive its first season, carrying on for 14 years until dissolving in 1850 (Inq 4/12/1850). It should be noted that the large numbers of investors and committee members associated with the Fremantle Whaling Company and the Northern Whaling Company have been excluded from the general analysis. However, Statham (1980a) has shown that of the five major shareholders in the Fremantle Company during the 1840s, three were merchant wholesalers, one was the harbor master and the last was the chief headsman, John Bateman, who would later become a major merchant in the colony.

The revival of whaling during the 1840s saw a diversity of station owners, usually with one or two readily identifiable principal investors. Figure 3.6 shows the first year in which owners became involved in the industry. When cross referenced to the biographical database it can be shown that 91% of the new owners in the period from 1841 to 1850 lasted only a single season. From this group and over the next decade emerged several major operators who engaged in the industry for lengthy periods, although other people did occasionally appear for varying spans.

The south coast industry shows a similar, but not identical, pattern of ownership. The first two shore parties were organized by local merchants through partnerships with eastern Australian and foreign whalers; although by 1839 both of these had ceased operation. After a hiatus in whaling activity during the early 1840s the revived industry also saw a brief period with a high turn–over of ownerships. As for the west coast, 80% of these people for the years between 1841 and 1850 survived for only a single season, with only John Thomas and Thomas Sherratt maintaining a consistent presence for the next two decades. The south coast experienced a brief revival during the 1870s, once again with a number of operators becoming involved for short periods until the close of the industry in 1879.

The duration of involvement for owners on both coasts is shown in Figure 3.7. On the west coast 55% of owners lasted only one season, with 90% lasting three years or less. On the south coast 54% lasted only one season, while 79% continued for three seasons or less. The most likely explanation for the short periods of involvement is that the industry simply failed to return a profit, and may have even not repaid the investment in equipment and other expenses. There is also some evidence to suggest that successful operation of the shore parties might have been associated with prior whaling experience on the part of the owner.

Eight (24%) of the west coast owners and five (21%) of the south coast owners had previous whaling experience. In some respects this was not an essential criterion, as each station also had a manager who directed operations. However, all of the more successful and long-term owners such as Bateman, Sherratt and Thomas had prior whaling experience and continued to take active roles in their whaling parties, often working as the manager and chief headsman.

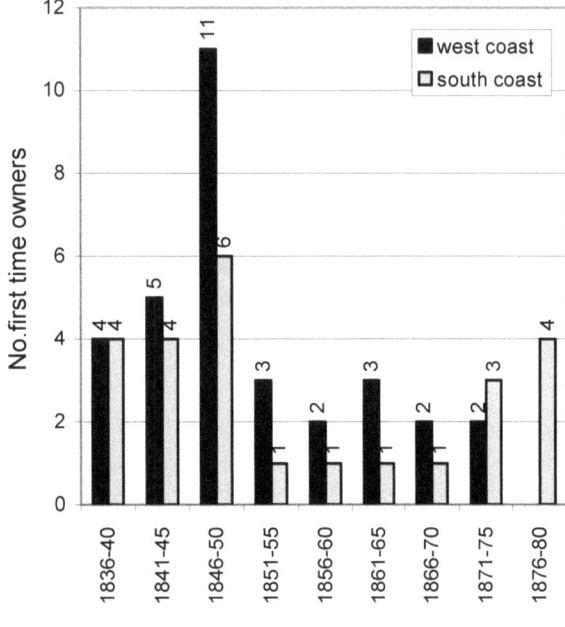

Figure 3.6 Frequency of first year ownership of whaling party - south and west.

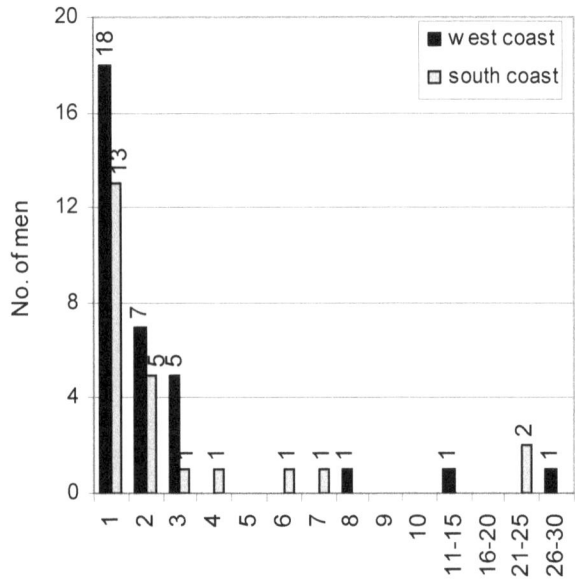

Figure 3.7 Duration of ownership of whaling parties

Although the biographical information in Erikson's (1988) dictionary has limitations in identifying the non-whaling interests of the party owners, it would appear that by far the largest and longest involved owner groups on both coasts were persons with other maritime concerns, particularly merchants and boat owners or people involved with the coastal trade. This includes at least nine of the 33 owners on the west coast and 11 of the 24 owners on the south coast. The remainder are listed as being farmers or land owners, hotel keepers, merchants without explicit maritime connections, or do not have identified occupations. As suggested by Statham (1980) for the early phase of the industry, it would appear that for the majority of the owners their involvement complemented or reinforced their other commercial interests.

The biographical analysis strongly supports the separation of activity between south and west coasts. Of the 575 entries, only three workers could be clearly identified as having moved between regions through the course of their career. Two of these (W. Parr and T. Hazelton) were headsmen, suggesting that they may have been engaged for their skills, although the other (M. Rockett) was simply a boat hand who sometimes doubled as a boat-steerer.

Ownership was also restricted between coasts, with only two cases of involvement in both regions. In 1846 Thomas Morton, a west coast resident and owner of the schooner *Thetis*, had his boat stationed at Torbay for the season. While he did achieve some success, he did not return to the station in the following year. An early and less certain involvement was in 1836 when David Dring, a settler in the Swan River colony, may have partially financed Cheyne's Doubtful Island Bay party. It is probable that the combination of distance between the two main settlements and a tendency to reinforce interests close at hand may have hindered a more widespread involvement.

WHALING PARTIES & STATIONS

Number and Size of Whaling Parties

Before proceeding it is necessary to explain the difference between the terms *whaling party* and *whaling station* as they are used in this volume. A whaling party refers to the group of people employed to work together as a team in both the industrial and domestic aspects of the operation of a whaling station. The whaling station was the place where the whaling party worked and lived, and included both industrial and domestic areas as well as more remote components such as look-outs. The distinction between party and station is necessary, as each whaling party could use a number of whaling stations in a single season, making the latter an unreliable measure of the extent of industrial activity.

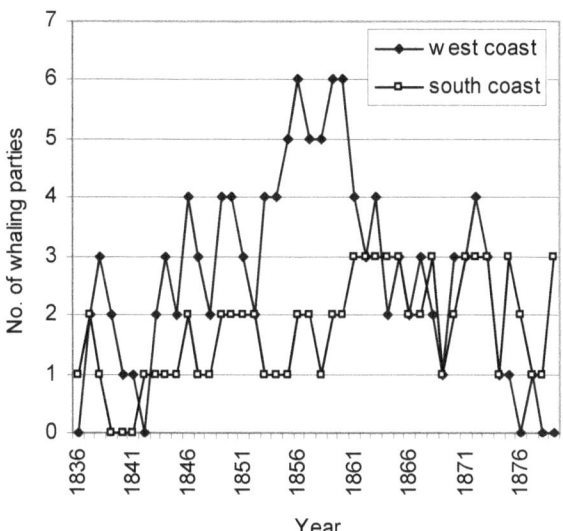

Figure 3.7 No. of shore whaling parties - south and west.

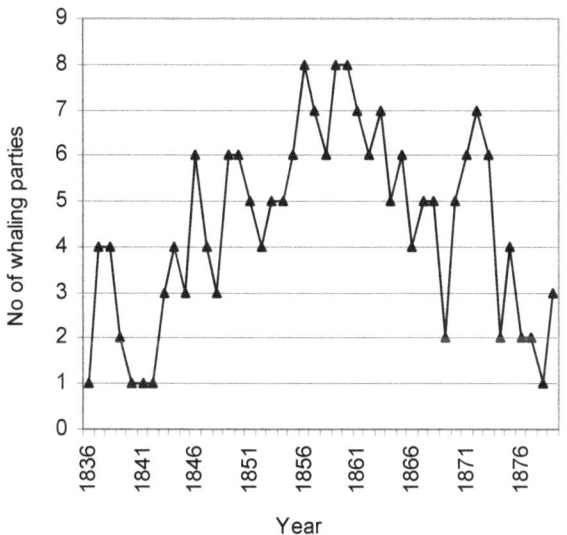

Figure 3.8 Number of shore whaling parties.

Figure 3.7 shows the number of whaling parties formed on both coasts, while 3.8 provides a total figure. The west coast peaked in activity during the mid–1850s, with five to six parties in operation at various locations each year. This was the period when Harwood and Bateman both ran two parties, one each at Fremantle and at Port Gregory. Bateman would then move his Port Gregory party down to the Bunbury station for the late season. The south coast industry reached its maximum development in the late 1850s, although only three parties ever operated in the region in any one season.

Establishing the number of whaling parties in each year is only an approximate way to determine the strength of the whaling industry. A more accurate assessment of the industrial capability can be gained through two closely related measures, the number of whaleboats which are known to have been in use, and the number of men known to have worked in the parties.

To deal with the first variable, the size of a whaling party was generally referred to in contemporary documents as being a 'two boat' or 'three boat' fishery and so on. This directly described the group's capacity to pursue whales and assist in their slaughter, and presumably suggested other capabilities or details of organization. The known number of boats at each Western Australian station, drawn from *Blue Book* records, newspaper reports and various other sources, is recorded in Appendix B1 and B2. This clearly shows that the west coast stations worked with an average of three boats, rising to a maximum of four. In contrast, the south coast parties consistently used two boats. In both regions there are isolated incidents of whaling parties working with one boat, including one at Toby Inlet in 1847 (Inq 25/8/1847), and one at Barker Bay in 1849 (CSR 189/249: 16/8/1849).

To give some idea of the changing strength of the total fishery, Figures 3.9 presents the minimum number of whaleboats in use on both coasts, with Figure 3.10 representing the total. It should be noted that the numbers of whaleboats recorded in the Blue Books are not always consistent with other sources. Some parties and their boats are not reported at all, while in the case of a party moving between locations such as Port Gregory and Bunbury, it is possible that the same three boats may have been recorded at both locations.

Where the actual number of boats at a station was not known, either the number of boats used at that station in immediately preceding years was carried over (if known), or the average figure of three boats for a west coast party and two boats for a south coast party was substituted. Where a party moved between locations, say from Port Gregory to Bunbury, its three boats used were recorded only once. For these reasons the graph should only be taken as an approximation and not as a strictly accurate record.

One factor which could not be represented in Figure 3.10 is the use of small vessels such as cutters and schooners to assist in the whaling process. These vessels appear to have played several different roles, the first being to transport the crews to the more distant stations, an operation which became more important with the evolution of early/late season mobility. Vessels which stayed with the station during the season could be used to move men and boats beyond the normal range of the station. Frederick Seymour's Castle Rock diary during 1848 has several entries which describe this (Seymour n.d. 15/10/1848, 14/10/1848), while in 1849 the manager of the Bathers Beach station hired the schooner *Pelsart* to cruise to the north of the station, equipped with two boats and a full complement of hands and gear (Inq 7/6/1849).

There is no evidence to suggest that the full processing of whales, including trying–out of oil, was carried out on these small craft. There are references to their use as 'cutting–in vessels' (Inq 25/5/1857, Seymour n.d. 11/10/1848), suggesting that the blubber may have been flensed at sea before returning it to shore, or that they assisted in returning the whale to the station and were moored alongside to be used as a flensing platform.

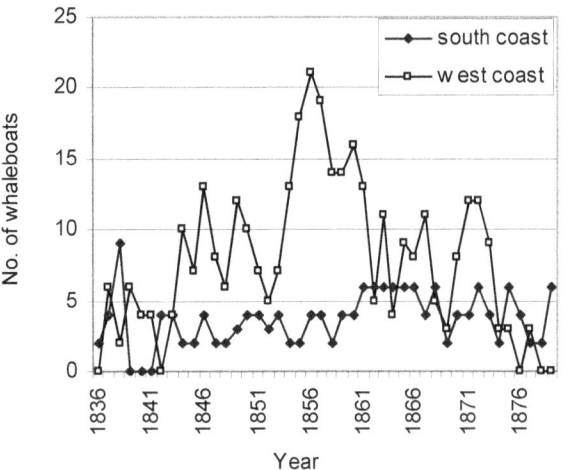

Figure 3.9 Whaleboats - south and west.

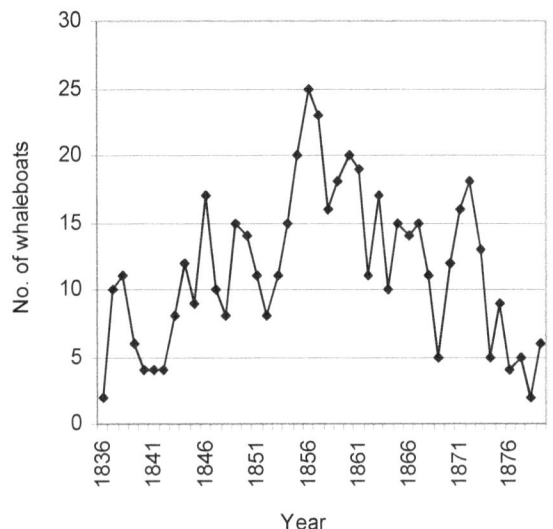

Figure 3.10 Total no. of whaleboats.

Table 3.1 lists the vessels known to have been associated with the operation of colonial shore stations. This is by no means a complete list, although in the absence of specific statements clearly associating vessels with actual whaling operations, other than in the capacity of supply ship, further details cannot be included. It can be assumed that other associations existed, particularly for parties such as those operated by John Bateman, which cruised between several stations every season. Although there are several references to small colonial vessels being built with whaling in mind (e.g. PG 10/12/1842; Garden 1978: 77; McKail 1927), it does not appear that any were built exclusively for that purpose. To remain an economic proposition, all of these craft would have been hired as coastal transport, trading or cargo vessels outside the whaling season.

It is not possible to make a direct statement about the extent to which these small vessels increased the effectiveness of a whaling party. However, their use could extend the range of a shore station well beyond its normal catchment area and increase the efficiency of the chase by taking the whaleboats out to the prey. The speed with which the animal could be returned to shore and processed also contributed to the process. While the use of cutting-in vessels appears to have been quite common, it is likely that the expense of hiring the craft and paying its crew for a whole season was beyond the reach of many shore parties.

Number of Workers

The number of men employed in a whaling party was closely related to the number of whaleboats in use at each station. Each boat required at least six men; the headsman, boat steerer and from four to six pulling hands, depending upon the size of the whaleboat (Little 1969). There might also be several other hands at the station performing duties such as cook, cooper, look–out, etc.

Vessel	Type	Location	Date	Whaling party	References
Vulcan	-	Two People Bay	1842–3	Andrews	Garden 1977
Vixen	-	Carnac	1845	Curtis	PG 20/9/1845
Julian	-	Torbay	1845	Sinclair	Garden 1978
Thetis	cutter	Torbay	1846	Morton	PG 5/9/46
Gazelle	-	Castle Rock	1847	Heppingstone	Inq 4/8/1847
Sonnet Bee	-	Castle Rock	1848	Heppingstone	Seymour n.d.
Pelsart	schooner	Fremantle Castle Rock	1849	Scott	PG 5/12/1849
Brothers	cutter	Castle Rock	1859	Layman	Inq 25/5/1859
Argo	schooner	Malus Island	1870–2	Pearse & Marmion	Inq 19/7/1870
MaryAnn	schooner	Malus island	1872	Bateman	Her 2/11/1872
Star	schooner	Malus Island	1877	Bateman	PG 26/6/1877
Star		Geographe Bay	1880	Bateman	Her 23/10/1880

Table 3.1 Small vessels associated with shore whaling operations.

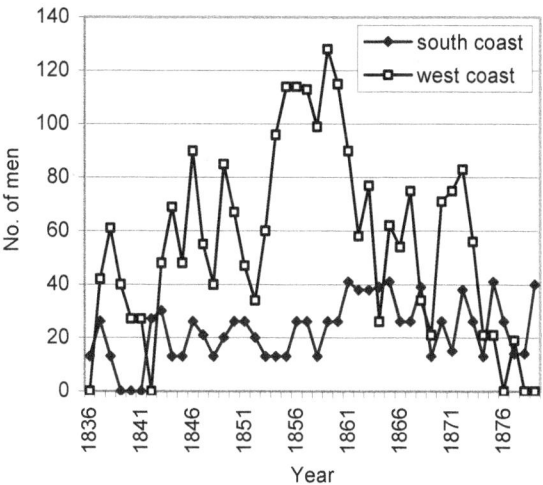

Figure 3.12 Estimated no. of whalers - south and west.

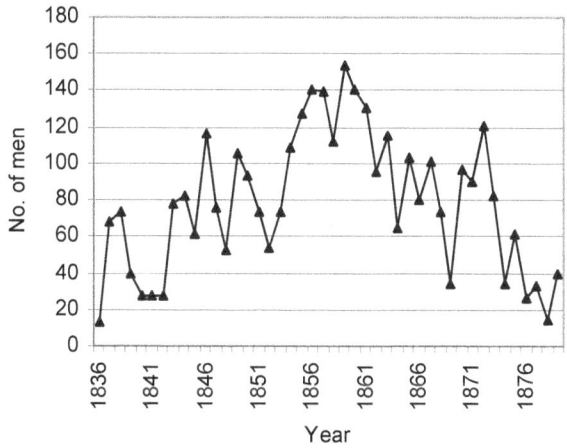

Figure 3.13 Estimated total numbers of whalers per year.

The whaling party registrations under the Statute 10th Victoria No. 16, passed in 1847, show the approximate sizes of various groups on both coasts. It is evident that the parties normally operated with a minimal number of employees. For instance, two boat fisheries, such as Castle Rock in 1851 (GG 16/9/1851) or Cheyne Beach in 1871 (GG 11/7/1871), sometimes listed only 13 men. This gave two six–man boat crews and an extra hand usually specifically registered as the cook. Even for a larger, four boat party such as at Bunbury in 1861 (GG 5/11/1861), only 27 men are listed. If we assume 24 men were required for the four boats, with one man registered as the cooper, there were only two 'extra' men, possibly cooks, look–outs or other supplementary positions.

To estimate the total number of men employed in any year, the most reliable data are figures giving the actual numbers of workers, usually through Government Gazette registrations. However, in most cases the size of the whaling party can only be derived by extrapolating from the number of boats operating. A fixed ratio of the number of men to number of boats derived from averaging the *Government Gazette* registrations has been used as follows: 13 men per two–boat party, 21 men per three–boat party, and 27 men per four–boat party.

The ratio of men to boats appears to have been fairly consistent through time and between coasts, with the number of men at the four–boat fisheries being the most variable. The most problematic aspect is that in many cases the number of men is extrapolated from an estimated number of whaleboats, resulting in some estimates of dubious reliability. Figures 3.12 and 3.13 are therefore illustrations to provide an approximation of the total workforce, rather than absolute or accurate counts.

Whaling Stations

Although a detailed discussion of the distribution and nature of the shore stations is presented in Chapter Four, it is appropriate to discuss briefly the number of stations in operation in various periods as an indicator of the scale of the Western Australian whaling industry.

One of the more interesting developments with implications for the archaeological record was the move towards using more than one station during each season. The relationship between the movement between regions and the seasonal migration patterns of whale species has already been proposed and will be examined in detail in the final part of this chapter.

Figure 3.14 shows the minimum number of whaling stations on both coasts with 3.15 showing the total, which can be compared to the number of whaling parties shown in Figures 3.7–3.8. I refer to this as the minimum number because there is no doubt that in the period after 1865 there was a greater number of stations in use than is plotted here. While the historical evidence suggests that most of the south coast parties split their season between two locations, there is often no firm statement as to which parties did so. Taking a conservative approach to the data, the use of multiple stations in this later period has not been assumed.

The first area for attention is the relationship between the size of the whaling parties and the size of the shore stations. The number and size of whaling parties operating on both coasts would have had a direct impact upon the physical nature of the stations. A party of four boats and 27 men would naturally require more or larger buildings to accommodate and supply the increased workforce and industrial capacity than a two–boat and 13–man fishery. This in turn should be archaeologically detectable in both the nature of the structural remains and the extent of associated deposits (see also Chapter Four).

It should also be considered that not only would the strength of the whaling parties have affected the size of the station complex, but also the capacity of existing stations may have borne upon the decision to form parties of a certain size. In addition to the capital required to make alterations to a station and lay in more equipment and supplies, an increased party would also have required a greater degree of management. Increased size might also have reduced flexibility, particularly with regard to movement between early and late season stations.

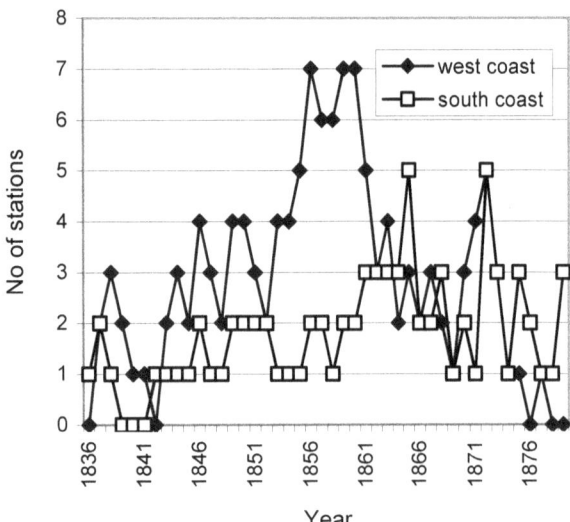

Figure 3.14 Minimum numbers of shore stations - south and west.

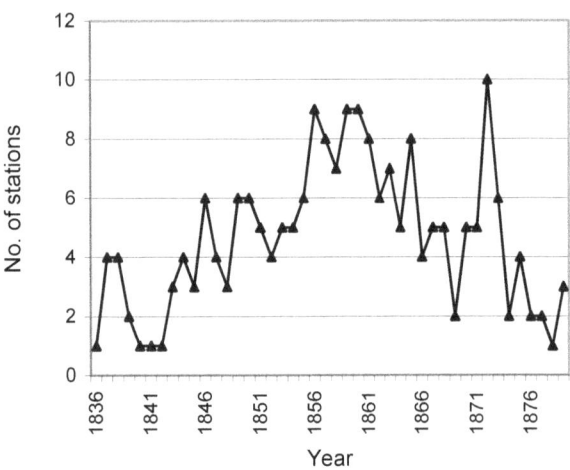

Figure 3.15 Minimum numbers of shore whaling stations.

WHALING TECHNOLOGY

The second half of this chapter focuses on aspects of the processes and production of the Western Australian shore whaling industry. The limited body of 19th–century Western Australian accounts of whale hunts and blubber processing (PG 10/6/1837; PG 29/6/1837; Landor 1847) shows no difference from international modes of commercial whaling at a general level (see Chapter One), so a separate study does not appear warranted. However, several associated areas have been investigated which relate to the success of the process. The first section discusses evidence for the diffusion of new technology into the Western Australian whaling industry, looking specifically at importation patterns and local production of whalecraft. In particular, it was thought that changes in the availability and nature of essential specialized equipment might be correlated to wider changes in the progress of the colonial industry.

Equipment supply

The common pool of specialized technology used by pelagic and shore–based whalers in 19th century has already been described in some detail by Pearson (1983) and need not be repeated here. As the concern of this current study is not with the technology of the whalecraft as such, it is only necessary to say that the historical record and existing museum collections suggest that the Western Australia whalers used the same range of items as those on the east coast.

Table 3.2 reproduces several auction catalogues from Western Australian whaling parties. The listing for the Northern Whaling Company (SRG 2/2/1837) is an almost complete assemblage of the whalecraft and supplies required by a shore fishery, although there are obvious omissions such as whaleline and extra boats. It is interesting to contrast this with the details of the items to be auctioned after the closure of the company in the following year (PG 17/2/1838). The other two lists also afford some comparison, the first being an auction advertisement from Daniel Scott of Fremantle, probably after he had decided to end his involvement with the Bathers Beach station (PG 1/3/1850). The other is a compilation of two lists of equipment received from Britain and sent northward to Henry Sanford, owner of the Port Gregory station, in 1855 (BL M385).

It is possible that the initial body of whalecraft used by the Western Australian whalers was drawn from the eastern Australian colonies, rather than through the lengthy process required to import items directly from Britain. For instance, the Northern Whaling Company called for supply tenders in February (SRG 2/2/1837, see Table 3.2) and by late May was ready for operation, an interval of only three months. Barring the unlikely scenario of an existing stockpile of whalecraft in the Western Australian colonies, this would have been sufficient time only for coastal traders to arrange importation from New South Wales or Hobart. More directly, Thomas Sherratt's Doubtful Island Bay party in 1836 was quite probably equipped through a partnership with an established Tasmanian whaler (PG 7/5/1836).

The arrival of foreign pelagic whaleships off the Western Australian coast coincided with the emergence of the shore whaling industry and immediately presented an alternative supply of whalecraft. With their vessels carrying a supply of equipment sufficient for a three or four year voyage, the masters of the whaleships were often willing to sell surplus to the colonial whalers. Even prior to the start of the 1837 season the Fremantle Whaling Company was able to purchase whalecraft from the *Cambrian*, one of the first American vessels to arrive off Fremantle (SRG 16/3/1837). On the south coast both of the 1837 season whaling parties at Doubtful Island Bay entered into agreements with an American vessel which amongst other forms of assistance probably provided them with some whalecraft (CSR 55/29:9/8/1837, SRG 29/6/1837).

1. Call for tenders to supply the Northern Whaling Company (*Swan River Guardian* 2/2/1837)

- 6 tons good sound hogsheads	- 48 strong sacks	- 4 buckets	- 2 mess kids
- 1 grindstone complete	- 2 spades	- 1 shovel	- 20 shark hooks
- 1 keg white lead	- 2 gallons paint oil	- 2 ladles	- 2 forks
- 2 skimmers	- 2 funnels	- 1 spirit pump	- 2 hand saws
- 4 hammers	- 1 seine	- 200 copper nails w. ruffs	- 20lb iron nails
- 1 doz. Gimblets [sic]	- 10 pounds seine twine	- 3 boat anchors	- 2 boat grappels
- 1 pair can hooks	- 2 pair grains	- 12 axe handles	- 12 harpoon & lance shafts
- 10 x 5 gal. breakers	- 2 x 15 gal. casks	- 1 large iron boiler	- 6 boat axes
- 3 large axes	- 10 muskets	- 2 boat compasses	- 12 ash oars 15ft
- 24 fishing lines	- 12 flinching knives	- 1 bag rice	- 100 bushels of wheat
- 10 gallons vinegar	- 1 chest tea	- 400 ft of scantling (10 ft)	- 1 1/2 cwt sugar
- 2 casks salt pork	- 300ft of battens (10 ft)	- 2 casks salt beef	- 1 ton salt
- 10 lbs pepper	- 1 telescope	- 50lb gunpowder	

- 1500 feet 3/4 boards, 8 inches in breadth.
- one full sized whale boat, with oars, mast & sprit sail complete   - one 12ft jolly boat; do. do., to be copper fastened.

2. Auction of Whalecraft from the Northern Whaling Company (*Perth Gazette* 17/3/1838)

- 4 whale boats	- 1 jolly boat	- 13 tons of new shooks	- cutting-in blocks
- coils of rope	- coppers	- 2 seines	

- 'a variety of gear...for a whaling establishment'

3. Auction of whalecraft by D. Scott of Fremantle (*Perth Gazette* 1/3/1850)

- 2 whaleboats	- 1 trypot	- 2 copper coolers	- lances
- harpoons	- ladles	- spades	- skimmers
- oil casks	- cutting-in blocks	- 2 new manilla fauls	- blubber hooks

- 'a variety of other useful whaling gear, and new hoop iron and rivets'.

4. Equipment sent to H. Sanford for the Port Gregory station, 1855   (BL M386)

- 20 lances	- 10 harpoons	- 13 boat spades	- 1 winch
- 1 half round spade	- 2 forks	- 2 copper coolers	- 2 trypots
- 2 mincing tubs	- 2 coils of whale line	- 1 lantern	- 1 signal lantern
- 1 boat bucket	- 1 chain head (?)	- 1 derrick chain	- 12 spare rowlocks
- 3 shovels	- 3 pikes	- 2 coils of whale line	- copper tacks or riveting
- trypots	- cutting-in block	- 120 hogsheads, or casks for 30 tuns of oil	

- 2 whale boats (various sails, anchors and gear specified)
- 'Galvanized iron roof for trying-out house with galvanized iron nails... 30ft by18ft... (width)

Table 3.2 Supply lists of whalecraft used at Western Australian shore whaling stations.

More importantly, as described by Pearson (1983:50) for New South Wales during the 1830s, 'a pool of imperishable equipment, such as trypots and coolers, had been established, and the need for new or replacement items would have been quite low'. Companies would rise and fall, but their equipment could now be resold to replace the plant of existing fisheries or to outfit newly formed parties (Inq 2/12/1846; PG 1/3/1850).

Despite reuse of some items, there would still have been a continued need for supply of harpoons, whaleline, lances and other pieces of gear which were regularly lost in the chase or through wear and tear. Importation records for Western Australia during its first several decades are either sketchy or non–existent, making it impossible to identify the arrival of whalecraft. It is equally impossible to gauge the level of informal trade with American whaleships for such items (see Gibbs 2000). Whitecar's diary of the cruise of the American whaler *Pacific* provides important insights into this activity, including the following passage.

Whalers, unless some serious accident befalls, do not usually enter ports where their necessities can be supplied at other than exorbitant prices, except the last one, where they calculate to dispose of surplus provisions, boats and rigging, being in a hurry to get home they make some port of note so as to be detained as short a time as possible in getting rid of them (Whitecar 1860:25).

By carrying cargoes of consumer items on the outwards voyage and then disposing of their whalecraft once a full ship of oil had been obtained, the captains obviously hoped to maximize the profit from each cruise and free up valuable space for the return passage. Even a single 'dumping' event of this kind could inject into the local market a body of equipment sufficient to equip two shore stations. While the Americans were competition to be discouraged, the colonial whalers must surely have valued this ready source of equipment supply. With the colonial parties operating on such a limited scale, it is probable that it was simply not necessary to organize a more formal source of supply.

It was only during the last resurgence of colonial whaling activity during the 1870s, when the number of American vessels had been reduced to a handful, that the improved records of imports in the Blue Books show the arrival of whalecraft from Britain and the other colonies (Table 3.3). Of these, only one record of exactly what items were being imported could be found in contemporary newspaper reports. In January 1872 the *Sea Ripple* arrived from Mauritius with two whale boats, two trypots, five coils of whale line and sundry whaling gear for J. and W. Bateman (Inq 4/9/1872), most probably to supply their new station in the Dampier Archipelago. However, this large quantity of whaling equipment would have been worth considerably more than the £15 recorded in the Blue Books for that year.

Year	Imported from	Value (£)
1872	Mauritius	15.00
1873	United Kingdom	136.00
	United States	53.16
1874	South Australia	8.17
1875	Victoria	26.00

Table 3.3 Imports of whalecraft (Blue Books 1872–1875).

Diffusion of Technology

The second factor considered in this section is the rate at which the Western Australian whalers received and were able to put into use technological innovations which might have improved the efficiency and success of their operations. Rather than undertake an overview of the total body of whalecraft, the focus is on the introduction of a single distinctive classes of instrument, the 'harpoon gun', which represented the most significant change in technology and practice for the 19th century whalers.

Because the harpoon lay at the heart of the whaling industry, determining to a large degree the success of any attempt to fasten to a whale, it became the most consistent focus of experimentation and innovation in whalecraft during the 19th century. Most efforts were directed at the design of the head in an attempt to improve the iron's ability to remain fastened in the blubber of the whale. This included variations in the number and design of the flues and the invention of special pivoting heads (called 'toggle–irons' or 'temple–irons') which would swing open once embedded in the animal (Pearson 1983). However, all of these designs still relied upon the harpoon being propelled by hand, thus limiting range and effectiveness to the throwing power of the headsman.

The alternative presented by the harpoon gun was that it fired an iron at the target using explosive force, with the whaleline attached along a slotted shaft. There had been experiments of this type since the 1730s, but it was not until the mid–19th century that these devices became an effective alternative to traditional harpoons. Many variations appeared, including combinations of harpoon guns and bomb lances, which were intended to kill the whale with the explosive charge (Pearson 1983; Shaw 1991). Whereas variations in harpoon head design were not remarked upon, the appearance of the gun harpoon was sufficiently conspicuous and interesting to merit comment in contemporary accounts.

The first report of a harpoon gun being used by a colonial party was in November 1849, when Captain Scott of Fremantle sent a newly–received weapon to be tested by his whaling party in Geographe Bay. Although no indication is given of the type of gun, it was described as having driven a harpoon 20 fathoms (120 ft/ 36.7m) in a direct line during an experimental trial, and with such force that it bent upon hitting the object at which it was aimed (Inq 7/11/1849). No reports were received of how the instrument fared in actual use, although in 1850 a report was made that the Bunbury station was having poor success, losing at least three whales through the attempted use of a harpoon gun (Inq 6/11/1850). The editor of the *Inquirer* advised them to lay the instrument to one side and use their old weapons.

In 1851 the American whaler *North Star* put in to Busselton, where the Master, Captain Brown, sold a number of harpoon guns of his own invention to the other whaleships resorting there. The gun was described as being entirely of brass (except the lock), weighing 35 lbs (16 kg), fired from the shoulder and capable of propelling its projectile 18 fathoms (22 m). No further details are given, other than that it was of a different construction to those previously employed, and was promoted as being 'infinitely more manageable at sea' (Inq 5/2/1851). Brown sold £500 worth of the guns at £25 each to the other captains, including one to Robert Heppingstone, the manager of Castle Rock.

Some months later a report noted that Heppingstone's party had experienced a poor season, with the harpoon gun tried once, 'and then unsuccessfully' (Inq 8/10/1851). Next month another article commented that although the gun had initially failed through mismanagement, it had more recently been all that could be asked of it, with three whales being taken by this means (Inq 26/11/1851). It is possible that the Castle Rock station was still using the same gun several years later, with the station manager's diary (Seymour n.d.) recording on 30th September 1853 that they had 'chased 2 Humpbacks and *fired* at them 3 times but missed'.

As it was in the interest of the American whalers to stay abreast of new and more effective means of engaging in their industry, it is probable that ships at the start of their cruise would carry the most recent innovations in whalecraft, even if only for testing purposes. If we assume the willingness of the American vessels to sell such gear to local parties, the colonial whalers could potentially receive new forms of equipment in as short a time as it took for the ship to arrive from the United States, possibly less than four months. Whether the colonials then chose to adopt the new technology or consistently use it is another matter.

Local Manufacture

The final consideration with regard to the supply of whalecraft to the Western Australian shore whalers is evidence for local manufacture. Some items, such as whaleline, harpoon guns, bomb lances and trypots were beyond the capabilities of Western Australian craftsmen. Whalers may also have preferred to purchase key equipment such as irons and lances from English or American sources as a means of ensuring quality. Even so, this still left a large body of whalecraft of a less essential nature, including flensing knives, forks, skimmers (etc) which could have been produced by local blacksmiths and carpenters.

The most significant item of whalecraft for which there is a body of evidence for local manufacture, even in the early period, is the whaleboat. The design and use of whaleboats have been extensively discussed by Ansel (1978) and again by Pearson (1983) for the Australian context. These small vessels needed to be fast and manoeuvrable with the general dimensions being '27–31 feet long (8.2m–9.4m) and about 1/5th that in width' (Pearson 1983:42). They could be clinker (lap–strake) or carvel in construction, and while primarily intended for whaling, were also frequently fitted with mast steps to allow a simple sail arrangement to be used. Whaleboats required from five to seven oarsmen, with a further man at the long sweep oar which was used to steer the boat.

Whaleboats were acquired from American vessels or wrecks and may also have been imported from Britain (Inq 4/9/1872). However, in the 1837 season the colonial shipwrights Mews and Cox, whose workshop shared Bathers Beach with the Fremantle Whaling Company, constructed the four whaleboats used by the Northern Company. Although these originally cost £30 each, after the collapse of the company they were auctioned for £25 and £26 (PG 3/3/1838). It is probable that Mews also repaired the several boats which were damaged during the season (PG 24/6/1837; SRG 20/7/1837). There are references early to ship-building at Albany (Chester 1927; Sale 1936; Garden 1977) which suggest a similar capacity for local manufacture of whaleboats. The construction and repair of whaleboats must also have been encouraged by their use for general purposes (Inq 23/3/1842; Inq 25/5/1842; Wollaston 1991:139).

There is no evidence for local variation in design, although local timbers were certainly used. A letter from Henry Sanford at Port Gregory complains that his new whaleboat from Mews & Company had been made with banksia (possibly *Banksia serrata*) rather than mahogany (jarrah - *Eucalyptus marginata*) both of which are local timbers (BL M386). The specifications for a new whaleboat for the Fremantle Harbour Masters Department listed in Table 3.4 (GG 6/2/1855), provides insight into the style of boat seen in Western Australia.

The capability for making minor and even major repairs to whaleboats was essential for a whaling party, as being damaged or 'stove–in' by injured or angered whales appears to have been a common occurrence (e.g. Seymour n.d. 20/9/1852, 7/8/1853). A detailed record of one such incident describes a whale striking the boat several times with snout and flukes, resulting in its destruction (Inq 4/8/1847). Although parties situated close to settlements (Bathers Beach, Bunbury or Barker Bay) may have employed the skills of professional shipwrights for repairs, those at the more distant stations would have been forced to restore their damaged boats themselves. The station cooper, also often doubling as one of the boat hands, most probably stretched his skills to effect minor boat repairs when necessary, rather than lose the use of the boat for the remainder of the season. Seymour mentions various repairs, including replacing 'stove–in' boards and putting in a false keel (Seymour n.d. 21/8/1852, 28/9/1852). In slack periods the boats also underwent maintenance such as repainting, explaining the presence of the kegs of white lead paint in the Northern Company's list (Table 3.2).

Length, over all, 28 feet.
Extreme breadth, 6 feet.
Depth, 2 feet 2 inches.
Keel, stern, sternpost and gunwales to be mahogany.
Planking, best yellow pine or Singapore cedar, plained on both sides, clear of all knots and rents.
Timbers and Floors to be notched to receive planking.
Thwarts to be dovetailed into rising.
Mast Thwart to be double–kneed.
Gunwales to be fitted with Iron Crutches, tack and sheet hooks and cleets.
Keel to be 3 inches deep clear, of garibard strikes.
The boat to have a good flat floor amidships with the usual spring of a whaler boat.
Bilge pieces filled to save the hands in hauling up and launching the boat.
The whole to be fastened with Wrought Copper, clenched with roves and to be covered with two coats of paint.

Table 3.4 Tender specification for a 5 oared whaleboat for the Pilot Service (*Government Gazette* 9/6/1857).

The necessity and capability to repair and maintain whaleboats at whaling stations suggests the potential for such activity to be archaeologically visible. This is discussed further in Chapter Five.

PRODUCTION AND EFFICIENCY

The following section examines the efficiency of the whalers and their success in terms of the catch record and income through exports of oil and bone. Because of the limited body of historical evidence which specifically concerns the operations of shore stations in Western Australia, this section combines a detailed analysis of the catch information contained in the Seymour diary of the Castle Rock whaling station (1846 to 1853, excluding 1851) with a general appraisal of the shore industry.

The Whaling Season

The two main species pursued by the 19th century Western Australian shore whalers were the southern right whale (*Eubalaena glacialis australis*) and the humpback whale (*Megaptera novaeangliae*), although other species were also sighted and pursued (Chittleborough 1965, Bannister 1985). The modern humpback population may arrive on the southern and western Australian coasts as early as April, although the majority of the north–bound group appears in June, moving to the sub–tropical waters of the northwest coast to calve and breed (Chittleborough 1965). Around mid–August they begin the southward journey, passing closer to shore and sometimes lingering in a bay or area with their calves for up to a week (Collier 1993). Although there are a few stragglers until late

November, the migration through Western Australian waters has largely ended by late October. The humpback population does not pass along the south coast on their southward run (Chittleborough 1965).

The extreme endangered status of the modern southern right whale populations has made them difficult to study in any detail, so at best only general statements on their modern behaviour can be made. The main group arrives on the southern and lower western Australian coast from mid–May to calve and mate, returning to sub–polar regions by mid–November (Bannister 1985; Cummings 1985). It is frequently said that right whales gained their name because they were the 'right' whale to catch, slow and easy to pursue in a whaleboat (see Table 3.15) and buoyant once killed, allowing them to be towed easily back to the ship or shore station (Baker 1990). Their oil was commonly referred to as 'black' oil (Cummings 1985) although some writers may have used the term for any oil which was not sperm whale oil. Black oil was regarded as inferior to that from sperm whales. Both right and humpback whales are plankton feeders and their mouths contain the baleen (whalebone) plates that also contributed significantly to the value of their capture.

The operational period of the 19th century shore whaling industry, normally referred to as the 'season', was based upon the coastal migration patterns of the humpbacks and right whale populations passing through each region. By the time of the 1836 and 1837 seasons, the European settlers on both coasts had observed these patterns for over half a decade, with further refinements after several years of more systematic assessment. Writing from the Fremantle region on the west coast, Ogle (1839) reported that whales frequented the west coast from June to September. Landor (1847) stated that from about June the whales (presumably humpbacks) proceeded northwards, generally returning southwards around six weeks later. Another correspondent noted humpbacks could arrive off the Fremantle coast as early as April (PG 22/4/1837), although a decade later there are statements that the Fremantle stations did not normally capture anything before August (e.g. Inq 2/8/1848). The shore whaling season for the Fremantle area appears to have closed in mid to late October (PG 6/11/1847; PG 23/10/1859).

The dates when whales appeared on the less populated south coast are even less certain, although the Cheyne Beach station reported making catches from late June onwards (Inq 7/7/1847; Inq 27/6/1850; Inq 15/7/1857; Inq 21/6/1865). The close of the southern season appears to have been in late October or early to mid–November (Inq 3/11/1847; Inq 21/11/1849). This is consistent with modern research on whale migrations (Jenner *et al.* 2001).

Although the start of the season in each area presumably reflected accumulated knowledge of when whale migrations passed that particular point in the coast, Seymour's (n.d.) records show that this was by no means a finely tuned system. The records for Castle Rock, summarized in Table 3.5, show a variation of up to three months for the starting date, although the close of the season was within a range of a just over one month. Both the opening and closing of the season may well have been arbitrary points within the general time frame of the migration, with the stations managers probably hoping to catch the peak of the herd without keeping the station open longer than necessary.

Year	Commenced	Ended	Total Days
1846	June 1	Nov 22	175
1847	Aug 3	Nov 30	119
1848	July 14	Dec 3	142
1849	Sept 1	Dec 3+	95+
1850	Sept 14+	Nov 14	62 +
1851*	July 16	Oct 30	107
1852	July 2	Nov 6	127
1853	July 26	Nov 5	103

(* Taken from Inquirer and Perth Gazette)
(+ Records incomplete; earliest or latest confirmed date)

Table 3.5 Whaling season - Castle Rock 1846–1853

There is also the likelihood that the whaling season in each region was affected by demands on the labour force to organize or participate in other seasonal rural tasks. In particular, November saw the movement of sheep and cattle to summer pastures, which may have provided men with several months work as shepherds, but also drawn them away from the whaling parties.

Catch efficiency

An analysis of the information in Seymour's journal (Seymour n.d.) provides insights into the efficiency of the operation of the Castle Rock station over the eight year period 1846 to 1853. This can been done by comparing the rate of success in each stage of the whaling process, detailed in Tables 3.6 to 3.11, and summarized in Table 3.12. Table 3.6 summarizes of the number of days each month in which whales, excluding killer whales, were sighted from the Castle Rock station. This can be contrasted with Table 3.7, which shows the number of days in each month in which whales were actually pursued. Seymour's diary suggests that the only reasons why the crews would not pursue a whale were extremely heavy weather or gales which might swamp the boats, or because the men were already occupied in processing a whale which they had previously brought to shore.

Although it is not possible to determine exactly how many whales were pursued by the Castle Rock boats, Seymour records how many times a day the crews engaged in chase (Table 3.8). As shown in Table 3.9, a mean of only 21% of these chases resulted in a whale being struck with a harpoon. Once the whale was struck a variety of incidents could occur, including the iron 'drawing' from the blubber, or the whale turning and destroying the boat. The whale might also run so far out to sea that the men would be forced to cut the line or risk not being able to make their way back to shore (Seymour n.d. 23/10/46). Between 29% and 86% of whales struck were eventually killed (Table 3.9–3.10), averaging 60%.

	1846	1847	1848	1849	1850	1852	1853	Total
June	2	-	-	-	-	-	-	2
July	1	-	1	-	-	8	-	10
Aug	6	14	6	1	-	12	6	45
Sept	21	13	23	17	13	14	11	112
Oct	25	19	26	23	18	30	26	167
Nov	17	13	22	2	5	1	4	64
Dec	-	-	2	-	-	-	-	2
Total	72	59	80	43	36	65	47	

Table 3.6 Castle Rock: days per month whales sighted.

	1846	1847	1848	1849	1850	1852	1853	Total
June	2	-	-	-	-	-	-	2
July	1	-	1	-	-	4	-	6
Aug	6	12	6	0	-	11	3	38
Sept	21	12	20	18	12	14	9	106
Oct	23	18	21	23	16	29	25	155
Nov	16	14	23	2	5	1	4	65
Dec	-	-	2	-	-	-	-	2
Total	69	56	71	43	33	58	41	

Table 3.7 Castle Rock: days per month whales chased.

	1846	1847	1848	1849	1850	1852	1853	Total
June	2	-	-	-	-	-	-	2
July	3	-	1	-	-	6	-	10
Aug	6	17	7	0	-	12	4	46
Sept	28	20	27	32	18	23	13	161
Oct	51	38	38	46	19	53	48	293
Nov	27	33	43	5	8	1	3	120
Dec	-	-	5	-	-	-	-	5
Total	117	108	121	83	46	95	68	

Table 3.8 Castle Rock: no. of whale chases per month.

	1846	1847	1848	1849	1850	1852	1853	Total
June	0	-	-	-	-	-	-	0
July	0	-	0	-	-	0	0	0
Aug	7	3	0	0	-	1	3	16
Sept	6	6	4	10	5	3	2	38
Oct	11	8	13	15	2	2	9	64
Nov	7	11	12	-	0	0	0	30
Dec	-	-	2	-	-	-	-	2
Total	31	28	31	25	7	6	14	

Table 3.9 Castle Rock: no. of whales struck per month.

	1846	1847	1848	1849	1850	1852	1853	Total
June	0	-	-	-	-	-	-	0
July	0	-	0	-	-	0	0	0
Aug	7	2	0	0	-	1	1	11
Sept	2	3	3	6	4	2	0	21
Oct	5	8	8	11	0	0	3	39
Nov	6	11	8	-	0	0	0	25
Dec	-	-	2	-	-	-	-	2
Total	20	24	21	17	4	3	4	

Table 3.10 Castle Rock: no. of whales killed per month.

	1846	1847	1848	1849	1850	1852	1853	Total
June	0	-	-	-	-	-	-	0
July	0	-	0	-	-	0	0	0
Aug	9	2	0	0	-	1	0	14
Sept	2	2	3	4	3	1	0	16
Oct	5	5	7	8	0	0	1	30
Nov	4	7	7	-	0	0	0	18
Dec	-	-	0	-	-	-	-	0
Total	20	16	17	12	3	2	1	

Table 3.11 Castle Rock: no. of whales brought to shore.

	1846	1847	1848	1849	1850	1852	1853	Total
Days sighted	72	59	80	43	36	65	47	343
Days chased	69	56	71	43	33	58	41	371
Chase events	17	108	121	83	46	95	68	538
Whales struck	31	28	31	25	7	6	14	132
Whales killed	20	24	21	17	4	3	4	77
Whales brought in	20	16	17	12	3	2	1	71

Table 3.12 Castle Rock: summary of operations 1846-53.

	1846	1847	1848	1849	1850	1852	1853	Total
% chases where whales struck	24	26	26	30	15	6	20	21
% struck whales killed	64	86	68	68	57	50	29	60
% killed whales successfully brought to shore	100	67	81	71	75	67	25	69
% chases resulting in whales killed & brought to shore	17	15	14	14	7	2	2	10

Table 3.13 Castle Rock: success and efficiency.

Seymour's diary suggests that once ashore, the process of cutting–in the whale and then trying-out and barrelling the oil took an average of three days. This could take longer if interrupted by whale chases, although Seymour (n.d. 16/10/1846) mentions the look–out not being kept while the process was completed. Cleaning whalebone seems to have been the least pressing task, done after the trying out was completed or at some later date (Seymour n.d. 21/8/1852).

It is interesting to note that over the eight years of records, the efficiency of the Castle Rock station actually appears to decline. Even though decreased whale sightings may partially account for diminishing performance, in general the rate of success at striking, killing and returning the whales to shore also fell. This cannot be easily explained by reference to Seymour's journal, although contemporary reports suggest some mismanagement by the crews (Inq 19/10/1853).

Species of catch and catch strategy

The species of whale involved in each chase by the Castle Rock whalers is summarized in Table 3.14, while the number killed (but not necessarily brought to shore) is presented in Table 3.15. Humpback whales dominate the sample, forming 79% of the species chased, and 77% of the total killed. Right whales form the next and considerably smaller group at 15% of the species chased and 15% of the total kill.

The location of the Castle Rock station on the lower west coast placed it within the migratory path of humpbacks and right whales. While Malus Island in the Dampier Archipelago is positioned at the northern end of the humpback migration, Castle Rock's situation at the northwest corner of Geographe Bay makes it one of the last places on the west coast passed by the whales on their southward journey. The opportunity to take two shots at the main body of the humpback migration provides ample explanation for Bateman's decision to open a station at each of these locations during the early 1870s (see Chapter Four and Appendix A).

Overall, the catch of humpbacks versus right whales at Castle Rock was in a ratio of 5:1. However, for both species there was a 14% success rate between chasing and killing the animals, suggesting an equal degree of ease (or difficulty) in the pursuit of each type. This is despite the differing swimming speeds (Table 3.16).

	Hback	Right	Other	UnID	Total
1846	87	23	3	4	117
1847	91	14	3	0	108
1848	103	12	6	0	121
1849	69	11	2	1	83
1850	41	4	0	1	46
1852	70	21	4	0	95
1853	45	13	3	7	68
Total	506	98	21	13	638

Table 3.14 Castle Rock: Species of whales in each chase.

	Hback	Right	Other	UnID	Total
1846	11	2	7	0	20
1847	20	4	0	0	24
1848	19	2	0	0	21
1849	16	1	0	0	17
1850	3	1	0	0	4
1852	1	2	0	0	3
1853	2	2	0	0	4
Total	72	14	7	0	93

Table 3.15 Castle Rock: Species of whales killed.

Species	Feeding	Cruising	Fleeing
Right	1.2–2.5	3–6.5	7–11
Humpback	1.2–2.5	3–9	15–16.5
Sperm	1.2–3.5	3–9	21–27
Blue	1.2–4	3–20	24–30
Fin	1.2–4	3–22	25–33
Sei	1.2–4	3–22	36–40

Table 3.16 Swimming speeds of whale species in miles per hour (after Cousteau and Paccalet 1988:126).

The next most commonly–pursued species at Castle Rock was the blue whale (*Balaenoptera musculus intermedia*), referred to in Seymour's (n.d.) journal as 'sulphur bottoms'. These animals also migrate north from the Antarctic and along the Western Australian coast as they head towards Indonesian waters (Cousteau and Paccalet 1988). Up to half a dozen sightings of blue whales were made from Castle Rock each year, with the main migration apparently passing between August and November like the other whales. In August of 1853 Seymour (n.d. 19/8/1853) also recorded sighting a cow and calf sulphur bottom passing by the station.

Despite chasing blue whales whenever they were within range of the station, the Castle Rock crews were usually unable to strike these animals with their harpoons.

This was presumably due to the 'famed swiftness' of the species (Inq 24/9/1851), which was able to flee twice as quickly as humpbacks and three times as quickly as right whales (Table 3.16). There is only one report of the Castle Rock party fastening to a blue whale, although on that occasion they were forced to cut the line for unspecified reasons (Inq 24/9/1851). There are in fact only two records of Western Australian shore–whalers being able to kill blue whales, at Bunbury in November 1858 (Inq 1/12/1858), and at Fremantle in March 1859 (PG 1/4/1859). Although the Fremantle whale was lost in transit, the carcass brought in at Bunbury was reported as not yielding as much oil as an ordinary right whale, while its bone was also inferior, if better than that taken from humpbacks (Inq 1/12/1858).

There are several references by Seymour (n.d.) to sightings of 'finbacks', possibly referring to fin whales (*B. physalis*) or sei whales (*B. borealis*) (cf. Baker 1990). Both species are similar to blue whales, although shorter, with the modern populations thought to spend summer off the northwest of Western Australia and winter in the Antarctic (Cousteau and Paccalet 1988). The Castle Rock crews are recorded as unsuccessfully chasing finbacks during the 1840s, so that by the 1850s there are sightings of 'lots of finbacks' without any indication of pursuit (Seymour n.d. 16/9/1853). As for blue whales, it is quite possible that the swimming speed of these animals simply put them beyond the capabilities of the open–boat whalers, who could only row at about five miles per hour (Ansel 1978). There are no historical references to other Western Australian shore stations chasing finbacks.

There is a single account of the Castle rock whalers capturing sperm whales (*Physeter macrocephalus*), a species which normally feeds along the continental shelf and does not approach the shore. In mid–August of 1846 Seymour (n.d. 14/8/1846) recorded that 'a score' of sperm whales was raised in Geographe Bay, while a contemporary report states that there were over 200 seen (PG 22/8/1846). Although Seymour's diary suggests that only seven were taken by the Castle Rock crews, it is possible that as many as 25 were eventually killed by them and another nearby station (Inq 2/9/1846). A cow and calf sperm whale was also taken by the Castle Rock boats just over a decade later (Inq 30/9/1857). The only other report of a shore station killing a sperm whale was in 1846, when the Torbay crews, with assistance from a small vessel, took a single animal (PG 3/10/1846).

Although the Castle Rock crews did not hunt killer whales (*Orcinus orca*) for oil, Seymour's diary suggests that a pod of these animals became associated with the station over a period of years. In the first year of the station's operation in 1846, killer whales were sighted cruising around Castle Rock on the 24th of July. In subsequent years they would continue to appear within a week or so of this date, with Seymour especially noting their arrival in his journal (Seymour n.d. 17/7/1848).

Unlike the co–operative arrangement at Twofold Bay in New South Wales where killer whales herded whales toward the whaleboats (Mead 1961), the relationship between the Castle Rock whalers and the killer whales was competitive. On several occasions the whalers salvaged humpbacks slain by the killers (Seymour n.d. 13/11/1846, 10/10/1848) and chased others which 'the kilers ad [sic] been at' (Seymour n.d. 2/11/1852). On at least one occasion the killers took advantage of the whaler's work, attacking a carcass being towed behind a whaleboat and dragging both beneath the surface (Inq 24/9/1851).

There are no explicit references in Seymour's journals to the catch strategies employed by the shore whalers. However, one clue is provided by Whitecar's observations of the fisheries at Castle Rock and Bunbury during the mid–1850s.

> If a whale is attended by a calf, they always fasten to the latter first, knowing that the mother, in her solicitude for her offspring, is very careful not to use her tremendous flukes; or if a humpback, her sweeping fins: but woe betide the boat, unless an experienced boat–header directs it, that is in the vicinity when she discovers that her calf is dead (Whitecar 1860:91).

The consistent capture of cow and calf pairs is borne out by Seymour's records. Over the seven years covered by the diary, 18 cow and calf pairs of humpbacks (36 individuals) were killed, representing 50% of the total humpback catch, or 39% of all whales taken by the station in that period. A high proportion of the remaining catch also represents cows or calves which were taken while the other half of the pair escaped. No cow and calf pairs of right whales are recorded as being taken at Castle Rock, although there is little doubt that the whalers would have used similar tactics. The capture of cow and calf pairs was obviously a successful strategy at Castle Rock, and it is highly probable that it was also used at the r shore stations. For example, in a single fortnight during September 1837 the Bathers Beach station was reported as catching four whales and their calves (PG 19/81837).

While there are insufficient historical data to undertake a comprehensive analysis of whale catch for all of the stations throughout Western Australia, an attempt was made to determine whether the trends detected in Seymour's records were exhibited by the whole of the colonial industry. Two contemporary newspapers and the Blue Book reports were analysed to extract information on the species of individual catches.

The reports on the success (and failures) of local fisheries which were published in the *Inquirer* and *Perth Gazette* newspapers were irregular and variable in quality over time, particularly with regard to the south coast. The extent of coverage appears to have been dependent upon the current perception of the significance or potential of the whaling industry, with interest waning rapidly after the mid–1860s. Prior to the mid–1840s the newspaper reports rarely provided information on which species were being captured. The analysis of the two newspapers is presented in Figures 3.15 and 3.16. The Blue Book listings are also variable and infrequently mention the number of individuals of each species taken (Figure 3.17).

Year	PG Rt	PG Hb	Inq Rt	Inq Hb	BB Rt	BB Hb	Bannister Rt	Bannister Hb
1845							20	0
1846	2	1				26	32	7
1847	1				2	10	10	44
1848	2	3				4	14	9
1849	2	2				3	0	27
1850	3	5					2	27
1851						2	8	10
1852							4	16
1853			5	1			5	12
1854	2		4	1			8	11
1855							19	11
1856	1	4				5	6	25
1857		16				3	14	18
1858	1	8				3	18	19
1859		4				4	0	29
1860				7		10	0	10
1861			1	4		3	1	11
1862				7			2	16
1863	1						0	29
1864							0	26
1865							1	39
Total	15	43	10	20	2	73	164	396

Table 3.17 Comparison of reports from different sources of right and humpback whales caught 1845–65.

	Inquirer Hback	Inquirer Right	Perth Gazette Hback	Perth Gazette Right
West Coast				
Port Gregory	11	2	13	0
Fremantle	10	9	5	12
Bunbury	8	5	5	4
Castle Rock	17	11	19	9
South Coast				
Torbay	5	0	-	-
Barker Bay	2	0	-	-
Cheyne Beach	20	1	0	1
Total	73	28	42	26

Table 3.18 Distribution of whale species caught 1836–79.

Comparison of the results from the three sources shows some differences (also see Appendix B8), although in general they all demonstrate that a greater number of humpback whales was being returned, especially in later years. Although the *Perth Gazette* accused the *Inquirer* of deliberately 'puffing' catch reports in an attempt to raise public and foreign confidence (PG 19/12/1846), there appears to be little reason why either source might try to misrepresent the species returned. However, it is possible that the reported right whale count may well have been skewed upwards as a result of its less frequent capture and greater (and slightly higher quality) oil return making them more newsworthy. Because of the incompleteness of the data and the sampling biases involved, these graphs are only indicative of the catch record. It was not possible to confirm the 5:1 humpback to right whale catch ratio suggested by Seymour's diary, and despite there being a number of cow–calf pairs reported, there were insufficient data to lend firm support to the catch strategy suggested by the Castle Rock material.

An indication of the 19th century distribution of right and humpback whales catches by foreign whalers is seen in Townsend's (1935) analysis of catches by American whaleships (see Wace and Lovett 1973:13). The American catch of humpback whales was focused on the northwest coast of Western Australia, around the area of the Dampier Archipelago, between July and September. In contrast, right whales were taken from the south and extreme lower west coast of Western Australia between September and January. However, the lack of humpbacks shown as taken in the southwest, despite known catches by Americans (Whitecar 1860:219), would suggest that these charts are only plotting major trends in the record.

Although no attempt has been made in this current study to calculate the number of individual whales killed, Bannister (1986) previously estimated a total of at least 266 right and 591 humpback whales taken by the Western Australian shore–whalers for the period 1836 to 1878. This includes an upper estimate of 311 right whales if no humpbacks were taken prior to 1846. There are, however, a number of difficulties with these figures and the way they were obtained.

Year	Right	Hback	Year	Right	Hback
1836	3	-	1858	18	19
1837	23	36	1859	0	29
1838	24	-	1860	0	10
1839	0	9	1861	1	11
1840	0	-	1862	2	16
1841-42	26	-	1863	0	29
1843	3	-	1864	0	26
1844	16	-	1865	1	39
1845	20	-	1866	7	13
1846	32	7	1867	0	7
1847	10	44	1868	0	10
1848	14	9	1869	0	5
1849	0	27	1870	0	27
1850	2	27	1871	0	30
1851	8	10	1872	0	22
1852	4	16	1873	0	15
1853	5	12	1874	0	3
1854	8	11	1875	0	11
1855	19	11	1876	0	4
1856	6	25	1877	0	3
1857	14	18	1878	0	0
			Total	266	591

Table 3.18 Estimated catch of individual right and humpback whales by Western Australian shore–whalers 1836-1878 (after Bannister 1986).

Bannister's (1986) calculations are mainly based on Blue Book records, which report oil and bone returns for each region and sometimes for individual stations, but only infrequently provide information on species (see Chapter One). His methodology can be divided into two parts, the first being the use of a ratio of whalebone to oil to ascertain which species was being taken at each station (when this is not stated in the original report). By taking several instances where the bone and oil returns for a known number of individuals of a particular species are provided, Bannister determined that if the reported ratio of oil to bone is greater than 25:1, the animals which had been taken were most likely humpbacks, while a ratio of less than 25:1 indicates right whales. Morton's (1982:53) research on New Zealand's shore–whalers produced a figure of approximately 100 tons of oil to 5 tons of bone (20:1) for right whales, which validates at least this part of Bannister's methodology, although Morton does not indicate a comparable ratio for humpbacks.

Once the whale species had been established, the second part of Bannister's methodology was to determine the number of individuals from the reported oil return by an using an average of 5 tuns of oil per right whale, based on only three instances in historical (presumably Blue Book) records. He acknowledges that this is low in comparison with other areas and may be as much as two tuns lower than the average figure obtained using a much wider range of reports (see Table 3.18). Bannister is not specific as to what figure he used for humpback whales.

The major difficulty with Bannister's calculations is his apparent assumption that individual whaling stations only caught humpbacks or right whales. Newspaper accounts and other records such as Seymour's diary clearly show a combination of both species being taken, with occasional contributions from other species. Not surprisingly there are discrepancies between his figures and those suggested by contemporary sources (see Figure 3.18). One example is in 1846, where Bannister estimates 32 right whales and seven humpbacks taken, while figures obtained from newspaper reports suggest at least 36 humpbacks and only two right whales.

The general pattern of the figures presented in Table 3.18 is, however, consistent with the trends suggested by contemporary accounts and reports (Figures 3.15 and 3.16). In particular, Table 3.18 suggests that after the late 1840s the number of right whales being taken by the shore whalers decreased sharply, with the catch being increasingly dominated by humpbacks. Bannister's (1986) figures and these other sources raise the possibility that in the early period the shore–whalers may well have expressed a catch preference for right whales, extending to humpbacks only as the more favoured resource diminished.

Bannister (1986) attributes the reduction in right whales to the activities of American whaleships during the pre–1850s period. This is also the conclusion reached through the analysis of whaleship activity along the Western Australian coast (Gibbs 2000), summarized in Figure 2.3. Foreign whaling peaked in the early 1840s, probably decreasing thereafter as the right whale population was fished out. This left the colonials with the harder to catch, lower yielding and consequently less valuable humpbacks. The resurgence of American activity in the mid 1850s (Figure 2.3) may well have prevented any slight recovery in the right whale population which could have been exploited by the colonial whalers. Combined with the hypothesized colonial strategy of targeting the breeding stocks, it is not surprising that the right whale population was almost reduced to extinction.

Oil Yield

The return of oil from the various shore stations, and its value on the export market, are the main measures of the success of the Western Australian shore whaling industry. Once again I will examine the changing production at individual stations before turning to an analysis of the industry as a whole. While the records of oil production and value are incomplete, it is possible to trace the progress of the Castle Rock and Cheyne Beach parties through the period 1846 to 1866. Castle Rock was a three–boat west coast fishery, while Cheyne Beach was a two–boat south coast fishery. The standard unit for measuring oil was the *tun,*, equal to 252 gallons (1146 litres), or seven *barrels* of 36 gallons each.

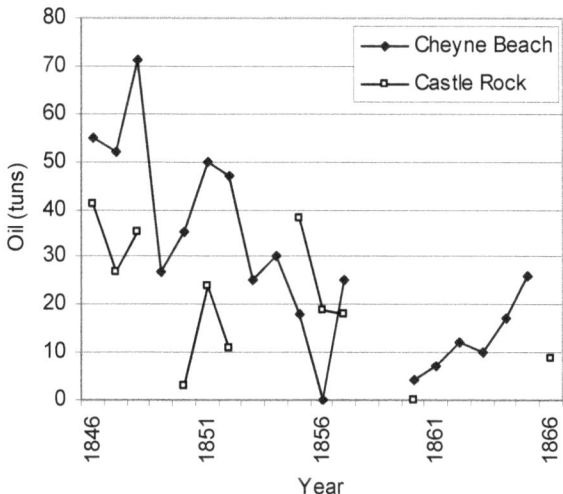

Figure 3.19 Reported yield of whale oil (tuns) from Cheyne Beach and Castle Rock stations 1846–1866.

While it might be expected that increasing skill and experience would result in increased production, Figure 3.19 shows that the returns of oil from Castle Rock and Cheyne Beach gradually declined over time. From peak yields of 41 tuns and 71 tuns respectively in the late 1840s, by the early 1860s both parties appear to have been reduced to annual returns of consistently less than 15 tuns (also see Appendix B7).

Source	Humpback (tuns)	Right (tuns)
Perth Gazette	2.9	6.2
Inquirer	3.2	6.8
Blue Books	3.5	5.4

Table 3.19 Average reported oil yield for individual right and humpback whales in Western Australia.

Analysis of reported oil yields from individual whales caught throughout Western Australia, taken from newspaper and Blue Book accounts shows that while right whales were frequently reported as producing eight tuns of oil or more (up to a maximum of 12 tuns), humpbacks did not usually produce more than four tuns. The mean yield by individuals which is presented in Table 3.19 represents a combination of bulls, cows and calves, and should not be confused with an average yield from an adult of either species. There are, unfortunately, insufficient data to see if the mean yields for humpbacks and right whales change over time. The most important result from this is that all three sources show that on average a right whale produced double the oil as from a humpback. With the decreasing right whale population the shore parties would have had to catch more humpbacks to produce the same quantity of oil.

It is interesting to note that even though Cheyne Beach was the smaller of the two fisheries, it achieved a better result. While this may be the product of greater efficiency or skill on the part of the whaling party, it may also reflect some as–yet unidentified natural factor associated with the migratory patterns and availability of whales, or some other environmental difference within each region.

The value of the oil taken by the two parties is harder to trace, although some figures are available. It can be seen in Figure 3.20 that the value of the season's catch frequently fell below £500, not to mention the several seasons where there was no return at all. Considering that it was necessary to pay the 13 to 21 crewmen, boat steerers and headsmen their proportional lays, as well as meet operating costs and equipment expenses for the station, the shore fisheries clearly operated on the extreme margin. Using the pay scales discussed earlier, the shore whaling industry appears to have been remarkably unprofitable for either workers or owners. After four to six months of what must have been extraordinarily hard labour, a boat hand may well have been left with far less than £10 for his efforts. This naturally raises the question of how or why the industry was able to continue at this level.

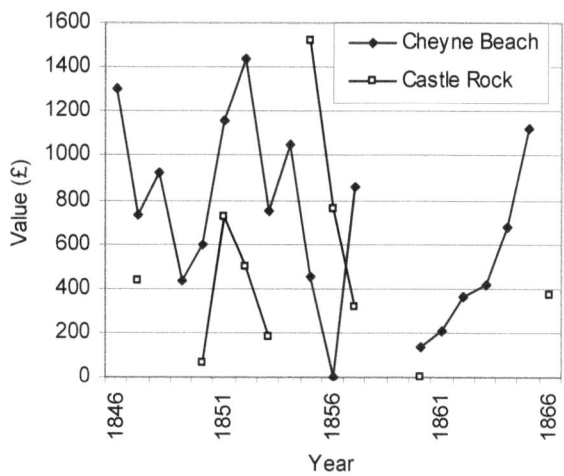

Figure 3.20 Reported values of whale products from Cheyne Beach and Castle Rock, 1846–1866.

For the whaling industry as a whole the Blue Books provide the only consistent reports of oil yields, although the accuracy of these reports can be questioned for a variety of reasons. Statham (1980) points out that irregular communications sometimes prevented outer ports from submitting their statistical reports by the due date, with the information either being omitted or simply added to the following year without explanation. The 1844 peak of £5314 for bone and oil, after the 1843 value of £450, is pointed out as being one such example.

Figure 3.21 shows the reported production of oil by the Western Australian shore whaling stations on the south and west coasts, while Figure 3.22 provides the total for the colony. Many of the fluctuations shown have already been discussed in Chapter Two and need not be repeated here, although once again there is clearly a general decline in the output from the fishery.

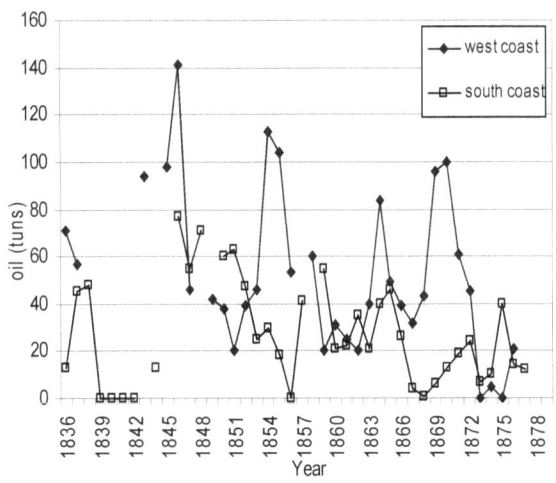

Figure 3.21 Reported oil productions – west and south.

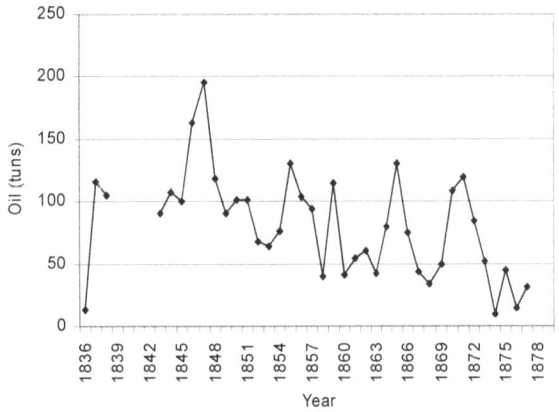

Figure 3.22 Reported total production of whale oil.

In addition to deliberate or inadvertent misreporting, the declared quantities and values might vary from the actual catch, particularly if oil had been directly sold to American or other vessels. An example is in 1851, when the early capture of eight right whales at Castle Rock raised hopes of increasing the circulation of capital into the Vasse district 'if the oil has not already been parted to some of the American Whalers, whose notions [trade goods] may have proved too great an attraction' (PG 10/10/1851).

The average return of oil per whaleboat, seen as the basic industrial unit of the fishery, has been shown in Figure 3.23 as a means of examining the productivity of the Western Australian whalers over time (also see Appendix B2). Higher returns per boat were achieved in the pre–1850s period, possibly because of the greater availability of whales and the higher yields from the right whales. Although the number of whaleboats in operation continued to increase during the 1850s (See Figure 3.10), the output per unit declined. This may have been the result of either the heavy fishing during the 1840s leading to a decline in the available whale stocks, or the increased number of colonial parties (and whaleboats) competing for a finite resource.

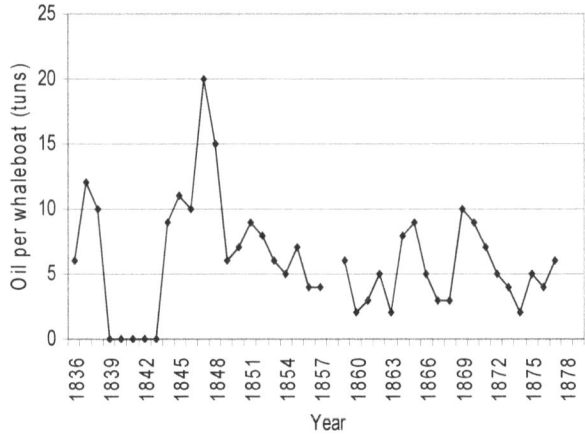

Figure 3.23 Mean volume of whale oil per whaleboat.

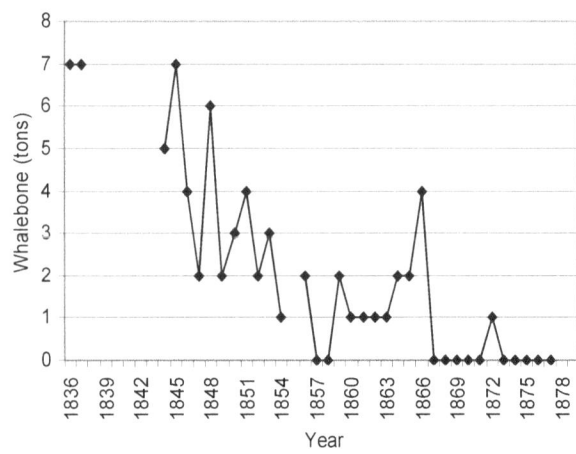

Figure 3.24 Reported total yield of whalebone.

Comparing Figures 3.8, 3.10 and 3.23 it is also worth noting that despite the decreased returns per boat during the period 1853 to 1863, the number of whaling parties and whaleboats remained high. The major internal economic development in Western Australia at this time was the introduction of convicts, which raises the possibility that the market had suddenly become flooded with cheap free (non–convict) labour. As the introduction of convicts appears to have been primarily aimed at breaking the high wages demanded by free workers (Statham 1981b), it is possible (although there is no direct evidence) that the whaling party owners such as Bateman and Harwood took the opportunity to reduce the lays, or redirect capital to expand their operations.

The slightly improved performance after 1863 may indicate a recovery due to the reduced activity of American vessels, or may be a product of the falling numbers of whaling parties and whaleboats competing for the resource. Other speculations include the possibility that later improvements may have been the result of the introduction of new technology, greater stability of the workforce, or other factors which are not readily identifiable.

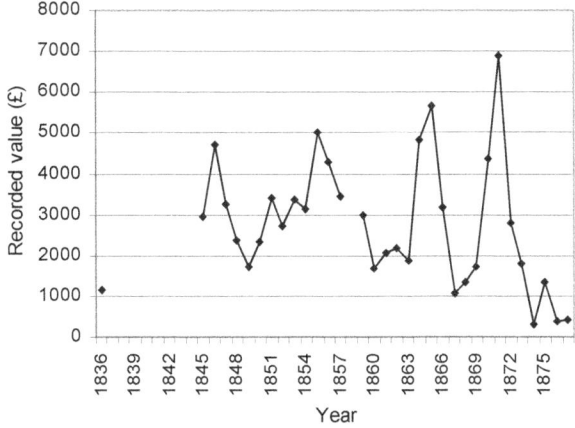

Figure 3.25 Reported value of oil and bone (Blue Books).

Although the annual return of whalebone, shown in Figure 3.24, exhibits the same pattern of decline as for whale oil, there is not the close relationship between the two measures which might be expected from following Bannister's (1986) ratios. As both humpback and right whales are baleen whales, any catch should have yielded some bone. However, despite oil returns exceeding 100 tuns in 1870 and 1871 (Figure 3.22), no bone is recorded in the Blue Book records. These and earlier omissions may simply indicate poor reporting on either the part of the whaling parties, or the compilers of the Blue Books. Some other mechanism may be at work, but this could not be determined through the available documentary record.

Figure 3.25 provides the gross annual value of oil and whalebone as reported by the Blue Books (see also Appendix B4). These figures were presumably calculated on the basis of the reported return by each fishery, and should not to be confused with the export returns. Returns from exports of oil and whalebone have previously been discussed (Figure 2.1), as has the diminishing contribution of whale products to the total colonial export income (Figure 2.2). Another component which bears on these latter two measures is the extent of local consumption of the whale oil which was produced. As there are no figures which describe this, an approximation can be gained by calculating the difference between the quantities reported as taken and the quantities reported as exported (Table 3.20).

Taken as a whole, during the period 1846–1877 over a third (34.7%) of the oil produced in Western Australia appears to have entered the local market. The only minor anomaly is in the first 5 year block, when 25 tuns more oil was exported during 1845–49 than recorded as produced in that period, indicating either a slight discrepancy in reporting, or supply from stockpiles. Consumption in different periods was presumably related to the growth in population, with the early (pre–1850) period having only a small European community with limited oil needs.

5 Year blocks	Catch (tuns)	Export (tuns)	Difference (local use?)	% Diff.
1846–49	667	692	-25	-3.7
1851–54	309	150	159	51.4
1855–59	484	319	165	34.0
1860–64	277	121	156	56.3
1865–69	332	156	176	53.0
1870–74	379	156	218	57.0
1875–77	91	59	32	35.0
Total	2539	1653	881	34.7

Table 3.20 Estimated local consumption of whale oil.

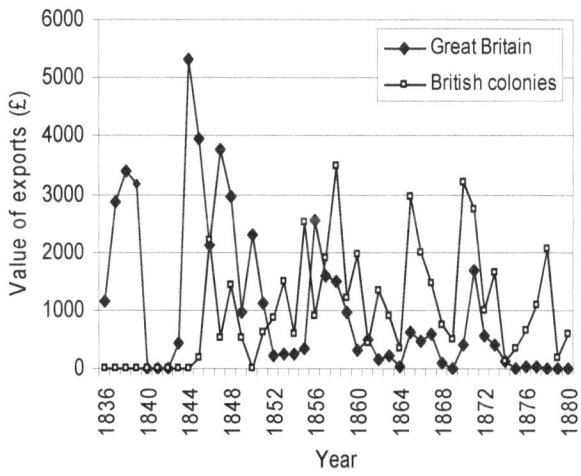

Figure 3.26 Destination of whale products exported from Western Australia 1836–1880 (Blue Books).

The period after 1850 saw the introduction of convicts, the rapid expansion of the civil establishment and a general increase in population, as well as construction of public works such as lighthouses which required oil. By the mid–1870s the local whaling industry was entering into decline while kerosene steadily became cheaper and more accessible for the colonists. In 1870 kerosene was reported at between £50–54 per tun, versus £36–40 per tun of whale oil (Herald 13/8/1870). By 1873 it had dropped to between £36–39 per tun with whale oil at £31–34 per tun (Herald 14/6/1873).

If the difference between production and export presented in Table 3.20 truly does represent the level of local consumption of oil, then there was obviously a wide variation in annual demand. The only indicator of the level of oil use during the early 1850s is a single report which states that a recent catch of five to six tuns of oil would be totally inadequate for the needs of Perth and Fremantle (PG 14/10/1853). There are several references to such oil shortages in the colony through the 1850s and 1860s (Inq 23/7/1851; PG 14/10/1853; Inq 24/5/1865), during which prices could be driven from around £30 per tun, up to £70 per tun (Inq 19/10/1853).

The Blue Book records show that prior to 1850, the majority of Western Australian whale products by value were exported directly to England (Figure 3.26). After this date the bulk of production was sent to the eastern Australian colonies of South Australia, Victoria and Tasmania. Whether the oil and bone were then dispatched from these colonies to England or America or kept for local use is unclear.

Before closing this section it is worth reiterating the relatively limited scale of the Western Australian industry compared to other parts of Australasia. For instance, on the southeast coast of Tasmania in 1838 Alexander Imlay's three shore stations employed 104 men, with another 31 on a whaling barque, taking 539 tuns of oil and 25 tons of whalebone. In 1843 in the Wellington region of New Zealand alone, there were 91 boats and 768 men, taking 1289 tuns of oil and 65 tons of whalebone (Prickett 2002:7). In 1841 it is estimated that New Zealand shore stations produced 1800 tuns of oil and 70 tons of whalebone worth at least £54,800 on the London market (Prickett 2002:2). However, by the late 1840s there were dramatic falls in production throughout Australasia and a rapid decline in the numbers and successes of shore stations. Further comparison is provided Chapter 8.

CHAPTER 4
WHALING STATION LOCATION AND ORGANISATION

The historical documentary record contains limited information on the physical and operational aspects of shore whaling in Western Australia. With few written descriptions of the actual location or organisation of the stations, or the nature of life and labour at these camps, it was felt that the archaeological record could make significant contributions to our understanding of the industry. The following chapter focuses on the nature of the Western Australian shore whaling stations, exploring patterns of site selection, use and abandonment, and determining the organisation and nature of the different site elements which comprised the stations. It also examines evidence for changes in locations and organisation over time. Comprehensive histories of individual stations are provided in Appendix A.

SITE SELECTION

At the time of the original study on which this volume is based there were few archaeological reports available on other Australasian shore whaling sites. An initial model of what might be expected of the location and organisation of a shore stations was drawn from several historical studies of Australasian whaling, including Dakin (1938:33), Little (1969:114), Morton (1982) and Pearson (1985:3):
- sheltered bay or beach.
- tryworks near the shoreline, usually covered by an open sided shelter or partially enclosed shed.
- ramp or shelving beach on which to haul the blubber up to the tryworks, sometimes with one or more capstans, winches or shearlegs.
- additional buildings such as a cooperage, and storehouse(s) for gear and oil.
- huts for the men, a cookhouse and gardens for food.
- watchtower or natural elevated look–out within audible hailing or visual range for signaling.

In more elaborate establishments there might be one or more jetties, a boat shed, ramps for hauling up boats, oil storage sheds or other facilities.

In the 1840s Charles Enderby, a noted British whaleship owner, suggested several other criteria for those considering establishing a shore station in New Zealand:

> a temperate to cool climate (to lessen leakage from the wooden casks); a reasonable distance from settlements from which plunderers might come; plentiful wood and water; good soil for gardens and pasturage for cattle; easy sailing distance from a supply base; a reasonably nearby source of recruits; and most important of all, a good harbour (Morton 1982:229).

Later archaeological studies have suggested various other factors and elements (Lawrence and Staniforth 1998; Prickett 2002; Nash 2003; Lawrence 2006), which will be discussed further below.

One of the most important factors in site location was presumably that a station was situated along the migration routes of the whales, preferably within bays known to be regularly frequented by the feeding or calving animals. Explorations of the Western Australian coast prior to permanent settlement, as well as the flurry of investigations by colonists searching for new harbours, rivers and fertile lands, saw whales reported in various bays on both coasts.

> Great numbers of fish [whales] are annually seen off Rottnest Island, and some come into Gage's Roads: Geographe and Augusta Bays are very superior stations; King George's Sound, Two People Bay, Many [Doubtful] Island Bay (not laid down in the charts), are good harbours and full of fish; and by the report of Capt. Pace, Shark's Bay is also a good station and harbour (Anon 1836:21).

Over the next several years the success of these and other bays as safe anchorages and good locations for whaling was proved by the increasing activities of American and French whaling vessels. Ogle's (1839:244) promotional report on the state of the Western Australian colonies even acknowledged the extensive contributions of the Americans, reproducing their sailing directions and stating that 'we are more indebted to them than to any others for our knowledge of the inlets and anchorages of the western seaboard'. The same situation clearly applied to the south coast as well (Garden 1977).

While the physical characteristics of what were judged to be desirable or at least suitable locations for shore whaling stations are discussed in a later section, the processes of selecting which locations to use, particularly in the first several seasons, can be considered here. Despite the inexperience of crews described earlier, presumably the headsmen or managers of prospective fisheries had some prior experience. Selection of a suitable location and the organisation of the station and the party would therefore have depended upon their breadth of knowledge and their ability to adapt this to the economic constraints and environmental conditions of the colonies. At least one of the colonists, Thomas Hunt (who became chief headsman of the Northern Fishing Company), had worked in the North American shore whaling industry being 'for some time the superintendent of a fishery at Cape Cod' (PG 3/9/1836). However, others may have drawn upon experience in the pelagic industry, or taken advice from visiting British or American pelagic whalers.

On the west coast the initial decisions on which locations to use were circumscribed in part by the limited number of suitable bays. Although Bathers Beach and Carnac Island both proved in later years to be quite good stations, their selection for the 1837 season reflects their close proximity to the major settlement at Fremantle. In contrast, on the south coast, which contains a far greater number of apparently suitable locations, the first stations were established at Doubtful Island Bay, over 160 km from the nearest European settlement at Albany. Given the considerable cost and effort required to move people, plant and supplies such a distance, particularly in the early phase of the settlement, the owners must have perceived the location as particularly desirable, or been advised as such.

During the 1830s and 1840s there appears to have been a strong correlation between the use of particular bays by foreign pelagic whalers and their subsequent occupation, usually within several years, by colonial shore whalers. On the west coast Safety Bay, Koombana Bay (Bunbury) and Castle Rock were all known haunts of American whalers. On the south coast Frenchman's Bay, Two People Bay, Cheyne Beach, Cape Riche and Doubtful Island Bay are known to have been successfully used by American and French whaling vessels (Gibbs 2000). More distant areas such as the Dampier Archipelago and Recherché Archipelago were frequented by foreign whalers in the early settlement period, but were not occupied by the colonial whalers until the later phase of the industry.

The predictable result of this pattern of occupying 'proven' locations was a series of conflicts as the colonials established their shore camps and attempted to assert their territorial rights by demanding that the foreign whaleships depart those areas. Chapter Two has already described how the Americans were well aware of their role in the coastal exploration of the region and the government's inability to enforce any restrictions (CSR 85/82: 24/1/1840; Gibbs 2000). However, they generally yielded by departing or offering to join in partnership with the local group.

As suggested previously, during the 1840s the initial formation of whaling parties was often the result of local entrepreneurs in each area establishing their operations in the nearest suitable bays. Due to restriction on the expansion of settlement, until the 1850s west coast whaling activity did not move far north of Fremantle. By this period the west coast whaling industry was increasingly under the control of merchants and other persons with maritime interests, so that the extension of the coastal trade network to the new settlements (such as Port Gregory and Roebourne) also made it economical to transport their own whaling parties to these regions (Bain 1975).

Despite the initial use of the remote Doubtful Island Bay location in 1836–37, the re-emergence of whaling along the south coast during the 1840s saw the occupation of bays in and around King George Sound, within a 50 km radius of Albany. Although Albany remained the only major settlement throughout the study period, by the 1860s several small pastoral groups had moved to the eastern coastal areas. For instance, in 1863 the Dempster family established a pastoral station close to what would later become the town site of Esperance. The initial movement of whalers into the Cape Arid ('East Coast') region dates to the same period and there is historical evidence of trade agreements between whalers and settlers (Erikson 1978). As on the west coast, the expansion of the coastal trade network into the more distant areas possibly allowed the owners of the whaling parties to offset the costs of transporting and servicing their crews against their trade interests with these small settlements. It should also be considered that by the 1860s there were also more vessels available along both coasts, which must have resulted in a general reduction in the costs of hiring a schooner.

There are at least two instances where highly regarded locations were never used for whaling. The first of these was Shark Bay, glowingly described as a potential fishery by the French explorer Baudin in 1803 (Cornell 1974: 512). In September 1834 a colonial survey party aboard the schooner *Monkey* also reported 'innumerable' black whales and good anchorages on the east side of Dirk Hartog Island, suggesting its potential as a fishery (PG 3/9/1836). Despite this information and later American use of the area (e.g. PG 20/11/1857), Shark Bay was never occupied as a base for colonial whaling, being by-passed in the 1870s for the Dampier Archipelago, near the new Roebourne settlement.

A similar situation occurred at Flinders Bay, on which the small settlement of Augusta was established in 1830. There are numerous reports of the successes of American and eastern Australian whalers in the bay (Inq 3/8/1842; Anon 1843; Hasluck 1955), yet colonial whalers did not come south of Cape Leeuwin or west of Torbay to use the location. Trade with Augusta was irregular and limited by the size of the population, while the rounding of the capes was acknowledged as a difficult passage. Transport would have been expensive for any west coast party, making it simpler to remain in Geographe Bay. For the Albany-based settlers, Flinders Bay was 300 km west of King George Sound and in the opposite direction to the spread of south coast settlement, making it impractical to use the area. Figure 4.5 illustrates the pattern of use and abandonment of west and south coast locations by the whaling parties.

While some factors associated with the initial occupation of locations such as proximity to settlements and proven use by foreign whalers have already been described, the reasons for abandonment often remain elusive. On the west coast it might be supposed that the limited number of bays encouraged the re-use of the same locations for extended periods. The historical record suggests that the several locations which were only used for a single season (Marmion, North Fremantle, Safety Bay, Toby Inlet) were selected because the more suitable positions in those areas were already occupied (Appendix A and B1). These sites lack many of the physical characteristics of the usual locations, especially a sheltered harbour, and may have proved too exposed and difficult to use as a base. It is also possible that sites closest to growing towns such as Fremantle and Bunbury may also have been forced to close in the 1860s because of objections to smell.

On the south coast the early abandonment of Torbay and Two People Bay was simply a result of the limited size of the local whaling industry. With the two parties operating between the mid–1840s and the mid–1860s occupying well–established bases at Cheyne Beach and Barker Bay, these other locations went unused. Their re–occupation came in the later period of whaling activity with the emergence of the split season and the move towards using two or more widely separated locations. The sites around King George Sound became the bases for the early season, with the new locations on the 'East Coast' around Cape Arid used in the later part of the year. Unfortunately, there is usually no specific documentary record of which late and early season locations were being used, particularly in the final phase of the industry.

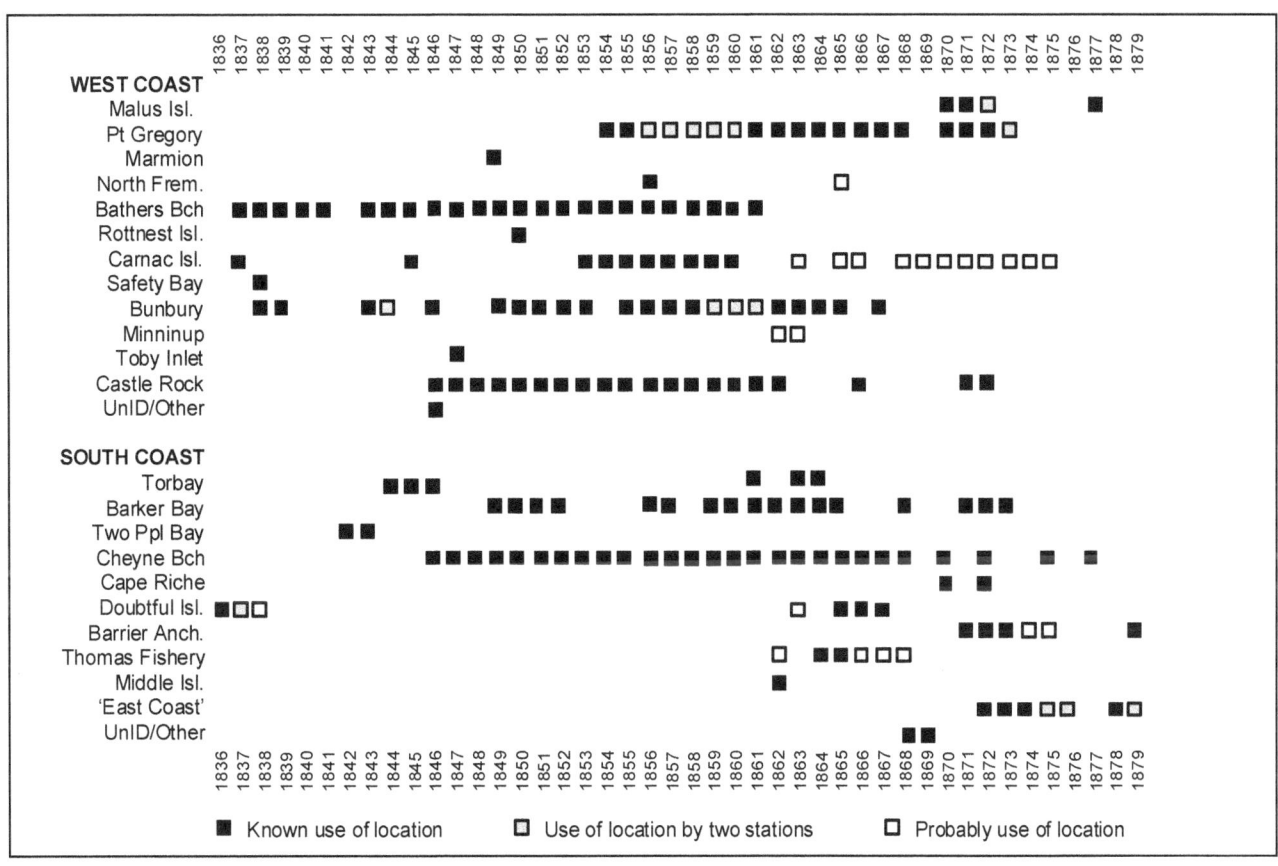

Figure 4.1 Timelines of shore station occupation

Year	station	period	water frontage	area	fee
1837	Doubtful Island	10 years	10 chains (182 m)	10 acres (4 ha)	peppercorn
1845	Castle Rock	1 year	3 miles (4828 m)	-	£30.0
1845	Migo Island	1 year	-	-	£1.10
1846	Cheyne Beach	1 year	-	2 acres (0.8 ha)	£1.75
1849	Sorrento	1 year	-	10 acres (4 ha)	no fee
1849	Castle Rock	1 year	-	3 acres (1.2 ha)	no fee
1856	Bunbury	1 year	-	-	£1.0
1872	Barrier Anchorage	1 year	16 chains (293 m)	50 acres (20.2 ha)	£1.0
1872	Barker Bay	1 year	25 chains (455 m)	22 acres (8.9 ha)	£1.0
1877	Malus Island	1 year	-	-	£1.0

Table 4.2 Whaling Station Lease Fees

Lease Agreements and the Occupation of Land

Aside from the physical and logistical considerations in selecting suitable locations for whaling stations, the occupation of particular sites and the development of infrastructure was constrained by the system of leases regulating the use of the coastal lands. With the Crown retaining ownership of foreshores and much of the hinterland, especially the harbour areas favoured by the whalers, it was necessary for the owners or managers of the stations to secure a lease for the land on which their station would be constructed. A number of lease requests, agreements, or at least fragments of information regarding land tenure were located during the course of this research, allowing some insight into how the system operated.

In general, leases were negotiated on an annual basis, usually some time before the commencement of the season. There were, however, instances during the early phase of the industry where the government was willing to allow quite lengthy leases of land for whaling purposes. For example, a section of Doubtful Island Bay was leased to John McKail for ten years (CSR 52/133:1836). Bathers Beach and Carnac were under either five or seven year leases, depending upon which reports are followed (SRG 11/5/1837; SRG 29/6/1837; PG 24/3/1838). This may reflect the early enthusiasm and anticipation of development into a major industry. There are also isolated cases of long leases being offered in later periods, such as the Barker Bay station being granted for a term of seven years (CSR 189/247: 12/9/1849).

The fees paid for the lease of the whaling stations were generally quite low (Table 4.2) and were sometimes waived completely in special circumstances. Correspondence for Barrier Anchorage, Barker Bay and Bunbury suggests that charges remained consistent from year to year, although there were some variations. For instance, in 1845 the government originally set the lease of the Migo Island anchorage at £5, although after several months of negotiation the license records a sum of only £1.10s being paid. It should be noted that the high fee (£30) charged for Castle Rock in 1845 included a substantial section of coast and hinterland.

Whaling station leases performed two functions. The first and ostensibly only reason was to get formal permission to erect the station buildings. In cases where large areas or adjacent islands were included in the arrangements, the stated aim was to run sheep or cattle for the use of the station. However, the second, ulterior reason for taking a lease was to exclude other whaling parties from using that beach, either for their camp or as a landing place for boats or whales. This was the probable concern of Viveash at Castle Rock in 1845, with his attempt to secure several miles of beach frontage possibly associated with a desire to force Hurford and Penney's rival party out of the area (CSR 140/107: 20/9/1845). In 1872 Hugh McKenzie's challenge of Thomas Sherratt's right to use the leases in this way resulted in the Commissioner for Crown Lands cancelling all licenses on the south coast (BL Acc. 346: 16/1/1873; Acc. 346: 12/2/1873). Leases do appear to have applied on the west coast for the several remaining years of the industry, with John Bateman obtaining a permit for the Malus Island station in 1877 (SDUR B10/1144C: 12/1/1877).

The leases set a number of conditions upon the users, the first being that the arrangement would be forfeit if either the fee was not paid or the land was not occupied for whaling purposes during the season (CSR 189/247: 12/9/1849). The latter provision was to ensure that land and stations, particularly those granted in long lease agreements, were not needlessly locked out of use. In the case of Bathers Beach it seems that the Fremantle Whaling Company was allowed to sub–lease to other operators, although there were peculiarities in their occupation of the land which may have permitted this situation (see below).

The other significant aspect of the lease agreement was that at the end or cancellation of the license, the government not only regained the land, but also 'all houses, buildings, wells, fences and appurtenances' which had been erected (CSR 52/133: 10/2/1837). It was this clause which was the final downfall of the Northern Whaling Company. After deciding to cease operations as a result of the unsuccessful 1837 season, the company attempted to recoup some of its losses by offering its seven year lease of Carnac Island and all improvements at the station back to the government 'for a reasonable consideration' (PG 24/3/1838). It was at this time that the lease was produced and the directors shown the clause indicating that upon the dissolution of the company the land and buildings reverted to the Crown anyway. The discovery of the same condition in the Fremantle Whaling Company's lease (PG 28/4/1838) may well explain why that group chose to continue, hoping for at least some future success in the fishery rather than instantly losing its considerable fixed assets by closing.

Later whaling station licenses are less precise and generally do not mention the ownership and removal of the improvements at the completion of the season (CSR 189/247: 12/9/1849; BL Acc.346: 8/5/1872). This may indicate that the government's attitude had eased after the early incidents, letting the companies recover whatever capital they could from the sites. It is also probable that the later, smaller and less well–financed whaling parties would have seen the example of Carnac Island and the general lack of security of the leases as further reason not to over–develop the fixed assets of a station. There were instances where long–term occupation by a single party probably lent some level of security. On the south coast, Cheyne Beach was occupied by John Thomas for at least 22 years, while Thomas Sherratt appears to have used Barker Bay for as long as 24 years. On the west coast, Castle Rock was used by Robert Heppingstone and then his son–in–law George Layman for 14 years.

A variation on the leases was seen at Bunbury and Fremantle, the two 'urban' stations. In these cases not only was the land leased, but also the existing tryworks and barracks buildings, with different parties putting in tenders for their use during the season (CSR 338/204: 4/9/1855).

ARCHAEOLOGICAL SURVEY

Environmental background

The wide geographical dispersal of the Western Australian shore whaling stations along both the west and south coast means that the sites are located in areas with markedly different geologies and climatic regimes, particularly during the winter months when whaling took place. The three major environmental zones were:

1. Dampier Archipelago (Pilbara Block) – a collection of islands up to 15 km long and 3 km wide clustered along the west and north sides of the Burrup Peninsula. The archipelago is a drowned landmass 'characterised by rock platforms and storm boulder beaches interspersed with localised accumulations of sand and silt in the more protected embayments' (Vinnicombe 1987:2). The area experiences large tidal variations and has warm and dry winters (Woods 1980).

2. Lower west coast - characterised by long, straight sandy beaches with few significant bays or interruptions (Woods 1980). Old limestone dunes have become islands and headlands in some areas, with southwest swells and waves creating crescent–shaped northward opening bays behind these hard points. This varies slightly in the area close to Cape Naturaliste, where the granite of the Leeuwin–Naturaliste Ridge outcrops on the coast, with several small, sandy bays forming in between. The Castle Rock station is situated in one such bay. Tidal range is very small and for the most part the areas behind the headlands are well protected. The region experiences a Dry Mediterranean climate with mild, wet winters.

3. South coast - characterised by large granite outcrops which form mountains, headlands and islands. The action of heavy southwest swells and easterly littoral currents upon these granite hard points has resulted in the formation of numerous crescent–shaped sandy bays opening towards the east (Woods 1980). Tidal variation is generally less than one meter. The climate west of Doubtful Island Bay is characterised as Moderate Mediterranean with wet winters. To the east of this the climate is classified as Dry Mediterranean. On the coastal fringe the cold winds, rain and squalls blowing in from the Southern Ocean during winter can make maritime work difficult.

Archaeological Survey

As noted in Chapter One, several 19th century whaling station sites had been identified during the 1970s and 1980s. The National Trust (W.A.) survey of whaling stations in particular drew on Ian Heppingstone's historical research to identify 20 probable locations for whaling activity, with MacIlroy's survey identifying seven sites with structural remains or artefacts (MacIlroy 1987:1). These studies provided a solid basis for the current study, commenced several years later.

Based on a more comprehensive historical analysis, several of the locations suggested in the 1987 study were eliminated as misinterpretations of the historical records (Ten Mile Well, Collie River and Augusta). A total of 21 locations, such as specific bays known to have been used as the site of one or more shore stations, were identified. In addition, further clues were generated as to probable site locations in bays which had previously been surveyed unsuccessfully.

Surveys were undertaken in several stages between 1990 and 1993, with the very limited funding available meaning that the more distant or inaccessible locations could not be visited. Initially the most accessible sites on the west coast between Port Gregory and Castle Rock were surveyed, followed by the south coast sites between Torbay and Cape Riche. Finally, the remote sites of Barrier Anchorage and Thomas Fishery were surveyed. Four locations (Malus Island, Carnac Island, Middle Island and Doubtful Island Bay) could not be visited. For these places it was necessary to speak to local informants and use other sources of information to assess the existence or condition of the sites.

Archaeological remains with a high probability of being associated with the whaling industry were identified at 11 locations and will be discussed below. However, a number of the other locations without visible structural or artefact evidence, or where later development or use had obscured or obliterated evidence, still exhibited topographic and other features which were felt to be relevant to the organisation and operation of the stations.

In many instances the features which had made locations attractive in the 19th century, such as sheltered anchorages, sandy beaches, a water supply, etc, were also attractive to subsequent users. Post–whaling fishing camps, wool sheds, jetties, camping grounds, car parks, boat ramps or other features occupied, often overlay and obscured, if not destroyed, the original whaling station sites. In some respects this re–use became a marker of a potential site, although in many cases the rare surviving whaling stations features had survived through pure chance on the edges of these later disturbances. In several cases the potential for excavation was eliminated by bitumen sealed surfaces or heavy traffic.

Several sites (Port Gregory, Castle Rock, Barker Bay and Cheyne Beach) were test–excavated to determine their archaeological potential. It was intended to excavate one site on each coast and compare the results, but this proved logistically difficult. Cheyne Beach provided the best combination of structural and artefact deposits, and was chosen for detailed investigation (Chapter 5).

The results of the survey are presented in detail in Appendix A. This includes location and site plans and historical information specific to each station. While the archaeological data have been synthesized in the following discussion, Table 4.3 summarises which features were recorded at each site during the survey. The survey strongly suggests that the determining factors of station location and organisation were closely inter–related. Common characteristics exhibited by the sites are described, as are exceptions or variations from the norm.

Location	Tryworks structure	Domestic structure	Surface artefacts	Subsurface potential	Lookout structure
WEST COAST					
Malus Island	■	o	■	■	-
Port Gregory	o	-	■	■	-
Marmion	-	-	-	-	-
North Fremantle	-	-	-	-	-
Bathers Beach	■	■	-	■	-
Rottnest Island	-	-	-	-	-
Carnac Island	(not surveyed)				
Safety Bay	-	-	-	-	-
Bunbury	-	-	-	-	-
Minninup	-	-	-	-	-
Toby Inlet	-	-	-	-	-
Castle Rock	■	■	■	■	o
SOUTH COAST					
Torbay	-	■	-	■	o
Barker Bay	■	■	■	■	-
Two People Bay	-	■	-	-	-
Cheyne Beach	-	■	■	■	■
Cape Riche	■	-	-	-	o
Doubtful Isl. Bay	(not surveyed)				
Barrier Anchorage	■	-	-	-	■
Thomas Fishery	-	o	-	o	-
Middle Island	-	o	-	o	■

- = No archaeological features identified or potential unknown.
■ = Identified archaeological features or subsurface deposits.
o = Arch. features of uncertain association, or reported but not located or inspected.

Table 4.3 Summary of archaeological features located during survey.

Location - Bays and Headlands

The main landscape feature in the location of shore whaling stations is a bay or sheltered section of coast. Along the Western Australian coast these have been formed by the action of swells and currents upon geological hard points, namely granite outcrops on the south coast and limestone on the west (excepting Castle Rock). Immediately behind these hard points or headlands are usually the sheltered sandy coves which were favoured as sites for the whaling stations and are still used as anchorages for small vessels.

Three main possibilities can be advanced for the use of bays for whaling.
1. Humpbacks and right whales are known to visit and sometimes spend lengthy periods in bays and sheltered areas during the course of their migration.
2. The curve of the bay may have allowed the whalers to trap the whales against the shoreline.
3. Bays provide some shelter from the swells, currents and winds of the open sea, both for the whaleboats during the process of hunting and for the station complex during processing of the catch.

The first factor is the most difficult to verify, given that by the time systematic scientific research was undertaken on whales in coastal Australian waters, they were mere relics of the original populations. However, scientific, historical and anecdotal evidence suggests that migrating humpback, right and other whale species do appear to favour particular bays and areas. The use (and non–use) of bays by whales is therefore a potentially significant factor in the use, success and abandonment of particular stations.

The situation of the whaling station at the projecting peak or headland allowed the boats to radiate outwards to intercept whales entering or swimming past the bay. Careful placement of two or three whaleboats would allow the whalers to trap the animals in the curve of the shoreline. However, the initial hunting range of a station using only whaleboats might be roughly defined through the observational limits of the look–out, with or without optical aids. This would naturally include the adjacent ocean, to whatever distance it was felt practical or possible to send the boats in pursuit. Use of a larger vessel such as a schooner as a launching platform and for cutting–in could extend this range considerably.

The final factor takes into consideration that shore whaling in Western Australia was pursued during winter, a season when (with the possible exception of Malus Island) extremely heavy swells, gale force winds and other difficult environmental conditions are the norm, particularly on the south coast. The inner areas of the bays could be expected to afford some protection for the small whaleboats and their crews. With the whaling station on the lee side of the headland the carcass could be drawn into sheltered waters for flensing, the boats could be beached out of the surge of the waves, and the buildings of the camp would not be subjected to the worst of the winds and rains.

Look–outs

A look–outpoint for a shore–based whaling station required two main attributes. The first was that it command a wide view of the bay, adjacent seas and if possible neighbouring bays. The second was that the look–out had to be visible from the whaling station, or at least the person stationed there would have had to be able to signal without major difficulty. The normal position for the look–out was atop the headland or high dune which sheltered the station, usually at a distance of no more than several hundred meters. There is some evidence that the Bunbury station used a series of look–outs on high dunes between Casuarina Point and Minninup, 19 km southward, to signal the approach of whales (Lally n.d.; Mitchell 1927).

Another option was to place the look–out on the peak of a nearby island, which appears to have been the case at Torbay (Migo Island), Middle Island (Goose Island) and possibly the small island in Barrier Anchorage. Although there is no specific information to suggest that the Cape Riche party used Cheyne Island as a look–out, Gorman's memoirs (AA 22/8/1929) show that the whalers visited it on occasion. An early survey of the area noted the existence of a 'whaler's look–out' on the southern slope (Gregory 1850), although as this was nearly 20 years before the first recorded use of the bay by colonial whalers, it is possible that it originated from the foreign whalers who had frequented the area during the 1840s. The Bathers Beach (Fremantle) station was even reported as receiving signals from Rottnest, 18 km westward, when whales were sighted near the island (Inq 21/8/1861).

There is limited historical or archaeological evidence of whether particular station lookouts had shelter structures, although some protection would not be unreasonable given their winter usage. The Bunbury station appears to have had a wooden watchtower on Lighthouse Hill, above the town, the timber for which was later used to construct two houses (Barnes 2001:62). However, this is the only evidence for such a construction.

At Barrier Anchorage and on Goose Island (Middle Island) there are low dry–stone walls on the hills above the station (Figure 4.7, 4.8; Pearson 1988). Although Cheyne Island (Cape Riche) could not be visited during the survey, there is some historical and oral suggestion that a stone windbreak also survives near its peak. There are oral reports about another structure on the adjacent mainland, although its position could not be pin–pointed. This may be the unidentified low granite wall described as a whaler's look–out in a photograph at the Albany branch of the Western Australian Museum.

Cheyne Beach has a granite boulder on the headland above the station with a small ledge which makes an ideal seat for a person watching out to sea. Unfortunately, the rock is too weathered to determine if this ledge is a natural or artificial feature. Castle Rock also has a 'look–out rock' on a hill nearly 500m east of the station, but still within direct line of sight. There were formerly several stone walls and small buildings on the cliff above Bathers Beach which would have served to shelter the spotter for the station (Bavin and Gibbs 1988).

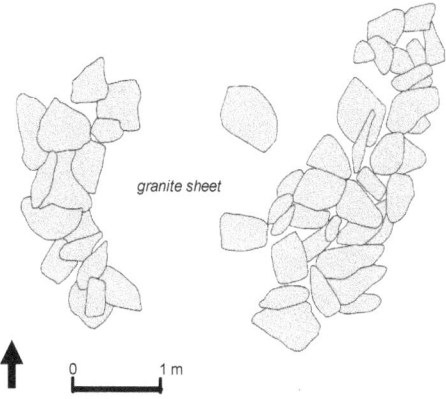

Figures 4.7 Barrier Anchorage Look–out.

Figures 4.8 Barrier Anchorage Look–out.

The dry-stone walls of the south coast look-outs are a meter or less in height, and were probably meant as windbreaks behind which the look–out could crouch to avoid the worst of the icy gales off the Southern Ocean (Figure 4.7). It is possible that wood and canvas structures were used to provide a roof or upper sides, although there is no evidence for this. On the west coast the much more moderate winter conditions made protection of this kind less important.

There is only a limited mention of signaling methods for alerting the station and directing the whaleboats. In many instances a strong pair of lungs and the cry of 'whale–ho' (Mitchell 1927), 'blow' (McKail 1927), or the well–known 'there she blows' (PG 19/7/1850) would be enough to rouse the men. It is less certain how more distant points transmitted their message, although it is possible that horns, guns, or even small charges may have been used. Oral information collected by Lally (n.d.:55) states that in the Bunbury area the spotter on the sand dunes had 'a high flagpole next to him, with a specific number of flags, and armed with a telescope'. The signals received at Bathers Beach from Rottnest may well have been broadcast by flags, smoke, or heliograph (mirror flashes) (Inq 21/8/1861), which later became a favoured means of communication from the island (Moynihan 1988).

Flensing areas

A popular misconception, fostered by observations of modern whaling facilities, is that the whale carcass was hauled out of the water and onto some form of deck or ledge for flensing. Images from other parts of Australasia, as well as the archaeological evidence from the Western Australian sites suggests that carcasses were beached in the shallows and secured by ropes or chains. The blanket pieces would be stripped from the body, with the whale rolled to retrieve the whole of the blubber. To assist this process the rope to which these strips were attached may have passed over shearlegs. The blubber would then be winched across logs or a granite surface and up to the tryworks for mincing and pitching into the trypots.

The nature of the flensing area is one of the major differences between the west and south coast stations in Western Australia. The majority of the south coast stations surveyed, particularly those with evidence of their tryworks remaining, suggest that the whales would be secured below a sloping granite shelf, sometimes (as with Cheyne Beach), in an adjacent scour channel. The granite would provide a smooth winching surface for dragging the blubber to the tryworks, in some cases up to 40 m away. Examination of the granite surfaces also suggests that some edges might have been removed or modified to reduce snags. Torbay was the only south coast station where such a stone ledge was not immediately evident. Similar use of granite sheets for flensing is also noted for South Australia (Kostoglou and McCarthy 1991:27).

The limestone geology and sandy shores of the west coast do not provide such natural advantages. It was in this environment that the jetties or timber ramps described in Dakin's (1934) or Little's (1969) descriptions would have been important if not necessary parts of the operation. The archaeological and historical evidence at the Bathers Beach presents the best picture of a working station, albeit the most elaborate operation in the colony. The jetty meant that the whale could be flensed in deeper water at the end or sides (Reece and Pascoe 1983:8), making it easier to roll and manipulate. The shearlegs and winch mounted on the end of the pier would aid this process. The blubber may have then been carried on trays or in carts across to the tryworks.

Direct evidence for jetties at other west coast sites is extremely limited. Early reports from the original Carnac Island station state that 'considerable advance had been made on the construction of a jetty' (PG 6/5/1837), but fail to mention whether this was to assist in processing. Bateman's Bunbury station of the 1860s has been variously described as being in the area of the jetty or breakwater (Mitchell 1927; Anon 1936), although it is difficult to determine if these existed during the whaling period. There are no historical or archaeological indicators for the other west coast stations. However, at Castle Rock and Port Gregory it would have been necessary to transport the heavy blubber up to 30 m over sand to the tryworks. It is possible that a simple ramp or surface of logs or planks would have allowed the blanket pieces to have been winched over the beach.

Malus Island, the northernmost whaling station, uniquely presents the difficulties of wide tidal variation. Whereas the southwest stations experience a tide range of no more than 1 m, the sea level around the Dampier Archipelago fluctuates by 3 m to 4 m or more daily during the winter months. It is possible that the whale carcasses were beached at high tide when they could be brought in close to the station, although whether or not flensing was easier at low tide with easy land access around the whale is unknown. As noted, flensing might have been carried out with the assistance of the schooner or 'cutting–in vessel', meaning that only the blubber had to be transported ashore.

An interesting piece of oral information collected at the Cheyne Beach site is that punts were used to assist in the flensing process (Charles Westerberg, pers. comm. 1989). Although there is no supporting textual evidence from Western Australia, Davidson (1988:126) shows a photograph of a small boat being used for just this purpose at the Kiah Inlet station in New South Wales. It is also possible that the 'cutting–in' vessels noted at some stations (see Chapter Three) were moored alongside the whale and used as platforms from which to flense, and if sufficiently large could have ropes passed over their masts or yards to assist in rolling the whale during the process (e.g. SAR 1/1/1842).

Carcass Disposal

During the 19th century the only body parts of right and humpback whales considered usable were the blubber and other oil–rich portions such as the tongue, and the baleen or 'bone' of the mouth. It was suggested early in the history of the Western Australian industry that the waste portions of the whale could prove to be a valuable source of fertilizer (PG 17/6/1837), although there is no evidence for this use being pursued. There is a single report of a German settler in Albany proposing to purchase whale skeletons and crush them (Inq 15/11/1871), but no further mention is made of this. This left the bulk of the whale carcass to be disposed of in some way, and in the case of the Fremantle Whaling Company the removal of the waste formed an essential part of the lease agreement for use of the jetty (PG 17/6/1837).

In the absence of historical documentation about disposal, the most likely method would have been to tow the carcass back out into the bay and let it sink in deep water. Sharks, ever–present around the whaling stations, would quickly strip the meat away and, it would be hoped, prevent it from washing back into shore. The archaeological support for this is the large quantity of whale bone which continues to be washed up on the beaches adjacent to the sites, even 150 years later. An 1880s visit to Cheyne Beach described it as the 'valley of bones' (Albany Mail 18/12/1889). Retired commercial fishermen interviewed during the survey invariably described the floors of these bays as being 'covered' in whale skeletons and recalled that their nets frequently snagged on or pulled up bones.

Processing Area and Tryworks

Once the blanket pieces had been winched up from the beach and into close proximity with the tryworks, further processing was required to reduce the blubber into a size and form suitable for the trypot. The blanket pieces would be sliced into horse pieces, which were thrown onto a wooden trestle or 'horse' and minced, but not cut right through, to produce the 'sliver pieces' (Pearson 1983) or 'bible leaves'. This latter process could be done manually, although a mechanical mincing machine, now in the collection of the Western Australian Museum, was recovered from the Malus Island site. This is the only archaeological evidence for this intermediate stage detected on a Western Australian site.

Archaeological evidence for tryworks was identified at three sites on the west coast and three sites on the south coast. Five of the tryworks (Malus Island, Castle Rock, Barker Bay, Cape Riche, and Barrier Anchorage) were situated immediately above the probable flensing area, at the junction between the beach or granite shelf and the vegetation line. Historical maps of the original topography of Bathers Beach show that the tryworks was constructed against the cliff edge close to the jetty, the closest approximation in terms of position. It is presumed that these positions were chosen not only because they were above the high tide mark, but also to provide a stable surface on which the structures could sit. Unfortunately, most of the tryworks are still very susceptible to damage or destruction through storm surges and erosion. For this reason, with the exception of clearing the portion of the Castle Rock tryworks previously excavated by MacIlroy (1987), it was decided not to excavate, clear vegetation or undertake other investigations which might endanger the stability of these structures. Unfortunately, this means that their internal design remains unexplored. The structure of the tryworks is similar to contemporary examples elsewhere in Australasia (e.g. Lawrence 2006:53; Prickett 2002).

The historical and archaeological record suggests that two trypots were the norm in a Western Australian whaling station, although some stations apparently tried to make do with only one, sometimes resulting in the loss of oil (Inq 16/11/1864). In contrast, Bathers Beach is the largest surviving tryworks with excavations revealing a substantial three–hearth structure, indicative of the grand intentions at the time when the station was established(MacIlroy 1987; see Figure 4.14). With the exception of Malus Island, all of the trypots from the stations examined had been salvaged either historically or by 20th century collectors. From the remaining evidence it is obvious that as the trypots had originally been built into the tryworks structure (or more correctly the sides of the tryworks had been built around them), their removal required the demolition of the tryworks down to the foundation or base on which the trypots sat. However, the general dimensions of the surviving features allow a broad estimate of the original capacity of the tryworks (Figures 4.9–4.10).

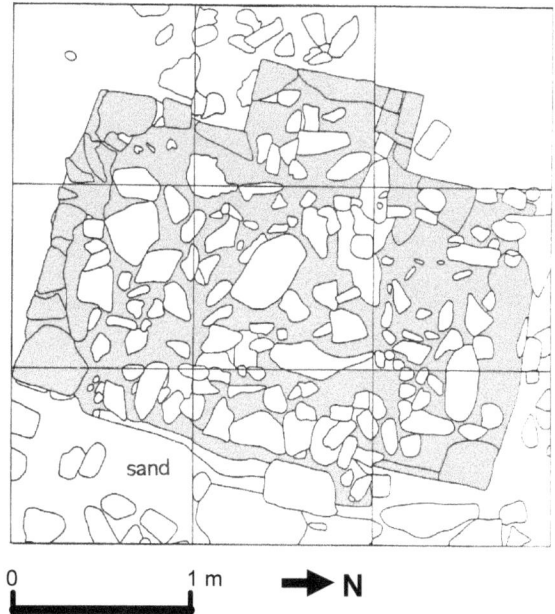

Figure 4.9 Castle Rock tryworks.

Figure 4.10 Castle Rock tryworks.

Figure 4.11 Cape Riche tryworks.

Figure 4.12 Barker Bay tryworks.

Figure 4.13 Malus Island tryworks (photo: E. Bradshaw).

The materials from which the tryworks were constructed vary slightly between sites. All of the surviving south coast tryworks only used the local granite, mostly mortared–together rubble, although some of the corners and edges might have been slightly dressed or squared. At Castle Rock and Malus Island the local granite was also used, but with brick quoins and edges. At Bathers Beach the whole of the structure is of brick, as was suggested for the Marmion station. It is not known whether granite provides better thermal qualities, or whether its use (rather than brick) was simply an economy measure which also obviated the need to transport heavy construction materials up. Brick was possibly used of necessity along the west coast as the local Tamala limestone reduces to powder under sustained heat. In the bases of the tryworks was a consolidated black organic substance presumed to have been the residue of the skin or 'scrap' which was fed into the hearths.

Descriptions and photographs from other areas of Australasia suggest that a tryworks shed, even if only a crude roof cover of some kind (Trotter and McCulloch 1989; Sinclair and Harrex 1978), was necessary, presumably to protect the oil from being spoiled by rain. Tryworks sheds are mentioned for Port Gregory (Inq 13/8/1837), Fremantle (Bavin & Gibbs 1988), Carnac (PG 22/4/1837), Bunbury (CSR 338/204) and Port Gregory (BL M386). The Bunbury 'blubber house' is described as being '30–40 feet [9–12 m] long, open on one side, and also shingled but only partly floored' (Barnes 2001:62).

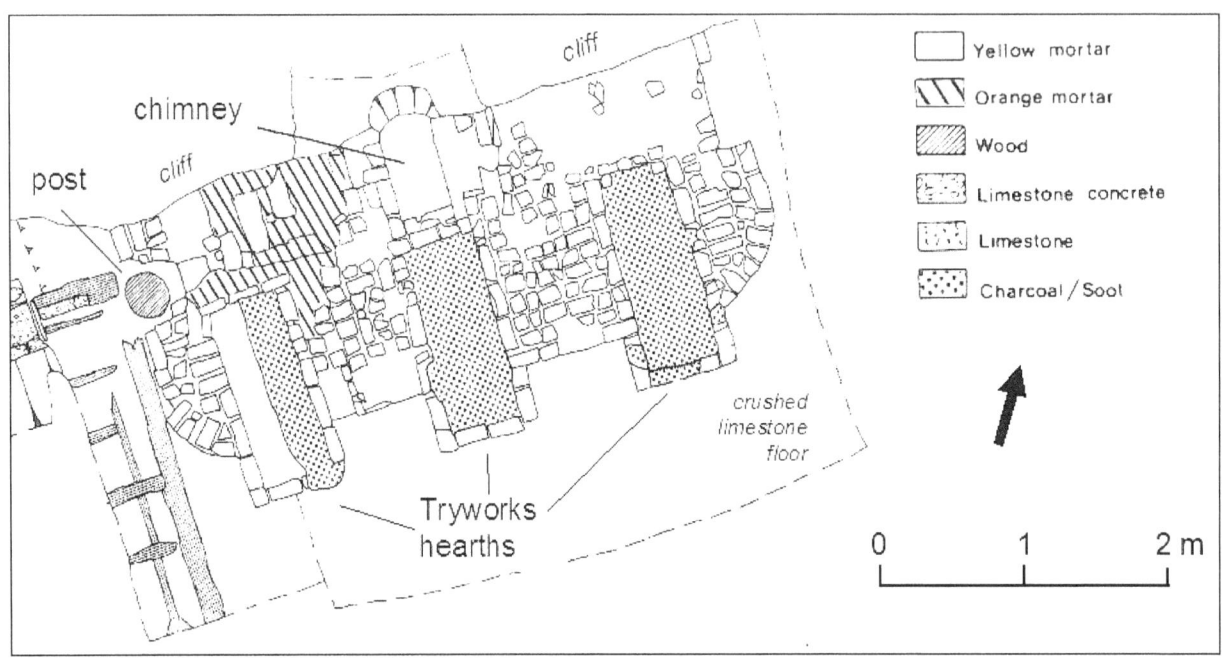

Figure 4.14 Bather Beach tryworks (Modified from MacIlroy 1986:47, original drawing by D. Meredith).

In the case of the Port Gregory station run by Sanford and Harwood, the initial list of equipment needed to establish the station includes sheets of iron to roof the tryworks (BL M386; see Figure 3.2). Evidence that the rest of the Port Gregory tryworks shed was constructed of wood comes several years later, with a report that flame escaping from the hearth had 'entirely consumed' the building, including 'a considerable quantity of fishing gear' (PG 13/8/1858). Although there would have been precautions to prevent spillage of oil, it is almost inevitable that accidental losses over time would soak the timbers, making the structure susceptible to fire.

The only archaeological evidence for a tryworks shed is from the excavated Bathers Beach site, showing the tryworks situated within a building of considerable size (MacIlroy 1987). This building is depicted in Samson's 1840s sketch as an open–sided structure, with what appears to be a shingled roof supported by large wooden posts (Reece and Pascoe 1983). It is possible that the adjoining floor space could have been used to accommodate mincing horses, tubs and coolers.

No historical or archaeological evidence was found to describe the cooling tanks which sat immediately alongside the tryworks, ready to receive the oil as it was bailed out of the trypots (c.f. Lawrence 2006:56). One exception may be the stone lines adjacent to the Barrier Anchorage tryworks which were conceivably used as supports for a cooling tank, rather than the base of another hearth.

Oil Storage

To prevent shrinkage of the wooden barrel staves, which would result in the loss of oil, it was necessary to store the casks in conditions of stable temperature and humidity (Pearson 1983). Although it is possible that the Bathers Beach station used either their two storey station house or a cave in the cliff to store their oil (Bavin and Gibbs 1988), there is no archaeological or historical evidence at the other stations for the construction of a shed or shelter to protect their casks. It is possible that barrels were simply covered with canvas or seaweed or, as in one documented instance, buried in the sand until the time of retrieval (CSR 372/40: 21/8/1857).

Nash (2003:71) describes Tasmanian shore stations having a wood and/or clay lined storage pit (a 'blubber hole') for keeping any flensed blubber that could not be tried out immediately, such as due to a shortage of barrels. There is no historical or archaeological evidence for these structures in the Western Australian records, although their use seems likely.

Boat ramps & launching areas

All of the whaling station locations have a gently sloping sandy beach nearby which would allow whaleboats to be drawn up and if necessary out of the water. Positioned behind the headland, these beaches are also sheltered from most of the swell and surf of the open sea, although it is obvious at some of the sites that they are susceptible to heavy storm surges. It was also there, just below the station house, that the boats would rest in full readiness to be pushed out when the call came from the look–out.

There is no direct archaeological or historical evidence for rails or slips to let boats in or out of the water, although it is probable such structures existed at many stations. As described previously, the 1840s drawing of the jetty at Bathers Beach appears to show davits which could draw the boats vertically out of the water. This sketch, probably drawn during the off–season, also shows one whaleboat stored in the tryworks shed and another in the storage cave nearby. There is, however, considerable evidence to show that out of season the owners of whaling stations deployed their whaleboats for other purposes (Chapter Three).

Whalecraft storage and work areas

Shore whaling required a large body of specialised equipment for both the catch and processing phases of the operation (see Chapter Three), including sufficient replacements of irons, lances, shafts and whalelines which would be expected to be lost or broken during the normal course of the season. These items, including other necessities for both industrial and domestic functioning, would require a shelter or storage room to protect them from the inclement winter weather. A description of the Carnac Island station includes a building used as 'residence and storehouse' (PG 6/5/1837), suggesting that some portion of the barracks, possible even a second room or a lean–to, was used for this purpose. As an additional structure would involve increased cost and effort, it seems consistent with the limited scale of the stations to have such an arrangement. If an independent storage room was constructed, presumably out of wood as for the barracks (see below), the lack of a chimney would drastically reduce archaeological visibility as a structure.

Both before and during the whaling season there were also routines of maintenance and repair, with at least one member of the boat crew doubling as carpenter/cooper. The cooper would be required to put together the shooks (bundles of staves) in anticipation of the catch, a task requiring some judgment lest the station be caught without sufficient storage and the oil be lost (Inq 3/11/1847). Whaleboats also required maintenance during the season, ranging from repainting to major repairs when struck or 'stove in' by a whale during the chase. Finally, there must have been a stream of other minor chores to replace equipment, repair the stations buildings, and so on. Although a covered workshop was not essential, coopering and the repair of metal items would require at least a fire, although this could presumably be built on the beach.

Barracks and Domestic Buildings

Aside from their industrial function, most whaling stations were also the home for between 12 and 20 men for four to five months during the middle of winter. In later years the two stations closest to towns (Bunbury and Fremantle) may have opted for allowing the men to stay in their own homes nearby, only meeting daily for work (Inq 30/5/1849). In all of the other stations the distance from settlement demanded that accommodation and food be provided for the workers. At Fremantle the 1837 station house and storeroom was a substantial two–storey building constructed out of stone, and was consequently one of the main objects of expenditure by the company. However, for many stations it appears that the barracks and other buildings were at least partially pre–fabricated wooden or possibly canvas structures.

This use of wooden buildings is suggested by the archaeological remains found on the south and west coasts. Stone or brick bases of domestic chimneys were located at Malus Island, Castle Rock, Barker Bay, Two People Bay, Cheyne Beach, and possibly Torbay. A quantity of brick rubble, probably originating from a chimney, was also found at Port Gregory, while oral evidence suggested a stone domestic chimney was also located at Thomas Fishery. In all of these instances only sufficient rubble was found to reconstruct the lower portions of a chimney. There were insufficient extra material and no structural evidence to suggest stone or brick walls, with the possible exception of Cheyne Beach, as will be shown below.

It is possible that timber and bark was collected for slab huts at the start of each season, although the areas north of Fremantle and east of Cape Riche have little timber close to the stations which is suitable for structural purposes. A prefabricated wooden frame and stock of weatherboards, or heavy canvas sheets, could be transported by ship and re–erected on a site in several days or even less, eliminating the need for time–consuming collection and preparation of local materials. A timber building could also be removed at the end of the season and re–used elsewhere, rather than be left for resumption by the government at the end of the lease, destroyed by bushfires, or damaged by transient users. There are several references to wooden structures being sold to or from whaling stations (PG 22/4/1837; CSR 24/118: 4/12/1847). The Bunbury 'dwelling house' was a weatherboard building, '25 feet by 15 feet [7.5 x 4.5 m], shingle battened and floored (CSR 645/112: 28/6/1870; Barnes 2001:62). In 1871 John Bateman applied for permission to erect a two–roomed 'portable house' at Castle Rock for the use of his whaling crew (MacIlroy 1987: 22).

Use of timber structures did not necessarily mean transience, as locations such as Cheyne Beach, Barker Bay and even Castle Rock were occupied consistently by the same parties for long periods. In the case of Cheyne Beach the station was operated by John Thomas for at least 22 years and for at least some time may have been his family's permanent home. At the other end of the scale there is no information on living conditions during the late period of whaling, when the south coast parties moved between two or more stations per season. Whether they had buildings constructed at several sites, moved a wooden structure with them, or reverted to tents, is unknown. Even with a canvas hut it is possible that a stone or brick chimney for the hearth might be constructed.

The position of the station house/barracks falls into a recognizable pattern, usually situated on or just behind the foredune, directly above the beach. This was presumably to afford rapid access to the boats once a sighting was made. In the case of sites located adjacent to settlements (Port Gregory, Fremantle, Bunbury), the locations were circumscribed to varying degrees by the need to fit into the formal town subdivisions. Port Gregory exhibited the most anomalous station house location, with the site presumed to be the barracks situated some distance behind a substantial set of sand dunes which make access to the beach an arduous task (see also Rodriguez *et al.* 2006). However, in this instance the whalers were housed in a storehouse constructed by Captain Sanford within the subdivision of the proposed Packington town, rather than in an especially built beachside barracks.

The locations of the habitation sites is usually upwind of the flensing and tryworks areas. To a degree this is a function of the morphology of the bays, and the swell and wind conditions which create them. However, in many cases the site chosen for the barracks is about 100 m from the processing area, still in close proximity, but sufficiently removed to avoid the worst of the smell.

Other Structures

As noted earlier, in the interests of economy and expediency, as well as the nature of the lease of land, the number of buildings at each station was probably minimized. However, there remains the possibility of other structures beyond those mentioned above. To use Cheyne Beach as an example again, there is archaeological and structural evidence to show that there were multiple buildings in the habitation area of the site. In an anecdotal account of the station there is an incidental mention of a 'cookhouse', presumably a kitchen separate from the barracks (McKail 1927). This may correspond to the small hut located east of the main building excavated at the site. There was almost certainly a house for John Thomas and his family, also probably in fairly close proximity to the other station buildings.

Water Supply

It is presumed that all of the stations would have had wells or otherwise attempted to secure stable supplies of fresh water, although historical evidence is limited (e.g. Albany Mail 18/12/1889). While the southwest of Western Australia can be dry during summer, the fact that the shore whaling industry was carried on in winter meant that there would have been less concern about water. When the various sites were surveyed between July and November all had readily visible water supplies through seasonally active streams and large volume runoff from adjacent hills and headlands. Water is less certain to the north of the Swan River, although at Port Gregory fresh water could be collected from the nearby Hutt River pools, or by digging wells in the inter-dune areas near the station. It is not known if there is fresh water on Malus Island.

No physical evidence of wells directly associated with any of the whaling stations was located, although lined wells of some antiquity have been reported in the general vicinities of Doubtful Island Bay and Middle Island, neither of which could be visited during the survey.

Gardens

Although the question of food supplies is dealt with in the following chapter, clearance and preparation of ground for vegetable gardens to supply the needs of the station should be considered. In several instances foreign whalers were reported as planting gardens on both the mainland and offshore islands (PG 30/1/1841; Eyre 1845; Gibbs 2000). However, the only direct reference to gardening by a colonial party is the 1880s description of Cheyne Beach (Albany Mail 18/12/1889) and oral evidence which suggested the low lying swampy area behind the site had been used for this purpose (C. Westerberg, pers. comm. 1989).

Burials

Despite there having been a number of fatalities in the whaling industry (see Chapter Three), the only instance where the bodies seem to have been buried at a station is the two graves reputed to be at Doubtful Island Bay. Unfortunately it was not possible to visit the site during the survey.

Aboriginal Sites

The historical evidence for Aboriginal groups frequenting whaling stations during winter has been discussed in Chapter Two. If we assume that large groups did seasonally congregate at or near the stations for several months, it is probable that Aboriginal sites containing a high proportion of glass and other European materials should exist within several hundred meters of the whaling station sites.

Given the constraints on the survey and the low surface visibility in the coastal zone around the whaling stations, it was not possible to extend the investigation to locating Aboriginal sites. The potential of such sites as a valuable source of information on the archaeology of the contact period is recognised, as is the greater probability of their survival in those places still at some distance from intensive urban development.

DISCUSSION

The historical and archaeological evidence demonstrates that despite environmental differences there were common characteristics in the majority of the whaling station sites which suggest what were considered desirable features in terms of location and organisation. The following list summarizes these features and the results of the survey.

a. Shore whaling activity was based in bays or other semi-sheltered areas, while the station itself would be situated in a protected area, frequently adjacent to a headland or high dune.

b. A look-out would be based on the headland or dune, within view of the station. A nearby island might be used if this location increased the view or range of the spotter. On the south coast a low windbreak or shelter might be constructed to protect against the worst of the wind and rain.

c. On the south coast the whales would be fastened and flensed in a channel below a granite sheet. The blubber would be winched across the granite to the tryworks, which was sited along the edge of the vegetation line (presumably above the level of most storm surges). On some west coast sites the whales were brought in next to jetties for flensing, while at others they must have simply been brought into the shallows and the blubber either carried up to the tryworks or possibly winched across logs or planks. West coast tryworks were also situated on or just above the vegetation line.

d. Although a triple tryworks was constructed at Bathers Beach, most stations appear to have used only one or two trypots. The construction materials varied depending upon the friability of the local stone and access to bricks. The design of the tryworks appears to have been similar, with the opening to the hearth at the front of the base, and a flue or chimney at the back, although internal design could not be investigated. With the exception of Bathers Beach, evidence for covering shelters or sheds was limited to historical references.

e. All of the sites had a sandy beach, presumably on which to pull up the boats.

f. The domestic areas were constructed above the sandy beach, usually on or behind the first dune. In most instances the visible structural evidence was limited to a single chimney or a scatter of bricks or stone suggesting such a structure. It is probable that a wooden pre-fabricated barracks were used at most stations.

g. There was only limited historical and archaeological evidence for other buildings such as storerooms or oil stores, cooperages or boat sheds.

h. Potential sources of fresh water (at least during winter) could be identified near each site.

In considering the various characteristics of the whaling station sites, it appears that the most significant feature influencing selection was the sheltered harbour. This was also the feature most noticeably lacking from those places used for only short periods, including Sorrento, North Fremantle, Minninup and Toby Inlet. As noted previously these locations were occupied only after the more desirable positions in each area had been claimed. However, even these locations exhibit some of the features of the other sites, such as slight curves in the line of the coast, adjacent high dunes, or visible water sources nearby. It is probable that another shared characteristic was that whales were known to pass near these points on the coast.

Despite the historical evidence that some stations had different periods of occupation, while others had whole or partial re–buildings of tryworks and station houses over time, there was little surface archaeological evidence found at the sites indicating different phases of use. The one exception is Malus Island, where the two sets of tryworks might be interpreted as the remains of Pearse and Marmion's 1870–72 station, as well as Bateman's 1877 plant. The simplest explanation for the lack of archaeological evidence for successive occupations is that structures were re–built or materials re–used as necessary.

The general impression gained from the surveys is that over time the whaling stations on both coasts became simpler, with minimal permanent infrastructure. On the west coast the stations opened with elaborate buildings, jetties and other site improvements, while later sites have no historical or archaeological evidence for these major developments. On the south coast the whaling establishments were always fairly simple, taking advantage of natural features where possible. However, the stations at Barker Bay and Cheyne Beach, which were occupied for considerable periods of time, do show evidence of quite well developed domestic areas, compared to the scant features of the later camps. The long–term use of Castle Rock by the same party also seems to have resulted in more substantial domestic arrangements.

The apparently decreasing sophistication of the whaling stations corresponds to what might be expected from the historical patterns outlined previously. The high hope for expansion which characterised the first phase of the industry is reflected in the capital intensive development of the stations. The failure during the first several seasons to achieve significant returns resulted in a simplification of the industry, while the short terms and nature of the lease agreements discouraged efforts towards making expensive fixed improvements. In the later phases of the industry the move towards mobility and the use of multiple stations for shorter periods would also have encouraged the establishment of only simple (and possibly easily transportable and removable) facilities.

Comparison to other Australasian whaling industries

Given the similarities of the industrial processes and requirements of the workforce, it is not surprising that the basic site location and organisation of the Western Australian shore station is comparable to other documented Australasian sites: a sheltered bay or inlet, tryworks constructed above the beach, and housing for the workers on the hill slopes or dunes above, often with a freshwater creek nearby (e.g. Kostoglou and McCarthy 1991; Lawrence and Staniforth 1998; Prickett 2002; Nash 2003; Lawrence 2006). Without a better documentary record or large–scale excavations on several sites (c.f. Lawrence 2006) it is difficult to make definite statements about the nature of the sites. However, it seems safe to conclude that the Western Australian stations come at the lower end of the scale in terms of size and apparent complexity. The substantial stone buildings found at many of the Tasmanian, New Zealand and even South Australian stations (Kostoglou and McCarthy 1991; Prickett 2002; Nash 2003; Lawrence 2006) do not have clear equivalents in the Western Australian sites. The majority of the Western Australian station quite probably come closer to the small cluster of timber and bark 'whalers huts' drawn at Wilson's Promontory in Victoria in 1843 (Lennon 1998:65). The exception is the elaborate two–storey Bathers Beach barracks and storehouse, which bears some resemblance in form and scale to the 'whaling barn' at Mosman, New South Wales (Gojak 1998:12).

Whereas the Western Australian whaling parties frequently consisted of only 12 men and station sites have archaeological evidence for only one or maybe two domestic chimneys, some of the Tasmanian and New Zealand stations were veritable villages, with semi–permanent populations of 80 or more men and an unknown number of women and children (Morton 1982; Evans 1983; Prickett 1998:50). The nature of the New Zealand stations was also influenced by the close social and economic relationships with local Maori groups, including the whalers taking of Maori wives (Coutts 1976; Morton 1982; Prickett 2002). While these large stations were the upper end of the industry, figures of between 20 and 50 men still appear normal. In consequence, the domestic areas recorded during archaeological surveys of whaling station sites reveal evidence of multiple domestic buildings (Campbell 1992; Prickett 1983; 2002; Jacomb 1998; Kostoglou and McCarthy 1991; Bickford, Blair and Freeman 1988; Prickett 2002; Nash 2003; Lawrence 2006).

CHAPTER 5
EXCAVATION OF CHEYNE BEACH WHALING STATION

The historical evidence of shore whaling in Western Australia rarely extends to descriptions of industrial activity, with almost no information on domestic activities at these sites. There are no diaries or descriptive accounts of life on the maritime frontier. Consequently, questions about material culture, diet and the 'lifeways' of the inhabitants of the whaling stations can only be addressed through excavation and analysis of artefacts.

The historical research and results of the archaeological survey generated several broad categories of questions to be addressed by intensive investigation. The first concerned the nature of the industrial workforce and its social organisation and domestic conditions. As described previously, the documentary evidence shows that a Western Australian shore whaling party could be composed of between 12 and 30 men who would work together almost continuously for between four and six months during the coldest and wettest seasons of the year. The majority of the stations were situated at some distance from settlements, meaning that the owner or manager would be expected to provide at least housing and food during this period. As noted in Chapter Four surface surveys generally only identified a single chimney in the domestic area, presumably attached to a wooden structure. Whether these represented a single barrack or the sole surviving chimney of a wider complex is unclear. Similarly, the size or arrangement of building(s) remained uncertain.

The second area for investigation was the material culture of the whalers, both as an example of the lifeways on an industrial frontier and for what it might tell us of the early European settlement of Western Australian. In the first instance the artefacts allow a reconstruction of how the whalers lived and what they used in the context of these isolated camps or communities. In a wider sense it indicates the trade networks which provided consumer items to the small Western Australian settlements that then presumably filtered through to the whaling stations.

Finally, the underlying theme of adaptation could also be followed, with the whaling stations affording insights into how the European settlers of that period dealt with the environment and their remote situations. The focus for this investigation was be the dietary evidence and in particular the balance between domestic and native faunal components. Although the documentary evidence presented in Chapter Three indicates that food was a potentially sensitive issue between employers and workers, the nature of the diet, alcohol consumption and other aspects of domestic behaviour in these remote locations were unknown.

This chapter describes the excavation and analysis of the Cheyne Beach Whaling station. The first section traces the progress of the excavation itself and provides relevant topographic and stratigraphic information. The second section describes the artefacts recovered, using the framework of a functional typology. The final section discusses the evidence of the site and addresses aspects of the questions raised above.

SITE DESCRIPTION

The original intention of the project was to sample deposits from at least one site on each coast to provide a comparative dimension. However, it was eventually decided to focus efforts on a single site in return for a more detailed analysis of lifeways. Cheyne Beach presented several advantages which resulted in its selection. The 1987 National Trust survey (MacIlroy 1987) had already indicated interesting subsurface structural evidence in the form of a floor composed of whale vertebrae. The presence of a well–defined foundation meant that a more detailed analysis of artefact distributions and activity areas might therefore be possible. The second factor was that the Cheyne Beach station was known to have been occupied almost continuously between 1846 and 1877, the longest use of any Western Australian shore whaling station. This not only increased the chances of finding substantial refuse deposits, but also presented the possibility of investigating change over 30 years or more.

Environment

Cheyne Beach is located 50 kilometres northeast of Albany (Figure 2.1) and is the southern–most end of Hassell Beach, a long, sandy bay typical of the south coast (Figure 5.1).

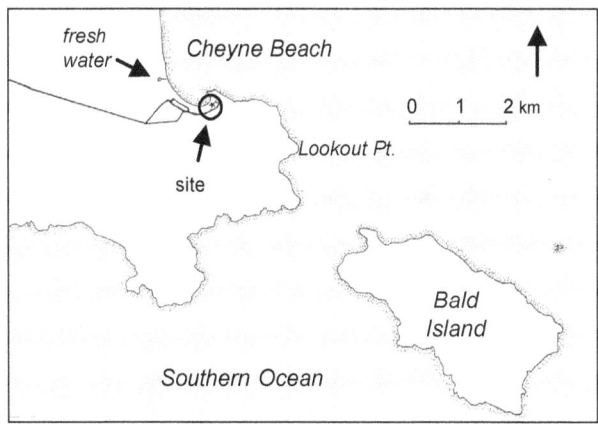

Figure 5.1 Cheyne Beach

Cheyne Beach is protected from the worst of the weather and swells coming up from the Southern Ocean by a range of granite hills which extend south and east behind the bay. The granite headland which forms the southeastern point of Cheyne Beach, together with the small reef which extends from it, creates a sheltered harbour although the area is still susceptible to storm surges and cold weather fronts blowing across from the southwest.

Temperatures between June and November, the normal months of occupation of the whaling station, vary from 6°C to 21°C, with August being the coldest month (Beard 1981). Rainfall peaks between June and August, each month having more than 20 days of rain with the area receiving an annual total of about 750 mm. Conditions can fluctuate widely and rapidly throughout the course of a single day, with cold fronts from the south sweeping over the peninsula and replacing sunshine and warmth with rain and cold winds.

Figure 5.2 Cheyne Beach from south–west

Figure 5.3 Cheyne Beach site from look–out (looking south). Structure One in reeds to right (west) of cars. Squares P93, U93 and Z93 directly beneath the cars.

During the winter months there is abundant fresh water available, with run–off from the granite slopes collecting in the inter–dune swales such as those immediately behind the whaling station site. There is also a perennial freshwater spring and small lake situated behind the dunes approximately one kilometre northwest of the site. The spring water flows onto the adjacent beach and, as suggested in Chapter Four, may have been used by foreign whaleships prior to the colonial occupation of the bay.

The site of the whaling station is located in the sheltered southeast corner of Cheyne Beach, adjacent to the granite headland. To the west of the station a white sandy beach extends for several meters above the high tide mark, before rising to a low, grassed area which is now used for boat–trailer parking. The eastern edge of this area is marked by the low sand dune, approximately 1.5 to two meters above high tide, on which the structural remains of the station were found. While the dune is heavily vegetated, in the vicinity of the site the natural cover has been reduced to an area of only 15 meters width. Beyond this the ground has also been cleared and levelled as a grassed picnic area, with a gravel car park along the northeast edge. To the southeast of the dune is a low and sometimes swampy area which, as will be discussed below, may have originally extended further north and west of the site and through what is now the picnic area and car park.

Figure 5.4 Cheyne Beach site from north–west Structure One in reeds on left. TP1 located right foreground.

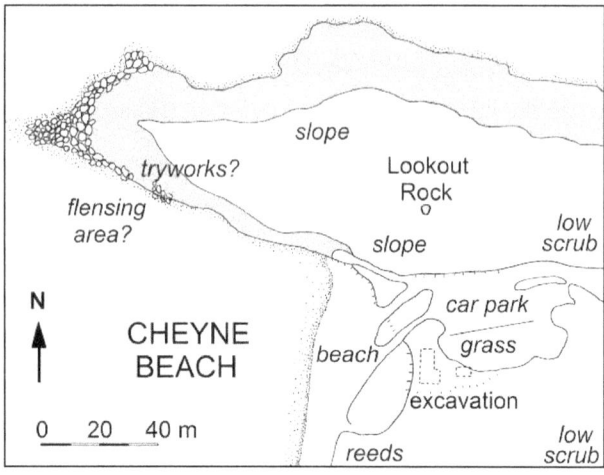

Figure 5.5 Cheyne Beach site plan

The foredune on which the site rests is covered by an extremely dense growth of knotted club rush (*Scirpus nodosus*) and coast sword sedge (*Lepidosperma gladiatum*), which then gives way to peppermint scrub (*Agonis flexuosa*) and tea tree (*Melaleuca pubescens*), and eventually to sand plain species (*Proteaceae, Leguminosae* and *Epacridaceae*) (Storr 1965:191). In summary, while there are limited stands of low woodland to a height of several meters, most of the vegetation within several kilometres of the whaling station site is scrub–heath, with no timber suitable for construction purposes. Although there is now a single small farm and a small fishing settlement nearby, much of the area surrounding Cheyne Beach is a floral reserve with the original vegetation relatively untouched.

When the site was first surveyed in August 1989 the area which had been cleared of vegetation and shovel–trenched by the 1987 National Trust survey (MacIlroy 1987) was still visible. The outlines of the excavation could be roughly traced, as could the stone wall which forms the southeast corner of what is referred to below as Structure One. However, further survey through the dense sword–sedge to either side of this clearing proved almost impossible, as the only means of passing over the area was to literally wade through the vegetation while walking on a pad of reeds at least thirty centimetres or more above ground level. This also made it unfeasible to either see artefacts and features or even detect indicative variations in the surface level. As the reeds are also prime habitat for several poisonous snake species, great care had to be taken at all times.

The work permits from the Shire of Albany required any clearance of vegetation be strictly limited to those areas under excavation to try to reduce foredune erosion, with re–vegetation to follow. This prevented a more widespread clearance for the sake of survey or more extensive excavation. It also was not permitted to disturb the surface of the car park, situated adjacent to the site.

EXCAVATION METHOD

The site was divided into a grid of one meter squares based upon north–south and east–west baselines. These squares also formed the basic unit of excavation, although a combination of open areas, trenches and single test pits was used in different parts of the site. Excavations were undertaken over several seasons, in part dictated by limited funding, seasonal opportunities to attract volunteers and permit constraints on clearance.

Excavation proceeded with arbitrary spits of 5 cm unless natural stratigraphy was detected. Artefacts were plotted in situ where visible, with deposit also sieved through screens of 5 mm or smaller. Bulk samples which were later sieved through a 2 mm mesh confirmed that, other than small, undiagnostic bone fragments and the very occasional pin or small glass bead, most material had been recovered through the larger mesh. All artefacts were bagged for sorting and analysis upon return to the laboratory. Aside from representative samples, all loose structural materials including brick, stone and whalebone remained at the site.

The area being excavated expanded as the form of the main structure, not visible from the surface, was progressively revealed. The logical starting point for the first season in November 1989 was a re–excavation of the area uncovered in 1987, extending the pits slightly beyond and below the disturbed zone. The fragile nature of the whale vertebrae floor surfaces meant that particular care had to be taken. In some areas it was decided to excavate down to within several centimetres of the floor, probe to confirm the presence of the surface, but not uncover the surface. Those areas of whale bone are shown on Figure 5.4 as stippling.

Over the next two seasons the excavation area progressively extended to uncover the whole of Structure One, including the foundation of a fireplace at the northern end and low stone walling along the eastern edges. The whalebone surface did not extend across the whole floor area, although it did continue to edge some areas (described further below).

A stone flagged path was discovered leading from the eastern doorway, heading southeast. This proved to connect Structure One to a small second building, also with a whale vertebrae floor (Structure Two). There was insufficient time to excavate this building, although test pits established its dimensions.

In addition to the main building excavations, a line of small test pits was also extended westward towards the beach (not shown in Figure 5.5). Within a several meters of the western edge of Structure One it was clear that although some artefacts were present, the deposits had been substantially re–worked by storm action.

Test pits were also excavated to the east of Structure One and the remnant dune it sat on, through what was then a grassed picnic area. This had originally been avoided on the incorrect assumption that the vegetation clearance and levelling by machines would have removed any deposit, such as encountered at several other whaling station sites. A test–pit excavated in square U98 at the start of the 1989 season had revealed a high density of bone and artefacts within the first ten centimetres, after which the pit was backfilled and attention given to the main structural features. In the final weeks of 1991 and with a temporary surplus of volunteers, the square was finally fully excavated. The continued high density of bone to a depth of twenty centimetres and the presence of a possible posthole led to the opening of several adjoining squares to determine if the latter was evidence of a wooden structure or fence line. While no further postholes or structural features were found, a similar density of material was encountered in squares T98, T99 and U99. It is possible that the excavation of a wider area to the south may reveal other postholes.

It was decided to sample more widely in this grassed area, with squares opened at Z93 and U93. These pits revealed from 20 cm to 30 cm of relatively undisturbed ash and bone deposit which strongly suggested that this was the sought–after refuse area for the whaling station. With time running out and an already appreciable volume of material for analysis, an attempt was made to determine how far the deposit extended. This resulted in the excavation of squares P99, P93, U87, Z87 and E87, all of which also contained what was obviously domestic refuse and dietary remains to depths of between 30 cm and 70 cm. The area further north of this was the car park and could not be disturbed. At this point, having excavated a total of 105 meter squares, it was decided that more than sufficient material had been recovered to address the questions.

STRATIGRAPHY

Although there were common elements in the stratigraphic sequences across the site (summarised below), the excavated areas can be divided into five main zones. A longer description is available in Gibbs 1996, while only samples of the stratigraphic sections are provided here for illustration.

Structure One

In broad terms, the stratigraphy within the walls of the larger of the two structures can be divided into five major units. The upper layer was composed of organic–rich brown sand (10YR 4/3) with heavy root penetration and modern artefacts. Immediately beneath this was a lighter grey/white sand layer in which the first 19th century artefacts appeared, increasing in density with depth (Figure 5.6)

The occupation surface of the building (if not the floor surface) was probably indicated by a 5 cm to 10 cm layer of orange–tinged sand (7.5 YR 6/8, but varying), mixed with small nodules of clay which could possibly be deteriorated brick, occasional fragments of charcoal and shell, and some artefacts. The thickness and consistency of this layer varied over the total area. The lack of compaction suggests that this was not the floor itself, although the upper surface was roughly level with the top of the whalebone vertebrae seen around the edges of the wall, and particularly in the southern portion of the hut. Further discussion of floor surfaces is provided below.

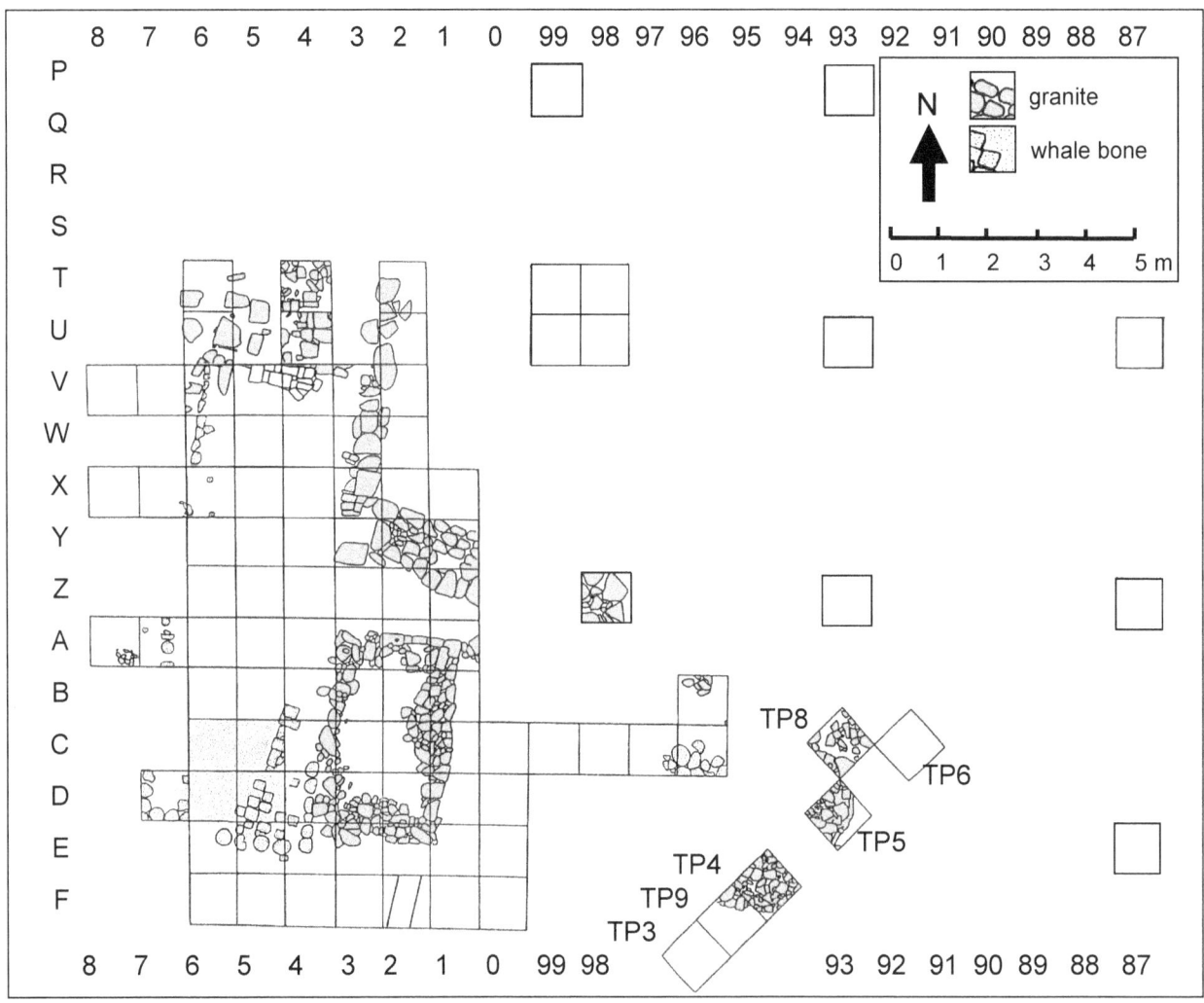

Figure 5.5 Plan of Excavated Features at Cheyne Beach.

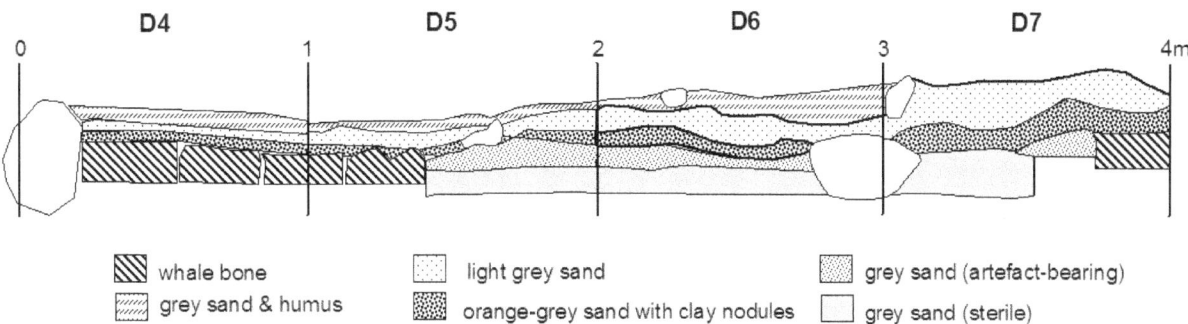

Figure 5.6 Stratigraphic Profile - Squares D4–D7 (east to west across floor of Structure One).

Beneath the under–floor layer was a dark grey sand unit (7.5YR 3/0) with a sharply decreasing density of artefacts, which in turn overlay a sterile unit of lighter grey sand (2.5YR 3/0). The break between these two layers was not always clear, and was often indicated simply by the absence of cultural material. There were minor variations to this sequence, including some modern disturbance and intrusive pits.

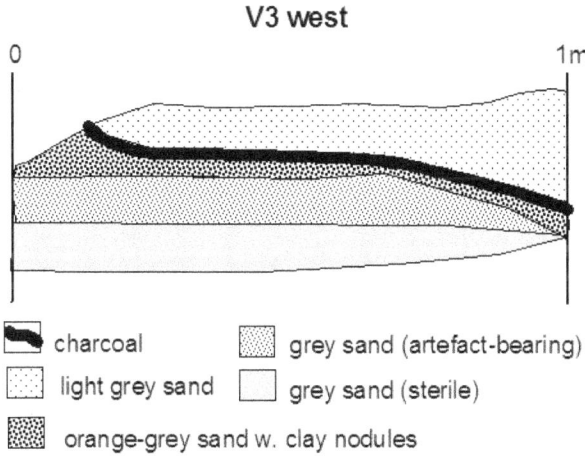

Figure 5.7 Stratigraphic Profile – Square V3 (west face) adjacent to fireplace in Structure One.

Rabbit warrens penetrated the sections in C6 (west) and A6 (west and north), but were confined to the sterile lower layer. Directly above the probable floor level around the east side of the fireplace was a 2 cm layer of ash and charcoal (Figure 5.5). As the usual lighter grey/white sand continued above this layer it was potentially an early deposit, although it may represent either a cleaning out of the fireplace, or even a small campfire after the removal of the floorboards and the end of the use of the building as a whaling station. The remains of a whole smashed (19th century) bottle just above the floor level in square B2 was presumably from a similar post–occupation event.

During the 1987 National Trust survey (MacIlroy 1987) a continuous shovel pit had been dug around the stone–walled section in the southeast corner of the structure. This roughly fell within the boundaries of squares A1 to A4, B1, B4, C1, C4, D1, D4 to D6 and E1 to E6, with the latter two areas including a two by two meter section of whale bone floor surface. Although this trench was partially backfilled, a 10–15 cm overburden of spoil remained mounded over squares A5, A6, B5, B6, C5, C6 and D6. This contained some artefact material which was removed as overburden but also sieved and retained for analysis.

Western and Southern edge (ext. Structure One)

The stratigraphy in the test pits along the western and southern edges of the grid but external to Structure One ((A8, X7–8, V7–8) roughly corresponds to the upper layers seen within Structure 1, with an organic rich surface with heavy root penetration giving way to light grey (possibly wind–deposited) sands. A darker grey unit containing a low density of artefacts underlay this, giving way to grey–white sterile sands. There were several areas with variations to the stratigraphic sequence or higher density deposits. For instance, on the western side of Structure One, Square A8 included a surface of orange–tinged sand (5Y 4/1) mixed with clay/brick fragments and small stones. This layer, sloping gently downward to the west, may have indicated a pathway from a door (in the unexcavated square B7, running to the beach.

The trench in square F2 is approximately 65 cm wide, roughly aligned with the east wall of Structure One. Unfortunately the 1987 shovel trench passed through the adjacent E squares, obscuring the possible relationship with the structure. It was clearly contemporary with the occupation of the station, cutting through the sterile grey sand unit and with the upper two thirds filled with occupation debris which the artefacts suggest was from one episode. The lower third, (to 55 cm depth or 85 cm below current surface), was filled with compacted white sand (Figure 5.11).

The trench visible in the wall of square D0 and along the southern edge of C0 is 75 cm wide and less well defined than the F2 feature. The trench was excavated to a depth of 20 cm, (50 cm below the current surface) but no artefacts were recovered. The 1987 shovel trench also obscured the relationship between this features and the adjacent structure.

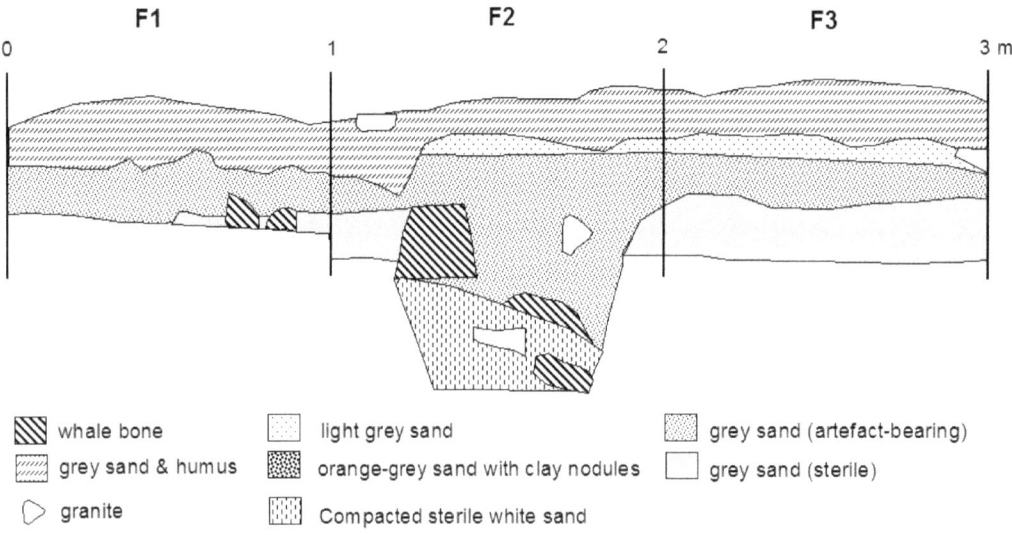

Figure 5.8 Stratigraphic Profile - Squares D4–D7 (across floor of Structure One)

Structure Two

The interior of Structure Two was encountered in two squares, TP5 and C96. The latter square provided less than 5 cm of vegetable matting and organic–rich grey sands over a whalebone floor surface. While TP5 intersected a stone wall, it was still possible to examine a small area of internal deposit in the western corner of the square. This contained the dark grey topsoil, underlain by a gritty orange sand/clay mix seen in both the interior and exterior portions of the square, which was probably a mortar associated with the rubble. At the base of this unit was a layer of charcoal and ash which contained artefacts, including a nearly complete clay tobacco pipe, supporting the working hypothesis that this was originally the hearth. Excavation did not continue below this level.

Midden Area

As noted, the area east of Structure One and north of Structure Two was originally avoided as it was thought that to have been disturbed. However, while some intrusions are evident, it would appear that this area retains a high level of stratigraphic integrity.

A simple three unit stratigraphy extended from the eastern wall of Structure One to at least T98 and U98. The upper layer of between 5 cm and 10 cm was the organic–rich light–grey sand which covers the rest of the site, heavily penetrated by roots and containing modern artefacts reflecting the use of the area by recreational fishermen and campers. Immediately below this another 10 cm band, were the grey sediments containing a dense layer of 19th century material, with the density of bone increasing to the east. Another break then occurred with a change to a sterile light–grey sand layer (Figure 5.7).

The squares to the east and north of this area proved to have a markedly different stratigraphic profile. Square U93, four meters east of the earlier squares, contained a 30 cm layer of archaeological deposit beneath the upper grassed layer. The artefact–bearing unit was composed of faunal material intermixed with charcoal, a limited amount of metal and other materials. Only small quantities of the bone are actually burnt, suggesting that the ash may have been a secondary deposit, perhaps emptied from a hearth, rather than the result of a fire in situ. A dark grey, almost black sterile layer underlay this, damp with the feel (and smell) of a peaty swamp. The same basic sequence is repeated throughout the seven squares between P99 and E87. It would appear that the artefacts seen throughout this area were originally discarded into a natural depression behind the foredune, similar to that seen to the southeast (Figures 5.8–5.10).

Squares P99 and P93 fell along the southern edge of the gravelled car park area, with the top 20 cm and 30 cm respectively of each pit being dolerite roadbase fill. Immediately below this was the grey artefact–bearing sand with a density of bone comparable to the other pits, followed by the very dark grey or black 'swampy' unit which, while mostly sterile, had some artefact penetration to a depth of 10 cm. It is not known how much of the original upper deposit had been removed by grading or preparation of the car park, although comparison with the adjacent squares suggests it may have been more than half of the artefact–bearing unit (Figure 5.7).

Squares TP3 and TP9 formed a two by one meter trench from the southeast corner of Structure Two (Figure 5.11). Beneath the humic layer was a 10 cm to 30 cm artefact–bearing unit of grey sand with high clay content, unlike that seen in F0, but similar to TP6 on the northeast side of the Structure Two. As for the pits to the north of Structure Two, it would appear that artefacts were discarded into a natural depression which has also subsequently filled with sand and sediment, but remains lower than the level of the building.

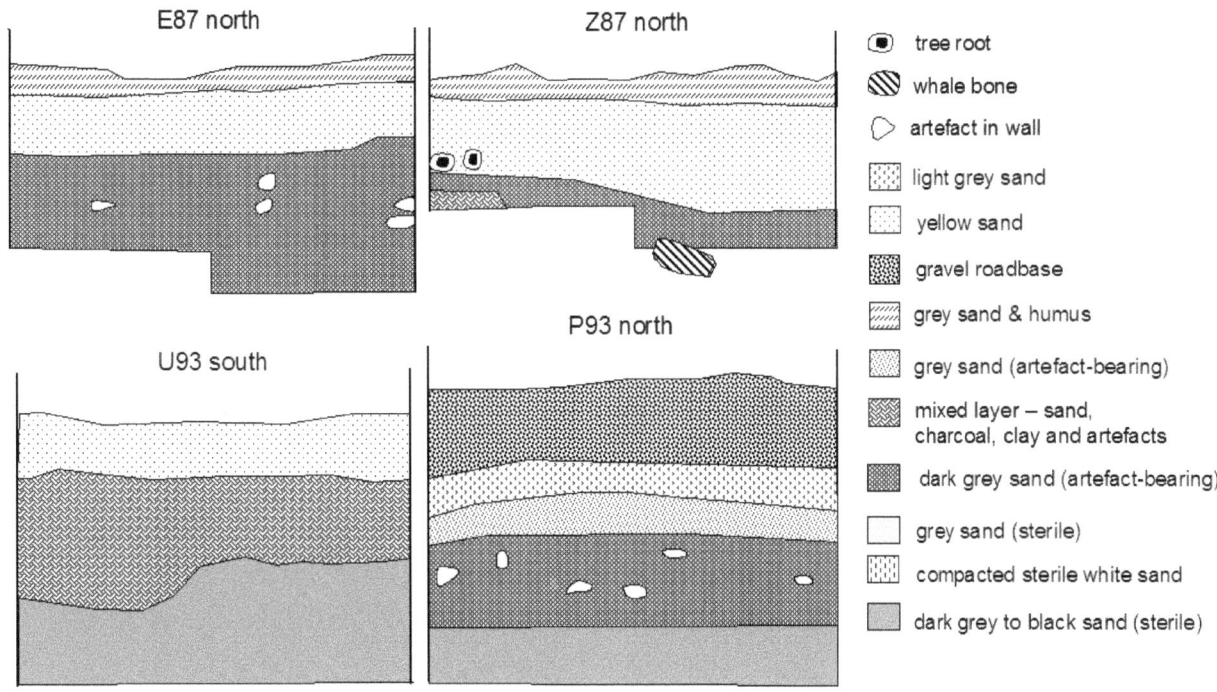

Figure 5.9 Stratigraphic Profiles – E87 north, Z87 north, U93 south, P93 north

Figure 5.9 Section E87 (south wall).

Figure 5.10 Section Z93 (west wall).

Summary of Stratigraphic Units

With minor variations, the stratigraphic sequence is vegetation above organic sands, underlain by loose grey sands which postdate the occupation of the site. An artefact bearing layer sits below this, which in the case of the structures included a floor–level indicator of orange clay mixed with sand and/or whalebone. Artefact density decreased below this to a sterile layer which varied from white beach sands to black peaty sands.

The squares excavated on the east side of the site contained the greatest depth of cultural deposit, with some layering evident within the artefact–bearing unit. However, it has not proved possible to make an inter–pit correlation of these finer divisions, either on a purely stratigraphic basis, or through the use of diagnostic artefacts.

Even within the individual pits the manufactured artefacts mixed in with the primarily faunal deposits do not provide an indication of either the ages of particular units, or the rate of deposition in general. Artefact mobility through the often loose beach sands, slippage down dune slopes, and reworking by storm action are other factors at work in various parts of the site which make stratigraphic relationships and dating difficult. Possible temporal indicators in the artefact assemblage are discussed in a later section.

BUILDINGS AND STRUCTURES

Structure One is comprised of two components: the main or western section which has an internal measurement of approximately 9.5 m by 3.5 m (approximately 31 feet by

12 feet) and the eastern section which is 2.5 m by 3.0 m (approximately 8 feet by 10 feet). This provides a total floor area of approximately 41 m². A plan of the excavated features is shown in Figure 5.2.

The construction of the walls of Structure One is still uncertain, although it appears probable that they were wooden. The large, unmortared stones along the edges are more suggestive of retaining walls to allow the floor to be built up level, rather than being the lowest course of a whole wall. The several fragments of whalebone floor which survive in this section are level with the tops of these boulders, providing further support for this interpretation. The walls around the southeastern section of Structure One use smaller field stones in several layers rising up to half a meter in height. However, this still seems to be a retaining wall rather than the base for a more substantial wall. The difference in style suggests this may have been an extension to the original cottage.

Figure 5.11 View looking north–west over Structure One (Fireplace to rear and stone pathway in foreground).

Figure 5.12 Walls in South–east corner of Structure One.

Unfortunately, no further indicators of a timber structure such as postholes or footings for wooden slabs were identified. The stump of a single wooden post was found at the edge of the whalebone floor at the juncture of squares E4 and E5 and may be a structural timber.

The hearth at the northern end of the cottage appears to have been primarily constructed out of stone, although the large quantity of orange clay spread over the upper layer suggests that low fired brick might also have been used. The flagstones across the front of the hearth would suggest a width of as much as 1.5 m. Although the excavations did not extend to the north side of the hearth, the ground surface shows a spill of stone rubble from the chimney extending for several meters. The ground level slopes slightly downward to the north, and it is apparent that the level of the chimney base had been built up slightly to compensate for this.

Figure 5.13 Fireplace in Structure One (looking north).

Other than being used in the fireplace, it is uncertain what role bricks played in the construction of either Structure One or Two. No whole bricks were found on the site, although badly deteriorated fragments of varying size were recovered. In particular, the layer which is presumed to have marked the floor surface (or immediate underfloor surface) of the cottage often appeared to contain clay and small brick fragments. The nature of the bricks recovered from Cheyne Beach is discussed in the analysis of structural artefacts.

Interpretation of Structure Two is based on a far more limited sample. It is argued that squares C96 and C97 intersected the northwest corner of the building, encountering a surface of whale vertebrae, but once again with no evidence of a surrounding stone wall. The stone pathway also terminates on the northern edge of B96, presumably indicating the position of the doorway. Test pits 3, 4 and 8 intersected stone rubble with ash, interpreted as a hearth at the east end of the building. The probable dimensions of the floor of Structure Two are approximately 3.5 m by 2.5 m, giving an area of about nine square meters.

Perhaps the most interesting feature of both buildings was the use of whale vertebrae as a flooring material. The initial excavations over the southern end of Structure One showed that whole vertebrae had been trimmed and laid with their circular surfaces upwards along what was probably the edge of the wall. This wall edging continued to the northern end of the cottage, although in the northern half of the building the vertebrae had been cut in half. Several traces of bone were also found along the northeast wall. Also in the southeastern corner the floor had apparently been carefully paved with vertebrae cut in half and with the rectangular cut surface laid upwards (Plate 5.4 vertebrae floor). This extended only for several meters along the southeast corner, and had been heavily disturbed by the 1987 shovel pit. No whale bones were found in the southeastern section.

Figure 5.14 Whale Vertebrae floor in Structure One (looking north). Note wooden post in right foreground.

Figure 5.15 Whale Vertebrae Flooring in southwest corner of Structure One (looking west over Square D7).

There are two possible interpretations for the whale bone surface. The first is that it may have been intended as a floor, although if so this project was then abandoned after only the southern section had been completed. The second is that the edging was to assist in supporting a wooden floor, either directly, or as bearers for joists. As described previously, the top of the whale vertebrae are contiguous with the compacted nodule clay and sand level which covers the rest of the interior. It should be noted that even with its clay component, this loose matrix would have provided a poor floor surface, suggesting some form of covering. The single 24cm wide section of jarrah board (located in the northeast corner) which may represent a surviving floorboard rests directly upon this layer. However, the roughly north to south orientation (i.e. along the length of the building), may lend weight to the idea that it originally rested on joists running east to west across the floor. However, if the whale bone edging was simply used as bearers, there would be no need for the almost continuous, carefully cut line which extends the length of the west side, or the more extensive coverage along the southern end, features which are suggestive of a decorative function.

Although only a small section at the western end of Structure Two was excavated, it appears that a similar whale bone surface continues across its floor, rather than just along the edge. Although some pieces had been trimmed, the vertebrae were placed with the articular surface upwards. No whale bones were detected in the limited excavation at the eastern end of the building, although it is possible that this did not penetrate beneath the rubble of the hearth. A single trimmed 'brick' of whale bone (15 cm x 8 cm x 6 cm), possibly from a vertebra, was also recovered from square U98. A hole, presumably for a spike, passes unevenly through the brick, although it's possible function remains undetermined.

While the issue of the function of the whale bones in Structure One remains unresolved, it should be noted that whale vertebrae have been used for structural purposes at other early whaling station sites, both in Western Australia and elsewhere. Local informants at Busselton reported that the buildings at Castle Rock had whale bone floor surfaces which were destroyed when the site was graded in the 1970s. Several sections of this bone now survive in the Busselton Museum. During his excavation of the Thistle Island whaling station in South Australia, McCarthy (1993) encountered four whale vertebrae deliberately sunk into the floor of one of the former cottages, which he interpreted as being associated with supporting a timber floor. In the sites of houses at the 17th century Dutch whaling stations at Smeerenburg (Greenland), whale vertebrae and ribs have also been found supporting floors and the bases of hearths (Hacquebord 1981).

Artefacts associated with architecture, construction, fittings and furnishing are described in the 'household/ structural' artefact category, discussed in the following chapter.

CHAPTER 6
ARTEFACTS FROM CHEYNE BEACH

When the analysis of the Cheyne Beach artefacts was done in the late 1980s/early 1990s there had been almost no historical archaeological research carried out in Western Australia and no regional comparative assemblages or analyses were available. Similarly, much of what was then available from elsewhere in Australasia at the time was descriptive rather than quantitative analysis and of that most was unpublished or locked in inaccessible grey literature reports. There was little or no uniformity in the structure or presentation of data, nor a clear means of drawing these sometimes idiosyncratic results into a comparative framework.

Consequently, the artefact analysis and presentation of data for Cheyne Beach was a very deliberate exploration of how a comparative framework might be established. In the absence of a clear model for dealing with historical period assemblages, the approach was based on the author's previous experience with pre–historic assemblages. Jim Allen's 1969 analysis of the Port Essington assemblage faced similar issues and evolved a similar response (Allen 2008), but a copy of his work was unavailable until late in the Cheyne Beach analysis process.

---

1. **HOUSEHOLD/STRUCTURAL**
    a. Architectural/construction - flat glass, nails, spikes, mortar, bricks, slate
    b. Hardware - hinges, tacks, bolts, staples, hooks, brackets
    c. Furnishings/Accessories - stove parts, furniture pieces, lamp parts, decorative fasteners.
2. **FOODWAYS**
    a. Procurement - ammunition, fishhooks, fishing weights
    b. Preparation - baking pans, cooking vessels, knives
    c. Service - fine earthenware, flatware, tablewares
    d. Storage – ceramic jars, glass bottles, tin cans, bottle stoppers.
    e. Food Remains - faunal and floral
3. **CLOTHING**
    a. Fasteners - buttons, eyelets, snaps, hooks and eyes
    b. Manufacture - needles, pins, scissors, thimbles
    c. Other - shoe leather, metal shoe shanks, clothes hangers
4. **PERSONAL**
    a. Medicinal - medicine bottles, droppers, toiletries
    b. Cosmetic - hairbrushes, hair combs, jars
    c. Recreational - smoking pipes, toys, musical instruments.
    d. Monetary – coins, tokens
    e. Decorative - jewellery, hairpins, hatpins, spectacles
    f. Other - pocket knives, fountain pens, pencils, inkwells
5. **LABOUR**
    a. Agricultural - barbed wire, horse shoes, hoes,
    b. Industrial - whalecraft, boat-related equipment
    c. Other

Table 6.1 Functional Categories (after Orser 1988:233).

The primary analysis of the Cheyne Beach artefacts was on the basis of functional classes, broadly following Orser's categories (Orser 1988:233; see Table 6.1). Diagnostic artefacts were also identified for further analysis, while intrusive modern material was removed at this point. The following discussion is based upon the functional categories applied.

Another concern of the original study was the spatial distribution of artefacts. Although not necessarily advocating the sort of 'pattern recognition' proposed by South (1977), the potential for a nuanced examination of activity areas and discard behaviours seems reasonable. In this respect a deliberate effort was made to explore the distributions of different functional classes of artefact, using a variety of measures (number of elements, weight, etc). The total weight of artefacts in each square (excluding building materials), is shown in Figure 6.1. Larger structural materials (bricks, stone, whalebone) have been excluded.

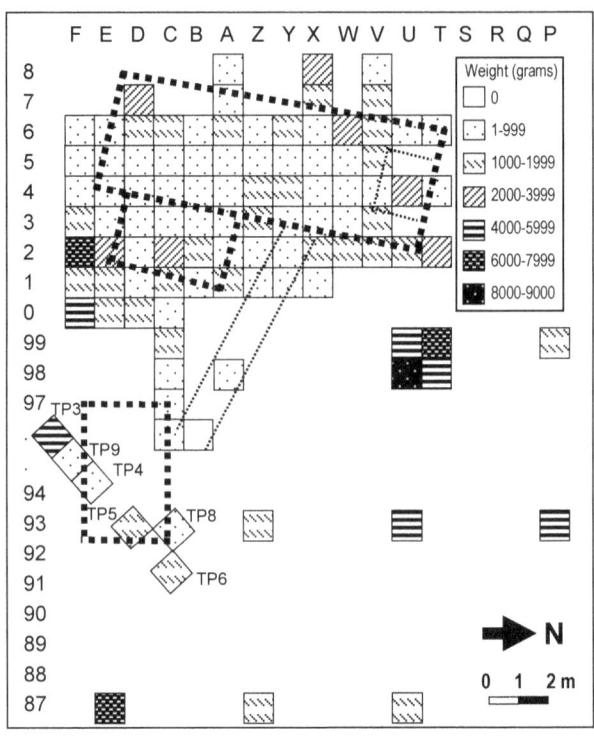

Figure 6.1 Total Artefact Distributions.

HOUSEHOLD/STRUCTURAL

Architectural/Construction related artefacts

Bricks

Only four brick fragments were sufficiently complete to take measurements of their ends, but not of their lengths. Munsell colours were also recorded (Table 6.2). Even allowing for the irregularity of the surfaces measured, there is wide variation in width and thickness. These measurements show a squarer end than for the 19th century standard sizes in either the UK (4.5" x 2.5") or the USA (4" x 2.25") (Pearson 1988; Gurke 1987). All of the bricks are hand–molded, with varying textures. The third fragment is the largest found, having a length of 12 cm, and showing part of a frog. All of the samples are low–fired, with deteriorated or uneven sides, making it difficult to be confident that these measurements reflect the original sizes. Smaller fragments found in the floor layer provided a similar range of colours to those noted above, including a deeper red (2.5YR 5/6), although much of the variation is probably the product of their position within the kiln or clamp when the bricks were fired.

width	thickness	code	colour
1. 7.9cm/3.1"	6.9cm/2.7"	5YR 7/4	pink
2. 8.6cm/3.3"	6.8cm/2.7"	5YR 7/2	pinkish grey
3. 8.2cm/3.35"	7.2cm/2.8"	10YR 7/4	very pale brown
4. 8.3cm/3.25"	7.9cm/3.1" to	5YR 6/6 10YR 8/3	reddish yellow, very pale brown

Table 6.2 Brick end measurements and Munsell colours.

Although there is clay in the general vicinity of Cheyne Beach, it is probable that the bricks were transported from Albany where brick kilns had been in operation since the mid 1830s (see Gardos 2004: 63, 258). A small quantity of a very light clay/lime mortar was recovered from around the hearth, but little from elsewhere which might indicate mortared stone or brick walls.

Nails and Fastenings

Initial sorting of the metal fastenings suggested that five centimetres (or two inches) constituted the upper range for iron nails, above which were appreciably larger bolts, spikes and other fastenings. This provided the basis for the major divisions in both the iron and copper fastenings (Table 6.3). Each of these groups was initially further subdivided into subcategories such as nails, screws, bolts and other, but the degree of rust and corrosion affecting the majority of the artefacts made these divisions impractical.

Material	Length	weight (kg)	% total
iron	less than 5cm (2 inches)	12.788	65.35
iron	greater than 5cm	5.940	30.36
copper	less than 5cm	0.679	3.47
copper	greater than 5cm	0.159	0.82

Table 6.3 Metal Fastenings.

Iron nails were by far the most numerous fastening, although these were invariably in poor condition and heavily fragmented as a result of the salty, alkaline environment of the site. However, all of those examined show the rose–head and flat shank tapering to a wedge which is characteristic of wrought or forged nails (Varman 1980). Although no attempt was made to count individual specimens, an average weight of 3.4 g obtained from identifiable complete specimens from squares A2, C2, T98, V6 and X2 produces a minimum number estimate of 3761 nails. The larger iron fastenings and spikes varied greatly in form and their functions are uncertain.

The relatively few copper alloy nails are of maritime origin; that is, they are types normally associated with boat or ship construction rather than structural uses in buildings. The most common of the smaller class are sheathing tacks, used to fasten wood or copper sheathing to ships' bottoms (Figure 6.2). These are characterised by flat, round heads and square shanks tapering to a point, and are up to 1.5 inches (38 mm) long (McCarthy 1983). In addition to clearly identifiable sheathing nails, there are various other nails and tacks in the size class, usually with square shanks and ranging upwards from 0.5 inch (12.7 mm) in length.

Figure 6.2 Small Copper fastenings.

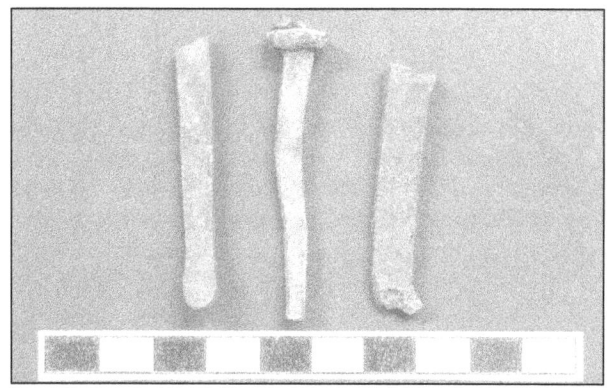

Figure 6.3 Larger Copper fastenings.

The larger copper fastenings are relatively consistent in shape, having square shanks (tapering down to rectangular), and wedge–shape ends, often with a wider or flattened area at the extremity (Figure 6.3). Although most are broken in some way, generally with the head missing, they are consistent with 'boat spikes' (or simply 'spikes'), used for securing large timbers and decking (McCarthy 1983:12).

Both the sheathing tacks and the spikes are types normally associated with larger vessels (McCarthy 1983), rather than the small and lightly built whaleboats which did not require sheathing. While it is possible that these items were simply kept on–hand for mid–season repairs, this seems an unlikely explanation. Two other possible explanations arise, the first being that these fastenings represent salvage from the 95 ton brig *Arpenture* which was wrecked within two kilometres of the station in 1849. The other possibility is that John Thomas undertook ship construction or repair which required these fastenings, such as on his schooner *Mary Ann*. In either circumstance, it is possible that at least some of these nails ended up being used for repairs to the station buildings.

Window Glass

A total of 3.36 kg of flat clear glass, presumed to be window glass, was recovered from across the site. The thickness of these fragments varies from 1.30 mm to 2.12 mm, with a mean (taken from 100 fragments in C6 and V6) of 1.78 mm. These measurements are well within the range for 'Crown glass', a manufacturing method (involving blowing and spinning the glass) which was common until c.1870 (Boow 1991:101). The Crown method produced glass with a maximum thickness of 2.8 mm (1/9th inch), compared to other contemporary and later techniques which had minimum thicknesses of 3 mm (1/8th inch).

Because Crown glass was lighter and attracted lower excise duties, it was the type most commonly exported from England (Boow 1991). It was normally cut into panes of approximately 16 inches (400 mm), although Boow (1991:101) suggests that glass with a thickness of less than 2 mm, such as that seen at Cheyne Beach, was used in smaller panes. By calculating an average weight of 0.35 g per square centimetre from a sample of flat glass taken from squares C6 and TP3, it is possible to estimate that the total area of glass recovered would be 9586 cm^2, just less than one square meter. The window glass was concentrated within and immediately adjacent to Structure One (see further discussion below), whilst the small fraction closely associated with Structure Two (100.5 g/ 35 cm^2) indicates a presence only slightly denser than the general background scatter (Figure 6.3).

Other structural

The whale vertebrae used for flooring have been described previously. Although several small fragments of slate were found in and around Structure One, these have been interpreted as writing slates, rather than as roofing or a decorative structural material.

Hardware

Architectural hardware was limited to several probable hinges and a padlock. An example from E2 (spit 5) appears to be a complete, if very rusted, two–piece hinge. The other two hinge parts are of the 'hook and eye' type (Cuffley 1984). The eye, a 26 cm piece of flat iron with a curled end (which would be fixed to the door) was located in E2 (spit 5), while a matching hook which would be bolted through the door-frame and on which the eye would hang, came from C99 (spit 5), four meters northeast. The latter was in an undisturbed context, although the two items in E2 were in an area disturbed in 1987 and may originally have come from a closer point.

A large padlock was recovered from C99 (spit 3), approximately 10 cm above the hinge. Rust and deterioration meant that further details could not be discerned. The association with either Structure One or Two is unclear, although C99 is only two meters from the latter building's presumed doorway.

Furnishings/Accessories

The only furnishing items were 13 hooded brass tacks, of the type normally associated with leather or fabric upholstery for chairs. These were clustered in several areas, with five in squares Y3, Y4, X4 and Y6, three in T99 and U98, and four in B5 and C6 which are quite close to a final example in D3. Several curved and ribbed fragments of glass from squares T99 (spit1), TP4 (spit 2) and F1 (spit 3) have been tentatively identified as belonging to the bowls of oil lamps.

Artefact Distributions in the Structural Category

The distribution of flat glass in Structure One appears to indicate windows in the vicinity of C7 and V7 on the front or eastern /beach side (Figure 6.4). It is highly likely that a large quantity of window glass remains in the adjacent unexcavated squares. The wider distribution across the site and midden areas could relate to various discard and post-occupation activities smashing and scattering material across the area. Removal and burning of window frames in a later fire could account for the concentration of melted flat glass, vessel glass and iron fastenings in squares Z3 and Z4. Despite rubble limiting the area available for excavation in TP5 (the interior of Structure Two), the density of flat glass is slightly greater than that for surrounding squares. This suggests that there may have been a window somewhere in the building, although it is not possible to determine the location.

The distribution of metal fastenings (by weight) and some hardware items is shown in Figure 6.5. No clear pattern emerges and the nails of both material types may have come from roof, walls or even the floor. The higher densities in U98, U99, T98 and T99 are due, at least in part, to the presence of several larger iron bolts. The concentration within the fireplace (U4), Z3, Z4 and C2, probably represents post–occupation campfires using structural timbers.

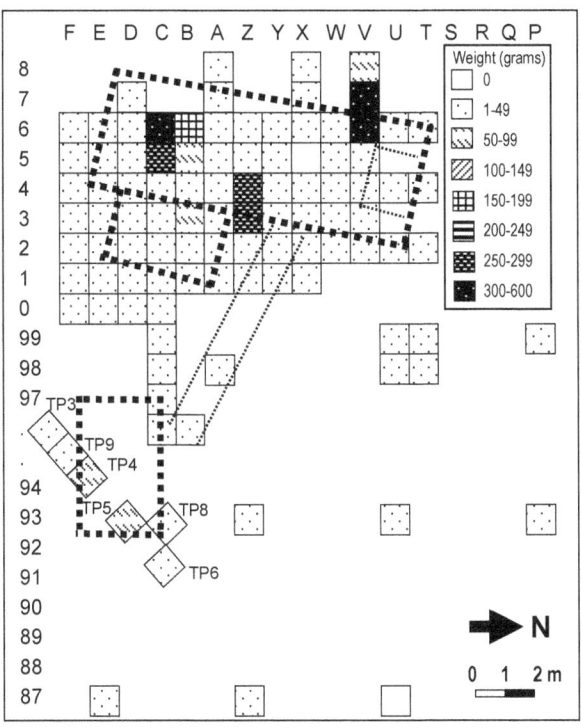

Figure 6.4 Distribution of flat glass.

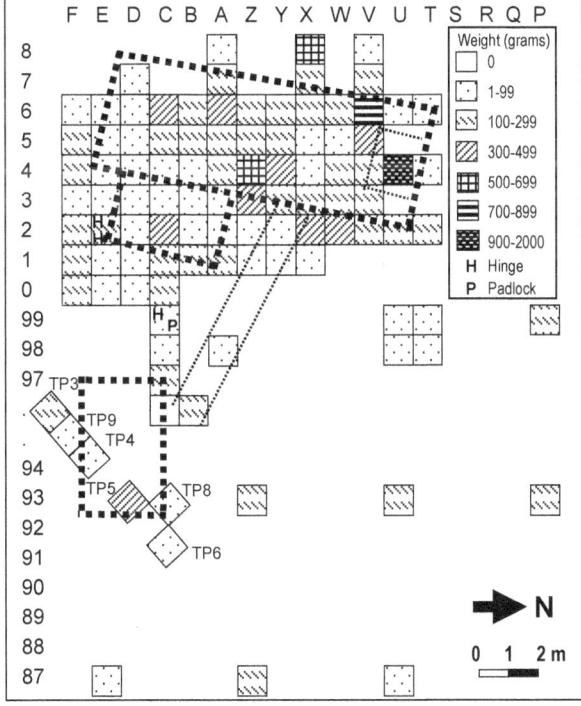

Figure 6.5 Distribution of nails and metal fastenings.

FOODWAYS

Artefacts associated with foodways easily comprise the bulk of the assemblage recovered from Cheyne Beach, including a diverse range of materials and functions.

Procurement

Ammunition

The only artefacts which could be associated with food procurement are various forms of ammunition. Of these, the only firmly identified 19th century items were the 58 copper percussion caps which were found both within the huts and the refuse areas. Percussion caps were a priming charge which replaced the highly erratic flint–lock mechanism. The capsule was placed externally on a piston (or nipple) which would be hit by the hammer, while the actual ammunition, usually a lead ball, was still muzzle–loaded into the barrel (Müller 1980). From the 1850s onwards cartridge–firing rifles began to replace the percussion–locks (Durdick *et al.* 1981), although sales catalogues show percussion–caps were still available as late as the turn of the century (Sears 1906).

When plotted against known sizes for percussion caps, the Cheyne Beach artefacts, all fall within the range associated with use in a rifle (cf. Hunt 1993:96). There are also two smooth–sided 'top–hat' caps, although both are too badly damaged to measure for the purpose of determining what form of gun they were used in. None of the caps of type showed evidence of head stamps or maker's marks.

Figure 6.6 Percussion caps.

A slightly deformed lead ball of approximately 0.49 inch (12.5 mm) diameter was recovered from TP3 (spit 3) and may represent a musket ball for use in a 0.50 inch calibre weapon (Scott and Fox 1987). Other ammunition which may be contemporary with the whaling station includes a 0.50 calibre cartridge inches in length, which was recovered from X8 (spit 4). The base of the round is very similar to the "UMC typed–primed" illustrated in Scott and Fox (1987:65), and also shows a centre firing–pin mark. The bases of two shotgun shells (from X8 spit 3 and B4 spit 5) were badly corroded, making it impossible to determine details. Seventeen pieces of lead shot between 0.12–0.19 inch (3–4.8 mm) diameter were also found, mostly in T99 (spit 2) and U99 (spit 2), although there is no certainty that these are not modern pellets which have filtered down through the sandy matrix.

From the upper levels of the excavation were seven modern .22 calibre shells, including one 'short–round' and one unfired example. There was also a single .303 shell

83

stamped "1941" on its base. No parts from either 19th century or modern firearms were recovered.

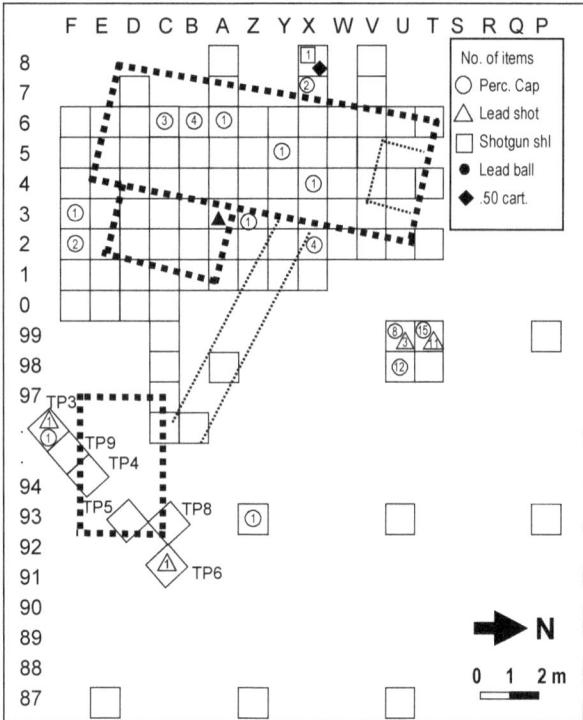

Figure 6.7 Distribution of ammunition artefacts.

The relationship between ammunition, presumably used for hunting purposes, and the faunal assemblage recovered at the site will be discussed later. The lack of fishing gear and agricultural or gardening equipment for tending a cottage garden is noticeable.

Preparation

No baking pans, cooking vessels, or implements such as large knives or utensils which might be associated with food preparation were recovered.

Service

Ceramics

The ceramic assemblage was used in two principal ways during this study. In the first instance it was used as a social and economic indicator, providing a view of the lifestyle at Cheyne Beach and in a broader sense examining the links between the settlement and the wider trade network. The second use, discussed later, was as a marker of discard behaviours across the site.

The ceramics are highly fragmented, with 1568 sherds weighing a total of 4.92 kg. All sherds sorted on the basis of fabric and decoration and where possible conjoined. Due to an absence of sufficient diagnostic elements, minimum numbers were determined on the basis of decoration and the profile of the rim sherds. Because of the high level of dispersion across the site, as shown by conjoins over distances of 11 m or more, unless sufficient of the vessel survived to demonstrate two or more parent vessels, rims with the same pattern and profile were assigned to the same individual. In some cases distinctive patterns, colours or forms allowed a fragment to be identified as an individual vessel despite the absence of a surviving rim.

A minimum of 128 tableware items were identified. Tables 6.4 summarises the identifiable forms with reference to diameters of bowls, cups and flatware. It is presumed that many of the fragments which were too small to measure accurately were from flatwares, so that as many as 25 or more further individuals might be added to the 41 items already in this category. An associated difficulty with the fragmentation is determining how many of the smaller flatware items, particularly in the 6 and 7 inch categories, were saucers rather than plates. Although the flatwares have been grouped together, the fact that saucers were frequently purchased with cups, rather than as separate items, may have a bearing upon the calculation of the CC index value, described below.

Rim diameter (Inch)	(cm)	Bowls	cups	flatware
3.5	8.9	-	1	-
4	10.2	-	11	-
5	12.7	2	3	-
6	15.2	4	-	4
7	17.8	3	-	6
8	20.3	1	-	4
9	22.9	-	-	14
10	25.4	-	-	10
11	27.9	-	-	3
12	30.5	-	-	2
UnID		3	9	25*
TOTAL		**11**	**27**	**68**

Other vessel forms
1 x ewer   1 x teapot
1 x teapot lid ? (unglazed)   1 x tureen + 1 lid
1 x oval platter   1 x vase ?
2 x strainers?

Table 6.4 Summary of ceramic forms.

At the time of the original analysis, Miller's (1980; 1991) 'CC Index Values' were still a relatively recent addition to historical archaeology and seen as an effective means of applying a standard measure to ceramic variability within and between sites. Subsequent writers have identified the difficulties with correlating vessel cost with wealth and status, and the importance of context in recognising nuances such as out-of-date purchases, heirloom pieces and other factors associated with the agency of the users (e.g. Brooks 2005; Crook 2005; Wurst 2006:192; VanderVeen 2007). Despite this, Miller's indices provide at least some notion of where purchases sat on the economic scale. Miller (1980:11) generated his index from English wholesale potters' prices, dividing the cost of 'CC ware' (the cheapest form of refined earthenware, sometimes referred to as 'creamware') into the cost of other forms of ceramic. 'CC ware' as the basic unit has a value of 1.00, with the relative cost of other forms varying over time.

Based on this research Miller (1980; 1991) suggested that decoration rather than fabric was the major cost determinant, defining four major categories, from 1 (low) to 4 (high).:

1. Undecorated (CC) earthenwares.
2. Minimal decoration, including shell–edged, sponge decorated, banded, dipped,
3. Painted wares with motifs such as flowers, Chinese landscapes or geometric patterns,
4. Transfer printed incl. willow pattern.

White–bodied wares (slightly more expensive than transfer printing) appeared in the late 19th century, post-dating the site (Majewski and O'Brien 1987).

Following Miller's formula, the index values of the Cheyne Beach ceramics have been calculated by comparing the assemblage against the values for 1858 (Table 6.6), the midpoint of John Thomas's occupation (1846–1869). This 24 year period is slightly longer than the 20 year maximum recommended by Miller (1991). The averaged index values for each class are 1.72 for bowls, 2.81 for cups and 1.51 for flatware/plates. Although the average index value of the flatware might decrease if some of the smaller transfer–printed flatware were placed among the 'cup and saucer' group, this has probably been offset by not including the large number of transfer–printed flatware fragments which were too small for their diameter to be measured. Several teacup handles were recovered which, if they could be associated with particular cup rims, could raise the value for teacups (e.g. Figure 6.8).

Although the CC index measures would really only be effective in reference to other Australian sites, a general comparison with U.S. sites (Spencer–Wood and Heberling 1987; Miller 1980) shows Cheyne Beach falling within the medium to high socio–economic range. A further consideration is the uncertainty as to whether the discounting factor used in Miller's (1991) revised index is reflecting a phenomenon only associated with the American market, or whether similar fluctuations in price extended to the Australian market as well (c.f. Crook 2005: 20).

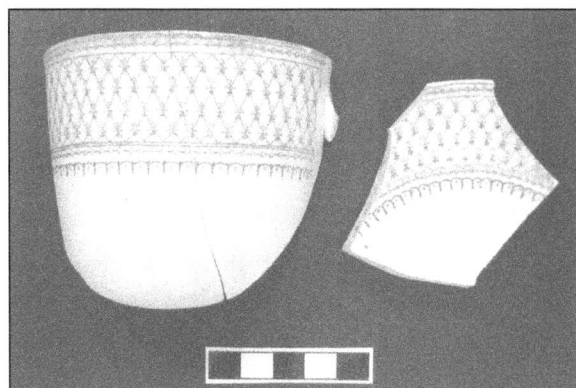

Figure 6.8 Purple transfer print cup and saucer.

There may be as many as 71 patterns or decorative designs in the collection although, despite conjoining, the high level of fragmentation makes comparison difficult. Because of this limitation, a comprehensive identification and dating of specific printed and painted patterns did not prove possible.

	No. of Styles	Min. No vessels	Production Range	Median Date	Max. Popularity
1. CC WARES	1	1	c1750s–		
2. MINIMALLY DECORATED					
dipped/annular	3	3	1830–1860	1845	
green glaze	1	1			
shell edged	1	17	1813–1834	1824	
sponged	1	1		1830–71	1850
redwares	1	3			
3. HAND PAINTED					
bone china	1	1			
lustreware	1	1	1805 –	1850s	
sprig pattern	1	4			
other e/ware	2	2			
4. TRANSFER PRINTED					
dark blue	20	24	1820–1860	1840	1820–1830
brown	3	6	1829–1850	1840	1829–1839
flow blue	7	8	1840–1860	1850	1840–1849
green	10	15	1829–1850	1840	1829–1839
grey/blue & black	9	9	1830–1860	1845	
purple	3	2	1829–1860	1845	1829–1839
anemone	1	9			
willow	1	16	1780s–		
pearl ware	2	2	1760–1820		
porcelain	2	2			
(other)	2	2			
TOTALS	71	128			

Table 6.5 Ceramic decoration, vessel MNI and date ranges (after Stelle 2001)

While many of the transfer printed patterns are probably variations of the same scenes, there are also matched or near–matched items within the collection. In particular, there is a minimum of 13–16 shell–edged plates in the 9–10 inch diameter (supper–plate) range. Despite minor variations, they are all of a sufficiently similar style that they could have been used as a set. In the same way, there are also 8–13 of the more expensive willow pattern plates in the 10 inch (table plate) category. There are matches between cups and smaller flatwares (saucers), although not between these and the larger tablewares, which is not surprising since large sets did not appear until the late 19th century.

In addition to cups, bowls and flatware, fragments of several other ceramic forms were recovered (Table 6.4). These included a willow pattern tureen and lid, a transfer printed oval platter, two 12 inch painted plates (possibly platters), a sponged ewer or jug, a willow pattern teapot and an unglazed earthenware lid of the right size to have come from another teapot. Several small fragments with perforated surfaces, some of earthenware and the others of porcelain, may be from strainers although there is insufficient of either to make a positive identification. A final item in the tableware category is a bone china vase, hand painted over a lustre finish.

Ware/style	Bowls	Cups	Flatware (inch diameters)						Misc.	UnID	Total Individuals
			6	7	8	9	10	UnID			
1. CC WARES	-	-	-	-	-	-	-	-	1	-	1
2. MINIMALLY DECORATED											
dipped/annular	3 (1.08)	-	-	-	-	-	-	-	-	-	3
green glaze	-	-	1 (?)	-	-	-	-	-	-	-	1
shell edged	-	-	-	-	-	12 (1.09)	1 (1.09)	3	1	-	17
sponged	-	-	-	-	-	-	-	-	1	-	1
redwares	-	-	-	-	-	-	-	-	-	3	3
3. HAND PAINTED											
bone china	-	-	-	-	-	-	-	-	1	-	1
lustreware	-	-	-	-	-	-	-	-	1	-	1
sprig pattern	-	-	-	-	-	-	-	2	2	-	4
other e/w	1 (1.38)	1 (1.13)	-	-	-	-	-	-	-	-	2
4. TRANSFER PRINTED											
blue pattern	-	7 (2.89)	-	2 (1.8)	1 (1.5)	1 (1.6)	2 (1.6)	2	1	8	24
brown pattern	-	3 (2.89)	-	2 (1.8)	-	-	-	-	-	1	6
flow blue	-	3 (2.83)	-	-	2 (2.5)	1 (2.4)	-	2	-	-	8
green pattern	3 (2.0)	7 (2.89)	2 (1.5)	1 (1.8)	-	-	-	1	1	-	15
grey/blue & black	2 (2.0)	2 (2.89)	-	1 (1.8)	1 (1.5)	-	-	1	-	2	9
purple	1 (2.0)	1 (2.89)	1 (1.5)	-	-	-	-	-	-	-	3
anemone	1 (2.0)	1 (2.89)	-	-	-	-	-	-	-	7	9
willow pattern	-	-	-	-	-	8 (1.6)	5	3	-	-	16
pearl ware	1 (2.0)	-	-	-	-	-	-	-	-	1	2
porcelain	1	-	-	-	-	-	-	-	-	1	2
TOTAL ITEMS	13	25	4	6	4	14	11	15	15	22	128
Items with index val.	12	25	3	6	4	14	11				91
Total values	(20.62)	(70.31)	(4.5)	(10.8)	(8.0)	(17.08)	(17.09)				
(Average Index values):		Bowls - 1.72			cups - 2.81				plates - 1.51		

Table 6.6 Summary of styles, forms and known CC Index Values (in brackets) c. 1858 (after Miller 1980, 1991).

Although fabric is not necessarily a significant indicator, it is worth noting that there are only three items of porcelain tableware. These include two transfer-printed porcelain vessels (possibly from a cup and another unidentified piece) and the possible strainer mentioned above. The (possible) bone china vase described earlier is the only other vitreous item.

There is little doubt that the Cheyne Beach ceramics originated in England, although there are only four partial maker's marks in the whole assemblage. The first is a brown printed mark on the base of a green transfer printed cup (or small bowl) from square TP9 (spit 3). The legend "COPELAND GARRETT" dates this piece to 1833-47. The second (P99 spit 3) has the words "PEARL ST[ONE]" on the visible portion of the outer oval, with the last three letters of a name, possibly "...NUS" in the middle. This is interesting as this does not correlate with any of the marks incorporating the word 'pearl' listed by Miller (1980:19). Only the far right portion of the third mark, a purple registration diamond on the base of a cup from U98 (spit 2), survives, although the fact that the day of the month is visible means that it comes from the period 1842–67 (cf. Majewski and O'Brien 1987).

The final partial mark (P93 spit 2) has a central crown with '[M]EAKIN' '[ENGL]AND' suggesting the J&G Meakin Staffordshire pottery which dates from 1851 onwards (Godden 1964). However, the use of the name 'England' on the mark could date the fragment to the 1880s or later (Majewski and O'Brien 1987). Unfortunately there is insufficient of the base to determine anything further about the form of the original item. The fragment lies immediately below the laterite road base which covers the area of P93, making its original provenience suspicious. A later date may well indicate association with the Hassell wool store, built somewhere in the vicinity of the car park area in the late 19th or early 20th century.

Table 6.4 lists the broad date ranges for the appearance and disappearance of some of the major ceramic styles represented in the assemblage. Overall, the dates reflect the known occupation of the site, although the midpoints tend to the earlier half. In particular, the even scallops and impressed buds seen on the Cheyne Beach shell edged wares are types generally dated 1813–34, with a median date of 1824. Does this suggest considerable curation, a time lag in supply as a result of the remote situation, or some other mechanism? Dating may also be better resolved with intensive analysis and identification of designs and patterns.

Cutlery

The handles of three cutlery items were recovered, all from exterior squares, although the first two were within close proximity of the buildings. Corrosion has seriously affected the first two pieces (which may be of pewter). The third spoon (U99) is less corroded and may be of electroplated copper alloy. It also shows a common 'tipped' ('Hanoverian') pattern at its head (cf. Sears 1906:109, Smith 1993:193).

Square	Type	Description
W2/3	Teaspoon	Impressed "[I]N GE NT IN"
TP6/3	Dinner Spoon	Impressed crown - letters unreadable
U99/3	Dinner Spoon	Impressed "*** ".

Table 6.7 Markings on Cutlery.

Glass Tableware

There are a number of fragments from drinking glasses, tumblers and glass tableware (Table 6.8). It is probable that other small fragments from items in this class have also been have recovered but not identified.

Square	Description	Reference
F1/3	Stemmed drinking glass.	Jones 1989:53
TP3/3	Tumbler - pressed panels.	Jones 1989:143
TP3/3	UnID. Press moulded floral panels.	
TP3/4	Decanter. Flanged lip and double neck rings.	Jones 1989:153

Table 6.8 Glass Tableware.

Storage

Glass Bottles

The most commonly recovered artefacts associated with storage were glass bottles. A total of 20.642 kg of bottle glass was recovered, although a small proportion is associated with medicinal purposes (see below), rather than food and alcohol. Analysis was hampered by the high level of fragmentation and dispersion across the site, with only one near–complete bottle (of a medicinal type) recovered (Figure 6.24). This made reconstruction of bottle forms and examination of diagnostic technological markers extremely difficult. An additional complication was heavy mineralisation of much of the clear and green glass, with a 0.5 mm or thicker crust resulting from the saline environment in which the artefacts were deposited.

Black glass comprised 5.6 kilograms, or 27.16% of the total vessel glass assemblage. Two basic bottle forms were determined; the first being the flat–sided containers associated with case gin, versus the usual cylindrical types. While the flat black glass was separated for analysis where possible, the fragmentation and mixture of the two groups made separate weighing of the two types unreliable.

None of the fragments of flat black glass showed signs of the embossing or ribbing often seen on this form of container and which might have provided further information on distillers or types. Only a single square base was recovered. While a minimum number count using these or other characteristics was not possible, the clustering of flat black glass fragments in different parts of the site (B2, E87, F5&F6, TP3&TP9, U93) suggests that at least five individual bottles are represented. An isolated applied lip of deep brown–black glass was also recovered from TP6 and may be from a 'bitters' type square bottle, although the body itself was not recovered.

The other black glass bottle form recovered from the site is the circular form with conical push–ups most normally identified on Australasian sites as 'beer' or 'ale' bottles (e.g. Coutts 1984; Boow 1991). Nine black glass applied lips were also found, rounded in form, with the string–rim collars which assisted a wire to hold the cork in the bottle. While most of the lips do not indicate the original body form (and may in fact be from the case gin bottles), three show evidence of a bulged neck which is consistent with the shouldered type of beer bottle. Other fragments in the collection also indicate the three–piece molding normally seen with this bottle type.

Although an attempt was made to separate 'clear' bottle glass from the various shades of green found at Cheyne Beach, mineralisation and crusting made this discrimination impractical. Most of the glass would appear to be from wine bottles, with a minimum of 11 individuals suggested by the number of complete or partial bases. Seven of these bases have low domes, with at least three having a small mamelon (a small, regular type of pontil scar (Jones 1989), although the presence of these might be obscured by the fragmentary or heat–affected nature of the other bottles. Three bases or fragments have higher 'champagne' kicks. A single base from Y4 (spit 2) has a low dome with an impressed "M" in its centre, suggesting a later origin from the Melbourne Bottle Works, c.1900-1915 (Boow 1991). Bottle glass clearly post-dating the whaling period was excluded from the analysis and distribution shown in Figure 6.13.

Nine whole or partial lips from green bottles were recovered. Eight were applied string-rims, including one example which was 'cracked-off' (Jones 1989). One also has a stopper-finish (or cork-seat) in its neck. A single glass stopper was also found in D0 (spit 3). The bases and necks of the green bottles are consistent with forms associated with wine. The large number of thin, flat scraps of lead recovered from around the site may represent the remains of the lead capsules used to seal some forms of bottle. Unfortunately, these are largely undiagnostic, pre–dating the period when capsule seals were stamped with various details.

In addition to the probable wine bottles, a light–green lip with glass stopper intact and in place was also found. This closely resembles the 'club–sauce' finish illustrated in Jones (1989:88). No other fragments of this container could be identified.

Unfortunately, the minimum number counts for both the black beer and light green/clear wine bottles based on diagnostic elements undoubtedly under–represents the actual number of bottles. Small quantities of black and green glass appear in most squares across the site, often at some distance from the nearest diagnostic piece. However, no attempt has been made to correct this imbalance by using presence/absence of fragments in more distant squares (such as across the midden area), although this has been done for the more distinctive bottle types such as in the medicinal class (see below).

A second major group of clear/light–green glass fragments results from pickle, chutney or vinegar bottles, which are characterised by an octagonal or roughly square cross-section and chamfered corners, and a wide neck (Roycroft and Roycroft 1976). The sides show some variation with concave and recessed panels and moldings. One almost complete base was reconstructed (C99 spit 3) with two other fragments in other areas (TP3 spit 4 and F0 spit 2). However, the total distribution across the site suggests there may be as many as nine individuals represented.

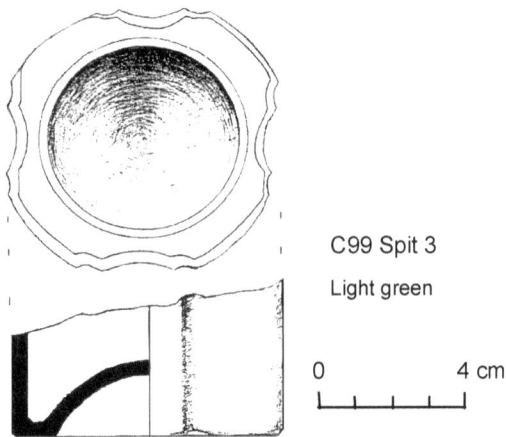

Figure 6.9 Pickle bottle base (C99 Spit 3).

Although no single pickle/chutney bottle can be sufficiently reconstructed to provide a more precise identification, the general class can be seen as associated with food flavouring and a means of making the diet more palatable. It is possible that a small bottle base recovered from T99 (spit 1) may be from a herb bottle.

Stoneware

A single base of salt glazed stoneware bottle of 4 inches (10 cm) diameter was recovered from F2 (spits 4 and 5). There are no distinguishing marks on the recovered portion of base. Bottles of this type are typically associated with stout or ginger beer (Roycroft and Roycroft 1976).

Cask Iron

The wooden cask was the most common form of bulk container for transport and storage used during the 19th century (Staniforth 1987). At Cheyne Beach casks would have performed a variety of functions, ranging from the storage of domestic items (foods, liquids and other commodities), to the industrial function of holding the oil produced by whaling activity.

A total of 5.69 kg of curved iron strapping was recovered, varying in width from 31 mm to 52 mm, and fragmented across the site in no readily detectable pattern.

The highest concentration was in the area of T99, U99 and U98, with the latter containing 1.76 kg, with a further concentration in F2 (see Figure 6.10). No single fragment was large enough to determine an approximate diameter which might have indicated the type or volume of cask in use, although the bent hoop shown in Figure 6.10 may have originally had a diameter of c.70cm (Staniforth 1987). No evidence of wooden staves was detected.

Figure 6.10 Barrel hoop in situ (F2 Spit 5).

Proximity to the domestic buildings and location away from the beach would suggest that the hoops found were from casks holding domestic items. It is probable that there is an area elsewhere on the site that would have been used for cooperage and may contain further concentrations of iron. During the test excavations at Barker Bay it was noted that fragments of barrel iron increased with proximity to the tryworks.

Distribution of ceramic tableware and glass vessels

Figures 6.11–6.12 illustrate the distribution of ceramics across the site by weight and by number of fragments. The reason for this dual presentation is that there still seems to be some level of uncertainty as to the most appropriate way of analysing and representing artefacts, particularly ceramics in circumstances of fragmentation. In this case there appears to be a close correlation between the measures, although there are several areas in the site where the higher number of fragments versus weight suggests greater fragmentation. These squares are not necessarily close to doors or obvious areas where trampling damage might occur, although more distant squares such as U87 and E87 which are presumably further from regular traffic do have larger pieces.

Most conjoined sherds came from within a radius of several meters of each other (Gibbs 2006, Appendix C.5). However, several examples record greater dispersion, including across distances of 11 m (U99 spit 3 to F2 spit 5) and 16 m (E4 spit 2 and U93 spit 3).

Figure 6.13 shows that glass appears in all squares, although there are several concentrations such as TP3, which contains 2.15 kg, or 9.6% of the total weight of the vessel glass recovered. Four squares within Structure One also show particularly high concentrations of glass. The fragments from B1 and V4 can be reconstructed into three almost complete bottles, two situated in the first square and one in the latter. The completeness of these vessels and their positions within the main structure, resting on the original floor surface in a corner of a room and on the base of the fireplace respectively, suggest they may post–date the whaling station occupation. The concentrations in squares W6 and Y6 are also green glass but melted in situ, suggesting they may also originate from a similar early and presumably casual post–whaling occupation. The base impressed with a Melbourne Bottle Works mark (Y4 spit 2) dated to just after the turn of the century can also be dismissed as a later discard, possibly even post–dating the demolition of the building.

If the several concentrations of glass within Structure One are dismissed as post–dating the occupation of the site, then at least one black and five green bottle bases, representing about one quarter of the alcohol bottles, must be eliminated from the minimum number count. Add to this the possibility that other glass in the assemblage may have a similar later origin, and there remain a surprisingly limited number of bottles to represent the 30 years of seasonal occupation by over a dozen men.

Figure 6.14 shows the locations of diagnostic elements used in the estimation of minimum numbers of glass and ceramic vessels. As noted above in the case of the alcohol bottles this was determined from bases, while individual pickle and medicinal bottles were sufficiently distinctive that body fragments could be used. While it is possible a more extensive deposit of glass remains unexcavated, alternative explanations include the use of bulk containers (such as the various types of cask) to transport and store liquids and other foodstuffs, or recycling bottles as a scarce resource.

Faunal Remains

The isolation, probable seasonality and industrial nature of the Cheyne Beach whaling station make diet and food supply an area of considerable interest. Of particular importance with regard to questions about adaptation and the relationship between the European settlers and the Australian environment is the use of domesticated versus native fauna in the diet. A version of this analysis is also available in a separate paper (Gibbs 2005).

The aims of the analysis were essentially the same as those expressed by Coutts and Aplin (Coutts 1984:391).
 a. Identify the principal taxa,
 b. Determine the relative abundance of the taxa and where possible their contribution to the diet,
 c. Define some aspects of the butchering, culinary and disposal processes.

Soil conditions at the site were highly alkaline soil conditions (8.0 or higher) resulting in 28.64 kg of bone and 18.41 kg of shell being recovered. Although general sorting, classification and distribution analysis was applied to material from across the site, only the eight pits with the highest density of faunal material were subjected to more intensive scrutiny. These squares (E87, F0, P93, TP3, T98, U87, U93, and Z93) contained 45.5% (13.03 kg) of the total bone and 40.6% (7.48 kg) of the total shell (Figures 6.17–6.19).

The enormous body of literature on quantification in archaeological faunal analysis presents varying thoughts on appropriate measures (Reitz and Scarry 1985; Brewer 1992; Lyman 1994). In the analysis of the Cheyne Beach fauna weight has been used to determine the distribution of the several classes of bone and shell across the site. MNI (minimum number of individuals) has been calculated for those parts of the assemblage which are the focus of the analysis. A NISP count was not made, and no attempt was made to determine meat weights.

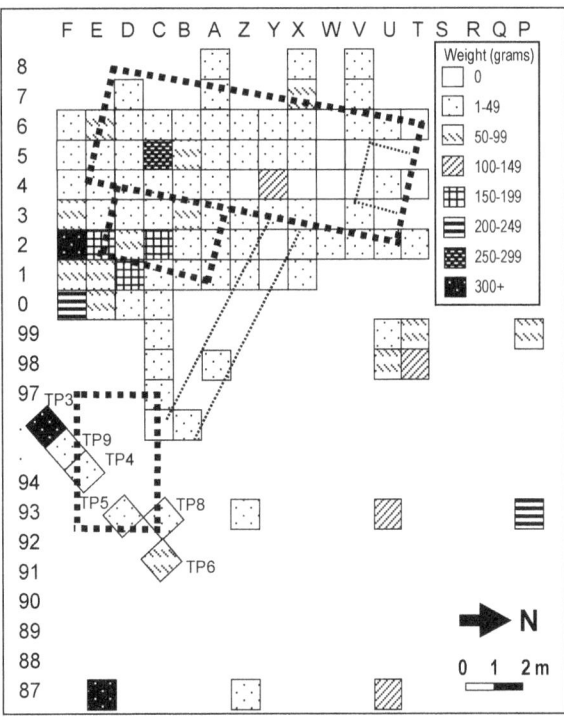

Figure 6.11 Distribution of ceramic vessels by weight.

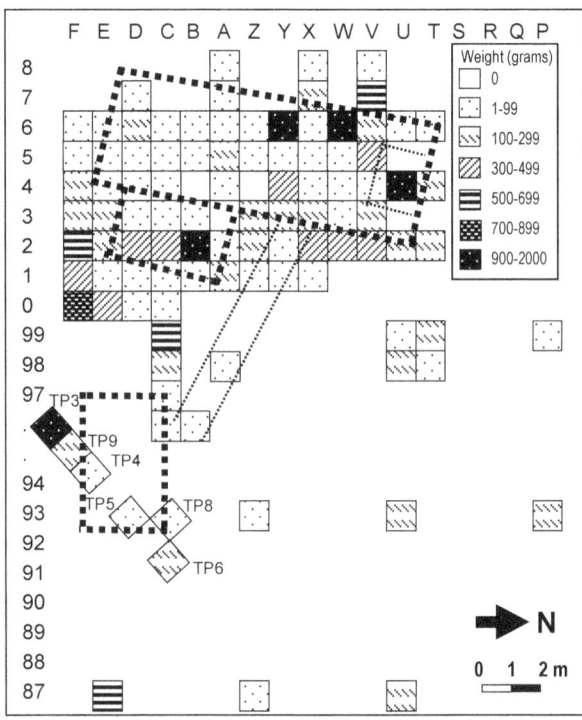

Figure 6.13 Vessel glass by weight.

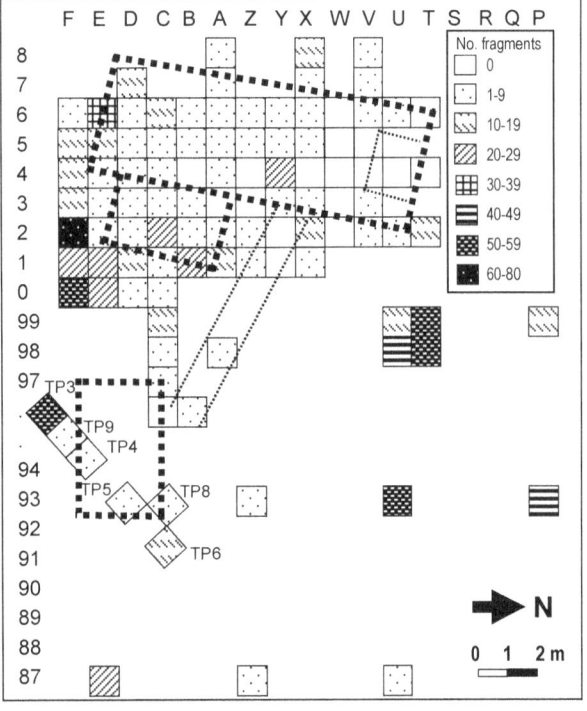

Figure 6.12 Distribution of Ceramic fragments.

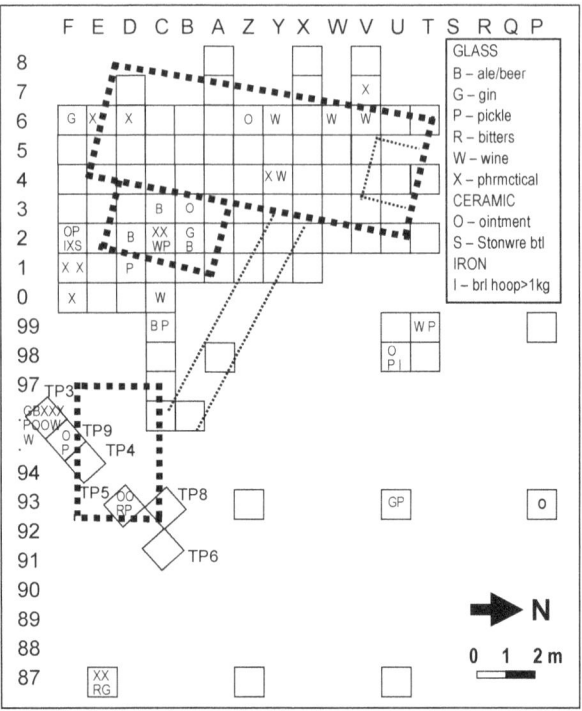

Figure 6.14 Vessels.

	Wt (kg)	% Total	% ID'd bone
BONE			
Domestic			
Sheep, Pig, (med–sized mammal)	13.621	47.56	76.38
Cow	0.385	1.34	2.16
Rabbit	0.006	0.02	0.03
Wild			
Quokka	0.878	3.07	4.92
Seal	0.391	1.36	2.19
Dolphin	0.054	0.19	0.30
Fish	2.265	7.91	12.70
Bird	0.235	0.82	1.32
Total ID'd Bone	(17.835)	(100.00)	(100.00)
UnID			
mammal bone frags	6.483	22.64	
bone fragments	4.321	15.09	
Total Bone Weight	28.639	100.00	
SHELL			
abalone	1.301	7.07	
periwinkles	10.544	57.27	
helmet	0.838	4.55	
limpet	1.006	5.46	
olive	0.235	1.28	
thaid	0.869	4.72	
turbo	0.329	1.79	
other	0.203	1.10	
Undiagnostic	3.086	16.76	
Total Shell Weight	18.411	100.00	
Crustacean (present but not weighed)			

Table 6.9 Summary of faunal weights.

The initial sorting for bone was based upon the most easily recognised categories of 'fish', 'bird', 'reptile', 'small mammal', 'medium mammal' and 'large mammal' classes, as well as 'unidentified mammal bone fragment' and 'unidentified/undiagnostic bone fragments'. Sea mammals (dolphin, seal) were separated immediately where identified. The detailed identifications undertaken for the eight selected squares were based on comparative collections at the University of Western Australia and from relevant literature including Schmid (1972) and Merrilees and Porter (1979). All shells were identified to species level using Wells and Bryce (1985). A summary of the total weights of bone and shell is provided in Table 6.9. For the purposes of this discussion the vertebral faunal material has been divided into 'introduced' and 'native'.

Introduced Species

Analysis of the eight selected squares shows that the assemblage is dominated by sheep *(Ovis aries)*, providing 5.46 kg of the bone by weight, or 76% of the identified total for these pits. An MNI count suggests the presence of at least 12 animals. For historical reasons (see below) there is a limited chance that the sheep bone includes the osteologically similar bones of goats *(Capra hircus)*. All body parts are present, although under–representation of some elements such as phalanges may indicate discard of non–edible portions in an early stage of butchering away from the site.

The other domesticate identified within the 'medium–sized mammal' bone class is pig *(Sus scrofa)*, although this only comprised 0.24 kg or 3.4% of the total identified bone weight within the eight selected squares. The available body elements do not allow a count of more than one individual, except the teeth, which clearly show at least one juvenile and one (possibly two) adults. That some of the bones come from spatially separated squares may suggest a greater number of individuals, although the majority of the pig bones come from a single square (U93). No other pig teeth were identified elsewhere in the site, although further scrutiny of the 'medium–sized mammal' bone class for the remainder of the assemblage may still produce other bones.

Short sections of butchered cattle *(Bos taurus)* bones comprise only a minor contribution to the assemblage, providing 0.18 kg or 3.4% of the identified bone weight from the eight squares analysed. The only other *Bos* body element clearly identified from the remainder of the site is another section of rib (0.17 kg) from U98, bringing the total weight to 0.385 kg, or only 1.3% of the total identified bone weight for the site. No limbs, cranial elements or other body parts, usually readily identified because of their size relative to other domesticates, have been recovered. The limited number and nature of recovered body elements suggests the possibility of salted meats (English 1990).

A small number of rabbit *(Oryctolagus cuniculus)* bones were recovered, with teeth identified in TP3 (spit 3), B2 (spits 2 and 3), D3 (spit 3), U93 (spit 2) and W2 (spit 2). The presence of open rabbit burrows as well as stratigraphic discontinuities indicating burrowing makes it uncertain if the bones are dietary or later intrusions. Rabbits were successfully released and bred on Mistaken Island (frequently referred to as Rabbit Island) near Albany by George Cheyne as early as the mid–1830s (Garden 1977). A mainland release occurred in the Albany area in 1866, with burrow sightings of at Cheyne Beach from at least 1890 (Stodart and Parer 1988).

A small quantity of bird bone was recovered from the sample squares, although most of this was hard to identify further (see below). While no domesticates were identified from the eight analysed pits, chicken bones were noted in several other squares elsewhere in the site (e.g. B6 spit 1, U98 spit 1).

Native Species

The native terrestrial fauna almost exclusively comprises of the remains of quokka *(Setonix brachyurus)*, a type of small wallaby. Quokka provides 0.24 kg or 3.3% of the total identified bone in the selected squares, with an MNI of two based on right mandibles recovered from E87 (spit 3) and U93 (spit 2). For the site as a whole, quokka contributed 0.88 kg, comprising 3% of the total bone. A total of nine right mandibles were recovered from across the site indicating a minimum of nine individuals, although wide spatial separation may mean that at least 11 individuals are represented. A more comprehensive examination of other body elements could provide a higher figure.

Figure 6.15 Quokka jaws *(Setonix brachyurus)*.

Quokka were once available in scrublands throughout coastal southwest Western Australia, but their range has now been restricted to relict populations on Rottnest Island, Bald Island (4km SE of Cheyne Beach) and several small mainland sites including the Waychinicup Valley (8 km SW) (Storr 1965).

A single tooth from a larger macropod (P93 spit 4), could not be identified to species level. A portion of a *Macropus* sp. mandible, also insufficient to make an identification, was recovered with other 19th century artefacts from the surface of TP1, which was located at some distance north of the site and in a context which suggest the material may have been re-deposited.

Several species of large macropod, including brush wallabies *(Macropus irma)* and grey kangaroos *(M. fuliginosus)*, are available in the general area, but are uncommon in the sand plains immediately behind Cheyne Beach (Storr 1965).

Skeletal evidence from the midden deposits indicates that both dolphins and seals were at least occasionally slaughtered for dietary purposes. Fragments of a lower right mandible of a dolphin were recovered from U93 (spit 4). Although the jaw is incomplete, the number of tooth sockets and the tooth size of 3 mm or less in diameter suggests that it may be from a common dolphin *(Delphinus delphis)* (Baker 1990). Fragments of four large tympanic bullae, part of the auditory structure of mammals, were also recovered (F2 spit 5, U98 spit 2, and two from T99 spit2). Although a firm identification has not been made, these probably originate from hair seals *(Neophoca cinerea)*, which are commonly seen on Bald Island as well as occasionally coming ashore on the mainland around Cheyne Beach (Storr 1965; Westerberg pers. comm. 1990).

Whale bones and fragments (as opposed to the whalebone or baleen strips described in Chapter Three) were recovered in varying quantities from most squares across the site, with the exception of the eastern and northern pits on the edge of the midden. This material is almost certainly present as a result of structural uses, such as the whale bone floors in both buildings, rather than as a result of dietary uses (discussed below).

Highly fragmented bird bones account for a very small proportion of the Cheyne Beach faunal assemblage, with a weight of approximately 0.24 kg, or only 1.3% of the total identified bone weight on the *site*. In the eight sample squares this rises only slightly to 1.5% from 0.11 kg of bone. The lack of diagnostic elements within the sample squares makes for some difficulty in discussion, and identification of native species will have to await a specialist study of the faunal assemblage. Biological surveys have identified a variety of potentially edible species in the area (Smith 1977), although the most likely candidates are the several nesting and burrowing species on Bald Island. These include brown quail *(Synoicus ypsilophora)*, little penguin *(Eudyptula minor)*, and great-winged petrel *(Pterodroma macroptera)*. The remains of fleshy-footed shearwater *(Puffinus carneipes)*, commonly referred to in Western Australia as the muttonbird, have also been found on Bald Island, but no burrows have been identified.

The skeletal evidence suggests that the most commonly consumed native fauna at Cheyne Beach was fish. The 0.77 kg of bone recovered from the eight sample squares provided 10.7% of the identified total for those pits, while for the site as a whole the 2.26 kg of fish bones recovered represented 12.7% of the total identified bone. Identification of fish species within the sample squares was made on the basis of diagnostic cranial material. A number of otoliths were recovered and have been identified as whiting, most probably King George whiting *(Sillaginodes punctatus)*. All the otiliths suggest quite large specimens.

Despite the limited identifications made from the faunal assemblage, it is clear that fishing provided a significant staple component of the diet. Cheyne Beach is now a popular and well regarded fishing spot, with the reefs and granite ledges near the site yielding a wide variety of highly edible species on a year-round basis.

Several shark teeth were found in the deposit, including one in square E87 (spit 2) and two in C0 (spit 1). Historical evidence and observations of modern whaling operations show that sharks were strongly attracted to whaling stations, often feeding off the carcasses as they were being brought into shore and while anchored in the shallows.

> Whenever whales were cut in Frenchman's Bay, we boys used to have some exciting times killing the sharks that were after the blubber; for the purpose we used the cutting-in spade (McKail 1927).

		Weight (grams)									
		E87	F0	P93	T99	TP3	U87	U93	Z93	Tot.	% of ID'd
DOMESTIC	sheep	904.7	215.2	724.9	701.6	949.7	88.7	1551.0	329.3	5465.1	75.88
	pig	0.	0	0	27.6	12.8	16.4	163.8	25.0	245.6	3.41
	cow	134.2	0	48.2	0	0	0.	0	0.0	182.6	2.54
	rabbit	0.	0	0.0	1.4	0	0	0	0	1.4	0.02
WILD	quokka	29.6	1.7	20.3	62.6	13.8	0.0	51.6	55.7	235.3	3.27
	hair seal	0	0	0	135.1	0	0	0	0	135.1	1.88
	dolphin	0	0	0	0	0	0	54.2	0	54.2	0.75
	fish	230.7	8.4	212.1	56.5	22.4	7.2	165.4	69.5	772.2	10.72
	bird	59.2	2.7	14.4	10.0	2.8	1.9	13.3	6.2	110.5	1.53
Tot. ID'd Bone		1358.4	228.0	1020.0	993.4	1002.9	114.2	1999.3	485.7	7202.0	100.00
UnID Bone		1400.2	95.6	1850.8	401.7	273.7	273.0	1312.2	220.4	5827.6	
TOTAL BONE		2758.6	323.6	2870.8	1395.1	1276.6	387.2	3311.5	706.1	13029.6	
TOTAL SHELL		1105.9	1007.3	386.0	2774.1	819.7	228.6	752.2	407.8	7481.6	
TOTAL FAUNAL		3864.5	1330.9	3256.8	4169.2	2096.3	615.8	4063.7	1113.9	20511.2	
Crustacean (presence in pits)		-	-	-	yes	yes	-	yes	-		

Table 6.10 Summary of faunal weights in sample squares.

Common Name	Family / Species	Environment	Tot. Wt (gms)	% Tot.
abalone	Haliotis (roei?)	rocks and reefs	1301.5	7.07
helmet shell	Phalium pauciruge	-	837.7	4.55
limpet	Patella laticostata	rocks and reefs	1006.3	5.47
moon snail	Naticidae	inter-tidal sands	146.7	0.80
periwinkles	Nerita atramentosa + Austrocochlea constricta	rocks and reefs	10544.0	57.27
olive shell	Oliva australis	shallow sands	235.1	1.28
thaid	Thais orbita	rocks	867.7	4.71
turbo	Turbo torquatus	shallow waters	329.3	1.79
Other & UnID	-	-	3143.6	17.06
TOTAL			18411.9	100.00

Table 6.11 Total weight of shells recovered from Cheyne Beach, including known environments.

	Weight (grams)									
Species	E87	F0	P93	T99	TP3	U87	U93	Z93	Tot.	%
abalone	47.0	194.1	12.1	185.5	323.2	4.9	27.3	33.7	827.8	11.1
Austrocochlea	231.0	41.9	38.8	830.6	41.2	24.2	165.2	65.3	1438.2	19.2
helmet	419.1	125.0	15.6	0	0	26.4	46.7	0	632.8	8.5
limpet	35.1	410.8	73.9	115.4	43.2	32.5	76.0	30.0	816.9	10.9
moon snail	10.5	3.3	0	13.9	7.0	0	4.7	2.4	41.8	0.6
Nerita	338.9	74.5	107.0	1464.1	156.4	132.8	335.8	192.5	2802.0	37.4
olive shell	3.9	0	5.7	16.9	9.3	1.1	0.4	4.8	42.1	0.6
thaid	17.9	12.7	0	98.6	5.8	0	2.3	15.5	152.8	2.0
turbo	0	0	0	0	0	0	3.5	0	3.5	0.1
unID/undiag	2.5	145.0	132.9	49.1	233.6	6.7	90.3	63.6	723.7	9.6
TOTAL	1105.9	1007.3	386.0	2774.1	819.7	228.6	752.2	407.8	7481.6	100.0

Table 6.12 Shell weights (grams) in sample squares.

	Number of Individuals									
Species	E87	F0	P93	T99	TP3	U87	U93	Z93	Tot.	%
abalone	6	14	2	14	3	1	5	6	51	2.9
Austrocochlea	87	10	10	119	14	7	47	33	327	18.3
helmet	10	4	2	0	0	2	2	0	20	1.1
limpet	2	13	3	8	3	1	11	8	49	2.7
moon snail	3	1	0	3	3	0	2	1	13	0.7
Nerita	158	33	27	621	75	52	222	92	1280	71.8
olive shell	2	0	4	8	1	1	3	4	23	1.3
thaid	2	1	0	13	1	0	1	1	19	1.1
turbo	0	0	0	0	0	0	1	0	1	0.1
TOTAL	270	76	48	786	100	64	294	145	1783	100.0

Table 6.13 Minimum numbers of shells in sample squares.

The equipment list for Carnac includes 24 fishing lines and 20 shark hooks (see Figure 3.2), supporting the probable use of shark as a dietary item.

Figure 6.16 Shark teeth.

Small quantities of crab shell were recovered from 11 squares spread from the eastern edge of Structure One and through the midden area (square C1, C5, E1, T99, U2, U93, U98, U99, X8, Z3, TP3). This evidence was limited to the tips of claws (dactyls), which are insufficient to make any identification to family or species level.

Shellfish

The small reef and granite shelves of the headland adjacent to the whaling station appear to have provided several varieties of shellfish. Table 6.11 provides a summary of the main species (by weight) recovered.

During the general sorting *Nerita atramentosa* and *Austrocochlea constricta* were grouped and weighed together, being of similar size, form, and environment, and generally being commonly identified as 'periwinkles'. For Tables 6.12–6.13 these two species have been counted and weighed separately. In addition to the species listed, single specimens or low numbers of several other shell species with possibly dietary use were also recovered, including tritons *(Charonia lampas)*, tun shells *(Tonna variegata)*, and *Camapanile symbolicum*, which apparently has no common name.

While it was not possible to undertake a minimum numbers count for the whole site, Tables 6.12 and 6.13 present a comparison of shell weights and numbers for the sample pits. Although no attempt has been made to calculate meat weights, *Nerita*, even without the *Austrocochlea* component, clearly comprises the bulk of the shell, followed by abalone and limpet.

Butchery and Disposal

Analysis of butchery marks and skeletal element representation was undertaken primarily to determine whether domestic species had been kept live on or near the site or brought in pre–prepared, probably as salted meats. Native terrestrial and marine fauna remains were not examined for butchery.

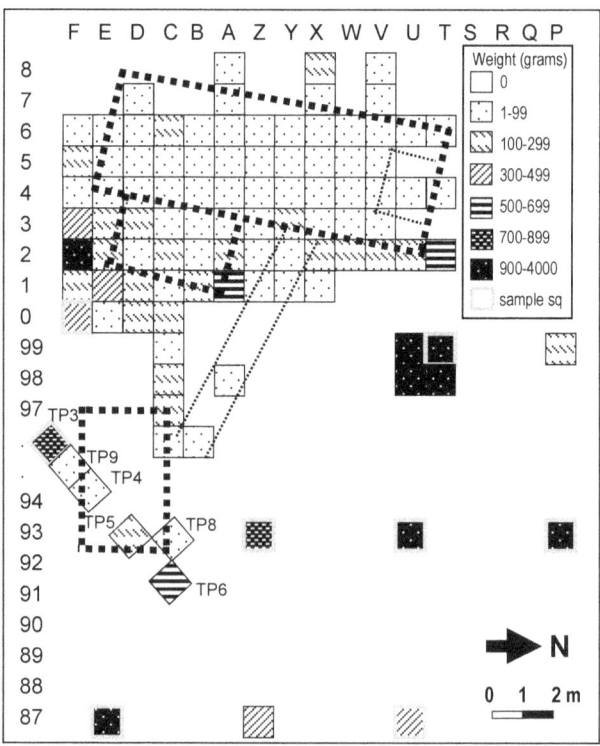

Figure 6.17 Distribution of animal bone.

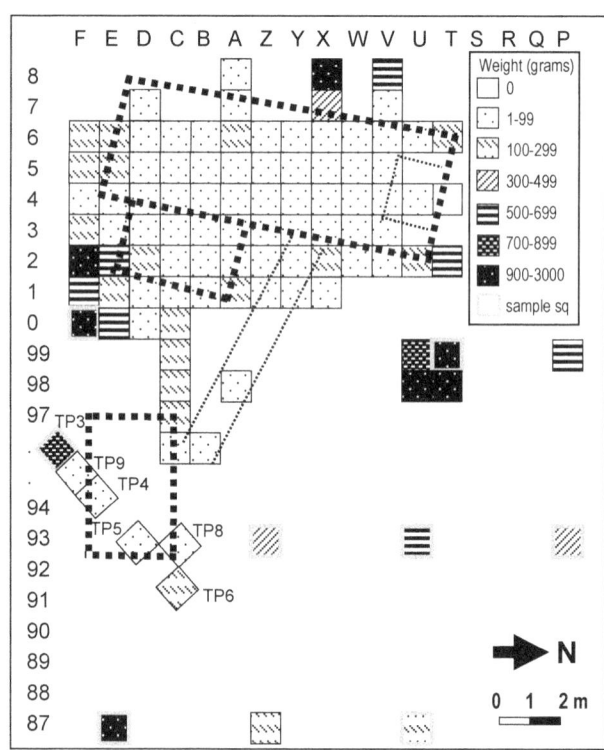

Figure 6.18 Distribution of shell.

As noted previously, virtually all body elements of sheep are represented, which is suggestive of butchery on–site, probably as a function of keeping meat 'on the hoof' (a detailed breakdown of elements is available in Gibbs 1995: Appendix C). Most of the bones are broken, with only two unbroken long bones in the whole sample, although some of this may be a result of post–depositional factors. Visible cut marks are only present on 19% of the sheep bones and 4% of the pig bones recovered. Although a detailed analysis of butchery patterns such as that undertaken by Ritchie (1986) would be useful, this current study was constrained to making only preliminary comments on the most notable or frequent cuts.

a. Crania: There was a considerable quantity of cranial material, mostly visible as whole or partial mandibles and maxillae, with many more free teeth. The craniofacial portions of the skulls were normally highly fragmented, although one example clearly shows the top of the calvarium neatly sawn off, presumably for the purpose of cleanly removing the brain. Mrs. Beeton's Cookbook (1861) contains several recipes for sheep's head and sheep's brains *(en matelote)* which might require this.

b. Vertebrae: All of the five epistrophei (axis vertebrae) recovered had been cut at various angles as a means of removing the head. Most of the other vertebrae had been cut longitudinally as a result of splitting the carcass in half.

c. Scapula and Humerus: The scapulae have frequently been cut across or near the articular surface, with some corresponding cuts across the end of the humerus. This might be a by–product of the removal of the neck as a separate cut. The scapula and humerus would normally be included in the forequarter cut (McVicar 1993).

d. Radius. Cuts at the distal and proximal ends of the radius were probably to acquire the fore shank cut and to separate the extremities, although in the sample collection it was noted that these breaks were usually along the shafts, rather than in close proximity to the epiphyses. Metacarpals and phalanges were recovered in low numbers.

e. Ribs: Ribs appear to have suffered most from post–depositional breakage, which includes their removal from the archaeological context. Those fragments with visible cut marks suggest that at least in some cases divisions were made both towards the proximal (head/articulated) end and towards the distal end, possibly to provide more manageable portions. The distal portions themselves were probably included in the breast cut.

f. Pelvis and Femur: Cuts through the pelvic bone tend to be close to or through the acetabulum, although some of the bones from the sample squares showed divisions slightly lower (through the ischium) and much more rarely higher, through the ilium (hip bone). Most of these fragments were also broken, although these cuts would indicate removal of the chump. There does not appear to be particular evidence of further cutting into chops. The proximal joints of the femurs bear corresponding marks, while divisions through the distal joints suggest division into a leg cut.

g. Tibiae and rear extremities: There was an almost equal number of breaks at the proximal and distal ends of the tibiae, separating the hind shank cut and removing the rear extremities. Several metatarsals were also recovered.

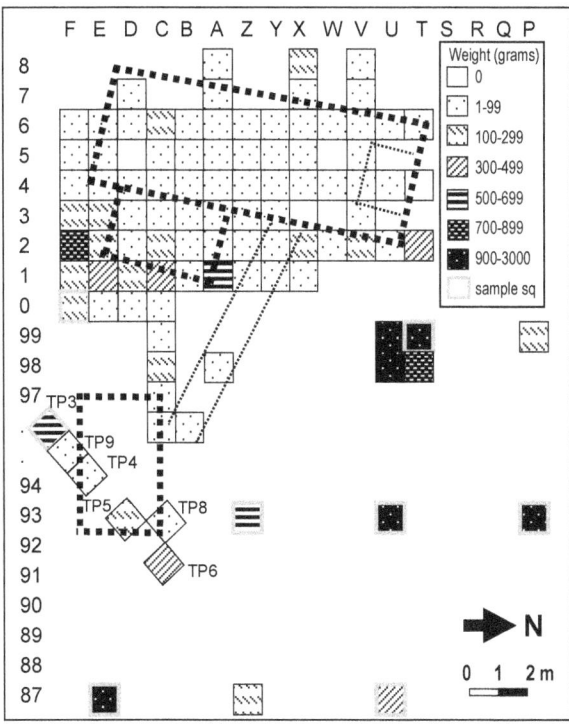

Figure 6.19 Distribution of mammal bone.

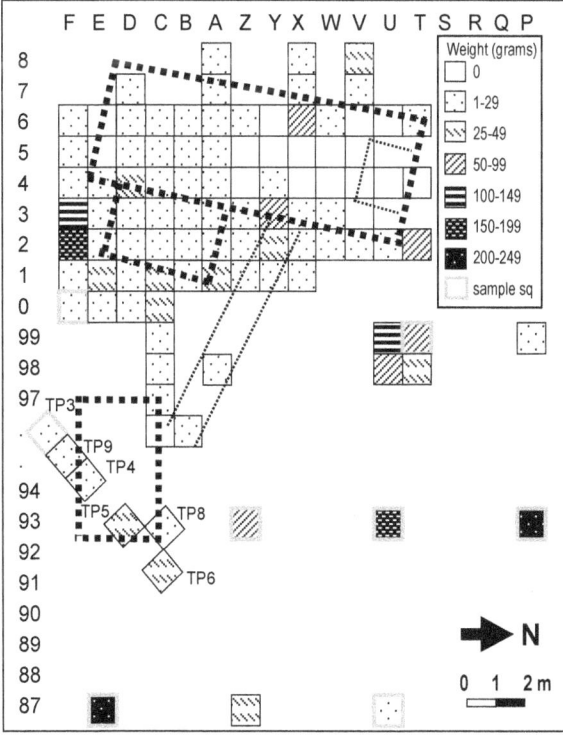

Figure 6.20 Distribution of fish bone.

From the evidence of the eight sample squares, it appears likely that the sheep were slaughtered and butchered at the site, rather than brought in as prepared and salted meats. The meat cuts suggested by the bone breakages are similar to those which might be expected for a European diet (McVicar 1993), although as noted the position of the divisions are sometimes away from the joints, presumably reflecting the fact that this was not done by a professional butcher. While no attempt was made to determine the ages of the sheep represented in the deposit, many of the bones had un–fused epiphyses, suggesting that both lambs and older animals were consumed.

In contrast, there is limited quantity and variety of bones from pig; mostly upper body and cranial elements, with the exception of a single fragment of pelvis. Cattle bones are even more limited, and comprise predominantly of short sections of rib, possibly indicating these were cut to fit into a barrel, which was the normal means for transporting prepared and salted meats (English 1990).

Less than 20 of the bones and fragments were burnt or charred, and even this may well have been post–depositional burns rather than a product of cooking. Given the close proximity of the midden to the cottage and kitchen, disposal of hot ashes onto the bones, or even a periodic deliberate fire to reduce the smell or volume of rubbish, may have been possible. Potential scavengers impact is discussed below.

Artefact Discard in the Foodways Category

Discard patterns for bone and shell are represented in Figures 6.17 and 6.18. While both classes have similar distributions across the site, a greater proportion of bone is present in the midden pits (P93, U93 and Z93), while shell is focused slightly closer to the buildings. Figures 6.19 and 6.20 compare the distributions of mammal bone and fish bone, with the latter increasing in density towards the middle and far edge of the midden. Two concentrations of fish bone within Structure One, at X6 and Y3, correlate with the concentrations of glass which are thought to result from an early post–occupational use of the building.

CLOTHING

Fasteners

Buttons

The clothing worn by the occupants of Cheyne Beach is best represented by the variety of fasteners found, including buckles, buttons, hooks and eyelets. Buttons are the most numerous form of fastening, with 99 whole and broken examples. These were classified into 30 types on the basis of material and stylistic characteristics, described in Appendix C.5 and summarised in Table 6.14. Only a small number of the metal buttons exhibit more diagnostic characteristics, such as manufacturer's names (Table 6.15), although it has not proved possible to date these.

Material	Description	No. of types	Tot
Bone	4 hole / 1 piece	4	15
Glass	2 hole / 1 piece	1	1
	4 hole / 1 piece	2	12
Shell	2 hole / 1 piece	2	4
	3 hole / 1 piece	1	1
	4 hole / 1 piece	5	15
Metal	2 hole / 1 piece	3	9
	4 hole / 1 piece	3	12
	2 hole / 2 piece	2	7
	sew-through / 3 piece	1	1
	soldered loop / 3 piece	3	9
	too rusted to determine	-	9
Composite	shanked/metal w. fabric cover	1	2
	soldered loop/metal w. glass insert	1	1
	sew-through/metal and UnID	1	1
Total		30	99

Table 6.14 Summary of button types

Two of the more interesting items are two two–piece metal buttons with wire loops from squares U98 spit 2 and E1 spit 5. The former appears to be a British naval button, 8 mm in diameter, slightly raised with an anchor and cable within a circular 'rope' rim, but without the crown which characterises naval buttons after 1832. This example most resembles an 'unauthorised' button, in particular a surgeon's button from the 1827–1832 period illustrated in Lewis (1945:136). The second button is of similar size and motif, but is flatter and without the rope rim.

Square	Description	No.
T99 s1	Braces/suspenders buckle. Triple tang. Brass. Impressed "REGISTERED 25 AUGUST 1856"	1
A6 s.2	Braces adjuster?. Brass.	1
X3 s.2	Serrated buckle. Brass. Leaf/fleur design?.	1
C3 s.2	Single tang roller buckle. Iron?	1
U93 s.4	Double tang, roller (external) buckle. Iron ?.	1
F0 s.4	Double tang, roller (external) buckle. Iron ?.	1
T99 s.1	Double tang roller (external) buckle. Brass.	1
U99 s.2	Button Hook?. Brass. Light leaf pattern. Impressed "C. ROWLEY PATENT" on rev.	2

Table 6.15 Buckles.

Buckles and Clothing Hardware

In total 19 hooks and 27 eyelets were recovered, with some variation in size evident. The five clothing buckles from Cheyne Beach are similar to the more common iron and brass examples in Cameron's (1985) types A, C and D, which include both tanged and serrated edge varieties. In addition, there were two brass braces–adjusters, and a probable braces fitting through which a metal button would be hooked.

Figure 6.21 Buckles.

Figure 6.22 Thimbles.

Manufacture

Thimbles and pins represent the only items clearly associated with clothing manufacture or repair. Two brass thimbles were recovered from within Structure One (squares A3 and A6 – see Figure 6.24). The 13 dressmaking pins were found both within and outside of the structures. These range in length from 31 mm to 34 mm and one 64 mm example, with several forms of round, tapered and flat head (c.f. McGowan 1985).

Other

Glass beading

Nine small glass beads were recovered from the site, in diameters of approximately 2 mm, 3.5 mm, 4 mm and 5 mm. These are the smallest cultural items recovered from Cheyne Beach, with a high probability that an unknown number passed directly through the standard 3 mm and 6 mm sieves used during the excavation. Four colours are represented, blue/green (4), amethyst (3), white (1) and amber (1), with various shades within each group. Beads of this type might also be attached to clothing and other items of apparel.

A badly deteriorated fragment of boot heel was excavated from F2 (spit 5). This consists of four layers of leather, of approximately 4 mm thickness each, held together with 18 small iron tacks. Several other small scraps of leather, probably parts of the same fragment, were also found in close proximity, although there is no evidence of the body of the shoe, other than two eyelets from F1 and F2.

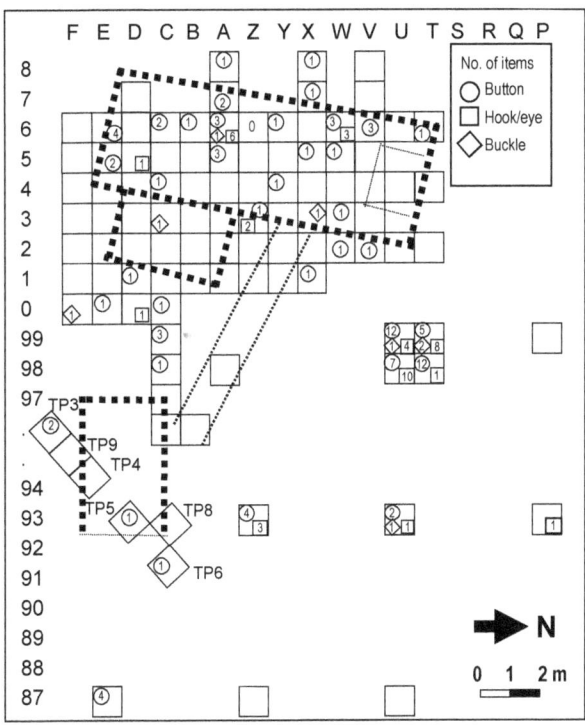

Figure 6.23 Distribution of clothing items I.

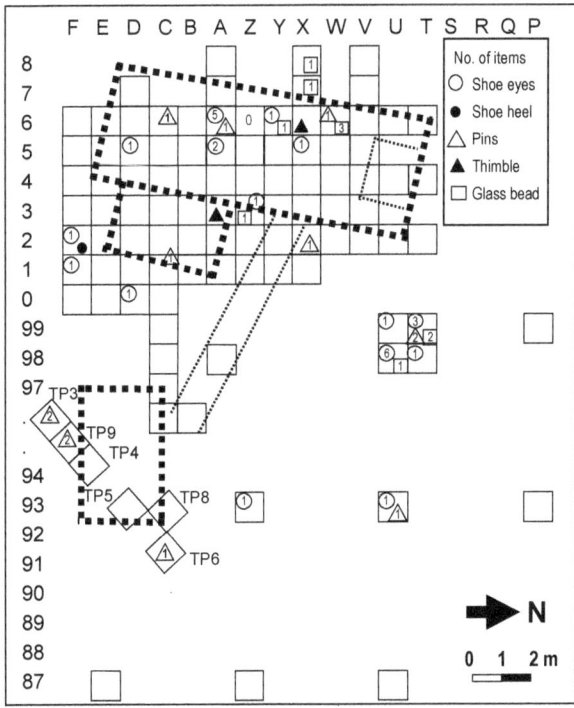

Figure 6.24 Distribution of clothing items II.

97

Whalebone strips

Several short strips of a semi–flexible dark brown material, 5 mm wide, were recovered from F0 (spit 3) and F1 (spit 4). Although not of the thickness or width of whalebone stays examined in museum collections, the flexibility itself suggests this material. While collection of whalebone was one of the functions of the station, the provenience of these pieces makes them more likely to have been from an item of clothing.

Artefact Distributions in the Clothing Class

Figures 6.23 and 5.24 describe the locations of the majority of clothing related artefacts. A scatter of small items is seen throughout the interior of Structure One, particularly around square A6, although the main concentration is in the four squares (T98, T99, U98, U99) located some distance from the doorway.

PERSONAL

Medicinal and Toiletries

The most common evidence for the use of medicines by the inhabitants of Cheyne Beach is provided by the remains of small glass bottles, described in Table 6.16.

In most instances individual bottles are represented only by a few fragments. All conform to the general shapes associated with patent medicine bottles for this period, although the several pieces which exhibit embossed lettering do not have sufficient to allow identification. As shown in Table 6.16, the fragments have been grouped to provide a minimum number of 13 probable medicinal or toiletry bottles.

Medicinal or Toiletry Bottles
C2/6   Clear/ pale green circular base, 48.15mm/ 1.895". Low dome with mamelon. Blown & moulded.
C2/5   Clear glass. Patent lip.
D6/2   Pale blue glass. Oval base, 39.5mm/1.55" by 59.5mm/2.34". Recessed base. (English). medicine for lung/stomach disorders?}
E6/3   Clear glass. Cylindrical base, 24mm/0.84". Slightly flared lip (12.4mm interior, exterior 17.0mm). Embossed "../MOMILE". [Pill bottle]
E87/3 Clear glass. Section of rectangular side, 1mm/0.83" width, with recessed panel. [pill bottle?].
E87/4 Pale green glass. Rectangular , 68.26mm/2.68" by 38mm/1.5", with flat chamfered corners and concave base. Blown & moulded.
F1/1&2 Clear glass. Rectangular base 41.5mm/1.63" wide by 50mm+,with recessed concave panel. Moulded.
F1/3   Clear glass. Cylindrical body approx 23mm/0.92". Embossed "../ORT/...". May be associated with section of base in F2 s3.
F2/3   Clear glass. Lower section of rectangular side approx 26mm width with recessed panel. Embossed (first line) ".../ORAS " (second line) ".../RISTOL ".
TP3/3 Clear glass. Straight finished lip, slightly tapered. Rect. base 42mm/1.6" x 48mm/ 1.9". Flat chamfered edges. Two piece mould. Embossed (first line) "…/ABINA " (second line) "RO/ .../ No 23".
V7/2   Pale blue glass. Complete bottle (174mm/6.7" length), oval base 59mm/2.3" by 42mm/1.6". Two part mould, applied lip, short neck and high, sloped-down shoulders.
F0/2, Y4/1, TP3/3 & 4 Cobalt blue glass fragments
Ceramic Ointment Jars and Lids
B3/3 & C2/5 White granite jar. 96mm diameter. No marks.
TP3/2 & 3 White granite jar fragments. No marks
TP9/2 & TP6/2   White granite jar fragments. No marks
F2/9 White granite lid. Partial design (Holloway's ?)
P93/2   Small Holloway's ointment jar.
TP3/3   Small Holloway's ointment jar.
U98/2   Small Holloway's ointment jar.
T2/3, TP6/3, & Z6/1 Fragment of small jars. No marks

Table 6.16 Medicinal and toiletry containers.

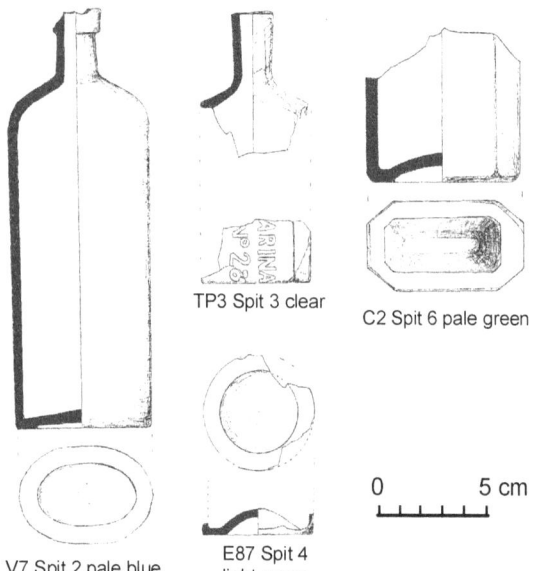

Figure 6.25 Medicinal bottles.

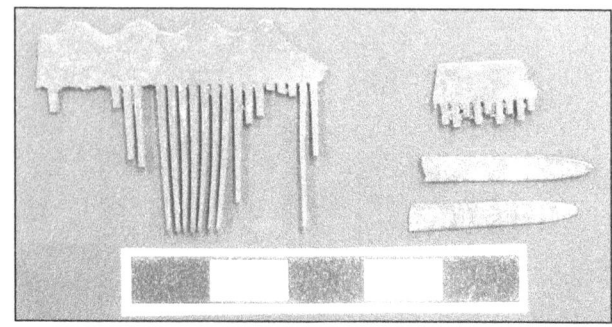

Figure 6.26 Combs.

Also within the medical category are pieces of white granite earthenware which originate from ointment pots or lids. The fragments of three small ointment jars and one larger–size lid would all appear to be from the ubiquitous Holloway's Ointment. Although it was not possible to determine precise dates, the Strand address partially visible on the three smaller jars (representing two different designs), dates them before 1867 (Roycroft and Roycroft 1977:25). The distribution of fragments suggests a minimum of 10 ceramic ointment containers

A fragment of the rim of a chamber pot, recovered from U87 (spit 3), might also be included in this category. The rim suggests a diameter of 10"/25.4 cm and is of a plain cream glazed earthenware with a flat upper rim embossed with a feather design.

Cosmetic

Combs

Fragments of several combs were recovered from the site, all made of an unidentified black material. Suggestions have included an early celluloid (although this would date from the 1870s onwards), or possible gutta percha. These include a fine–tooth comb with 19 mm long teeth from U98 (spit 2), and small piece from the back of another fine–tooth comb (with no remaining teeth) from X8 (spit 4) (Figure 6.26). Eight 22 mm long teeth from a larger comb were recovered from T98, T99, U98 and U99, with a further single tooth of similar size and type found in U7 spit 2, 8 m west.

Recreational

Toys and Gaming pieces

A number of small items suggestive of gaming activities were excavated from within Structure One, with particularly notable items being a small bone die and a Chinese coin, both found in Y5 (spit 3). The die is badly deteriorated, although the irregular dimensions (11.0 mm x 10.1 mm x 10.4 mm) and uneven placements of the dots on the faces strongly suggest that this was home–made. An artefact found in U98 (spit 2) looks as if it were in the process of being squared, possibly for use as a die and appears to be either ivory or a fragment of a large tooth, possibly whale or seal (Figure 6.27).

Figure 6.27 gaming pieces.

The Chinese coin is copper, measures 24.8 mm (0.983") in diameter, but is damaged, with the normally square central hole being roughly cut and dented out of shape (Figure 6.28). The two characters on the reverse can be read as "Boo–ciowan", indicating that it was minted by the Board of Revenue in Beijing (Krause and Mishler 1988). The right and left hand characters on the obverse are "T'ung–pao", or 'universal value', meaning that the coin was legal tender throughout China (Ritchie 1987). The deformed central hole and wear along the face obscures the top and bottom characters which contain the name of the emperor at the time it was struck. This is, unfortunately, the crucial element for dating purposes. However, it is possible that it is a coin from the Ch'ien Lung period with the emperor Kao Tsung (1735–1796), and may be of a type known as 'coin of celestial benefit' (Cresswell 1979:44). It is unlikely that this piece performed a monetary function, possibly being kept as a gaming token or lucky piece.

Figure 6.28 Chinese coin – face and obverse.

A 6 mm thick fragment of rectangular bone with six regularly spaced and deeply drilled holes may also be associated with game purposes (Figure 6.27). This piece, found in D7 spit 2, bears resemblance to a peg–board used for cribbage, although this is by no means a certain identification. Two bone pegs of 22 mm (13/16ths") in length, but each split in half down their length, were excavated from E87 spits 3 and 4. These may be associated with gaming purposes, or may have some other as–yet unidentified function not associated with recreational purposes.

Figure 6.29 Harmonica.

Marbles were a highly popular game during the 1860s and 70s, and consequently have been found on a variety of 19th century Australasian sites As noted by (Birmingham 1992). The first of the two examples found at Cheyne Beach (T99 spit 1) is a 'stoney' of brown clay with swirls of orange and red/maroon, and a diameter of 14.8 mm (0.58"). The other is white with faint grey swirls, possibly earthenware, of 19 mm (0.78") diameter, and may be an 'alley' (TP3 spit 1). The final artefact within the 'toy' category appears to be a fragment of a small porcelain saucer from a child's tea set (C99 spit 2). Unfortunately, no further pieces from this set have been identified.

Musical Instruments

Several fragments of the sound–board of a harmonica were excavated from U98 spit 2 (Figure 6.29). The reeds are brass, while the base plate is possibly a lead alloy, similar to an example excavated at the mid–1860s site of Omata Stockade in New Zealand (Prickett 1981). Small fragments of wood with iron clasps were closely associated with these, and would appear to be the remains of the body. Single brass reeds from another harmonica or similar wind instrument were also found in squares V5 (spit 3) and X8 (spit 4).

Clay Tobacco Pipes

Fragments of clay tobacco pipes were found throughout the site, with Table 6.17 summarising the key attributes identified during the study. A minimum number count was attempted using several different attributes, including stem/bowl joins, lips (mouthpieces), and bowl rims. The stem/bowl junction provided a count of at least 36 individuals, although there are at least 38 stems with makers' marks. A comprehensive analysis using combinations of attributes would undoubtedly increase the minimum number.

Attribute	No.
Bowl/stem joints (min. no. count)	36
Number of stems with makers marks	38
Min. no. of decorated bowls	18
No. of decorated stems	2
No. of feet/spurs	10
Lips	22
Sharpened stems (mended?)	3
Teeth marked (clenched) stems	6
Glazed fragments	12
Total number of fragments	411
Total weight	628.6 grams

Table 6.17 Attributes of Clay Tobacco Pipes.

Fragments from as many as 18 bowls, or just under half of the minimum number of pipes recovered, show evidence of decoration, not including plain makers' marks. The decorations include anchors, ships, line, leaf and geometric designs, although in most cases the size of the fragments made a more specific identification impossible. Only two stems were decorated, although six had manufacturer's names within rope borders.

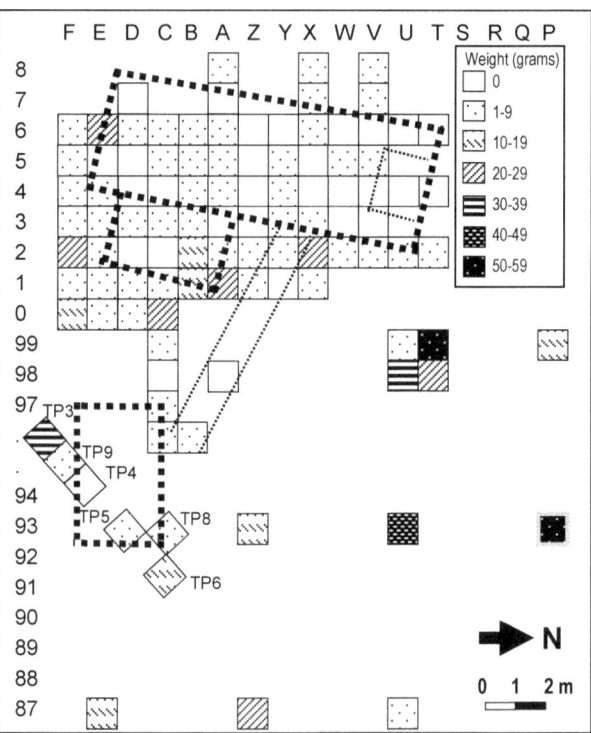

Figure 6.31 Distribution of clay pipes by weight.

Maker	Location	No	Date
English			
[CROP] = (Charles Crop?)	London	1	1856-1924
Theosophilus Milo	Strand	2	1860-1870
Scottish			
[CHR...] = (Wm Christie?)	Glasgow	1	1857-1962
Thomas Davidson & Co. (Caledonian Pipe Works)	Glasgow	6	1863-1910
Duncan McDougall & Co.	Glasgow	4	1847-1968
William Murray & Co.	Glasgow	3	1830-1861
William White & Sons	Glasgow	5	1806-1955
[..OP. LO...]	Glasgow	1	-
Unidentified			
[Baltic Yachter]/ [Yachter]	-	4	c.1862?
[Baltic] / [Baltic 32]	-	2	c.1862?
[Burns... / ...P]	London	1	-
[Bu... / ...on]	-	1	-
[..OP. LO... / ...iscu..]	-	1	-
[Prince of Wales]	-	1	-
[Ernest Bend... Adel...]	-	1	-
[G... / ...N]	-	1	-
[D... / ...Pipe]	-	1	-
[...don]	-	1	-
[B...]	-	1	-
TOTAL		38	

Table 6.18 Clay tobacco pipe marks (Oswald 1975).

The assemblage contains other features which clearly indicate modes of use. Breakage of the fragile stem lip, either being bitten through or snapped, appears to have been a common occurrence. Three stems have been sharpened, presumably for fitting to a new (possibly wooden) mouthpiece (Figure 6.30), although none of these replacement pieces was recovered and there is no clear sign of bindings on the stems. Six of the stem fragments have teeth marks where the broken stem has been clenched, often quite close to the bowl.

Figure 6.30 Clay pipes showing sharpening for refitting (top row) and teeth clench marks (bottom row).

Monetary

The only coin located during the excavation was the Chinese coin which has already been described above. Despite the absence of other 19th century coinage, rumours of buried money at Cheyne Beach were heard from several persons visiting the site during the excavation. This story appears to have been current since at least the 1950s, with a newspaper of that time reporting the popular belief that money (with which to pay the whalers) had been buried somewhere on the site for safe keeping (W.A. 17/5/1950).

In itself this discovery is quite interesting, both for the high value of the find, and the fact that if it really was made up of half crowns, the cache would have contained at least 168 coins. In some ways it is difficult to understand how such a significant sum could have been lost, particularly given its worth in the mid 19th century. No further information could be found on the fate of these coins.

Decorative - jewellery, hairpins, hatpins

Only two artefacts clearly fall within this category. The first is a carved piece of pearl shell (F0 spit 2) with a flower design which looks as if it were the head of a hairpin or hatpin. The other appears to be a finely carved piece of bone (C6 spit 3), possibly with a leaf design, although its original function has not been identified.

Figure 6.32 Pearl and bone decorative personal artefacts.

Other

Writing Materials

The most numerous artefacts associated with writing are the ten pieces of slate pencil, the majority of which seem to have been snapped during use. Seven of the ten have a utilised end, either sharpened or flattened through wear along one or more sides, with the longest segment (3.8 mm long) pointed at both ends. Most of the fragments are 3 cm or less in length. Four of the fragments of flat slate have chamfered or straight edges, such as would fit into the wooden edging of a slate writing board (Davies 2005). No markings were found on these pieces.

There are also two copper/brass artefacts which may come from writing implements. The first (from U99 spit 1) appears to be the base of a 'stub' style pen nib (Sears 1906) with the tines broken off. The second piece (X1 spit 2) may be the seat by which a nib is fitted onto the pen shaft, although if so, in this case it would have been a small nib. A single small piece of square pencil lead was recovered from U98 (spit 2).

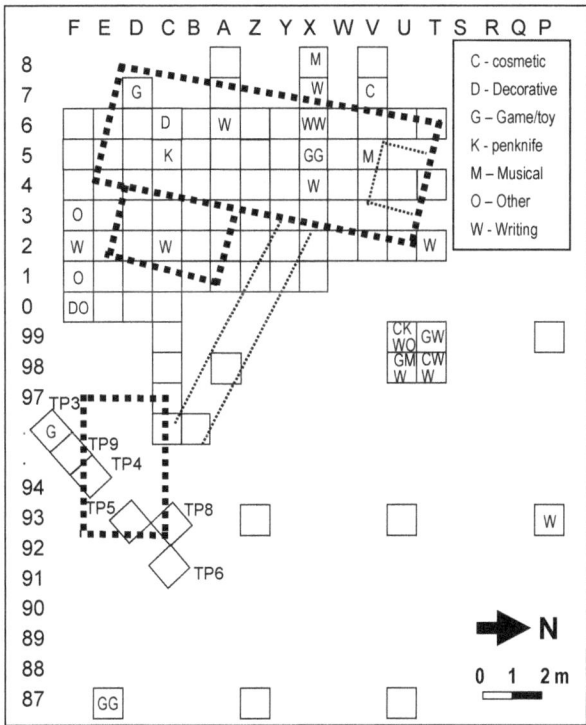

Figure 6.33 Distribution of personal artefacts.

Penknives

The first example, from C5 (spit 2), is a badly corroded folding pen–knife, with the body length suggesting a blade size of approximately 5 cm. Strips of bone facing from both sides of the case were recovered from spits 2 and 3. A similar fragment of bone facing from a larger pocket–knife was found in U99 (spit 3), although there was no evidence of the knife itself.

Miscellaneous

There are several further items which may well fall under the 'personal' category. The first is a threaded brass lock fitting with an opening for a small key (U99 spit 3). The second is a small flat brass hook (F0 spit 2). One or both of these may be associated with small personal storage boxes. No identification has yet been made for either the 9 cm long flat brass hook (F3 spit 5) or a small brass embossed fitting (F1 spit 3).

LABOUR

Whalecraft and Boating equipment

It was hoped that some indication of the industrial nature of the site might be located in the deposit. Ideally and perhaps a bit fancifully this would have been some specialised whalecraft item such as a harpoon or lance. However, this was not to be the case. The most relevant artefacts are boat–related hardware such as the copper sheathing tacks (described earlier) and a ring–bolt (17 cm/6.5" shaft with a 11.5 cm/4.5" ring) which was excavated from F2. A small sheet of copper, 14 cm by 25 cm with a number of nail holes through it, may also be associated with boat sheathing. The ring bolt is of a type normally fastened into mast or deck and used to fasten ropes or lashings (McCarthy 1983). Both the nails and the ring–bolt are associated with vessels larger than a whaleboat.

Despite some barrel hoop iron being excavated, its proximity to the house makes it likely that it was associated with food storage rather than the oil production of the station. However, as the re–assembly of oil storage casks in either 'barrel' (36 gallons/164 litres) or 'hogshead' (54 gallons/245 litres) size was vital to the functioning of the station, it is likely that a concentration of discarded hoop iron exists elsewhere on the site.

In the broadest terms, whale bones might also be construed as being indicative of the nature of the industry at the site, although as already discussed above it is best considered as a structural material. A single horseshoe found in A1 (spit 3) has been included in this category, although whether horses played some active role in the operation of the station or were simply present for transport purposes is unknown.

ABORIGINAL ARTEFACTS

Only one item has been identified as a probable Aboriginal artefact (X7 spit 3). This is simply a flake with a bulb of percussion, but no retouch. The fine–grained white material on which is based has not been firmly identified, although it is possibly chert. All the glass analysed was inspected for evidence of Aboriginal utilisation. Although some pieces had random flakes detached, there was no clear evidence of deliberate modification such as retouch or flaking from the bases of bottles (cf. Allen 1969; Allen and Jones 1980).

ARTEFACT DISTRIBUTION

The distribution and density of artefacts and the stratigraphic information from the excavations provides insight into the original topography of the site, the nature of the whaling era structures and activities, and the pattern of discard by the inhabitants. The different functional classes clearly have different distributions across the site.

The stratigraphic record from the excavated pits indicates that Structures One and Two were constructed on a low dune which sloped away to the south and east. Overall, the immediate doorway area outside Structure One and along the stone pathway contains relatively low densities of artefacts. However, this rises sharply after about four meters, with high densities of all classes of materials within squares T98, T99, U98 and U99, and to a lesser extent in T2. The four T and U squares are on the edge of the original dune and are therefore relatively shallow in depth. A similar pattern appears outside of Structure Two with low densities in B97 and C98, increasing in Z93 and C99. It is probable that in addition to being the area into which sweepings were pushed, the T and U squares also indicate the 'toss zone', that is the area into which larger items could be casually tossed from the doorway, beyond which a more deliberate discard effort would be required. This is akin to the 'Schlepp effect' in artefact discard distributions described by Schiffer (1977:20).

The north–eastern squares suggest a large, possibly seasonally damp inter–dune depression up to a meter deep. There is no reason to believe that the dense deposit of faunal material, discarded to the 'front' (north) of the probable kitchen (Structure Two), is not a continuous deposit throughout the area and for some distance beyond. The decreasing artefact densities in squares P99 and U87 may suggest an outer boundary to the discard zone, although in the former instance an unknown quantity of the upper part of the deposit may have been removed or disturbed. Despite a distance of nearly 12 m from either doorway, the artefact densities in U93 remain quite high, particularly in the bone and shell classes. It is probable that the disposal of material into the midden area required a more deliberate process, that is, the refuse would have had to be carried away from the building to be discarded into the depression. This distance presumably reduced smell and kept insects, rodent and larger scavengers away from the immediate doorways. There are some differences in the distributions of mammal and fish bones, with the latter increasing slightly at a distance from the buildings. Minimal amounts of bone were recovered from within the buildings. Shell appears to be focused slightly closer to the buildings.

Personal category artefacts such as ornaments, clothing items (pins, beads and buttons) and recreational items are clustered within Structure One. These are generally small items which might have filtered through gaps in floorboards or between whalebone floor blocks. However, it would not be possible to claim that these internal distributions are sufficient to make any claim for activity areas within. However, the high densities of this class in the interior areas can be contrasted to the low densities of larger (ceramic, glass) or dietary items. Although there is a surprisingly low number of these artefacts immediately around the eastern doorway, several meters away in squares T98, T99, U98 and U99 there is a very high concentration. Clay pipe fragments mostly within the latter area, rather than inside Structure One. However, almost no personal items are located within the deeper midden deposits to the east which contain the majority of faunal remains.

Ceramic tablewares and glass share a similar distribution, concentrating along the southern margins of the excavated area (such as TP3 and F0–F2). As noted, some or all of the internal concentrations of glass almost certainly represent post–whaling casual occupation of the cottage. It is interesting to note that the similarities and differences between these and faunal material discard patterns of, which shares high densities on the southern margin, but also in the farther set of squares to the east (e.g. F87, U93). This might indicate similar processes of removal of larger and/or sharper edged refuse into low traffic or recognised discard areas and contexts.

CHAPTER 7
LIFE AT CHEYNE BEACH

The excavations at the Cheyne Beach whaling station were intended to address a variety of questions regarding the living and working conditions of the whalers and other persons living in this type of industrial maritime frontier community. The almost complete absence of historical description of life on the stations creates a particularly powerful ambiguity which could be approached only through exploration of the archaeological record. The original hope was that excavation would provide insights into how the whalers lived; the ways and conditions in which they were housed, and the diet and material culture of the labour force. If possible, the question of status difference within the workforce and other elements of social organisation within the frontier community could also be examined. A parallel aim was to examine the economies of the station for insights into trade and supply systems into these remote areas, as well as evidence of engagement with and adaptation to the environment.

As described in Chapters 5 and 6, the scope of the investigation narrowed into an intensive excavation of a single archaeologically rich part of the site, with the intention that this provide detailed insights. Interpretation of this material record is therefore made with reference to the known historical context of the whaling station and the development of European settlement within the Albany region and the known history of the Cheyne Beach station. In particular, it will be argued below that the excavated components of the site and the material remains within relate to the occupation of John Thomas, his wife and family.

THE ALBANY SETTLEMENT

Chapter Two has already described some aspects of the history of Western Australia, including the migration boom and bust, the difficulties in adapting agriculture and pastoralism to local conditions and the social and economic troubles which arose from these situations. Although the situation stabilised during the 1840s with a slow re–commencement of immigration and industry (including whaling), the population remained small and short of capital. New agricultural and pastoral settlements spread along the lower west coast harbours and inland across the Darling Ranges, assisted in part by the improvement of land routes resulting from the 1850s introduction of convict labour. New outposts were also established to the north of the Swan River, opening frontiers for miners, pastoralists, pearlers and whalers. Even into the 1860s and 1870s the colony remained focused on primary production, rather than development of manufacturing industries.

European settlement and population growth along the south coast proceeded at an even slower. Considered part of the Swan River colony, the harbour town of Albany had been established several years earlier in 1826 as a military outpost and penal settlement. In March 1831 it was officially handed over to the new Western Australian administration and declared a free settlement, but for many years was to remain a marginal and often moribund frontier village. As well as sharing most of the woes of Perth's early crises, Albany's distance from the administrative centers on the west coast and consequent delays in communication further exacerbated problems. Contemporary writers observed that by sail from Fremantle it took a week or ten days just in rounding Capes Naturaliste and Leeuwin (Burton 1954:37). The overland route proved to be an equally long and arduous trek of twelve days or more and it was not until 1872 that a telegraph link was finally created between the two communities (Glover 1979; Garden 1977). Despite King George Sound being a superior harbour, it was in the interests of the Perth administration to keep Fremantle as the focus of trade.

Contemporary descriptions of the Albany settlement are disparaging.

> The population of the Sound is approximately 200 or 250 persons. It is really surprising how they continue to live, as there appears to be scarcely any trade or means of support. The settlers are chiefly employed in hunting the kangaroo, for the sake of that animal's skin. The settlers depend chiefly, not upon agriculture, but upon the sale of kangaroo skins, whale oil, and the other sales and barterings effected during the occasional visits of the few American whalers that call at the Sound for wood and water (PG 10/2/1849).

While possibly exaggerating, these comments do contain an element of truth. Blue Book statistics show the population remained under 300 persons for over 20 years and, despite some gaps in the colonial records, does not appear to have passed 1500 persons for another 15 years after this (Table 7.2). Between 1852 and 1880 Albany rose to prominence when it was selected over Fremantle as the Peninsular and Oriental (P&O) Steam Navigation Company's coaling depot. During this time it became the regular port–of–call for steamers, received the mails from England and was the main contact point between Western Australia and the rest of the world. The construction of a jetty and facilities, as well as the permanent employment of over 30 people at the P&O depot and offices (Bulbeck 1969), were also important stimulators to the local economy. However, aside from these monthly diversions, the tone of the settlement often remained depressed until later in the 19th century.

CHEYNE BEACH

The establishment of a whaling station at Cheyne Beach followed the familiar pattern of choosing an anchorage already frequented by American whalers. The 1846 season was a partnership between John Craigie, Solomon Cook and John Thomas. In the following year this association had dissolved, with the party run by Thomas as owner, manager and chief headsman. Cheyne Beach operated as a two boat fishery with a crew of 12 to 14 men under Thomas's control until 1868 or 1869. Details of the industrial history are presented in Appendix A. From 1870 to 1877 the station was used by a variety of shore parties, although it is possible that for some of this time it was actually Thomas's party under different management. John Thomas was therefore associated with the Cheyne Beach whaling station for at least 22 years of the 31 year period during which the location was used, and can be seen as a major influence on the formation of the archaeological record of the site. Unfortunately, the historical record of Thomas and life at Cheyne Beach is scant and confused.

The Western Australian Dictionary of Biography suggests that John (or James) Thomas was born in 1818 and arrived in Western Australia with his parents in 1829 (Erikson 1988:3039). It also states that in early 1835 he was sentenced to seven years transportation to Tasmania for participating in the plundering of the schooner *Cumberland* after it was wrecked approximately 30 km south of Fremantle. Contemporary court records contradict this, reporting that John Thomas (junior) received only six months hard labour (CSO 37/86, 12/1/1835), with some suggestion that he did not actually leave Western Australia. This is unfortunate for our story, as a Tasmanian connection would have provided a convenient explanation for his whaling skills. However, Cheyne Beach whaler Capt. John Sale's (1936) memoirs also suggest that the John Thomas of Cheyne Beach was of Tasmanian origin. With several persons in Western Australia bearing the same name, we can only be sure we are following the career of the correct man from 1846 and his first involvement at Cheyne Beach.

In 1851 John Thomas attempted to purchase the Cheyne Beach station site, but was refused because it would have included the anchorage area. His second attempt to obtain this property came in April of 1855, when the Government negotiated with Thomas to purchase his Albany town lot which was required for the expansion of the neighbouring Convict Depot. Thomas offered to swap this land for 10 acres at Cheyne Beach, later reducing this to a request for only four acres. The government appears to have made a counter–deal, offering instead a remission of £10 on the (unstated) purchase price of this land (Surveyor General 1354:226, 30/4/1855). Thomas must have accepted these terms as soon afterwards he was also granted an eight year tillage lease for Bald Island (Surveyor General 1430:242, 5/9/1855). Curiously, a study of title and lease records for both the Kent and Plantagenet districts failed to provide any supporting evidence for either Thomas's ownership of the town lot, or for a subsequent purchase or lease of either the Cheyne Beach or Bald Island areas.

The few documents which mention John Thomas provide little real information about the man. The later memoirs of McKail (1927) and Sale (1936) appear to afford him a level of respect as the recognised leader of Albany's whaling community. In addition, he is known to have trained or employed key identities such as Thomas Sherratt, John Cowden, Nehemiah Fisher, Hugh McKenzie and Cuthbert McKenzie, all of whom would later form their own whaling parties and become key identities in the last phase of shore whaling.

Thomas is referred to in most accounts as 'Captain Thomas' (McKail 1927; Sale 1936; Erikson 1988:3039), while on a petition of 1855 he signed himself as "Whaling Master" (CSR 338/60: 3/7/1855). It is possible that outside of the whaling season Thomas was involved with the coastal trade, with an 1855 document referring to him as the owner of a schooner (CSR 338/23: 20/3/1855). In 1871 he was also listed as a boat owner (Erikson 1988) although the craft was unnamed. Sale (1936) claims that Thomas salvaged material from the *Arpenture* which wrecked opposite the Cheyne Beach whaling station in 1849 and employed a Mr. Metcalf (possibly the American deserter known to have worked at nearby Cape Riche (Erikson 1988:2151) to build a small vessel called the *Mary Ann*. The registration of this vessel has not yet been confirmed.

Perhaps the most significant pieces of anecdotal information concern John Thomas' personal life. He was married to Fanny Davis and had three daughters, Mary Ann (born 1849), Fanny Sophia (born 1850), and Katherine Ellen (birth date unknown, but known to have been the youngest child) (Erikson 1988; McKail 1927). Sale (1936) notes that

> Mr. Thomas continued to work at Cheyne Beach where he brought up his family of three, and all married at Albany to become Mrs. Geak, Mrs. John Cowden, and Mrs. George Broomhall.

This brief statement introduces two significant factors into the consideration of the occupation of Cheyne Beach. The first is that Thomas's wife and small children lived at the whaling station, possibly for a period of years. As will be argued below, the archaeological data provide strong support for the excavated structures and artefacts being associated with the household of this small family unit, rather than the seasonal labour force.

The second factor emerging from Sale's memoir is the possibility that John Thomas and family lived at Cheyne Beach throughout the year, rather than just during the whaling season. In an 1854 court action by Thomas he also describes himself as living 'at Cheyne's Beach, 30 miles from Albany, where I carry on a whaling station' (PG 24 March 1854). In May of 1855 there is a report that Thomas and three others had been swept out to sea for several days on Thomas's schooner while en route to Cheyne Beach (CSR 338/23: 20/3/1855; Inq 4/4/1855; Inq 18/4/1855). Even allowing several weeks for pre–season preparation, this would be nearly two months earlier than might be expected if the station was only used for whaling purposes.

As described above, tracing Thomas's land ownership has proved difficult. Even prior to selling his town lot to the Government sometime after April 1855, there is no clear evidence for him living in Albany.

Having noted the historical evidence suggesting that the Cheyne Beach whaling station was not a purely male–inhabited seasonal camp, it then becomes necessary to consider a range of other factors. These include effects upon the social organisation of the camp, the nature of the site and buildings, as well as possible variations within other aspects of the material culture. Even greater differences might be expected if Thomas and his family did maintain a year–round occupation of Cheyne Beach throughout some or all of the 22 years or more of his involvement with the station. In this latter case, the possibility of a more permanent use of the site did not arise until late in the analysis, and therefore was not specifically tested. The implications of these various scenarios will be investigated as part of the interpretation of the archaeological evidence, provided below.

INTERPRETATION OF THE ARCHAEOLOGICAL EVIDENCE

Some years after the original research for this volume was completed a brief account was found of an 1889 visit to Cheyne Beach, just over a decade after the abandonment of the whaling station. The anonymous traveller records an overland trip from Albany to the 'fishery reserve', describing the bleached bones of whales scattered on the shores of the bay and the 'ruins of a number of stone huts'.

> The walls are composed of stones or whalebone cut into blocks and used as large bricks. Invariably these bone bricks have been used as flooring. The stone used for walls seems to be a soft sandstone nature, red and yellow. The fishing settlement must have looked very bright and picturesque in the days of its existence as a fishery (Albany Mail 18/12/1889).

The writer also notes the remains of flower gardens at the front of 'the cottage', a freshwater well situated behind the site, and that the station look–out had been posted on the high rock on the adjacent hill.

The description of Cheyne Beach correlates with some aspects of the archaeology, but also raises ambiguities. As described in Chapters 5 and 6, the surviving stonework associated with Structure One appears unlikely to have supported full height walls. The stones are roughly laid, unmortared and often comprise of only a row of large boulders, suggesting low retaining walls to allow the floors to be levelled rather than foundations. The single wooden post found in–situ in the southeast corner also suggests a wooden framed wall. Of course, the 1889 description does not eliminate the possibility that the station originally had a mixture of stone and wooden buildings. Insufficient of Structure Two was excavated to be certain of its construction. Whalebone flooring is certainly evident in the archaeological record for both buildings, while several fragments of whalebone trimmed into blocks or bricks were also found.

The overall size and nature of Structure One is comparable to the standard domestic cottage plan commonly seen throughout much of 19th and early 20th century Western Australia (Oldham 1968; White 1979). Iron and copper nails were found across the site, although it is impossible to determine if these might have come from walls or roofs. The 1870 census which includes the first attempt to document the building stock of the colony, provides little insight into the latter, noting that of the houses 'of less than four rooms' in the Albany/Plantagenet district, 68 were shingled, 69 were thatched, and four roofed in iron or slate (Knight 1870:40). The distribution of flat glass is suggestive of windows in the area of squares C7 and V6, roughly equally positioned along the western side of Structure One. There was no clear evidence for a beach side (front) door, other than a possible path surface, although only a few squares were excavated along the western wall.

Although there is no physical evidence of an internal division in Structure One, this is not particularly surprising given the apparent absence of post–holes or footings trenches for several of the external walls and the damage from the 1987 trenching. The almost complete lack of structural hardware and furnishings also makes interpretation of internal areas difficult and there is no clear evidence for internal walls. If the structure functioned as barracks for the men, their needs might have been best served by a single large room. If it was John Thomas' residence an internal wall may have been a more appropriate, particularly as his three daughters may well have lived there until their late teens (Erikson 1988). The 2 x 3 m addition to the southeast corner may have formed an additional sleeping/storage area. Further evidence supporting Structure One as Thomas' residence is provided below.

The limited excavation of Structure Two means little can be said, although it is possible that this was an external kitchen connected to the main cottage by the stone flagged pathway. The proximity of this structure to what appears to substantial amounts of dietary refuse, discarded into what were originally natural depressions around its edge, also supports this sort of usage.

There is no doubt that the station would have included the same variety of industrial and domestic structures common to other whaling stations, and the 1889 description certainly makes it clear that there were several buildings on the site. The only other historical reference to another structure is a rare anecdotal account of life at the station which incidentally describes one of the whalers walking to 'the cookhouse' to ask the station cook for cups of tea and cakes for the men (McKail 1927). Presumably the men slept in a separate barracks or several cottages. Elements of this description might fit with Structures One and Two as barracks and cookhouse, although as will be argued below the artefact evidence suggests these were associated with the Thomas family.

Where the living structures and cookhouse for the whalers were situated is uncertain. However, based on the topography of the site and especially the low–lying swampy ground to the south of Structure One, it is very likely that these were to the north and northwest of the excavated areas. If Structure One was the home of the Thomas family, there may have been some separation between the areas. Regardless, this would place the workers' buildings within the area of the current car park; although there is a possibility they may have been in the fore dune area immediately west of Structure One.

Excavation within the car park was not permitted and it is probable that any structural remains would have been graded away, although deeper deposits may exist below the fill such as seen in pits P98 and P93. A test pit (TP1) dug approximately 30 m north of Structure Two along the northern edge of the car park on a small sandy ridge at the base of the slope contained artefacts (sheathing nails, transfer print ceramics, bone fragments) comparable to the excavated areas to a depth of 10 cm. This ridge stands more than a meter higher than the adjacent car park level and provides further support for extensive grading and destruction of deposits. Several small test pits in the dunes north of Structure One, as well as close inspection of vehicle access tracks cut through to the beach, failed to recover evidence of further structures or significant artefact deposits.

In the late 19th–early 20th century a wool store was constructed at Cheyne Beach by the Hassell family, allowing wool from hinterland farms to be gathered close to the harbour awaiting shipment (C. Westerberg pers. comm. 1992). Although no historical evidence survives on the nature of the building, which was situated in the area of the current car park, a wool store of similar age which survives at Cape Riche, the next closest harbour, is constructed of stone. It is therefore possible that the stone from the buildings of the Cheyne Beach whaling station were salvaged for foundations or walls of the wool store.

There is even less evidence for the location of industrial buildings such as tryworks, whalecraft and oil storage, or boat sheds. As described in Chapter 4 there is a flat area on the southwest edge of the point, immediately above a granite sheet leading down to a deep scour channel. Although close to the end of the point, the ridge of the headland still provides some shelter from the worst of the weather. An eroding surface on this flat area shows a layer of ash, rusted iron flakes and some 19th century artefacts. Excavation was not possible, although this may be a reasonable position for a tryworks. Once barrelled the oil could have been rolled to a storage area closer to the beach. The beach area to the front and north of Structure One continues to be ideal for small boat launching and anchorage.

Domestic Life

Tablewares

In the first instance it is the nature, diversity and context of the Cheyne Beach tablewares, mainly in the form of ceramic fragments, that indicate Structure One and the associated refuse deposits are unlikely to have been associated with the all–male seasonal labour force. Despite the complexities of consumer behaviour making simple correlations between ceramic values and status problematic (Klein 1991; Crook 2005; Wurst 2006), tablewares are arguably still the main archaeological markers of economic level and social affiliation available to us. The simplest understanding is that households with high income and upper social status will have more and better ceramics than low socio–economic households. It might be expected that the isolated situation and the heavy usage likely to result from feeding a dozen or more men would necessitate the use of cheaper and sturdier creamware tablewares, or metal tablewares. However, the ceramics recovered are of the expensive transfer–printed earthenwares, generating a high CC index value, with attention apparently paid to creating near–matching sets of shell–edged and willow pattern. There is also the use of handled tea cups with matching saucers and other service forms such as tureens, unlikely to be of concern to a male industrial labour force in a frontier situation, although as discussed in Chapter 8 this may be another assumption that should be challenged.

The second level of interpretation is the symbolic nature of the ceramic assemblage, suggesting that selection and purchase is gender based (i.e. women have greater control of the domestic domain into which ceramics fall) and that changes in the nature of ceramics can be linked to changes in domestic modes and rituals. If we follow Yentsch (1991) in perceiving ceramic selection as a female domain, we might envisage Fanny Thomas having insisted upon maintaining the symbols of status and the significance of domestic ritual despite distance, isolation and other prevailing social conditions. Given the limited precision in dating the use of the ceramics, it is possible that some these were slightly out–of–style and cheaply purchased items (Lawrence 2006:111). Non–ceramic tablewares such as the goblet base, tumblers and decanter provide further support for maintenance of desired domestic patterns. This is discussed further in the concluding chapter.

The historical record gives no specific indication of the socio–economic level of John Thomas and family. However, Thomas' ownership of the whaling station, property and a vessel, plus the eventual marriage of his daughters to middle echelon public servants, the Albany Harbour Master and Post Master (Erikson 1988), are suggestive of the equivalent of at least middle class status or higher within the settlement. Remaining conscious of and performing current fashion would have been of some importance in maintaining that status.

Finally, the tablewares can be used to inform on access to markets, with an implication that more remote communities will have limited access to consumer goods and a reduced choice, which will potentially also be of lower quality. It is also assumed that the time lag between factory production and local purchase will be significantly greater for more isolated households. Cheyne Beach is a decidedly 'frontier' situation, at the site of an isolated outpost of an isolated settlement of the British Empire at the extreme far end of the trade network. The role of the ceramics in understanding the trade systems in operation during the early settlement period will be discussed further below.

Beyond the tablewares, the preparation and storage categories are under–represented. As stated earlier, no preparation wares such as pots or pans or associated implements such as knives were recovered. Given between 20 and 30 years of occupation of the site, more cutlery and non–flatware tableware items might have been expected. Although it is possible that a separate kitchen was located elsewhere on the site, the large quantities of faunal material still suggests that Structure Two was a food preparation area, or that one was nearby. It is possible that the under–representation of these other wares is a function of the excavation strategy, and that further sampling to the south of Structure Two, adjacent to TP3, might yield relevant items.

Personal

While many of the individual artefacts within the Personal category could easily be used by the male workers at the station, collectively the assemblage lends weight to the picture of a family maintaining particular social and domestic standards. The harmonica, clay tobacco pipes, and penknife are most likely to fall within the domain of John Thomas, rather than the female members of the family. Similarly, there are items which are closely associated with the female members of the household, including the pearl shell hairpin, the small comb and decorative carved bone piece. The sewing activities represented by the many pins, thimbles and glass beads are part of a female domestic and leisure realm. The dice, gaming board pieces, and marbles can be linked with the toy tea set to create an image of the family's, and especially the children,

amusements. Conversely, the fragments of slate writing tablets and pencils indicate that their schooling, probably through Fanny Thomas, remained important (c.f. Davies 2005).

Clothing

Despite a variety of metal, bone, glass and shell buttons and the several metal buckles recovered from Cheyne Beach, most are of plain types not described or discussed by collectors and have limited diagnostic value (e.g. Epstein and Safro 1991; Whittemore 1992). It seems that most of the bone buttons and the one–piece and two–piece stamped brass and composite buttons are cheap, mass produced items (Cameron 1985).

Many of the fastenings are associated with utilitarian work clothing, including pants, trousers or overalls of canvas or leather (Cameron 1985:20; Birmingham 1992). This is consistent with what might be expected from John Thomas' roles as whaler and sailor. Although there are no specific descriptions of the forms of clothing used by the whalers, one could suppose that it would have been similar to that used by fishermen. During the mid–19th century this would have comprised canvas trousers, possibly with woollen leg warmers, an oiled smock or knitted wool guernsey, oiled leather boots, and an oiled or tarred hat (Levitt 1986; de Marly 1986). In heavy weather a mackintosh might be worn, although the traditional heavy oilskins remained the most commonly used protection (Levitt 1986). There could of course be variations, such as oiled bib–and–brace overalls or dungarees, sometimes with all–in–one boots (Williams–Mitchell 1982). The freezing winds and sudden squalls of the southern coast would require boatmen to wear warm and waterproof gear. Many of the above clothing items would require buttons, presumably of the common types recovered from the excavations.

The two possible naval buttons are interesting but may have come to the site through a variety of processes. Rather than speculate on Thomas' maritime connections or the possibility of a visiting naval vessel, the most parsimonious explanation is simply that they came as slops or clothing traded from a passing ship.

A proportion of the buttons can potentially be ascribed to the presence of women (and children) at the site, although care needs to be taken. It is possible that some of the smaller shell and glass buttons may have been clearly associated with women's clothing, although the most diagnostic items in this case are the metal hooks and eyes which were used to fasten items such as bodices (Sichel 1978).

Although alcohol bottles were found across the site, they are in remarkable low numbers, given that many almost certainly post–date the whaling period (Table 7.1). It has already been suggested that the shortage of storage items probably reflects the use of casks as bulk containers, in addition to which glass bottles may also have been considered a scarce resource to be curated and recycled. Alternatively, Thomas and his wife may have been temperate drinkers. The presence of a woman and several children might also have moderated the drinking behaviour of the other men at the station.

Container type	Minimum no.
ALCOHOL	
Bitters (brown)	1
Gin (square black)	5
Beer/ale (cylinder black)	5
Wine (circular green)	11
CONDIMENTS	
Pickles	9
Sauce and herbs	2
MEDICINAL	
Medicine/toiletry	15
Ointment	10

Table 7.1 Summary of Glass and Ceramic Containers

The assortment of patent medicine containers is similar to many urban and rural 19th century sites with limited access to medical care or more potent medications (e.g. Davies 2001). Albany was at least 50 km distant from Cheyne Beach by boat and it is possible that at times there was no qualified medical practitioner available at the settlement to assist in any case. Consequently, it is likely that all but the most severe ailments would have been treated at the station.

The interpretation that the deposits from which the patent medicine bottles were recovered are associated with the Thomas family, including Fanny Thomas and several young children, suggests a range of possible ailments and medical concerns beyond what might be expected in a male industrial workforce. However, the fragmentation of the bottles makes it difficult to identify specific treatments.

Diet

While it was felt that diet may have been the area in which adaptation to local conditions and resources would be most evident, this proved to not be the case. The Cheyne Beach faunal assemblage shows that, despite the whaling station's isolation, the diet of the inhabitants of Structure One was dominated by introduced species.

In particular, sheep bones greatly outnumber those of pig or cattle. While this may have been a function of personal taste or preference, historical data on stock numbers in the Albany/Plantagenet region suggests it may simply have been a matter of availability. The summary of Blue Book and census data presented in Table 7.2 shows that throughout the study period sheep were by far the most numerous and successful of the livestock and therefore the cheapest of the available domestic meats. Although focused on the 1830s period, Gardos' documentary analysis and excavations at the Old Farm Strawberry Hill in Albany recovered a similar pattern of utilisation of sheep as the major source of meat (Gardos 2004:52–54).

Blue Books indicate that in 1845 a sheep cost 8s. while a cow cost £10, although Cameron (1981) states that prices could vary wildly as settlers either tried to conserve their stock for breeding, or sold them to solve liquidity problems. Accounts of Albany during the 1840s and 1850s repeatedly describe the shortage of meat in the settlement (Burton 1954; Hassell n.d. a.). One memoir (Hassell n.d. a.) recalls that in the late 1850s beef was only available once a month and that even then this consisted only of the surplus from what was required by the regular P&O steamer. Most other times only mutton was available.

Another important indication of the state of food supply comes from a memorial of July 1855, signed by most of the adult European male residents of Albany and the surrounding region (including John Thomas), pleading with the government to lift the heavy harbour fees which were discouraging ships from visiting.

> We are deserted by the steamers and apparently by all other vessels, our stock of flour is exhausted, and many parties are now suffering great privation in consequence, and the prospects of the place are alarming (CSR 118/60: 3/7/1855).

This situation contradicts some of the historical claims that Albany's income was largely derived from supplying whaleships with fresh produce and meat. It may indicate distortions in the economy and agricultural practices of the region (e.g. a focus on livestock rather than agricultural production) which might have resulted in the dire shortage of certain essential foodstuffs. However, Garden (1977) also describes at some length the apparently lethargic attitude of many of the early Albany residents towards performing public works or even towards producing sufficient food.

Given the high representation of all skeletal elements of sheep at Cheyne Beach, it appears probable that animals were brought in live and slaughtered as necessary. Keeping meat on the hoof would have negated many of the difficulties of storage, even with the cold winter climate of the southern coast during the whaling season. A further advantage of sheep over cattle was ease of transport, as it is considerably easier to convey a live sheep, particularly in small boats. A small flock could also have been kept at the station for immediate needs.

It is possible that the tillage lease of Bald Island allowed John Thomas to run his sheep there without the need for pens or shepherds, a practice which continued during the late 19th and early 20th centuries (WA 17/5/1950; C. Westerberg pers. comm.). It would also have protected the flock from Aboriginal hunters.

With the evidence for exploitation of larger native fauna limited to a single macropod tooth, quokka appears to be the only regularly hunted terrestrial animal. Given their small size and limited meat content,

Quokka must have provided occasional variety, rather than a staple dietary item. While there may have been a mainland quokka population in the immediate vicinity of Cheyne Beach during the early settlement period, it appears likely that the animals consumed at the whaling station were taken from Bald Island. A possible scenario is that the whalers snared or chased down the small marsupials while visiting the island to round up sheep. If this was the case, their exploitation should be seen as harvesting of a captive resource, rather than hunting.

Another possible scenario for the quokka and seal remains is that sealers were still resident on Bald Island during the early occupation of the whaling station and that these animals formed part of a trade relationship between the two groups. William Nairn–Clarke's report on sealing activity along the south coast during the early 1840s stated that Bald Island was frequently occupied by sealers on account of the "wallabees" on it.

> One of the sealers, named 'Gemble' or familiarly 'Bob Gemble', originally from Van Diemen's Land, used to reside there with his black gins and his children for months together, and for aught that I know may still be there, or somewhere in the Archipelago, to this day. This man seals on his own account and his wives perform the part of a boat's crew (Nairn–Clarke 1842).

There is no documentary evidence to confirm that Gemble or other sealers were still present on Bald Island during the mid–1840s, contemporary with the Cheyne Beach whalers. It is probable that after Thomas was granted the lease of the island in 1855 these groups, if they were still active in the region, would have been prevented from camping there.

The relatively small proportion (by weight) of bird bones suggests that these also provided variety rather than a major component of the diet. While chicken is present in small quantities, the majority of the bone is from native species which might also have been collected on occasional forays to Bald Island. It is probable that the quantity of bird bone has been affected by post–depositional attrition, such as scavenging, described below.

Firearm artefacts in the form of percussion caps might be associated with foodways, especially the possibility of hunting. However, as percussion caps were detonated at the site of firing it seems incongruous that so many discharged examples were located in and around the station buildings. As hunting from the back door of the station appears implausible (except for possibly shooting at birds), the caps might be associated with post–whaling occupation of the buildings by fishing and hunting parties. Other evidence of this sort of casual use includes the high concentration of nails around the fireplace which is suggestive of the burning of old structural timbers or shingles, as well as smashed 'black' beer bottle in same area.

Dolphins, seals and sharks would have been regularly encountered during the course of whaling activities and may well have been slaughtered on an opportunistic basis, using the harpoons, lances and other implements normally carried in the whaleboats. The possibility of supply from sealers has also been mentioned above. The fish, crab and shellfish species recovered from the excavations reflect collection from the beach and reef within the immediate vicinity of the station. Despite the large quantities of fishbone recovered, no evidence was found of fishhooks or other procurement items, suggesting netting or lines were stored elsewhere.

One of the major unknowns in the diet of the whaling station is the consumption of whale meat. Whale meat, blubber, brain and some internal organs are certainly edible and are still valued foods for several cultures (Cousteau and Paccelet 1988). As described in Chapter Two, Aboriginal groups considered whale meat and blubber preferred foods and spent the whaling season close to the shore stations. However, whale meat is reputed to have a strong taste which does not necessarily appeal to the Western European palate. While pelagic whalers were known to eat whale meat on occasion and Mawer (1999:171) reproduces several recipes, it was neither a preferred or regular part of the diet (Shoemaker 2005). The same is likely to have been true for Cheyne Beach.

Archaeologically it is difficult to detect consumption of whale meat, blubber, or other body parts. Because of the size of the animals, meat could easily be carved off without cutting bone which would ultimately end up in a archaeological context. In the case of Cheyne Beach, whale bones were scattered over many areas of the site, particularly in close proximity to the buildings, although this is almost certainly from its structural use rather than as dietary discard.

Although the Cheyne Beach site offers good preservation, other taphonomic factors need to be considered, in particular the potential impact of dogs, dingoes and other scavengers. Walters' (1984) study of bone attrition from around a modern campsite is especially relevant given the midden–style disposal pattern not unlike that proposed for Cheyne Beach. Walters recorded the number of butchered bones of several taxa (including kangaroo, sheep, goanna and chicken) disposed of over a six month period and the levels of recovery of each type at the end of that period. In summary, the small animal bones suffered drastic reductions in number, with only 1–2% later recovered from the site, while the larger animal bones provided a recovery of between 9–14%. Dogs were identified as the primary scavengers, although rats, crows and goannas also contributed.

While there is no specific evidence that domesticated dogs were kept at Cheyne Beach their presence is not unlikely, while dingoes were still being reported in the immediate area as late as the mid–1960s (Storr 1965). With a substantial midden of animal bones plus whale carcasses beached in the shallows, the site must have presented a very attractive focus for scavengers. Piper's (1990) consideration of taphonomic factors on historic sites suggests that removal and reduction of bones by canines, pigs and other animals can be identified by the presence of gnawing marks. No such evidence was detected on any of the Cheyne Beach bones, although scavenged bones may have been removed beyond the site periphery (cf. Walters 1984).

If we follow Walters' (1984) study, it is probable that a high proportion of the smaller bone content of the midden, including quokka, fish and bird bones, has been removed or destroyed.

The larger bones (primarily sheep and pig) would also have been reduced in number, although the sheer mass of material discarded in the midden would guarantee a higher level of survival. A further influence on scavenging activity may well have been the (potential) seasonal occupation and abandonment of all or part of the site, influencing scavenger access to the midden.

YEAR	POPULATION			LIVESTOCK				CROPS* (acres)
	Male	Female	Total	cattle	sheep	goats	swine	
1835	103	47	150					
1836	120	50	170					
1837	122	52	174	45	534	0	30	30
1838	122	51	173	120	1200	2	55	30
1839	126	67	193	106	1734	9	0	27
1840	106	46	152	148	2210	9	6	67
1841	109	48	157	158	2300	15	15	76
1842	141	72	213	321	4983	25	64	81
1843	170	90	260	321	6090	10	43	103
1844	172	97	269	370	7500	10	43	125
1845	173	97	270	513	6980	0	67	89
1846	178	102	280	476	9220	0	120	168
1847	175	104	279	565	9716	5		235
1848	186	114	300	515	9582	0	85	212
1849	184	122	306	572	10407		232	258
1850	181	127	308	626	12618		126	250
1851				700	13220	0		259
1852	173	151	324	703	17271	0	136	286
1853	308	195	503	748	21017	5	339	267
1854	290	238	528	703	19432	7	204	286
1855				757	24000	5	277	414
1856				700	27897	17	280	483
1857				718	29434	9	438	512
1858				776	31646	32	674	624
1859	590	261	851	1223	36736	35	706	800
1860				820	36168	48	505	841
1861	605	275	880	832	29201	55	451	805
1862				980	43418	22	561	973
1863				1209	50837	30	561	1126
1864				1556	59181	31	913	1297
1865				1331	61639	32	813	1186
1866				1388	74411	25	685	1256
1867				1268	74390	19	739	1184
1868				1351	82648	43	771	1386
1869	1064	587	1651	935	89337	80	723	1679
1870	998	587	1585	1139	88707	32	480	1978
1871				978	89951	70	649	2037
1872				1121	92559	67	1128	1825
1873				1350	112446	74	1419	2355
1874				1301	103333	28	514	460
1875				1538	124005	42	272	473

* 'Crops' includes wheat, barley, oats, rye, potatoes, maize, vineyards, kitchen gardens, beans and pulses, and artificial pastures.

Table 7.2 Albany District Population, Agricultural and Stock returns (Blue Books 1835–1875 & Census reports).

The non–faunal faunal component of the whaler's diet would have included flour, potatoes and other vegetables. Considering the number of men to be fed, the largest proportion of this would have to have been brought into the site, probably from Albany. However, it is probable, particularly given the presence of Fanny Thomas and children, that there would also have been a small cottage garden to grow at least some fresh produce. The 1889 description of the station describes the ground near the fishery being 'covered in clovers and grasses, doubtless the result of the whalers' cultivation' (Albany Mail 18/12/1889). Cheyne Beach farmer Charles Westerberg related that a son of one of the Cheyne Beach whalers whom he had met at the site had indicated that the 'vegetable patch' had been in the low area to the southeast of the site. No landscape or floral evidence was found in this area, nor were there any agricultural implements located during the excavation. No large seeds were recovered from the excavations. Palynological study might be possible, although the alkaline conditions of the site are not conducive to preservation.

The glass bottles included at least 11 which contained pickles, sauces and other condiments including vinegar. Condiments such as pickles and sauces were common methods of flavouring food. On the frontier they could also make stored or unfamiliar foods more palatable. Heavy fragmentation means the real count is likely to be much higher, with the same problems of curation and recycling as for the other glass vessels.

The analysis of the faunal material provides the most significant insight into the relationship between the inhabitants of Cheyne Beach and the surrounding environment. In many respects the diet at Cheyne Beach was maritime or marine in nature, with little evidence of intrusion into the hinterland behind the station for the purpose of hunting. Even the sheep and quokka would appear to have been captive populations on Bald Island, accessible only by boat and waiting to be harvested when necessary. With an eight year lease of the island, Thomas could have simply left his stock for long periods of time. Similarly, the more obvious marine resources are all readily accessible along or very near the shores of Cheyne Beach itself. The emphasis on these resources may well indicate both a reluctance and limited need to move beyond the immediate coastal zone. The whalers lived the season in almost constant readiness for the hunt, which would have been interrupted by excursions away from the coast. It is worth noting that the Cheyne Beach crew registrations always included a cook, which is also reported in anecdotal accounts (McKail 1927).

As there is strong evidence that Structures One and Two and the adjacent midden deposits are associated with the Thomas family, the question arises whether their diet was the same as the workers. Undoubtedly they suffered similar constraints of supply and availability, although their diet is unlikely to have been identical to that of the whalers. Similarly, Fanny Thomas is likely to have prepared the food for herself and her family in her own kitchen, separate to the cook. Consequently, while the Cheyne Beach faunal material provides an insight into supply and diet preference on the maritime frontier, it does not allow us to make any statements regarding the diet of the whaling workforce itself.

There are few historical indications of the foods consumed by whalers at other Western Australian stations and there are few comparable analyses of non whaling sites. The Carnac station equipment lists various items, including 100 bushels of wheat, 10 lbs of pepper, 10 gallons of vinegar, 1.5 cwt (168 lbs) of sugar, one bag of rice, two casks of beef, two casks of salt pork, one ton of salt and one chest of tea (see Table 3.2). Furthermore, there was fishing equipment including a seine, 24 fishing lines and 20 shark hooks, clearly indicating the intention to exploit marine resources. Seymour's diary from Castle Rock frequently mentions the slaughter of cattle ('bullocs') for the station (Seymour n.d.). This diary also suggests that headsmen were given preferred meat cuts.

Thomas Sherratt's 1835–36 accounts ledger includes purchases associated with his 1836 Doubtful Island Bay whaling operation. Although it is difficult to be certain that these large quantities of food were solely for the whalers and not for his other stores and enterprises, the ledger includes nearly purchases of 2500 lbs weight of flour, over 250 lbs (and possibly as much as 550 lbs) of sugar, 160 lbs of biscuit, 672 lbs of beef and 418 lbs of pork (including 2 casks of beef and 1 of pork), 48 lbs of tea, almost 50 gallons of spirits, 17 gallons of rum, 4 pounds of pepper, as well as 4 dozen hooks and 8 fishing lines (Sherratt 1836). The remoteness of Doubtful Island Bay compared to Carnac and even Castle Rock's proximity to other settlements presumably meant that supplies for almost the whole season were required.

Curiously, sheep are not mentioned in any of these sources. Does this indicate that whalers expected beef rather than mutton, and that if excavations had been elsewhere a different faunal assemblage would have been obtained? Lawrence's work with the extensive documentary records for James Kelly's Tasmanian whaling operations, including crew agreements, indicate that whalers could be supplied mutton or beef depending on availability (Lawrence 2006:106). Presumably at Cheyne Beach mutton was more available.

Import Patterns and Local Manufacture

The bulk of consumer items arriving in Western Australia arrived through the normal process of local merchants being supplied from Britain. In terms of Cheyne Beach's position on the formal trade network, it should be considered that between 1852 and 1880 Albany's position as the P. & O. coaling port put it into regular direct contact with the trade route from Britain.

This presumes that the steamers would carry at least some cargo for the colony, other than the mail. If so, despite Albany's marginal status as a settlement, at times its access to the centers of production (in Britain) would have been comparable or possibly even better than that of the larger colonies of the west coast. Many of the Western Australian colonists maintained their links with relatives and friends in Britain, ordering specific items (sometimes requesting the 'latest fashions') directly through them or having standing annual orders via agents, to be sent out each year (e.g. Shann 1926; Hasluck 1955). New fashions in clothing, ceramics or other items could therefore have arrived from London within months of their debut. Consequently, the time–lag on the maritime would potentially be a matter of months, rather than years (c.f. Klein 1991).

The mean dates for the Cheyne Beach ceramics (particularly the shell–edged wares) are suggestive of a lag time, that is, they tend to date to the first half of the period of occupation. This may be a function of curation rather than a product of the trade networks, or purchase of cheaper, out–of–date ceramic styles and patterns. Apart from several slightly mismatched transfer prints, there is no evidence for Cheyne Beach or the colonies being a dumping ground for inferior goods or 'seconds'.

By the late 1860s the combined imports from other British colonies (Victoria, New South Wales, South Australia, Mauritius and Singapore) were rapidly approaching levels equal to those from Britain (Knight 1870). It is not possible to determine if this included colonial manufactured items, although the majority was most likely to have been re–exported items from Britain which would have added further delay to their arrival.

An unknown quantity of material also entered through the 'grey market' of American whalers. The whalers were willing (and preferred) to engage in barter with smaller settlements in return for meat, fresh produce and other supplies, including oil (Gibbs 2000). However, it is not possible to identify this component of the trade and supply within the archaeological record. In one respect the isolation of Cheyne Beach, particularly if it was occupied year–round, would have made it a possible contact point for American ships wishing to shelter or water in the bay. However, the antipathy between colonial and foreign whalers, and Thomas's previous objections to an American presence in the area (CSR 189/254: 23/8/1849, and see Appendix A) suggest that direct contacts may have been limited. Despite this, it is possible that Thomas might still have received American materials indirectly through George Cheyne's private supply depot at nearby Cape Riche, or through any of the other Albany merchants.

With the exception of several small and probably home–made artefacts in the 'personal' class, the Cheyne Beach assemblage provides no evidence for colonial production of consumer items. The Blue Books, census reports and other documentary sources suggest that besides primary producers there were only a limited number of manufacturers, mostly associated with garments (including a number of tailors and shoemakers) or various forms of carpentry. In 1870 there was only one nail maker listed and several gunsmiths, and the latter probably did not manufacture new firearms (Knight 1870). Although there were numbers of brickmakers, no potters or potteries are reported. In Albany in 1870 most of the male population registered was involved in pastoral and agricultural pursuits.

Aboriginal Contact

In many respects it is not surprising that the evidence for an Aboriginal presence at the site is extremely limited. First, the historical evidence suggests that the Aboriginal workers at the station were well integrated with their non–Aboriginal colleagues. They were presumably housed in the same barracks, or if not, were housed nearby. They were supplied with food, had access to steel knives and other manufactured items, and so had no need for recourse to flaked glass or stone. It is possible that, as at other stations, Cheyne Beach was regularly visited by large groups of Aboriginal people intent on feasting on the whale carcasses. Their camp, which has not been located but was probably at some point away from the main station, may contain flaked stone or glass tools or other evidence.

CONCLUSIONS

There is strong evidence to suggest that while the structures and artefact deposits excavated at Cheyne Beach were part of the whaling station, they were associated with the household of the manager, his wife and their three daughters, rather than with either the domestic or industrial activities of the whalers proper. For this reason the main questions based on investigating the operation and lifeways of a whaling station, focused on the nature of the industrial workforce, remain unresolved. However, the Cheyne Beach assemblage provides in many instances a range of far more interesting insights into the wider themes surrounding colonial adaptation, subsistence and supply on the maritime frontier.

The faunal evidence suggests a conservative diet based on mutton and less frequently beef and pork. The sheep were probably brought to the station live and may have been allowed to run free on Bald Island until needed. The pigs may also have been brought live, although the limited quantities and cuts of cattle bones would suggest the beef was probably a salted meat (i.e. brought in pre–butchered). There is little evidence for adaptation of diet or practices to take advantage of the native terrestrial fauna, although a variety of marine fauna was exploited. The emphasis on marine resources rather than terrestrial hunting may be interpreted as an attempt to minimise absences by those who procured the fauna from the immediate coast.

Despite a relatively isolated position at the end of the trade network, the consumer items, particularly the ceramics, are of an expensive kind, suggesting attention to status and domestic rituals was being maintained. The occupants of the buildings were still clearly dependent upon imports from Britain for most manufactured consumer goods, with little or no evidence for local industry beyond building materials and small personal and recreational items.

Although it is possible that women and children were present on other whaling stations, Cheyne Beach is probably the exceptional case resulting from the continuous association with the same manager/owner for over two decades. The only comparable situation of extended occupation, at Castle Rock, has no historical evidence of a family being present (Seymour n.d.). It can be expected that other parts of the site contain archaeological evidence of the industrial processes and the domestic arrangements for the crews. However, it is possible that the presence of women and children may have subtly influenced many of the behaviour patterns of the men, particularly in areas such as the consumption of alcohol.

CHAPTER 8
LIFE ON THE MARITIME INDUSTRIAL FRONTIER

The first chapter of this volume introduced the notion of the frontier as both geographical area and process, discussing the latter with respect to current archaeological and geographical models of colonisation and adaptation. Despite variations, most of these approaches incorporate elements such as information collection, environmental perception, cultural filters, positive and negative feedback through experimentation, and other learning processes. These learning processes contributed to the three basic categories of information which Rockman (2003:4) identifies as necessary for a colonising group: *locational* (location & characteristics of resources), *limitational* (cost and seasonal availability of recourses) and *social* (attribution of meanings to, or transformation of, environment). These contributed to the 'push' and 'pull' factors and decisions encouraging colonisation or making it unattractive.

As noted in Chapter One, Cameron's (1981) research on environmental factors and decision–making in the European settlement of Western Australia includes the period when the colonists first decided to engage in shore whaling. Undertaken as a study in historical geography, Cameron proposed that the settlers of the Swan River colony and its associated settlements (including Albany) had engaged in a process of differential learning about the environment, which they applied through agricultural and other land uses. A particularly relevant portion of Cameron's (1977, 1981) argument is his contention that the speed at which outcomes from particular learning and action sequences became available was a major determinant in the shift by Western Australian colonists from agricultural to pastoral production. Agriculture was seasonal, requiring six months or more before success or failure could be judged, and potentially many more years before the causes behind either could be determined. Even allowing that the success of certain staple crops was essential to achieve a stable subsistence base, the slow feedback loop, combined with the economic difficulties, land regulations and other factors described in Chapter Two, saw a shift in focus to non–agricultural concerns during the mid–1830s. Cameron (1981:152) suggests that while the raising of sheep was also seasonal, with the critical periods being shearing and lambing:

> the factors which were likely to have a detrimental effect were fewer (footrot, scab, poisonous plants), more immediate and apparent in their impact, and more easily avoided or treated.

In short, the increased rate of feedback on decisions and actions allowed faster learning and responses to environmental conditions. In addition to this, sheep and cattle could be easily moved within and between areas either to avoid hazards or exploit more favourable circumstances. This is not to say that the development of agriculture was set aside, or that pastoralism was immediately successful. It was not until the mid–1840s that either could be seen as achieving moderate success, with sheep emerging as the major export income provider.

While Cameron does not consider the role of shore whaling within his development sequence, the historical evidence of the emergence of the industry in Western Australia fits it neatly within his scheme. On one level the enthusiastic co–operation of diverse interests in the initial establishment of the colonial whaling industry during the mid–1830s can be seen as an attempt to tap into a flourishing international market and a means of raising much–needed liquid capital for the colony. On another level, while whaling had been promoted as a potential industry even prior to the settlement of the Swan River, its execution represented a significant departure from the original agricultural aims and efforts of the colonists. As noted above, while agriculture was never abandoned, the re–direction of capital, labour and enthusiasm towards whaling may be seen as a temporary conceptual retreat from the difficulties of adapting to the alien terrestrial environment, and a return to familiar marine resources.

As a conservative response to the utilisation of unfamiliar resources, the European colonisation of Australia is not unlike the 'coastal colonisation' paradigm which has been employed by some prehistorians (Bowdler 1977). Both groups colonised by sea, progressively occupied coastal areas, eventually moved inland along the river systems and finally populated the intervening areas. Despite obvious differences in the nature, style and rate of colonisation, both populations shared an initial attachment to the sea. During the 1830s, after the failure of their original agricultural ambitions (yet before the emergence of successful pastoral interests), the European colonists of Western Australia looked back to the sea as the environment most familiar *location* with respect to their points of origin. Unlike the land they had occupied, the resources of the sea were well known and readily visible.

Cameron's feedback loop would provide further support for shore whaling having been used as a retreat mechanism by the colonists. The nature of the industry is such that, unlike agriculture or pastoralism, the outcome of whaling required no lengthy waiting period before its short–term effectiveness could be measured. Despite the resource being somewhat capricious and difficult to understand (i.e. its *limitational* aspect), success or failure was almost immediate and could be readily measured in terms of barrels of oil at the end of the day. Because of this immediacy, the process also had an undeniable positive psychological effect upon the small non–Aboriginal population, who observed the spectacle with a high level of satisfaction. Even the partial success of shore whaling, when seen in the context of the limited local economic and social environments, provided an important bridge between the late 1830s and mid–1840s, and the successful development of stable pastoral and agricultural interests.

It is easy to dismiss the long–term economic significance of shore whaling by examining only the records of production and exports from the Swan River colony where, after the mid–1840s, whale products provided a limited proportion of the export revenues. However, in the context of the smaller settlements, whaling remained a significant component of the local economies until the 1870s. The fisheries supplemented the seasonal round of agricultural and pastoral pursuits, and in a broader perspective the presence of the foreign whalers provided a market for produce which simply would not have otherwise existed. In particular, the periodic resurgences of whaling may be seen as one of a series of activities including sandalwood gathering, gum and *Zamia* wool collection (the fiber from the butt of the *Zamia* palm which was used to fill pillows and mattresses), which all recurred, despite prevailing market values, during times of recession (Erikson 1974). The evidence provided in Chapter Three also shows that the industry supplied a regular and significant local demand for whale products, obviating or reducing the need for imports.

Another factor in the continuance of whaling into a period where it provided only marginal economic returns was that over the 44 years of the industry's existence it had become a well–entrenched part of the local scene, providing *social* value to the activity and the resource. Even if whaling was no longer vital to the well–being of the settlements, there are indications that there had developed a 'culture' of whaling, where it was a normal part of the seasonal round for at least some of the population. By the end of the industry there were second and even third–generation participants, as well as the continued involvement of men who had developed other, more significant interests. The most notable of these was John Bateman (Jnr), who, despite owning and operating a large and successful import and export company, apparently continued to act in the dangerous capacity of chief headsman for his whaling parties into his late 50s. John Thomas must have been a similar age by his retirement in the late 1860s.

The role of the foreign pelagic whaling fleets in the failure of the Western Australian shore fisheries to expand into a major industry cannot be overestimated. While the American whaleships provided the technology, skilled labour and intelligence on suitable locations which allowed the settlers to make their second (and to some extent even their first) attempts to establish a colonial fishery, the sheer number of these vessels provided a formidable degree of direct and indirect competition. The scale of foreign whaling activity had seriously depleted the stocks of coastally accessible right and humpback whales by as early as the mid–1840s, just about the time in which the colonial parties had begun to re–appear and the international oil market recovered. The decreased coastal whale populations effectively limited any opportunity for the less experienced colonial parties to generate sufficient profit to attract British investors, finance expansion of the shore stations, or develop the industry into the more lucrative pelagic industry. Despite the colonists' attempts to exert territorial prerogatives, American whalers were to remain a continual presence along the coast until the 1870s, with periodic resurgences of activity possibly in response to real or perceived recoveries of the whale stocks.

The further consequence of the foreign whaling presence was the instability which it created in the composition and skill levels of the colonial parties. Visiting foreign whalers were frequently in need of new crewmen to replace injured or deserted sailors. Members of the colonial fisheries, particularly those who had originally been deserters from whaleships, were often attracted onto these vessels by the offer of higher lays and the opportunity to leave the colony. The lack of off–season employment also encouraged skilled whalers to engage with passing American vessels.

THE MARITIME INDUSTRIAL FRONTIER AND THE EXPANSION OF SETTLEMENT

The relationship between whaling and the general expansion of European settlement on both the west and south coasts was not a particular concern of this study, although some comment might be made here. It has already been pointed out that colonial whaling, as a commercial activity, contributed to the survival of the smaller settlements, while the presence of foreign whalers provided a market for their produce. On the south coast the establishment of whaling stations generally preceded the pastoral settlement of the hinterland, with the fisheries often being established in the best harbours in each region. However, there appears to have been little direct relationship between the two activities, aside from some indications that whalers and pastoralists may have engaged in agreements associated with supply. On the west coast the appearance of whaling stations occurred as a function of the establishment of new settlements. They were often owned or operated by local settlers, although this changed over time with the emergence of the larger merchant owners. On both coasts the expansion of coastal trade networks to new settlements allowed movement into new areas.

In other parts of the world the activities of whalers have been clearly associated with the European exploration and colonisation of new regions, especially the Pacific, with some writers recognising a distinct 'whaling frontier' (Henderson 1975; Gibson & Whitehead 1993: x). The foreign pelagic whalers were acknowledged as making significant contributions to the early settlers' knowledge of the Western Australian coast and environment, including the *locational* aspects of the whale resource (Rockman 2003:4). There is no specific evidence that the colonial shore whalers made similar contributions, although they probably provided fellow colonists with information on the coasts, harbours, and hinterland areas they may have observed. This would have been particularly true on the more sparsely explored and less occupied south coast.

The spread and operation of the shore whalers corresponds closely to the notion of a maritime industrial frontier, featuring impermanent and/or short–term settlements of a specialised and resource focused nature, with limited concern or engagement with the surrounding environment, but a close link to wider economic fluctuations (Hardesty 1985:214; McNiven 2001:178). The seasonal whaling camps certainly fit the first criterion of being short–term and economically specialised, with no indication of any economic activities other than whaling occurring at the stations. Even Cheyne Beach, which may have had a lengthy occupation by the Thomas family, was abandoned after the closure of the station without transforming into a permanent settlement.

As part of the core–periphery relationship the raw materials of whale oil and bone were sent through the trade networks for sale on the London market, with a lesser amount retained for national (in this case Western Australian) consumption. Relative success of the industry, rather than of individual stations, was dependent upon the current market prices for oil and bone which were themselves affected by the totality of global whaling activity. The whaling industry and especially the American pelagic fleet as the main operator were sensitive to a wide range of natural and civil disasters, wars and other factors which affected production and therefore flowed through to influence the value of the Australian production. By the mid–1860s the shift to mineral oils, changing women's fashions reducing the need for whalebone, as well as the invention of plastics, also reduced market demand.

Despite its international aspect, the nature and intensity of Western Australian whaling also reflected local and national economic and social conditions. Hardesty's (1985) characterization of industrial frontier settlements such as mining camps is suggestive of at least semi–permanent (year–round) occupations, surviving for at least several years before the resource was exhausted, then resulting in either abandonment or change in resource focus. In contrast, most of the Western Australian whaling stations, with the possible exception of Cheyne Beach, were only seasonal camps closely associated with the coastal agricultural and pastoral settlements and offering a form of supplementary income, particularly during marginal periods. However, the other general features of the cosmopolitan frontier still apply however. The short occupation appears to have discouraged indigenous developments, with even the atypical settlement at Cheyne Beach showing minimal response to the environment with its reliance on domesticated animals for food. It can be supposed that the more typical stations and particularly the later short–term occupations of sites would have encouraged reliance upon salted or prepared foods.

Hardesty (1985) proposes that standardisation is a feature of industrial frontiers, with groups attempting to use the same technologies and adaptive solutions despite environmental differences. When innovations were produced, the connection between the industrial settlements and the regional/national system produced almost simultaneous changes throughout the industrial frontier. Both the west and south coast whaling parties in Western Australia seem to have followed the same series of adaptations, decreasing in size, reducing capital expenditure and fixed works, and later increasing their mobility and using multiple stations as the *limitational* aspects of whaling became apparent (Rockman 2003:4). As part of the international whaling tradition, the colonial fisheries could receive innovations in whaling technology almost immediately through their contact with American vessels. Whether innovations such as gun harpoons were immediately implemented (and consistently used) to replace the older forms is another question. Apart from harpoons and lances, the actual process of whaling carried on internationally appears to have undergone little change throughout the study period. It was only after the 1880s that the new, mechanised forms of chasing, killing and processing revolutionised the industry.

Another feature of the industrial frontier is the ecology of resource patch use, abandonment and possible re–use. In essence, the resource at a particular place will be used until its value or yield drops below the average for other patches in the area. Hardesty (1985:216) suggests that the rate of movement among patches is dependent upon

> the rate of patch renewal, variability of patch, size of patch, technological efficiency of exploitation ('capture' cost), transportation cost and market price.

Changes in transport methods, costs, or particularly in the efficiency of exploitation through innovations in techniques or technology may make a previously abandoned or unprofitable patch worth re–occupation, or encourage continued occupation of a patch currently being worked.

Although this model is normally applied to fixed resources of a renewable or non–renewable nature, it may provide some insight into some aspects of site use and abandonment evident in the progress of the shore whaling industry. The success of the shore whaling industry hinged primarily on the exploitation of two migratory whale species, the right and humpback whales, as they passed along the south and west coasts. Although we can presume that through an extended period of personal observation and collection of intelligence from other sources the shore whalers built up a fairly good picture of the migratory patterns of right and humpback whales, we do not know how these men understood or interpreted this information in ways that influenced decisions to change stations. For instance, which factors were associated with a change in location?

a. Perceived inadequacies in the nature of the station site, including its distance from Albany, versus the superiority of another site?

b. Real or perceived patterns of behaviour on the part of the whales, using or not using particular bays, or even learning to avoid particular bays after several seasons of shore whaling (in essence, the resource at that spot becoming 'exhausted')?

c. General reduction in whale stocks resulting in fewer whales visiting the less favourable bays?

There are other factors which might be mentioned, although the core of the question is: why were some bays abandoned for over 20 years, overlooked and then re–occupied later? The answer may well be the major innovation of the colonial whalers, the split season. Sites which had presumably been abandoned because the resource (migrating whales) had fallen below marginal value could be re–occupied for shorter periods at the peak of the migration through that point. Rather than wait for the normal decline in numbers as the increasingly reduced population of whales passed by, the party would then move to another position as much as several hundred kilometres away either to exploit the same migratory group, or attempt to catch the migration of a different species which might not have passed the first station. As suggested earlier, in the case of the Western Australian shore whalers the actual impetus to innovate and the cyclic pattern of the industry is as likely to have been the result of local economics as it was due to the effects of international market trends.

WHALING AS INDUSTRIAL PROCESS

The Western Australian shore whalers were clearly part of the tradition of shore and pelagic whaling that emerged during the late 18th and early 19th centuries. The constant flow of men and equipment through the medium of visiting American whaleships ensured that the colonial whaling parties employed the same terminology and techniques and rapidly received the latest technologies. However, the documentary and archaeological records demonstrate that the economic and social conditions of the colonies, together with increasing familiarity with environmental conditions and the nature of the resource, combined to encourage the development of several distinctive strategies in the operation of the Western Australian industry, or more properly industries. The growth of two parallel but almost completely unrelated shore whaling industries on the south and west coasts underscores the physical, economic and social separation between the two main Western Australian settlements through their first several decades. It also provides useful comparisons and insights into the responses of both groups.

Chapters Two to Four have shown that in their initial conception of a whaling industry the colonists, particularly on the west coast, attempted to form large, elaborately organised companies and stations presumably emulating the sorts of operations known from other parts of Australasia and elsewhere. The initial failure to make returns on investments (resulting from inexperience, mismanagement and lack of resources) combined with the advent of a recession to produce a rapid demise of the first several stations. The re–emergence of the industry in the 1840s was on a different basis, with smaller parties of two boats on the south coast and three boats on the west coast, often employing only the minimum crew to run the fishery. Ownership was now based on much smaller groups of investors, sometimes individuals, with an eventual dominance by merchants or other persons with vested maritime interests. Government control on the lease of stations also discouraged expenditure on fixed improvements, as these would revert to the Crown at the end of the term, sometimes limited to only a single year. Scour channels, granite slabs, sandy beaches and other natural features were utilised wherever possible in preference to construction of jetties, flensing decks or ramps, or other structures.

The most distinctive strategy which evolved on both coasts during the late 1850s was the split–season, with whaling parties moving progressively north to south or west to east, often between widely separated stations. One result of this pattern was the re–use of some of the earlier abandoned stations, although these shortened occupations (sometimes of two months or less) further discouraged the construction of semi–permanent camps or other infrastructure. The shift away from the traditional single station to the flexible mobile approach with smaller parties can be seen as a product of long–term learning processes. The whaling parties progressively scaled down to a size and form more appropriate to the local economies, and after a period of time were able to use the cumulative knowledge of both whale migration patterns and suitable station locations to optimise access to the resource. Unfortunately the other limiting factors, in particular the reductions of whale stocks, meant that despite increased experience, efficiency and innovations in strategies, the shore parties were unable to increase their returns significantly.

There is no doubt that the Western Australian whalers formed the bottom end of the spectrum of international whaling activity. As a whole the Western Australian whaling industry consisted of fewer parties with fewer boats and fewer workers than contemporary operations in other parts of Australasia. Modern historical studies of Australasian whaling (including those associated with archaeological surveys) have tended to stress examples of optimum operation, rather than exploring the normal or lower scale of the industry in terms of numbers of parties, boats or men. For instance, Pearson's (1985) discussion of whaling in Twofold Bay mentions that in 1842 there may have been up to 27 boats from several stations; that in 1844 Boyd had seven boats and that after the 1840s all of the stations scaled down operations. However, neither this paper nor the later study of Davidson's whaling station (Bickford et al. 1988) attempts to describe how many whaleboats might typically be found at the fisheries.

Table 8.1 compares the maximum number of whaling parties known to have operated a single, probably peak, year. Unfortunately, figures for Victoria and New South Wales are not available. In considering what might have been regarded as a 'typical' Australasian whaling party, Little (1969:114) suggests that a 'competitive station had at least three or four boats...and some maintained a double party of six boats', with the average fishery requiring 30 men. Morton (1982:224) echoes this statement, also describing a four boat fishery with at least 30 men as typical for New Zealand, with six or seven boat fisheries being considered 'larger' stations. He also notes that there were extremes, with one party of 11 boats at Otakou in 1835, as well as other reports of stations with 70 or 80 men, equivalent to 10 or more boats (Morton 1982:228). However, these are descriptions of larger companies, with Morton casually dismissing the 'tiny 'co–operatives' or other locally owned enterprises [carrying] on small operations' with local capital (Morton 1982:226) which appear to be the equivalent of the Western Australian whalers.

The composition of the several South Australian whaling parties listed in Table 8.2 probably represent the normal scale of operations for that region, although there is no explicit indication as to whether these were considered small, large or average sized stations. While of comparable size to the Western Australian operations it can be seen that, with the exception of D'Estrees Bay, the South Australian fisheries employed a higher ratio of men to boats than the Western Australian averages of 6.5 men per boat on the south coast and 7 men per boat on the west coast. Even if the larger eight–man whaleboats were being used in South Australia and a cook, cooper and look–out were included as part of the count, this would still leave as many as half a dozen men extra. Contemporary accounts suggest that these men were 'spare pulling hands' (SAR 1/1/1842) who presumably also assisted in processing the whales and other duties.

A further difficulty in comparing Western Australian whaling operations to the rest of Australasia is that there are no complete statistics of production (oil and bone) for all regions of Australasia. In addition, the available figures are the combined total for all fisheries, both shore and pelagic operations, of those colonies that are represented.

Colony/region	Year	No. of parties	references
Tasmania	1841	35	Dakin 1963
South Aust.	1840s	14	Kostoglou et al. 1991
New Zealand	1840s	50	Morton 1982
Western Aust.	1859	8	

Table 8.1 Peak number of Australasian whaling parties.

Station	year	boats	men	men-to-boats
Thistle Island	1838	4	35	8.75
Thistle Island	1839	3	-	-
Noarlunga Fishery	1841	2	25	12.5
Hog Bay	1841	2	20	10.0
Cape Jervis	1843	2	24	12.0
D'Estrees Bay	1843	2	13	6.5
Streaky Bay	1845	3	25	8.3

Table 8.2 Boats and men at South Australian whaling stations (after Kostoglou and McCarthy 1991).

YEAR	W.A. (£)	TAS. (£)	N.S.W. (£)	S.A. (£)
1828	-	11268	27000	
1829	-	12313	55000	
1830	-	22065	60000	
1831	-	33549	96000	
1832	-	37176	147000	
1833	-	30620	147000	
1834	-	56450	157000	
1835	-	64858	180000	
1836	1150	57660	134000	
1837	2860	135210	183000	
1838	3380	98600	198000	
1839	3190		172000	
1840	?		224000	7000
1841	?	98897		4000
1842	?			3000
1843	4081			6000
1844	5314			4000
1845	4228		96804	2000
1846	3338			2000
1847	4288			
1848	4377			
1849	1486			
1850	1220		29368	
1851	1766			
1852	1110			
1853	1820			
1854	829			
1855	2880			

Tasmanian figures from Evans (1993:30)
N.S.W. & S.A. figures from Linge (1979:89) and Little (1969)

Table 8.3 Export returns from whale products.

It is also possible that during the later period when Western Australian oil and bone were being shipped to the eastern colonies they may have been re–exported and included in the totals for other states. The partial record reported in Table 8.3 provides at least some basis for judging the Western Australian output. It is worth pointing out that the returns for Western Australia and South Australia, both of which were small colonies with limited resources and small whaling parties are similarly low in comparison to the larger colonies.

It is interesting to note that despite the vastly different scale of production in New South Wales, the percentage contribution of whale products to the export income of the colony followed the same pattern of decline as seen in Western Australia, with a drop from 42% of the colony's export earnings in 1830 to 1% in 1850 (Little 1969:125). The difference is that this decline was linked to falling production, whereas in Western Australia production remained relatively constant.

Chapter Four has already compared some of the physical characteristics of the Western Australian shore stations to those recorded historically or archaeologically for whaling sites in other parts of Australasia. From the evidence available the main differences appear to be those of scale, as might be expected from the consistently smaller operations of the Western Australian industry.

The similarities in the industrial processes and workforce meant that the basic nature of the location and organisation of the stations is comparable, yet while some of the New Zealand and Tasmanian fisheries virtually comprised small villages, the Western Australian stations were often no more than a tryworks shed and one or two huts or a single barrack. With the exception of the earliest west coast stations, particularly Bathers Beach, the Western Australian stations appear to have minimised their fixed improvements, particularly in the later phase when the adoption of the split season saw increased mobility and the use of multiple locations for shorter periods of time.

LIFE ON THE MARITIME FRONTIER

Although the Cheyne Beach assemblage does not provide information on the nature of the whaling workforce, it presents valuable insights into broader questions surrounding frontier life.

The inhabitants of Cheyne Beach appear to have been conservative in their adaptation (or lack thereof) to the surrounding environment and the isolated conditions. The faunal evidence shows that domesticates, in particular sheep, dominated the diet with much smaller contributions from pig and cattle. Native terrestrial and marine mammals are represented only in small proportions that would suggest occasional and opportunistic exploitation. Fish and shellfish collected from the adjacent reef are, however, present in sufficient quantities to suggest they must have provided regular contributions to the diet. As suggested in Chapter Seven, the nature of these resources presents a strong marine orientation, including the terrestrial fauna which were probably kept as captive populations on nearby Bald Island. While dietary preferences towards familiar food may have played a strong part, despite the distance from sources of supply, the reluctance of the fauna procurers to move beyond the coastal zone for the purpose of hunting may also have been a result of having to stay in close proximity to the station in readiness to respond to whale sightings. In this case the perceived conservatism may in fact be an adaptation appropriate to the whalers' purpose at the site.

The interpretation of the Cheyne Beach whaling station as a residence for women and children, presumably John Thomas and his family, adds flesh to the bare historical hints that these places could be more than male-only seasonal camps. The material culture items recovered from in and around Structures One and Two suggest that domestic and social norms were being maintained, despite the station being at least 50 km to the nearest European settlement.

In her critique of masculinist representations of the Australian 'bush', Lawrence (2003b) draws on the archaeological evidence from a variety of whaling, mining and pastoral sites, including Cheyne Beach, to highlight the apparent contradictions between remote frontier settings and the material culture used by those who dwelt in them.

> Archaeological evidence from nineteenth century rural sites in Australia indicates the commonplace usage of refined tablewares and other accoutrements of simple but respectable domestic dining etiquette. The inspiration for such practices can be found in contemporary British and colonial notions of decency, hard work and self improvement that characterised the Victorian age (Lawrence 2003b:211).

Lawrence's argument is that despite physical distance and even gender imbalance, these remote settlements remained firmly integrated with wider society. She also sounds a caution regarding simplistic equations of refined goods (such as teawares) as identifying the presence of women, as men might also use these as devices to demonstrate and maintain domestic respectability and ideologies, such as can be seen from her analysis of artefacts from the male–only Adventure Bay whaling station (Lawrence 2006). However, the nature and context of the Cheyne Beach assemblage as a whole, as well as the historical evidence, lends confidence to Structures One and Two being associated with at least one woman and probably children.

Quirk (2007) has explored the ideologies of Victorian 'gentility' as enacted through 'correct taste' and 'correct behaviour', based on analysis of artefacts from Paradise, a late nineteenth century mining settlement in Queensland. She argues that gentility expressed in various ways (including material culture), acted as a claim to and marker of (middle class) status. In particular she argues for 'gentility–as–strategy' which focuses on the agency of women in the settlement and examines demonstrations or symbolic performance of gentility to those around.

In contrast to Paradise, there is no clear evidence of other women at Cheyne Beach, which returns us to the notion of the embedded nature of such ideologies. Demonstrating and performing respectability, despite the isolation and regardless of the varied social and ethnic make–up of the rest of the (male) whalers, reinforced status but also recognised the continuing relationships and connections to a wider society. The marriage of the Thomas daughters to middle class public servants means that Fanny and John Thomas successfully negotiated and retained their respectability.

Structure One itself would appear to be a standard cottage design despite the unusual use of whalebone as a structural and possibly decorative feature. One poignant indicator of life at the station for Fanny Thomas or other women is from the 1889 account of the abandoned whaling station buildings, describing the remnants of flower gardens at the front of a cottage, possibly Structure One, which the author felt may have been an attempt to counteract the effects of the smell of the 'decaying monsters' on the beach nearby (Albany Mail 18/12/1889).

Excavation elsewhere at Cheyne Beach, accessing the deposits from the presumably male–only barracks, would provide a fascinating contrast. Unfortunately the increasing disturbance to the site (described below) has rendered this unlikely in the foreseeable future.

An important aspect of life on the maritime industrial frontier was that many of the whaling stations, including Cheyne Beach, represented the first sustained contact between Aboriginal and non–Aboriginal groups. Despite this, several factors seem to have combined to minimise conflict. The stations themselves were only occupied for short durations, they utilised small portions of land, and resulted in little or no modification of surrounding environments through agricultural clearance or pastoral activity. In addition, the whalers exploited resources not commonly available to the Aboriginal inhabitants and therefore not a part of their normal subsistence base, while also being willing to provide the un–needed meat for Aboriginal consumption.

The concept of the frontier as a place of innovation and adaptation is equally valid in two directions. The eventual incorporation of Aboriginal men into the whaling labour force may have been part of the traditional acceptance of ethnic diversity by whalers, as well as a means of overcoming potential labour shortages. However, for the Aboriginal workers participation in whaling provided access to the European economy, with goods received or purchased with their 'lay' payments redistributed among their kin along traditional lines. As for young Europeans, the experience of whaling was no doubt tinged with an attractive aura of adventure and danger, and the opportunity to show off their physical and hunting prowess. In symbolic terms this would have provided these men with greater power in both communities, particularly given the lack of clear distinction from the European whalers in pay scales and labour conditions (Gibbs 2003a).

CONCLUSIONS

To return to the opening paragraph of this volume, while it would not be fair to say that the 19th century shore whaling industry in Western Australia was a failure, there is little doubt that it was stifled almost from the point of its conception. The early combination of a lack of liquid capital, combined with the direct and indirect competition from the vastly better equipped and experienced foreign pelagic whaleships, ensured that there were limited opportunities for expansion. As the colonial whaling industry was unable to demonstrate the ability to produce a significant return, investors were understandably reluctant to invest in it. Meanwhile, the owners of the whaling parties were left without the means to expand into the lucrative pelagic industry. By the time that there was sufficient liquid capital in the colony to make this sort of move, interest was focused on other resources.

The shore whaling industry did achieve a level of significance in two areas. The first was during the early phase of Western Australian settlement, when it provided an economic and psychological link between the early difficulties of the agricultural settlement and the emergence of the successful pastoral interests. For several years during the late 1830s, shore whaling doubled the level of export income for the colony, providing evidence of its economic viability. At the same time the immediacy of the industry's success, as demonstrated through the spectacle of the pursuit and catch, provided an important source of excitement and reassurance to the colonists. The second area of significance, and the reason for continuation of whaling, was its role in the economies of the coastal settlements outside Fremantle. For at least some of the settlers, the extra income provided a further hedge against continuing difficulties, and whaling eventually developed into a normal part of the seasonal round. Operation at the threshold (or below) of economic viability indicates its role in the evolving social environment within at least some elements of the colony (c.f. Rockman 2003:4).

In terms of the operation and processes of shore whaling, the Western Australian whalers were part of an international tradition, using the technology, terminology and techniques employed throughout the European world. However, evidence for learning and adaptation can be seen in the changing nature and practices of the industry over the 43 years or more of its existence. The whaling stations themselves appear to have been located and organised on the basis of principles seen elsewhere in Australasia, although initial attempts to emulate the more successful companies from these areas were rapidly discarded in favour of strategies more suitable to the prevailing social, economic and environmental conditions. Ultimately this saw the Western Australian whaling industry operate on a much more limited scale than its contemporaries and develop new means of optimising access to the resource. The rapid integration of Aboriginal men into the workforce might also be seen as a means of not only overcoming an often crucial labour shortage, but incorporating a range of new skills into the local industry.

Adaptation is less evident in the behaviours exhibited at Cheyne Beach. Although not typical of the whaling industry, being derived more from an attached settlement than the core of the process, the archaeological evidence suggests a high degree of conservatism in diet, material culture and the social behaviours of the inhabitants. In part this may have been a function of the economic specialisation of the site which discouraged indigenous development and focused attention on marine rather than terrestrial concerns. In addition, the assemblage of ceramics suggests a strong attachment to the wider trade networks, even though Albany and Cheyne Beach were fairly isolated outposts of the British Empire.

ADDENDA

Almost a decade after the submission of my original dissertation and eventual departure from Western Australia to work elsewhere, I happened to be driving along the South Coast Highway not far from Cheyne Beach. In a fit of nostalgia I decided I had the time to take a diversion and visit 'my' site. From the start it was obvious that there had been changes, with what had been 30 kilometres of sometimes problematic dirt track now a sealed road. Cresting the final ridge and looking down at the glorious white sweep of the bay it was also evident that new holiday houses were replacing the fishermen's cottages, with freshly cleared bush suggesting more were coming. Talking to the owners of the caravan park, who only vaguely remembered the archaeology students who had stayed there, I learned that our main local informant had died several years earlier. Charles 'Snapper' Westerberg, descendant of a notable south coast fishing family, who had first seen the site as a child in the 1920s and later had taken up the small farm above the bay, had regularly come down to the site to chat and tell stories about the bay, fishing, and what he knew of the early whalers. Now that tenuous oral history was gone.

Driving down to the site the old loose gravel car park had been replaced with a bitumen surface, at worst meaning that whatever deposits were in that area had finally been scraped away, or at best that they were now sealed below. However, presumably as a consequence of the increased traffic and despite heritage listings and theses carefully packaged and sent to libraries and authorities, someone, possibly a well–meaning Council worker, had clearly decided to make it easier for boat trailers to access the beach. Where Structure One had sat for 160 years on its low dune covered in reeds was now a track, graded through to the beach. In the wheel ruts and to either side sat crushed or broken whalebone of what had been the floor, as well as the occasional brick fragment and sherd of transfer printed ceramic. Along the sides of the track the erosion which we had so carefully tried to avoid, minimizing our excavation area, backfilling and trying to re–plant the reeds each year, was now melting the heart of the site away.

As professionals we frequently experience the destruction of interesting, significant, exciting, or beautiful archaeological sites. Often their impending obliteration is the very reason why we are allowed to work on them. However, it is still possible to be shocked and saddened at the loss of these places, even if there is some consolation to think that at least you were lucky enough to capture something of their essence before they were gone. However, the vulnerability of these places and the idea that if the original study had only been several years later the Cheyne Beach site would already have been gone, can still leave me cold. Undoubtedly there are still archaeological deposits at Cheyne Beach, but I doubt that the story that emerged could have been the same.

By its nature the maritime frontier was ephemeral; a temporary presence with little intention or pretension of becoming more. Sites such as whaling stations had a tenuous position along the edges of coasts and perhaps the fragility of these sites to later natural and cultural forces simply underscores this. However, despite the marginal position on the edges of beaches and the edges of the empire, the archaeological evidence of the men, women and children who lived at Cheyne Beach shows they remained economically, technologically and socially linked and attentive to the wider system. Pursuit of a resource which could be fed back into that greater system and consequently reap them wealth and the comforts that could bring was the very reason for their being there. However, this was not necessarily true for all maritime frontier industries or settlements and there is certainly evidence that different whaling, pearling, sealing and operations pursued different strategies. Exploring these nuances promises to be a fertile ground for historical and archaeological researchers for many years to come.

APPENDIX A
SITE HISTORIES AND ARCHAEOLOGICAL SURVEYS

The following Appendix provides a brief history and archaeological description of shore whaling at 21 locations along the west and south coasts of Western Australia. A more detailed historical and archaeological description is available in Gibbs 1996. Analysis of the site histories and components is provided in Chapter 4.

SURVEY METHOD

As noted in Chapter One, several 19th century whaling station sites had been identified during the 1970s and 1980s. The National Trust (W.A.) survey of whaling stations in particular drew on Ian Heppingstone's historical research to identify 20 probable locations for whaling activity, with MacIlroy's survey identifying seven sites with structural remains or artefacts (MacIlroy 1987:1). These identifications provided a solid basis for the current study, commenced several years later.

Based on a more comprehensive historical analysis, several of the locations suggested in the 1987 study were eliminated as misinterpretations of the historical records (Ten Mile Well, Collie River and Augusta). A total of 21 locations, such as specific bays known to have been used the site of one or more shore stations, were identified. In addition, further clues were generated as to probable site locations in bays which had previously been surveyed unsuccessfully.

Surveys were undertaken in several stages between 1990 and 1993, with the very limited funding available meaning that the more distant or inaccessible locations could not be visited. Initially the most accessible sites on the west coast between Port Gregory and Castle Rock were surveyed, followed by the south coast sites between Torbay and Cape Riche. Finally, the remote sites of Barrier Anchorage and Thomas Fishery were surveyed. Four locations (Malus Island, Carnac Island, Middle Island and Doubtful Island Bay) could not be visited. For these places it was necessary to speak to local informants and use other sources of information to assess the existence or condition of the sites.

NORTHWEST COAST

Malus Island is part of the Dampier Archipelago, a collection of islands up to 15 km long and 3 km wide which are clustered along the west and north sides of the Burrup Peninsula. The archipelago is a drowned landmass 'characterised by rock platforms and storm boulder beaches interspersed with localised accumulations of sand and silt in the more protected embayments' (Vinnicombe 1987:2). The area experiences large tidal variations and has relatively warm and dry winters (Woods 1980). Winds are easterly during winter, although there is a west to northwest sea breeze. The swell is weak, arriving from the west, although the tidal variation is large. Winters within this region are relatively warm and dry, with cyclones through the summer (Woods 1980).

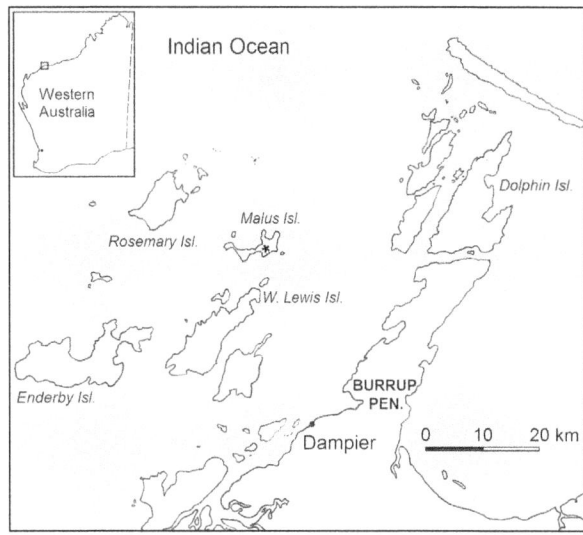

Figure A1 Dampier Archipelago.

MALUS ISLAND
Date Range: 1870–1877
Location: Whalers Bay, SW section of Malus Island.
1:100,000 AMG Reference: 2256 Dampier 672–311

History
Although intensively used by foreign whalers since at least the 1840s, colonial whaling in the Dampier Archipelago ('Rosemary Islands') only dates to the 1870s and the establishment of pastoral and pearling outposts in the area (Wace and Lovett 1973:13). Initial use coincides with the establishment of pastoral and pearling outposts in the Roebourne area. In 1870 W.S. Marmion and W.S. and G. Pearse, established a shore station on Malus Island, using the 34 ton schooner *Argo* to assist operations (Inq 20/7/1870). In 1872 John Bateman also sent a party northward in 1872, forming a partnership with the Roebourne merchant George Howlett and using his 104 ton schooner *Mary–Ann* (Inq 9/10/1872). It is uncertain where Bateman's shore base was located, although reports mention the *Mary–Ann* working around Rosemary Island (Inq 12/6/1872). It is interesting to note that the masters of the vessels were also required to sign articles with the rest of the men

(GG 4/6/1872; GG 25/6/1872).

After a poor 1872 season (Inq 9/10/1872) there was a hiatus until 1877, when Bateman leased Malus Island for the sum of £1 (SDUR B10/1144C: 12/1/1877). His son Francis managed the party and also acted as the master of the 70 ton schooner *Star* (PG 26/6/1877). This was the last recorded use of the station. The Blue Book records of oil taken at Malus Island during 1870–72 are unclear and it appears that at least some was recorded as 'Fremantle'. The 1877 catch by the *Star* was reported as amounting to 147 casks, probably totalling between 2.5 and 3.5 tuns of oil (PG 23/11/1877), but was not recorded in the Blue Book at all.

tryworks and a possible domestic fireplace. Until the late 1960s all four trypots were in situ, the only site in Western Australia where this occurred (Figure 4.13). Two trypots have since been removed, destroying one tryworks, while an amateur reconstruction has partially compromised the integrity of the other. The close proximity of the two tryworks may represent two separate phases of use of the site.

Figure A3 Whalers Bay, Malus Island.

MacIlroy (1987) also located a small stone structure, possibly the base of a domestic hearth or oven, approximately 20m northeast of the tryworks. The position, slightly inland and upwind (prevailing winds are westerly) of the tryworks is consistent with the spatial relationships seen at other sites. In the 1980 reconstruction of the tryworks the chimney was also rebuilt as the mounting for a commemorative plaque (E. Bradshaw, pers. comm. 1993).

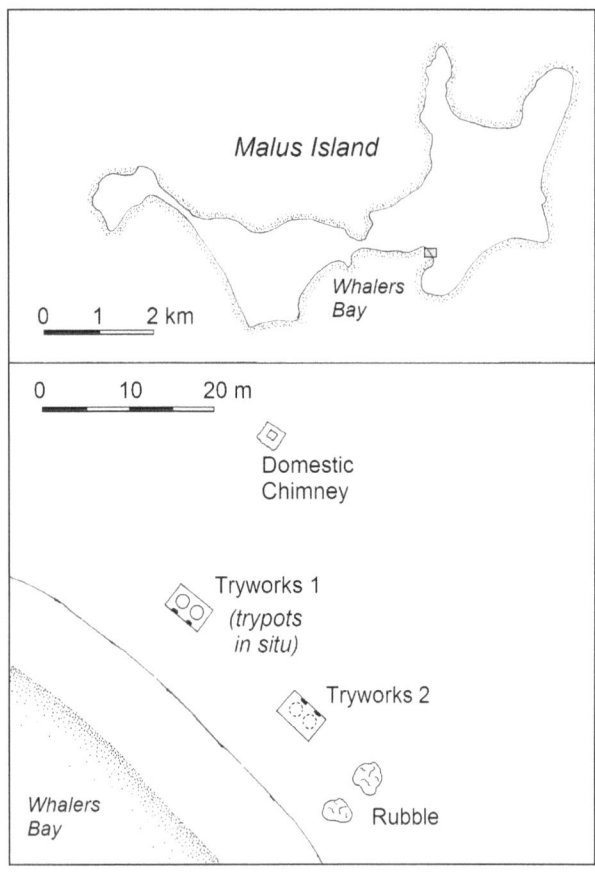

Figure A2 Whalers Bay, Malus Island.

Site Description

The site of the Malus Island whaling station was partially recorded by Western Australian Museum staff during the 1960s and 70s, and was re–inspected during the 1987 National Trust survey (MacIlroy 1979; 1987). While it was not possible to visit Malus Island during this current study, further photographs of the tryworks and samples of the char deposits in their hearths were collected by a colleague undertaking a survey for prehistoric sites (E. Bradshaw pers. comm. 1993).

The whaling station is located in Whalers Bay, a sandy cove on the sheltered SW side of Malus Island. The archaeological features include two double

LOWER WEST COAST SITE SURVEY

The lower west coast stretches from approximately Kalbarri to Cape Naturaliste and is characterised by long, straight sandy beaches with few significant bays or interruptions (Woods 1980). Old limestone dunes have become islands and headlands in some areas, with southwest swells and waves creating crescent–shaped northward opening bays behind these hard points. This varies slightly in the area close to Cape Naturaliste, where the granite of the Leeuwin–Naturaliste Ridge outcrops on the coast, with several small, sandy bays forming in between. The Castle Rock station is situated in one such bay. A strong south to southwesterly sea breeze is experienced along the lower southwest coast, although there are occasional strong northwest storms. Tidal range is very small and for the most part the areas behind the headlands are well protected. The region experiences a Dry Mediterranean climate with mild, wet winters.

PORT GREGORY

Date Range: 1854–1875

Location: North end of Port Gregory harbour, behind Eagles Nest Hill.

1:100,000 AMG Reference: 1741 Hutt 289–790

History

A whaling station was established at Port Gregory several years after the opening of the area to European settlement, following reports of sperm whales 'literally swarming' on the coast adjacent to the harbour (Inq 26/1/1854). Captain Sanford, owner of nearby Lynton Station, formed a whaling party in partnership with Fremantle businessman David Ronayne (Inq 3/5/1854). Although the whaleboats were lost as they were being shipped northwards (Inq 12/7/1854), replacements were found in time to proceed with the season. However, only one humpback was caught (BB 1854).

Sanford operated his station again in 1855, hoping to attract one of the major whaling parties up to the port (BL M386; Inq 22/8/1855). In 1856 he was partnered by Joshua Harwood of Fremantle to run a three boat, 22 man fishery (GG 10/6/1856). Harwood maintained a party at Port Gregory until 1860, after which he ceased all of his whaling operations. In 1857 John Bateman also established a station at the port, which he continued to use intermittently until as late as 1875. From the early 1860s Bateman kept his party at Port Gregory from June to September, after which he would move them southward to Bunbury or Castle Rock.

Harwood's crew is known to have lived in Sanford's storehouse, built on Lot No. 1 of the proposed Packington town (BL M386). Bateman would probably have also been required to lease land within the Packington town subdivisions, although no record of this has been found. There are no historical references which pinpoint the location of either Harwood's or Bateman's processing areas or tryworks, although several contemporary sources indicate that the station(s) were opposite Gold Digger Passage (e.g. Inq 29/6/1859). The only other reference directly relating to a processing plant is a report from 1858, which states that the tryworks building and a considerable quantity of whaling gear had been completely destroyed after catching fire from the tryworks furnace (PG 13/8/1858, Inq 18/8/1858). As Bateman had not formed a Port Gregory station that season this could only have been Harwood's plant. An 1883 plan of the area shows what might be a structure on the beach in front of Lot No. 1, although as this was 30 years after the whaling period the association is questionable (Rodrigues 2006: 3).

Site Description

Port Gregory is a lagoon formed by a reef running parallel to the coast for 3 km. The enclosed area of water forms a safe harbour for boats and small ships and is entered through one of three passages on the far northern end of the reef. High dunes surround the bay from juts above the high tide mark, with lower dunes behind. An early chart also notes that good water is available two feet below the surface (Roe 1854).

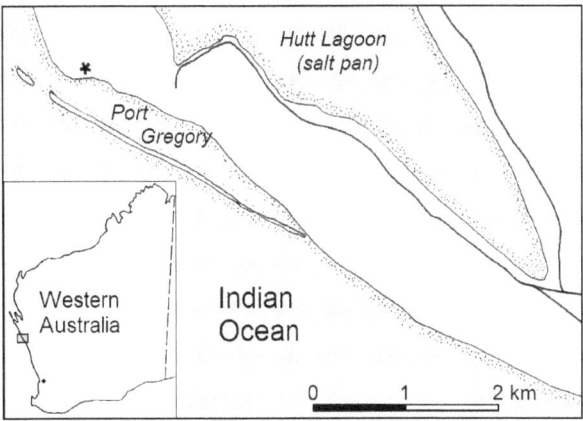

Figure A3 Port Gregory Location.

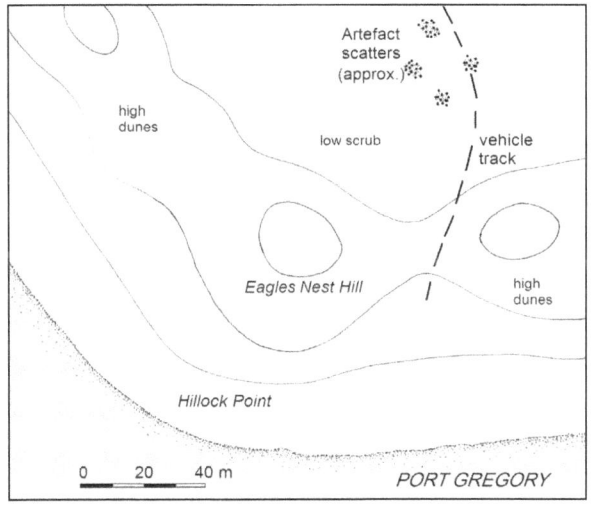

Figure A4 Port Gregory Site Plan.

As early as the 1950s, historical studies had associated the scatters of bricks and artefacts found behind the Hillock Point dunes with early whaling activity (Suckling n.d.; Kelly 1958). In 1986 the W.A. Maritime Museum relocated the site and collected surface artefacts (M. McCarthy pers. comm. 1990). Several features were recorded by the 1987 National Trust survey (MacIlroy 1987) and the site was visited again in 1990 as part of this study. A further inspection was made by the W.A. Museum in January 2006 to investigate reported disturbances and newly visible features eroding out of the dunes.

Possible archaeological evidence of the station is visible in two areas. Behind the dunes approx 250m ENE of Hillock Point are several scatters of early brick and squared limestone which may have come from hearths or chimneys, although the source of these is uncertain. This area also contains light surface scatters of 19th century bottle glass, shell, ceramics, ironwork and bone, exposed in some areas by vehicle tracks and dune deflation. A 1m² test pit indicates that artefact deposits exist to a depth of 50cm. It is difficult to determine positions relative to the original land divisions, although this material is likely to fall within or close to the position of Sanford's Lot No. 1. The 2006 survey identified what appears to be a pug floor surface eroding from a vehicle track cutting through the dunes (Rodriguez 2006: 17-20).

Figure A5 Port Gregory looking north towards point.

The second site consists of material eroding from the beach–side dune face. This includes further brick rubble and iron both on the beach and in the dune face, The 2006 survey also identified chunks of black organic matter which may be pyrolised animal fats such as from a tryworks, although these have not been analysed further. No evidence of a look–out was found, although the high sand dunes on Hillock point would provide good elevation.

MARMION/SORRENTO

Date Range: 1849

Location Approx. 25 km north of Fremantle.

1:100,000 AMG Ref: 2034 Perth 813–714 (approx.)

History

After unsuccessfully bidding for the 1849 lease of the Bathers Beach station, Patrick Marmion requested the lease of an area 20 miles north of Fremantle. The position was described as

> Eastward of a little Island which is about 2 miles from the main. The spot in question is also a mile, or perhaps two miles northward of the parallel of the northwest of Rottnest Island. It is also...about 3 miles west or west by south of

Wanneroo (CSR 4/7/1849 cited in Daniel & Cockman 1979: 6).

Marmion was granted permission to occupy the 10 acres rent free, with liberty to run sheep on the adjacent Crown land for the purposes of the station (Daniel & Cockman 1979: 6). Marmion regained his lease of Bathers Beach in the following 1850 and there is no further evidence that the Marmion station was ever used again. Physical evidence did, however, survive for some time. In his application to the Governor, Marmion stated his intention 'to erect a house for the whalers, to set a proper sort of tryworks with English bricks etc, and make this affair not a merely temporary concern' (CSR 4/7/1849, cited in Daniel & Cockman 1979: 6). While no further description is available, a small allotment with a feature marked as 'Marmion's Chimney' appears on various maps of the area through the rest of the 19th century which might indicate the tryworks or more likely the whalers' barracks (Daniel & Cockman 1979).

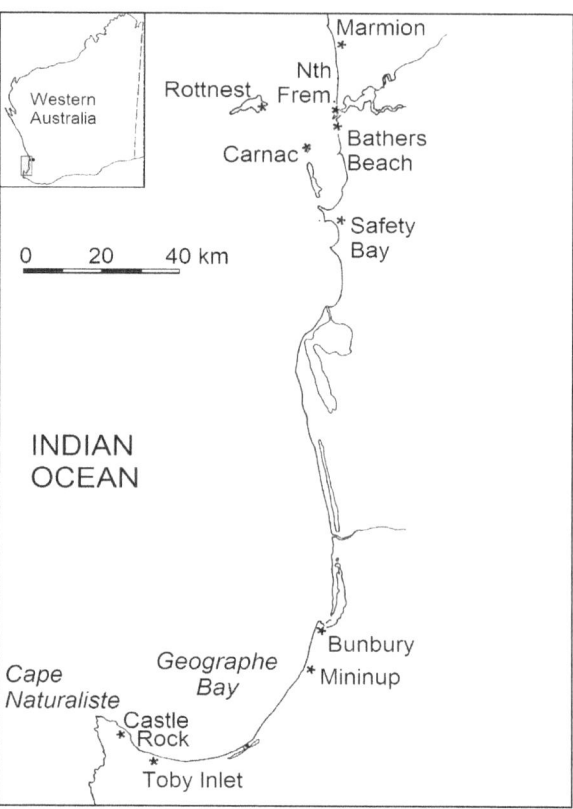

Figure A6 Lower West Coast Sites.

Site Description

There are few environmental features which would recommend the location for a station. There is a slight projection in the coast several kilometres northwards at Mullaloo Point, although this provides none of the advantages of a headland as a protection or look–out. The only particularly desirable feature was the presence of freshwater springs, noted on early plans (Daniel & Cockman 1979). Recent changes to the coastline and urban development makes it difficult to assess other contributing attributes. There is no remaining surface evidence for the station and its precise location cannot be determined, although a memorial plaque has been erected near the beach by the Royal Western Australian Historical Society.

NORTH FREMANTLE

Date Range; 1856

Location: Unknown, north side of Rous Head?

1:100,000 AMG Reference: 2034 Perth

History

Evidence for the existence of a shore–station at North Fremantle is limited to several minor references. The first is by Butchart (1933) in his childhood recollections of whaling activity about Fremantle, who simply states that 'Bateman had his plant on the south side of the river, and Harwood on the north'. Similarly, Hope (1929) recalls as a child in 1865 'when whales were caught in the harbour, there was a boiling down establishment at North Fremantle, near the present wheat sheds'. He notes that he last saw the remains of the station in 1875. It is possible that Crammond's (1935:5) description that 'in 1855 there was also a plant at North Fremantle, situated near the river where large boilers and vats were used for boiling down' is based these earlier comments.

No direct historical documentation has been found to support the existence of a North Fremantle whaling station, while Harwood's station would appear to have been located on Carnac Island (see above). However, during the 1856 season a third whaling party (other than Bateman's or Harwood's) was reported as operating in the Fremantle region. With the two most suitable locations already taken, North Fremantle may have been the nearest available position where a shore station might be established. The unidentified third party did not survive its first season before dissolving (Inq 24/9/1856).

Site Description

In the early period 'North Fremantle' included a large area on the north side of the Swan River, almost to Rocky Bay (c.f. le Page 1986:126). The area around the mouth of the Swan River has been massively altered by harbour development and it is unclear from early maps whether a small cove or sheltered area existed that might have been suitable for a station. Hope's (1929) recollection that men from the station sometimes quietly left the St John's (Fremantle) Church service when a whale was sighted would suggest that it was nearby, as does his reference to the wheat sheds, many of which were on the north side of the harbour at this time (Shaw 1979:336). There were various high hills and dunes which could have been used as a look–out, while Butchart (1933) mentions a 'Whaler's Hill' at Cottesloe.

As with the Marmion fishery, the North Fremantle station appears to have been based on the more desirable locations already being occupied. Except for its proximity to Fremantle, the area has little to offer for a whaling station, being directly exposed to winds and swell. The short period of operation and subsequent heavy landscape alteration makes the survival of archaeological remains highly unlikely.

BATHERS BAY / FREMANTLE

Date Range: 1837–c.1861 (-1875?)

Location: Bathers Beach below Arthur Head.

1:100,000 AMG Reference: 2033 Fremantle 809–524

History

The small bay immediately south of the mouth of the Swan River, later known as Bathers Bay (or Bathers Beach), was a focus for early settlement activities at Fremantle. All settlers and supplies were landed on this beach until the construction of deep–water jetties at the adjacent point and the eventual removal of a river bar in the 1890s. The other side of the headland was also where the first European colonists camped and is now the City of Fremantle,

In 1837 the Fremantle Whaling Company obtained a five year (in some reports seven year) lease on Bathers Beach, constructing what would prove to be the most elaborate whaling station in the colony. Improvements included a two story stone station house, a wooden tryworks and boat shed, storage rooms cut into the base of the headland, a stone jetty and a tunnel through the headland to the town beyond. The last two works were granted government assistance in the form of engineering expertise and convict labour, as the jetty would also become the main landing for the colony and the tunnel a means of easing access between the port and the town.

The 1837 and 1838 seasons were very poor (See Chapter 2) and from at least 1839 the company appears to have chosen to lease the premises to private operators, rather than attempt to form a party of their own. During the early 1840s the station was most frequently rented to Captain Daniel Scott, although other identities such as Patrick Marmion and Capt. Anthony Curtis are also known to have taken the lease for one or more seasons. The Fremantle Whaling Company was finally dissolved in 1850 and its equipment auctioned (Inq 4/12/1850).

An 1840s drawing of the station (Reece and Pascoe 1985: 8) provides an accurate representation of the station, showing the station house, tryworks shed, jetty and a cave–like opening in the cliff corresponding to what is shown in historical plans as the oil store. The jetty is stone between wooden pilings, with shearlegs at the far end, likely used to assist in stripping the blanket sheets from the whale. This suggests that whales were beached or secured at the end or sides of the jetty, rather than brought right in to shore. The horizontal beams projecting from the right hand piles of the jetty appear to be davits for pulling one or two boats out of the water, similar to those used at the Boyd station jetty in New South Wales (Davidson 1988:79). On the headland above is the platform and signal mast from which the look–out was kept (PG 6/5/1837).

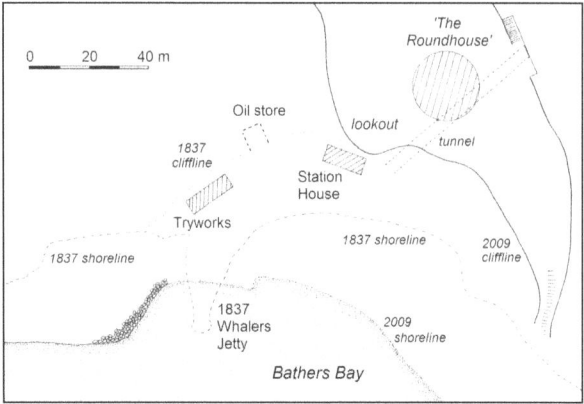

Figure A7 Bathers Beach Site Plan.

From the 1850s onwards John Bateman, merchant and former headsman for several Fremantle parties, became the regular lessee of the Bathers Beach station. However, this may have only included the jetty and processing buildings, as the station house had already been leased to the Convict Department (CSR 222/190: 7/7/1851). This raises the possibility that Bateman's crews were housed in his nearby warehouse or in their own homes. During the 1850s the catch from the Fremantle area fell to no more than 25 tuns of oil (Bathers Beach and Carnac Island) combined.

Increased traffic through the port and the growing town behind may have encouraged the abandonment of the station, with its last confirmed use by Bateman being in 1861 (Inq 21/8/1861). Despite this, in 1863, 1865, and 1867–1875 a 'Fremantle' entry is recorded in the Blue Books and reported as including between two and eight boats. This suggests that there were one and sometimes two parties in operation in the area, leaving open whether there were also stations at North Fremantle, or that it refers to a station on Carnac Island (see below). In several years the total catch for the area was around 40 tuns of oil, a considerable quantity for that period.

No contemporary sources confirm a continuing use of the Bathers Beach station. However, in 1865 a report of whales near Fremantle laments the absence of whaling equipment 'in the absence of Mr. Bateman's plant, which is now stationed near Bunbury' (Inq 18/10/1865). This leaves some ambiguity as to whether Bateman had moved to a southern station permanently, or had used Bather Beach in the first part of the season and shifted to Bunbury for the late part of the season.

The jetty and buildings may have remained in use for some time into the late 19th century, when progressive quarrying and landfill eventually covered the structures (Bavin and Gibbs 1988).

Site Description
MacIlroy's excavations at the site of the Bathers Beach whaling station have revealed substantial structural remains from the early whaling period (MacIlroy and Meredith 1984; MacIlroy and Kee 1986; MacIlroy 1986; MacIlroy 1990). Evidence for the station house, tryworks and workshop/boatshed, storage cave, jetty and a contemporary boat–builder's workshop has been excavated and recorded, although no analysis of artefacts removed during excavation has been made.

Figure A8 'View of the Tunnel under the Round House and Whaling jetty at Fremantle', 1840s by Horace Samson. (Personal collection, Mrs. Godbehear, Perth).

In several respects Bathers Beach is atypical of Western Australia whaling stations. The substantial brick foundation of the tryworks shows three hearths, significantly larger and more elaborate than any of the other tryworks located (Figure 4.14). This structure and the other substantial capital works are indicative of the grandiose intentions which characterised the earliest phase of whaling. However, despite their ambitions the parties of the Fremantle Whaling Company and later lessees never exceeded four boats. Although the largest and most elaborate of the Western Australian shore stations, in comparison to many other Australasian whaling parties this would still have only been rated as a modest establishment.

CARNAC ISLAND

Date range: 1837, 1845, 1853–c.1875

Location: East bay of Carnac Island, 10 km southwest of Fremantle. Precise location unknown.

1:100,000 AMG Reference: 2033 Fremantle 739–452

History

In 1837 the Northern Whaling Company, also referred to as the Perth Company or Carnac Company, established a shore whaling station on Carnac Island in competition with the Fremantle Whaling Company at Bathers Beach. The company was based on joint stock investment of £600, with 20 men, three whaleboats and a jolly boat (SRG 4/5/1837). Reports at the time suggest that the station was located in the sheltered eastern bay (SRG 4/5/1837) and that a jetty, residence and store were under construction (PG 6/5/1837). The store was constructed from the frame of the former first church in Perth, known as the 'rush church', which was purchased at auction for £25 (PG 15/4/1837).

As described in Chapter 2 the 1837 season proceeded very badly and at its end the company decided to dissolve, auctioning its equipment (PG 10/2/38; PG 17/2/38). However, when the company tried to offer the station and its seven year lease back to the government 'with all improvements thereon, for a reasonable consideration', they were reminded that upon dissolution of the company the land and buildings had automatically reverted to the Crown (PG 24/3/38). The company was formally dissolved on May 23 (PG 26/5/38).

In 1845 Captain Anthony Curtis attempted to establish a new station on Carnac (Cammilleri 1963), combining it with the use of his schooner *Vixen* to cruise the adjacent islands (PG 12/7/1845). Statham (1980) suggests that the effort of transporting supplies to Carnac and difficulties in hiring and retaining crews made the venture uneconomic, forcing its closure at the end of the season. The next occupation was more successful, with Joshua Harwood basing his whaling operations on the island from as early as 1853 (CSR 344/244: 24/5/1856). Details on the station are extremely limited, although it is probable that a schooner or other small vessel would have been used for transporting supplies, if not to assist with the whaling itself. A condition of Harwood's lease was that he kept the government quarantine buildings on Carnac in good repair, which suggests he may have been using them to house his crews.

The final year in which Carnac Island was used as a base for whaling is uncertain. Although 'Harwood's party' is last mentioned in 1860 (PG 19/10/1860), there is the possibility that Carnac was one of the unidentified 'Fremantle' stations reported operating until 1875.

Site Description

Carnac Island is a small limestone island of about 2.5 hectares in area, situated 10 km southwest of Fremantle. Although normally accessible by small boats, two attempts to reach Carnac Island to carry out a survey for this project were unsuccessful. No reports have been made of evidence for early occupation being found on the island.

From the limited historical evidence it is most probable that the successive whaling stations were situated in the sandy bay on the east side of the island. Adjacent limestone hills provide further wind protection and a vantage point for a look–out (PG 15/7/1837), giving a view to the area between the island and the mainland (Gages Roads and Cockburn Sound), and out to sea.

ROTTNEST ISLAND

Date Range: 1850

Location: Thomson Bay, east side of island, 18 km west of Fremantle. Precise location unknown.

1:100,000 AMG Reference: 2033 Fremantle

History

The earliest proposal to use Rottnest as a base for whaling activities was in 1832, with John Sweetman (Swetnam) being given approval to occupy land for that purpose (CSF 5/99: 17/3/1832; Erikson 1988:2996). The venture never proceeded, with the island being declared an Aboriginal prison several years later with all land grants revoked and whaling parties warned to stay away (Ferguson 1986; CSR 19/236: 29/7/1845).

The first and only attempt to form a whaling establishment on Rottnest was made in 1850, during a brief period when the island was not being used for penal purposes. James Dempster obtained the lease of the island including pastoral rights, use of the salt works and permission to form a whaling station (PG 21/9/1849). Dempster made arrangements with both Bateman and Harwood for use of whaleboats and equipment (Inq 19/9/1849). Local newspapers reported on his preparations for a three–boat fishery and wished him luck, but feared there were many obstacles to his success (PG 5/7/1850; Inq 10/7/1850). One major impediment was that despite two recruitment drives, local whaling hands were reluctant to join his party because it would mean they were isolated on the island for months. His party chased a humpback in late September before conceding defeat (Erikson 1978). Five years later in 1855 Rottnest was again declared a prison with no boats allowed to land there (GG 12/8/1856).

Site Description

Rottnest Island provides a good location for a whaling station, commanding both the area about Gages Roads and the seaward side of the island. Dempster and his men used existing buildings on the island, many of which are still standing and in use (Ferguson 1986). It is probable that the tryworks was located in Thompson Bay, the sandy, eastern facing bay on which the settlement is situated. The adjacent limestone headlands would provide excellent vantage points for a look–out. Unfortunately the short duration of the party, the fact that the tryworks was never used and the subsequent heavy use and remodelling of the foreshore has removed all trace of whaling activity.

SAFETY BAY

Date Range: 1838

Location: Approx. area would be the northern end of Warnbro Sound, 30 km south of Fremantle.

1:100,000 AMG Reference: 2033 Fremantle

History

In 1837 the American whaler *Pioneer* spent several months bay whaling in Warnbro Sound and surveying the harbour (PG 26/5/38; Ogle 1839: 243). In the following year the master of the vessel entered into a partnership with local landowner Thomas Peel (see Chapter 1; Hasluck 1965). In the same year the Western Australian Whaling Company was reported as establishing a station in Safety Bay at the northern end of Warnbro Sound. The company made claims towards establishing an ambitious bay–whaling venture, but probably failed to obtain adequate capital (PG 8/7/1837; PG 15/7/1837). A measure of this was that at the start of the season they had to refute claims that they did not have the means for catching and processing whales, or even for provisioning their men (PG 5/5/1838). There is no description of the progress of this party until October, when no return is given for "Duffield's party", despite the *Pioneer* taking 35 tuns of oil (PG 20/10/1838).

Although the nearby Fremantle Whaling party complained about foreign intrusion (CSR 61/14: 9/5/1838), the lack of complaint from the Western Australian Whaling Company suggests the possibility that they too entered into the co–operative arrangement described above. This agreement would have provided the company with the means of overcoming their difficulties with capital and equipment, as well as providing experienced hands for the fishery (PG 5/5/1838). Ironically, if this were the case, it contrasts with an early account of their prospectus, which claimed that no foreigner would be allowed to hold interest in the company (PG 22/7/1837). There is no evidence that Safety Bay was subsequently used by either colonial or foreign whalers. A final mention of the station appears in November 1839 when newspapers reported a dispute between the station owners and the former cook about whether the latter had agreed to work for a lay or wages (PG 31/11/1839).

Site Location

Safety Bay is the northern end of Warnbro Sound, a large bay fringed by a limestone reef which provides some protection from swells and high seas. The point at Safety Bay is a relatively low limestone outcrop and sand dune, although the hills on adjacent Penguin Island might have provided sufficient elevation for a look–out across the sound and adjacent seas. The beachfront area has been remodelled for recreational and residential purposes and no evidence has been found of whaling activity. It should also be considered that the 1838 arrangement with the American whaling ship may well have obviated the need for a shore–based processing plant or other buildings.

BUNBURY WHALING STATION

Date Range: 1838– c.1867

Location: Precise location(s) unknown, although probably along the east side of Point Casuarina (Koombana Bay), in the area of the small boat harbour.

1:100,000 AMG Reference: 2031 Bunbury 731–126 (approx. only)

History

During 1838 several reports appeared regarding the whaling potential of Koombana Bay, enhanced by the successes of Americans bay whaling there (PG 21/7/1838; PG 20/10/1838). By July of that year a small colonial 'tonguing' party salvaging the discarded portions of the whales had already recovered seven tuns of oil (PG 14/7/1838). In the following season the local settlers formed their own shore–station, although there are no reports on its nature other than it was making satisfactory progress (PG 6/7/1839; PG 10/8/1839).

No colonial party was formed in the next several years despite increasing American activity, with one reliable source reporting 14 vessels seen in a single day (Clifton 1841). The wreck of three American vessels in the bay during a gale in mid–1840 saw the captains auction off hulls and equipment (Table 2.1; Henderson

1980). One of the captains (Coffin) spent the remainder of the 1840 season with his crew bay–whaling (PG 1/8/40), although it is not known whether they established a shore station or continued to use one of the wrecked ships as a base. The colonial government also made legal attempts to limit possible foreign interference with any colonial party which might arise (CSR 85/82: 21/4/1840).

In April 1843 another American whaleship was driven ashore in during a gale, selling its equipment to J.K. Child who was forming a whaling party (PG 22/4/43; Inq 3/5/1843). The arrangement seems to have included some partnership, possibly with the captain, with a contemporary diary recording Child was

> enabled to enter into the bay–whaling by taking an experienced American into partnership, and he sees after all the work; the men are also paid by shares in the oil (Burton 1954:272).

Reports during the season showed the station achieving some success but also losing a number of whales, possibly through inexperience (Inq 26/7/1843; Inq 13/9/1843). Despite this, Child continued in the following year, now competing with The Koombana Bay Whaling Company, headed by John Scott (PG 11/5/1844). Child applied for and was granted the lease of an area of land on which to erect whaling buildings, with the Koombana Company granted the area immediately west (CSR 131/1: 1/2/1844; CSR 131/4: 8/2/1844). Both groups were moderately successful, although there were reports of competition (PG 27/7/1844). There was also friction over the Koombana Company's decision to take up an offer of assistance from two American vessels, offered by the latter as a means of being allowed to remain along the coast (CSR 131/59: 31/7/1844; CSR 131/60: 29/7/1844).

Throughout the 1840s and 1850s Koombana Bay hosted one or more colonial shore stations, operating under various owners and managers. It is uncertain if the same station sites were re–used over time, although at least one letter records that Child's original buildings were removed in 1847 'for the police station' (CSR 24/118: 4/12/1847), while another states that the boards of the 'whale house' were being re–used in a stable (CSR 24/313; 29/4/1848). In 1849 Messer's Onslow and Sillifant formed a new company which allowed their men to resided in their own homes, meeting only for business. The proceeds of the season, presumably increased by not having to meet the overheads of providing food and accommodation, were then divided among the men (Inq 30/5/1849; Inq 12/12/1849). The scheme worked well and the same group continued in 1850, although operations were hampered by difficulties with a new harpoon gun (PG 22/11/1850).

In 1855 John Bateman commenced his practice of sending a small party to one of the southwest stations, usually in September after the season had closed at Port Gregory. Although given permission to build his own tryworks (CSR 366/169: 11/3/1856), Bateman eventually leased the existing whaling buildings at Bunbury for a sum of only £1 (CSR 366/182; 22/4/1856), waiting until 1862 to build his own station (CSR 502/260: 6/8/1862). Sometimes in competition with local parties, Bateman's crews continued to visit Koombana Bay during most years until at least 1867 (Her 5/10/1867). In 1870 his weatherboard station house and tryworks were removed (CSR 645/112: 28/6/1870), possibly to Castle Rock where he continued operations.

Site Description

The historical record describes a succession of whaling stations constructed along the shores of Koombana Bay, presumably beneath Marlston Hill (also known as Lighthouse Hill) which provided the look–out point (Mitchell 24/3/1927).

An undated but possibly 1843 plan of Bunbury by John Wollaston (Poole 1979: 225; Parks 1990) shows several foreshore buildings noted as "Child's Buildings" close to the end of what may now be Eliot Street. However, the 1844 lease agreements (CSR 131/2: 18/1/1844), which placed the Koombana Company's lease as west of Child's station, suggests that both stations were probably further north of this, along what is described on the Wollaston map as 'The Strand'. Later reminiscences also suggest this area, facing out onto the bay proper, as the location for Bateman's station. The first report (Mitchell 1927) states that it was 'near the present breakwater', while another (Anon 1936) says that the 'old whalehouse', stood on the foreshore 'just a little the other side of where the jetty baths are now located'.

Various accounts from the 1840s onwards describe the demolition or removal of successive whaling station buildings, most of which appear to have been wooden, and were subsequently re–used. Harbour works on the Bunbury foreshore, including extensive land reclamation has substantially altered the topography of the probable area of the whaling stations. No surface evidence was located, although it is possible that remains are buried below later fill.

MININUP

Date Range: 1862–63+
Location: Possibly adjacent to Mininup Hill
1:100,000 AMG Reference: 2031 Bunbury

History

In 1862 Joseph Buswell registered a whaling party for 'Bunbury and Minninup' (GG 19/8/1862) and in the following year for 'Minenup, or elsewhere in the Wellington District' (GG 15/9/1863). There are no contemporary descriptions of this party's operation, although the Blue Books report that in the first year only one tun of oil was taken, with only 5.5 tuns in the second (BB 1862, 1863). A later account from a local octogenarian suggests that unregistered parties may well have continued whaling from this location on an irregular basis.

> When work for the men was slack on the farms and dairies, the settlers around Mininup combined and started whaling, but not with very great success. Mrs. Rose relates that a man with a spy glass was stationed on the highest hill near this place and also one on the Lighthouse Hill in Bunbury, who gave the alarm "Whale–ho!" or "Blow–ho!" whenever a whale was sighted. The boats would then be manned in a very short time and give chase. (Mitchell 1927)

It is possible that faced with the competition of Bateman's crews, it was hoped that a station at Mininup would sight and catch the whales before they proceeded north to Koombana Bay. However, as Buswell occupied Mininup House during this period (Erikson 1988: 417), the location of the station near to his holdings can be seen as an attempt to diversify from other pastoral or agricultural activities. An interesting report on smuggling in the colonies (Inq 8/5/1850) also states that 'Menninup' (sic) was one of the locations where American whalers would drop their illicit cargoes, being close to Bunbury, yet far enough away to escape detection.

Site Description

The area which is generally known as Minninup is approximately 19 km southwest of Bunbury, although no historical description has been found which provides a precise location for the Mininup whaling station. Adjacent to Minninup Homestead is a shallow cove backed by high dunes which is still used as an anchorage for small boats, and is the most likely position for the station. Several weatherboard buildings and sheds are situated in a gully between the sand dunes, immediately behind the anchorage. No evidence of whaling activity was located, although it is possible that evidence may be located on the private land behind the coastal reserve.

While not situated in a bay, Minninup provides several topographic features (anchorage, high dunes) which fit the pattern for whaling stations elsewhere on the west coast. The location is another compromise site, attempting to avoid direct competition with the Bunbury station, but also one of the few obvious attempts to combine whaling with the pastoral and agricultural interests of the adjacent hinterland.

TOBY INLET

Date Range: 1847

Location: Precise location unknown, but approximately 17 km west of Busselton.

1:100,000 AMG Reference: 1930 Busselton 309–759 (approximate only)

History

The operation of a shore station at or near Toby Inlet appears to have been limited to a single year, and then only appears in the historical record as a result of the fatalities which the party suffered during the season. In August 1847 it was reported that a Right whale taken by the Castle Rock party had previously been fastened to by the whale boat of another company which had come to grief (Inq 25/8/1847). After being struck by the headsman of this latter boat, the whale was said to have gone quietly for the first 400 yards, after which it turned and stove in the side of the craft, drowning three of the crew.

Little more is known of the station or its operation. Late in 1847 a summary of returns from the fisheries refers to 'Mr. Kerr's' party, but gives no location or quantities (PG 6/11/1847). As a Mr. H.T. Ker was known to be the manager of John Molloy's property which borders Toby Inlet (Erikson 1988: 1732), the connection with the whaling party appears certain. A pamphlet from the Busselton Historical Society, which states that the party consisted of only one boat, and that the drowned seamen were buried 'beneath the peppermint trees near Toby's Inlet' (Anon 1977). An alternative secondary source suggests that the bodies were buried 'under the peppermint trees near where Seymour's old cottage used to be in Dunn Bay Road' (Guinness n.d.:24), a considerable distance away in Dunsborough itself.

In 1846 another shore party, unrelated to Ker's venture, had also competed with the Castle Rock fishery from somewhere in Geographe Bay. The location of this station has not been identified, although it is possible that it was based at Toby's Inlet.

Toby Inlet held some significance in the early history of the area as the closest watering point for vessels visiting Busselton, there not being a supply readily available near the beach at the town itself. As a result, this became one of the points where both legitimate and black market transactions took place between settlers and visiting American whaleships (Inq 8/5/1850).

Site Description

Toby Inlet is located about 17 km west of Busselton and 10 km south–east of Castle Rock, opening onto the flat, sandy beach that forms the long curve of Geographe Bay. The area is an unlikely choice for a whaling station, exposed to the open sea without a headland or high dune for weather protection or look–out point. Toby Inlet itself is shallow and cannot currently be entered by boats, although it is possible that this was not the case in the 19th century.

In the absence of historical or topographic indicators which locate the station, the beachfront and adjacent vegetation were surveyed for 100 m to either side of the mouth of Toby Inlet. No surface indications were found.

The area about Toby Inlet contains virtually none of the topographic characteristics seen at whaling station sites elsewhere along the west coast. The main factors in its selection would seem to be the proximity to an existing land grant (Molloy's property), the need to operate outside of the lease boundaries of the adjacent whaling station (Castle Rock), and availability of fresh water (Toby Inlet).

CASTLE ROCK

Date Range: 1846–c.1872

Location: 25 km northwest of Busselton, between Sail Rock and Castle Rock.

1:100,000 AMG Reference: 1930 Busselton 231–826

History

The first colonial party was established at Castle Rock in 1845 after consistent use of the area by American vessels who had also reported on the potential of the site for bay whaling (Hasluck 1955; 212). Robert Viveash's 1845 lease of three miles of shoreline southward from Castle Bay as well as the adjacent pastoral land appears to have been aimed at excluding a rival colonial shore party from access to this area (CSR 140/107: 20/9/1845). Initially the lease payment was set at a staggering £40 for the 1845 and 1846 seasons, although this was later lowered to £30 after Viveash reduced the area of land under lease (CSR 140/108: 20/9/1845; CSR 140/110: 1/11/1845; CSF 19/392: 19/11/1845). In the following year the station operated again as the Castle Rock Whaling Company, possibly made up of a partnership of Viveash, Robert Habgood, Robert Heppingstone and Robert Sholl, all of whom are mentioned in connection with the station at various times (Seymour nd; PG 22/8/1846).

After 1847 Robert Heppingstone and George Chapman, took over management of Castle Rock. Heppingstone died in 1858, with his son–in–law George Layman then running the station until 1860 (SDUR L3/299: 18/3/1859). As described in Chapter 3, the diary of manager (and headsman) Frederick Seymour provides a daily record of the station's proceedings for 1846–53. During this time Castle Rock was a moderately successful small–scale fishery with two or sometimes three boats.

In 1861 a new partnership controlled by the Bunbury whaler 'Butty' (Maori headsman William Parr) and local land owner George Bridges, was listed as operating at Castle Rock (Erikson 1988:306; PG 21/8/1861). This lasted only a single year, followed by a hiatus in use until the late 1860s, when John Bateman decided to relocate his late season fishery from Bunbury. The exact date when Bateman commenced to visit the station is uncertain, although the first confirmed use is in 1871 (Herald 16/9/1871). The last recorded occupation by Bateman is a year later, with the catch of only five tuns of oil (Herald 30/11/1872).

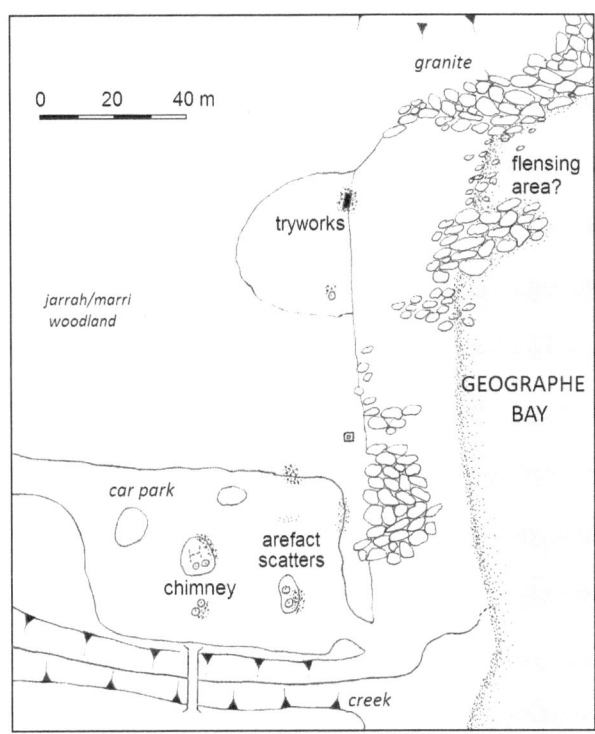

Figure A9 Castle Rock Site plan.

There are several reports over the years of Castle Rock parties using small vessels to assist operations (see Chapter Three). In 1847 Heppingstone arranged the hire of the newly–launched *Gazelle* to work with the shore party (Inq 4/8/1847), although this ship is not mentioned in Seymour's journal or subsequent news reports. In October 1848 Seymour (n.d.) notes the *Sonnet Bee* arriving to help 'cut–in', while in the following year the *Pelsart* came down from Fremantle to meet with Chapman's group (Inq 24/10/1849). George Layman is also known to have purchased the cutter *Brothers* in 1859 for use as a cutting–in vessel (Inq 25/5/1859), while Bateman would have also used his schooner *Twinkling Star* for a similar purpose (Herald 16/9/1871).

Despite Seymour's diary there is very little information on the physical nature of the station. The earliest reference is from March 1849, when it was reported that a bush fire had destroyed Heppingstone's whaling establishment. The loss of the whole of his gear, one whaleboat and all of the bone was estimated at several hundred pounds value, although the oil, presumably stored separately, narrowly escaped damage

(Inq 28/3/1849). It may have been in consideration of this situation that Heppingstone was allowed the lease of Castle Rock free of charge that year (CSF 27/205: 1/8/1849). The second reference is from 1871, when John Bateman was granted permission to erect at Castle Rock a two–roomed portable house for his whaling crew (CSR 9/6/1871). It is not known if the house was removed by Bateman at the end of his use of the station.

Site Description

Castle Rock is a relatively small, northward–facing sandy cove between granite outcrops, unlike the coastal formations seen elsewhere along the lower southwest coast. On the hill above Castle Rock is a white–painted granite boulder locally known as Lookout Rock, reputed to have been used by the whalers and more recently by salmon fishermen (Guinness n.d.). From this point there is an extremely wide view, both northwest into Castle Bay and southeast into Curtis Bay and Dunn Bay. A more accessible look–out with similar, if somewhat more limited views is from the top of Castle Rock, situated to the east of the site.

The site of the Castle Rock whaling station is well known and has been marked by a cairn and plaque erected in 1969 by the Royal Western Australian Historical Society. Several archaeological features still remain, although as a popular fishing and swimming place many of these have been destroyed through various processes. The habitation area was located on the west side of the winter creek, in the space now occupied by the car park. The foundations of at least two buildings were intact until the mid 1970s and at least one of the structures was floored with whalebone (J. Lord pers. comm. 1989). Several pieces of the vertebrae paving were rescued by the Busselton Museum after the local council graded away the remaining structural features to form the car park. Small scatters of highly fragmented ceramics and glass are still visible within this area, although no diagnostic pieces could be located. These artefacts, including some pieces of brick, worked stone and mortar are closely associated with the raised islands of soil surrounding the trees and vegetation left standing within the car park. The most substantial of these is a low mound located on the south end of the car park (furthest from the beach). While only several meters square in area, this appears to contain a fairly substantial section of masonry, possibly a chimney base.

The foundation of the tryworks is located approximately 60 m west of the memorial cairn, at the juncture between the beach sand and soil. Located well above the high–tide mark, the structure is of stone and brick, and of sufficient size to take two trypots (see Figure 4.9). There is no evidence of a covering structure. The flensing area was probably to the northwest of the tryworks, in or just beyond the clear area between two concentrations of boulders. There is no evidence for a ramp or platform, although the expanse of beach would require some sort of surface for winching the blubber to the processing area.

The tryworks were cleared of vegetation and surrounding earth during the 1987 National Trust survey, and the main dimensions recorded (MacIlroy 1987). This loose overburden was removed again in 1990, with the structure drawn and a sample of the ash removed from both hearths.

SOUTH COAST SURVEY

The south coast of Western Australia is characterised by large granite outcrops which form mountains, headlands and islands. The action of heavy southwest swells and easterly littoral currents upon these granite hard points has resulted in the formation of numerous crescent–shaped sandy bays which open towards the east (Woods 1980). Tidal variation is likely to be less than one meter.

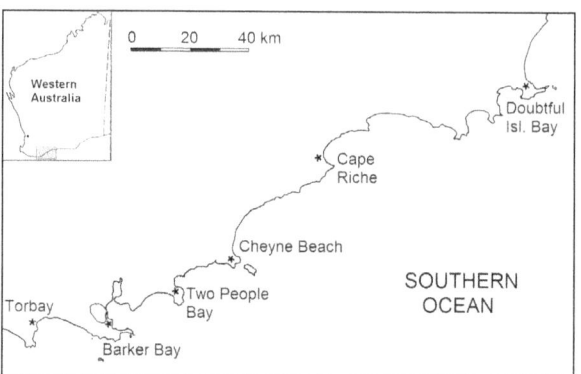

Figure A10 South Coast whaling stations.

The climate west of Doubtful Island Bay experiences a Moderate Mediterranean climate with cold and wet winters peaking in July–August. To the east around Cape Arid the climate is classified as Dry Mediterranean, with six or more dry months each year. On the coastal fringe itself, the cold winds, rain and squalls blowing in from the Southern Ocean during the winter months can make maritime work difficult.

TORBAY/ MIGO ISLAND

Date Range: 1844–1848, 1861–c.1864

Location: East side of Torbay, slightly NW of Migo Island.

1:100,000 AMG Reference: 2427 Albany 587–188

History

In 1844 a shore station was established in Torbay by John William Andrews (sometimes referred to as Williams), a sealer who had also previously conducted a whale fishery in Two People's Bay. During 1844 the operation employed Andrews' schooner *Vulcan* and two whaleboats, taking six tuns of oil and 500 pounds of bone worth £133 (Heppingstone n.d. b). In 1845 John Sinclair was granted the lease of Migo Island as his whaling establishment at an annual fee of £5, a move supported by the local Resident Magistrate as a means of excluding Andrews and his 'convict party' from the area (CSR 139/61; 20/5/1845). An appeal was made that the fee be lowered, clarifying that the island was only intended to be the look–out for the station (CSR 139/37; 20/3/1845), with the fee eventually lowered to £1.10s (CSR 139/61; 20/5/1845). During the season Sinclair used his boat *Julian* (Garden 1977), although no returns were reported to judge whether the party was successful.

Sinclair renewed his lease for the following year and left his trypots in place in anticipation (CSR 139/119; 14/11/1845; CSF 19/408: 2/12/1845). However, only Thomas Morton with his schooner *Thetis* is specifically mentioned as being at Torbay during the 1846 season (PG 5/9/1846), although one report does refer to 'the *parties* [my emphasis] stationed at Torbay' (PG 12/12/1846). The *Thetis* was recorded as taking 25 tuns of oil, three of which were sperm oil (PG 12/12/1846). Andrews may then have occupied the station in 1847 (CSF 23/208: 4/6/1847), with Sinclair possibly using it in 1847 (Heppingstone nd. b).

Torbay was next occupied in 1861 when Hugh McKenzie registered a party of 14 men for a two boat fishery (G.G. 18/6/1861). The season was either brief or unsuccessful, as the Blue Book (1861) records a total take of only two and a half tuns of oil (probably a single whale), worth only £90. There is no record of operations in 1862, although in 1863 and 1864 McKenzie organised a two–boat party, taking eight tuns and 18 tuns of oil in the respective seasons. A report from 1864 suggests that several tuns of oil had been lost through lack of a second trypot (Inq 16/11/1864). The location does not appear to have been used after 1864.

Site Description

Migo Island is a drowned granite mass in the northwest corner of Torbay. The island and an adjacent headland protects a strand of beach on the mainland, although this area is backed by a very steep ridge. The 1987 survey (MacIlroy 1987) located a stone feature on the mainland shore slightly northwest of Migo Island, at the foot of the ridge and close to the current landing area. The removal of covering vegetation and earth suggested that this was granite and mortar rubble from a structure, although no diagnostic artefacts were found which could positively identify this as the whaling station site. When re–inspected in 1989 and 1993 the area was heavily overgrown with limited visibility. The rubble covers an area of approximately 2 m^2, although in 1989 it was noted that further mounds or raised areas of earth and scatters of unmortared stone, possibly natural expressions, continued to the northwest. However, the lack of a clear pattern or distribution of the stone suggests that this material may have been pushed aside several meters by a bulldozer or other means to create an adjacent cleared area used by modern fishermen. No surface artefacts were seen.

The small beach where the stone material is located is on the lee side of Migo Island and sheltered from Southern Ocean swells, while the adjacent ridge provides further protection from wind and rains. Other than the beach itself, there was no location in the immediate area suggestive of a flensing or processing area. It was not possible to visit Migo Island to investigate evidence for look–outs, although the peak would provide good visibility throughout Torbay.

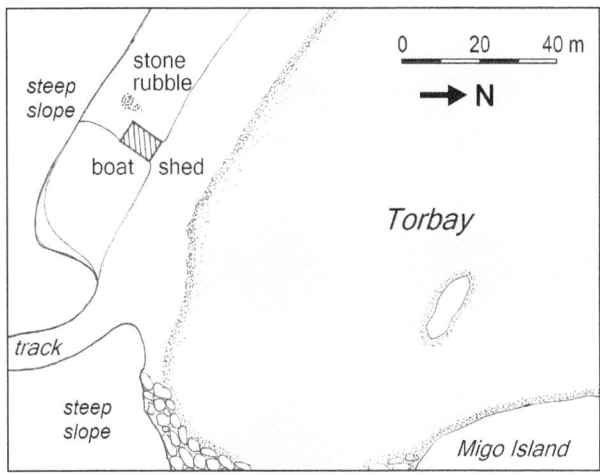

Figure A11 Torbay site plan.

An 1837 survey plan of Torbay shows a small building labelled 'Shipbuilder's Hut' in the approximate area of the site (Broeze and Henderson 1986:60). Immediately next to this are two parallel lines of points marked 'A vessel of 150 tons on the stocks here', almost certainly the vessel constructed for T.B. Sherratt (PG 14/4/1838), while nearby are further notes including 'sandy beach' and 'good water'. It is clear that prior to the whaling period the area was a known anchorage and already in use by colonial entrepreneurs. It is possible that the structural remains are associated with the early shipbuilders, the whalers, or both. Subsequently Torbay has been a centre for timber milling, boat–building and fishing, with the area of the site including a dilapidated modern fishing shed and the remains of segments of old railway line possibly formerly used to slip boats.

BARKER BAY/ WHALING COVE

Date Range: 1849–c.1873

Location: Whaling Cove, west side of King George's Sound, 5 km southeast of Albany.

1:100,000 AMG Reference: 2427 Albany 845–201

History

It appears that James Daniells, a publican in Albany, had already commenced the 1849 season with a one boat fishery elsewhere in King George's Sound before he decided (or was forced) to apply for a lease of land on which to form a station

> situated in Barkers Bay on the west side of King George's Sound, with about (20) twenty chains water frontage having a shelving rock above the centre running into the seas. And I also beg to apply for the lease of Mistaken Island to run a few sheep on for my establishment (CSR 189/249: 16/8/1849).

The Resident Magistrate supported the application, suggesting purchase or a long lease would allow Daniells to erect tryworks and buildings for his men in a substantial manner suitable for a permanent station (CSR 189/250: 26/8/1849). Although the land could not be sold because of its strategic value, the government allowed a seven year lease, renewable annually provided he occupied the site during the whaling season (CSR 189/247: 12/9/1849).

The King George's Sound station, presumably the Barker Bay site, is noted in various records as operating continuously between 1849 and 1852. A hiatus of several years follows in which there no mention of the station, until 1856 when several reports which suggest there was a party in the area (Inq 15/10/1856; BB 1856). In 1857 the station commenced operations under the control of Thomas Sherratt (Inq 15/7/1857), the son of Thomas Booker Sherratt who had operated at Doubtful Island Bay in 1836 and 1837. It is uncertain whether Daniells also maintained an interest in this party, as there is correspondence from him regarding a lease of Mistaken Island as a station (CSF 41/543: 10/8/1857). Alternatively, it is possible that he attempting to form his own party.

Sherratt occupied Barker Bay consistently until at least 1872, using it as his early season station before proceeding eastward to Barrier Anchorage. In 1872 he sought to renew his lease on both Barker Bay and Barrier Anchorage, once again describing the areas (BL Acc. 346 (14/73): 8/5/1872). The extent of the lease (Plantagenet license 928) had increased slightly in size from the original, taking in about 25 chains (502 m) of shoreline and 22 acres (9 ha) in area.

Besides the station at Barker Bay, several sources suggest associations with Mistaken (Rabbit) Island, and the use of the island to hold sheep for the station has been described above. In 1850 there is a report of a whaling party formed at Mistaken Island (Inq 31/7/1850), as well as Daniells' 1857 inquiries. Reminiscences from Sale (1936), McKail (1927) and Chester (1927) all speak of whaling activity in connection Mistaken (Rabbit) Island, especially use of the island as a look–out. However, it is difficult to determine if the site was a separate station from Barker Bay.

Site Description

The Barker Bay site retains structural evidence for both the processing and habitation areas of the whaling station. Fifteen 50 cm by 50 cm test–pits were excavated around these two zones to determine whether the archaeological deposits would be suitable for the more extensive excavation intended for this project.

The bay consists of a sandy beach between granite points, backed by sand dunes and a high ridge. The tryworks is located on the southern side of the sloping granite sheet forming the western edge of the small bay. Presumably the whale would be anchored in the water adjacent to this platform, and the blubber winched over the rocks to the trypot(s). The tryworks structure is reduced to a granite base measuring approximately 3 m by 2 m, situated at the juncture of the granite and the vegetation line (Figure 4.12). Within it is the solidified black organic deposit seen in other tryworks. Several test pits around the area of the tryworks produced a quantity of iron barrel hoops strapping. Other artefacts including clay pipe fragments were present on a eroding dune 15m east.

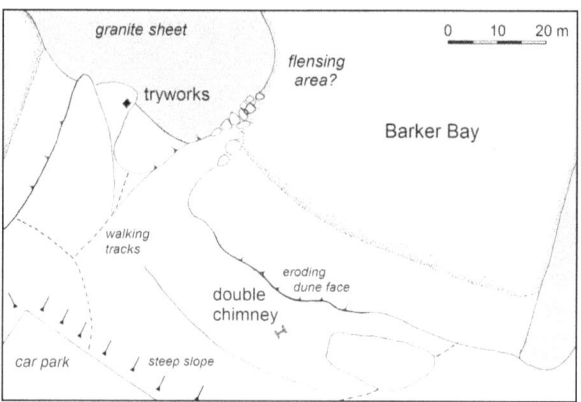

Figure A12 Barker Bay Site Plan.

On the dune ridge above the beach (now seriously eroded), sit the remains of an east–west facing stone built double fireplace, although no other evidence for walls or other structures is visible. Small test pits to the west of the fireplace revealed a stone floor surface, although the full dimensions were not established. Artefacts recovered from test pits adjacent to the structure included were largely undiagnostic 19th century glass, ceramic and faunal material, apart from a clay tobacco pipe stem stamped with 'MURRAY' 'GLASGOW' confirming a date range of 1830–1860 (Oswald 1975:205). Interviews with local residents suggested that various artefacts have been recovered as they erode out of the dune surfaces.

The headland to the east of Whalers Cove would provide a view across King George's Sound, and possibly into Frenchman's Bay itself. However, there is no immediately visible feature which suggests a look–

out point and a survey of the hillside did not reveal any structural or other archaeological evidence.

Although the beach immediately west of Mistaken Island was also briefly surveyed, no evidence was found to suggest possible use as a whaling station. The location provides some advantages with its outlook over King George Sound and Frenchman's Bay, with the disadvantage that the area is more exposed to winds and swells than Barker Bay. Slightly to the northwest of Mistaken Island is a sloping granite slab which might have suited as a flensing area, while south of this are sandy beaches which are afforded some slight shelter by the island and the reef which stretches between it and the mainland. These attributes make the location suitable for use, while it is possible that the clearly evident storm action has removed physical remains from the area.

TWO PEOPLES BAY

Date Range: 1842–1844, c.1870s

Location: North side of King George Sound, south end of Two People Bay, 34 km west of Albany.

1:100,000 AMG Reference: 2528 Manypeaks 083–295

History

In 1838 and 1839 a combination of American, French and Australian whaling vessels took catches of whales from within Two Peoples Bay yielding at least 650 tuns and well over 1000 of oil (PG 28/7/1838; PG 24/11/1838; PG 1/12/38; PG 17/8/1839; CO 18/26: 30/6/1840). Colonial use of the location dates from 1842, when James William Andrews requested protection for his fishery from foreign whalers (CSR 111/152: 2/5/1842). Despite the uncertainty regarding colonial powers to restrict foreign whaling, a letter was issued warning non–British ships that persons interfering with the colonial party or whaling within three miles of the coast would risk forfeiture of their vessel.

Little is recorded of the 1842 or 1843 season, although a second letter of protection issued in the latter year describes it as consisting of four boats and 30 men (CSR 119/98; 22/6/1843). It is possible that Andrews was using his vessel *Fanny* (PG 8/10/1842) or in the latter year the *Vulcan* (Garden 1977) to assist operations. Exports through Albany in 1843/44 included 13 tuns of whale oil and 700 pounds of bone, which could only have come from the Two Peoples Bay station (Garden 1977: 79). Another interesting feature is the 1843 census of Albany, which recorded a population of 260 persons, including 16 Americans employed at Two Peoples Bay (Glover 1952: 119).

Andrews moved his whaling operations to Torbay in 1844 (Heppingstone n.d. b) leaving another unidentified local party to form a station at Two Peoples Bay (Inq 6/11/1844). While an un–named brig from Tasmania was reported as taking 1000 barrels of oil in the bay, the local party took nothing, with several of the hands even deserting to join the Tasmanian ship (Inq 6/11/1844).

No other colonial party is reported as using Two Peoples Bay for at least the next two decades. In a set of reminiscences, Evidence for later use of the station is contained in a set of reminiscences of the 1880s and 1890s with McGaughin (1916) recounting the *Grace Darling* riding out a squall at the anchorage in Two Peoples Bay.

> The Mackenzie Brothers once had a shore whaling station in the bay, and near a shallow fresh water swamp we came across evidences of their sojourn, the rotting remains of a whaleboat, a discarded trypot, a broken steering oar, and part of a rusted harpoon.

There is no documentary evidence that the McKenzies, who commenced whaling in the early 1860s, used Two Peoples Bay as a station during that decade, preferring Torbay, Cape Riche or Doubtful Island Bay. However, it is possible that during the 1870s when parties were being registered for the 'east coast' (Cape Arid), Two Peoples Bay may have been used as an early season station. Webb (1963) suggests that in the 1850s Thomas Sherratt (Jnr) used the bay for whaling, but does not provide a source for this. She also states that 1873 and 1874 Mary Taylor of Candyup Station recorded in her diary several instances of men calling in en route to various whaling stations, including Two Peoples Bay. The possibility of later use therefore remains, but by which party is unresolved.

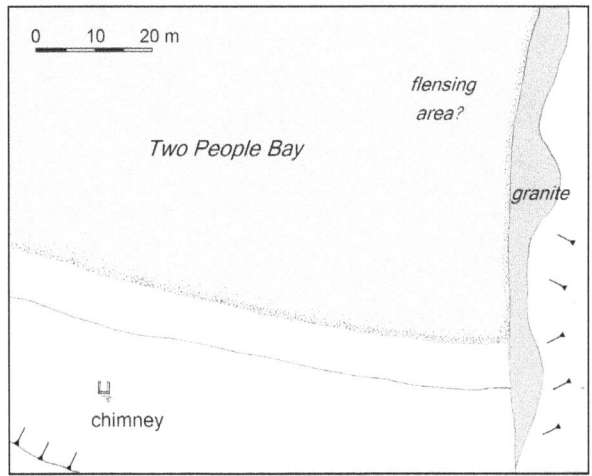

Figure A13 Two People Bay site plan.

Site Description

Two Peoples Bay is a semi–circular sandy beach between granite headlands. The historical record does not indicate the precise location of the station site, although there are several indicators. McGaughin's (1916) account records that the remains of the station were near 'a shallow freshwater swamp', which would place the site just west of South Point. Alternatively, Webb (1963) states that remains could still be seen 'at a little beach just south of the main one'. During the survey of Barker Bay, a local fisherman recalled a friend removing two trypots from Two People's Bay 'from the little beach past the granite boulders' (G. Brown pers. comm. 1990).

The cove located immediately southwest of South Point and separated from the main (western) beach by large granite boulders includes a protected sandy beach backed by a low, flat dune area, with a sloping granite ledge running up from the water along the east side. Survey along the vegetated dune behind the eastern corner of the beach located the base of a stone chimney base facing northwards, towards the water. The external dimensions were approximately 1.45 m along the sides and 2.25 m along the back, giving an internal area of 1.10 m by 2.35 m wide. There were no signs of other structural remains and no surface artefacts.

The higher end of the granite shelf was unsuccessfully searched for evidence for the tryworks. It is possible that vegetation cover, particularly the seaweed which has collected on the flatter areas of the ledge, had covered any structural remains. As noted, the trypots are reported to have been removed only this century, although their current location is unknown. A position on nearby South Point provides a wide view through the bay and adjacent seas and is visible from the site, although no structural or artefact evidence for a look–out could be found.

CHEYNE BEACH

Date Range: 1846–1877

Location: South corner of Hassell Beach, approximately 47 km northeast of Albany.

1:100,000 AMG Reference: 2528 Manypeaks 285–393

History

Cheyne Beach was known as a bay–whaling location for foreign vessels from at least 1840 (CO 18/26: 281, 30/6/1840), with the perennial fresh water spring 1 km NW of the headland used as a watering point.

In 1846 a whaling party was formed at Cheyne Beach through a partnership of Solomon Cook, John Thomas and John Craigie, also referred to in contemporary reports as 'Cheyne's party' (PG 3/10/1846, Inq 16/12/46). While it is possible that George Cheyne (a south coast merchant who had a whaleship supply base at neighbouring Cape Riche) held some interest in the station, this may simply be the colonial press confusing the name of the location with the man. A lease was granted for two acres of ground 'surrounding the boat harbour' at an annual fee of 35 shillings (CSR 149/31: 5/3/1846, CSR 149/64: 30/4/1846).

The season proceeded well, with 17 tuns of oil from eight humpbacks being taken by early August (Inq 5/8/1846), and 55 tuns of oil by early October (PG 3/10/1846). However, there were obviously difficulties in the management of the station, with Thomas going so far as to publish a notice during the following year stating that the partnership had been dissolved, and that his current whaling party had no connection with either John Craigie or Solomon Cook (Inq 14/7/1847). Thomas must have been granted the lease of the station, which would have included all of the buildings and improvements. His two–boat fishery had a successful year, but was forced to break up in late October with 52 tuns of oil and two tons of bone after running out of casks (Inq 9/6/1847; Inq 3/11/1847). It is uncertain if Thomas operated in 1848, although there is a report from the south coast that a two boat party with some Aboriginal crewmen had taken 70 tuns of oil and two tons of bone (Inq 29/11/1848).

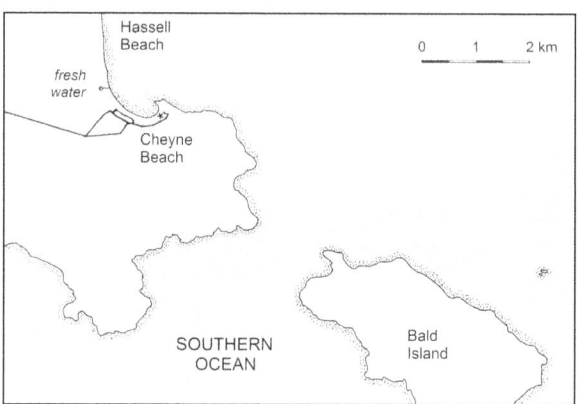

Figure A14 Cheyne Beach Location.

The Cheyne Beach station under Thomas's management appears to have operated continuously until at least 1868 or 1869, usually with a two boat party. The exception is in 1862, when Thomas is registered for Middle Island in the Archipelago of the Recherché, while Hugh McKenzie is listed for Cheyne Beach (GG 29/7/1862). Captain Thomas Sale (1936) recalled that when he was a hand at the station during the late 1860s, Thomas would use Cheyne Beach from June to August for humpback fishing, before moving eastward to Cape Riche or Doubtful Island Bay to catch right whales.

From 1870 John Thomas is no longer mentioned in connection with whaling. The Cheyne Beach station was subsequently registered by various other operators such as Thomas Sherratt (GG 5/7/1870), Nehemiah Fisher (GG 11/7/1871; GG 4/6/1872) and John Bruce (GG 29/5/1877). 1877 is the last year that whaling is known to have occurred at Cheyne Beach, although a later source stated that when he had visited the site in 1902 he was told that operations had ceased in 1889 or

1890 (WA 17/5/1950). This date is ten years later than the last reports of organised whaling off the south coast, but may indicate an undocumented and informal continuation of the industry.

Some anecdotal information regarding the Cheyne Beach station recorded in memoirs from McKail (1927) and Sale (1936) is discussed in Chapter **. After the closure of the whaling station the anchorage was used as a transshipment point for wool from surrounding stations, and a stone and wooden wool store was constructed in the area now occupied by a car park, slightly north of the site. It is possible that the stone foundation for this building, demolished in the 1960s, was taken from the whaling station. Salmon fishermen have also used the beaches, and the immediate vicinity of the site was a popular camping site from the 1950s onwards. Further historical information on Cheyne Beach is contained in Chapter 7.

Site Description

Cheyne Beach is the southernmost portion of Hassell Beach, an extremely long, sandy bay which terminates at its northern end with Cape Riche. The orientation of the bay, the granite headland and a small reef provide protection from wind and some swell, and the bay is currently used as an anchorage by salmon fishermen.

The 1987 National Trust survey was directed to the site by long–time resident of the area, Charles 'Snapper' Westerberg (MacIlroy 1987). Archaeological excavations conducted as part of the current project show that there are extensive subsurface structural remains and artefact deposits in the dune area approximately 50 m south of the headland. These are described in more detail in Chapter 5.

There was no historical indication of the location of the tryworks, although there are several features suggestive of the general area. The first is a scour channel which runs adjacent to the sheltered south side of the point, forming an area deep enough to haul a whale into. Oral evidence supports this, and includes the information that small punts were used alongside the carcass as a platform for flensing (Westerberg pers. comm. 1989). There are two areas where sloping granite sheets might have aided the process. The first is towards the end of the point, and has a level area above it which might have served as a working surface. Although there is ash and material shown in shallow erosion area, there is no clear evidence for a tryworks. A similar granite sheet is seen closer to the shore, although the area above this has been cleared and altered by modern fishermen to include a concrete floor. The final option is that the blubber was hauled up to a tryworks on the main beach, although no physical evidence was found to support this.

Historical information suggests that the look–out was on the ridge of the hill to the north of the site (McKail 1927; *Albany Mail* 18/12/1889), with the probable location being the large granite boulder at the peak of this. Although it was not possible to detect deliberate working of the stone, there is a small ledge near the top of the boulder which proves to be an ideal seat for anyone watching towards Hassell Bay and the open sea. No artefacts were visible around the base of the boulder. Large sections of whalebone can be seen along the shore at Cheyne Beach, and local fishermen state that these are often dredged up by the sea after heavy storms. Further information on the Cheyne Beach site is contained in Chapters 5–7.

CAPE RICHE

Date Range: 1870–1872+

Location: Southern end of Cheyne Bay, 3 km northwest of Cape Riche.

1:100,000 AMG Reference: 2628 Cheyne 606–701

History

As early as 1835 there was an application to use of Cape Riche as a whaling station, with Henry Ommaney applying for a grant of 2650 acres including the adjacent island (Cheyne Island), 'it being a very desirable and eligible situation for a whaling establishment which I contemplate shortly commencing' (CSR 46/20: 10/12/1835). The application was refused, despite Ommaney's appeals (CSR 46/22: 4/5/1836).

In 1842 Albany merchant George Cheyne established his homestead and an independent supply base for foreign whaling vessels at Cape Riche, providing 'water, fuel, vegetables and fresh meat, and other necessaries... at moderate prices' (PG 18/11/1843; Stephens 1951). The operation was a bold and astute move which proved highly successful, allowing the masters to avoid paying the excessive harbour fees of Western Australian ports and minimising the risks of desertion and drunkenness that arose on visits to settlements. The safe anchorage also made the area attractive to American and French vessels wintering and bay–whaling (Inq 6/11/1844; Inq 9/9/1846; Inq 7/7/1852).

Sale (1936) suggests that John Thomas from Cheyne Beach may have begun using the location as a late season station in the late 1860s, long after its demise as an independent port. The first firmly recorded use was in 1870, when John MacKenzie registered a two–boat party for that location, probably using it as his early season station (GG 5/7/70). The *Inquirer* also commented that Mr. MacKenzie was 'occupying his old berth at Cape Riche', implying an earlier association (Inq 20/7/1870). Two years later another party with 12 men was registered for that site by Cuthbert MacKenzie, although by early September they had returned to Albany, having taken only one small whale yielding 2 tuns of oil (GG 4/6/1872; Her 7/9/1872). The same report notes that they would depart the following week for the head of the Great Australian Bight 'in order to be in time for the right whale season'.

After this time registrations tended to be for 'east coast' stations, although it is possible that Cape Riche was still used.

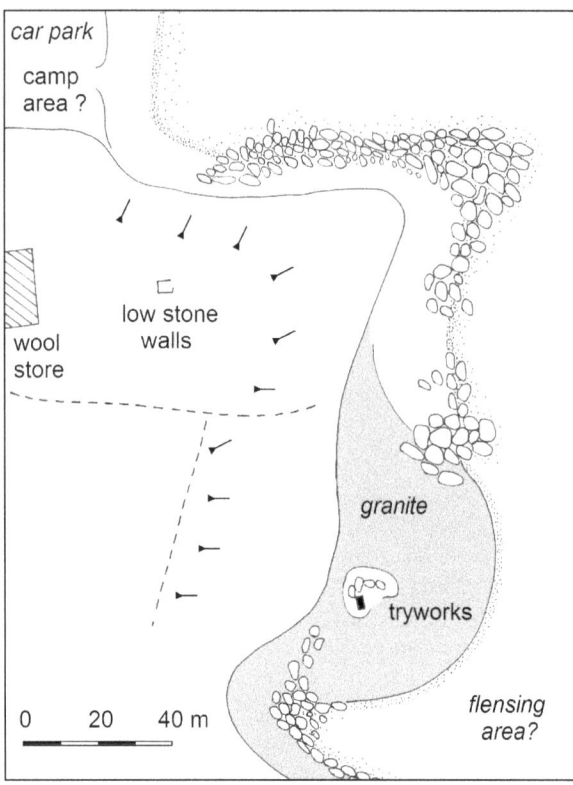

Figure A14 Cape Riche Site Plan.

Site Description

The site of the whaling station is 3 km northwest of Cape Riche at the end of Cheyne Bay, opposite Cheyne Island. These topographic features form a sheltered anchorage used during the late 19th and early 20th centuries as a transshipment point for wool from farms in the area. A late 19th century wool store has survived on the ridge above the sheltered sandy beach and it is probable that the whaling station camp would have been located nearby, possibly in the area now occupied by the modern campsite. No evidence of the campsite was located, although footings of later buildings related to salmon fishing are evident.

Approximately 160 m eastward of the car park is a granite shelf sloping up from a slightly protected area. Thirty five meters above the high tide mark is a small island of soil and vegetation which appears to contain the remains of a stone tryworks. Measuring 2.10 m (N.E. to S.W.) by 1.10 m, only the lower 30 cm of the structure remains. It did not prove possible to locate ash or other products of the trywork process in or around the structure, although access to internal deposits was limited by the overburden of rubble. A small trypot is located in the front garden of nearby Cape Riche station, although the Moir family (the long–term owners) has no specific knowledge of its origin other than it being from the whaling station.

Although it was not possible to visit Cheyne Island, historical records suggest it may contain archaeological features. A survey of Cape Riche by F.T. Gregory in 1849 includes one sighting from the Cape to a 'whaler's lookout' on Cheyne Island (Gregory 1850). As this predates the colonial use of the area it is probable that the look–out was for the foreign vessels anchored in Cheyne Bay. Reminiscences by Laurance Gorman, a member of McKenzie's 1870 whaling party, describe the graves of three French whalers on Cheyne Island, which he refers to as Oars Island, as well as several engravings on the granite including the date '1764' and '18 tuns' (AA 22/8/1829).

DOUBTFUL ISLAND BAY

Date Range: 1836–1838, 1863–1870s

Location: Corner Cove (House Beach), southern edge of Doubtful Island Bay.

1:100,000 AMG Reference: 2829 Hood Point 322–943

History

As described in Chapter 2, Doubtful Island Bay was the site of the first shore station in Western Australia, organised through a partnership of Albany Merchant Thomas Booker Sherratt and William Lovett, a Hobart whaling captain (Sherratt 1836). Sherratt made an application for use of land in Doubtful Island Bay for the 1837 season (SDUR S3/271: 6/12/1836), although the actual lease is made out to John McKail (CSR 52/133: 17/3/1837; L&S Red No. 522). The station lease, encompassing ten acres around Whale Point (now Whalebone Point), was taken for ten years at a peppercorn rent, with all improvements to revert to the Crown upon failure to pay or other cancellation of the arrangement (CSR 52/133; 17/3/1837).

A second colonial whaling party organised at Doubtful Island Bay for the 1837 season may not have required a shore station at all. George Cheyne, another Albany merchant, entered into an arrangement with the master of the American whaler *Charles Wright* which saw the colonial party embarking on the foreign vessel and joining with them in bay whaling (CSR 55/29: 9/8/1837). Sherratt, operating again in partnership with Lovett (CSR 53/45: 14/4/1837), complained about the presence of the American vessel and the government's responsibilities to protect the interests of the settlers (CSR 53/43: 14/4/1837; CSR 55/14: 5/5/1837). He was eventually pacified by entering into his own arrangement for assistance and sale of oil (SRG 29/6/1837; CSR 55/29: 9/8/1837). There is no record of the season's catch for either group.

There are no reports in either colonial newspapers or government correspondence to suggest that any whaling activity took place on the south coast between 1838 and 1841. There are some indications that Sherratt attempted to continue shore whaling (Stephens 1963), but quit in frustration at the inability of the government to prevent foreign interference, declaring that

> a man must be a fay idiot to fish with a land party if foreigners are allowed to come into this port, take our men, proceed to the bay...and blockade the land party (CSR 55/14; 5/5/1842).

Renewed interest in the location came with the introduction of movement between early and late season stations. During the 1860s Hugh McKenzie used Doubtful Island Bay in conjunction with Torbay, although in later years he may have used it in tandem with an east coast (Cape Arid) station. Government Gazette registrations show that he maintained a two boat party but was only moderately successful, usually taking fewer than 20 tuns of oil (Inq 16/11/1864; Inq 22/11/1865). In 1866 two of his men, J. Raison and A. Appleyard were killed at Doubtful Island Bay after a whale struck their boat (Inq 15/8/66; GG 17/7/1866). The bodies were buried close to the station (Hassell n.d). The final date at which the station was used for whaling is uncertain, but may well have been in the 1870s.

After the close of whaling activity the anchorage at Doubtful Island Bay was used by the Hassell family, who had a pastoral property at Jerramungup. A shearing shed and living quarters were constructed in the 1890s and the bay used as the transshipment point for wool.

Site Description

On two occasions (1989 and 1993) unseasonal weather prevented access into Doubtful Island Bay. It is likely that the whaling station(s) were located on House Beach, a NE facing sandy cove which from the late 19th century was also the site for a Hassell family homestead and shearing quarters, as well as a mid–20th century salmon fishing camp (Heberle 1985). Given the prevailing swells and similarities with other south coast sites, the processing area is likely to have been in the sheltered SE corner.

Hassell (n.d.) mentions two features at Home Beach which may relate to the whaling period. The first is a stone–lined well approximately 3 m deep (said to have now been filled). The other are the two whalers graves which, while no longer visible, are thought to have been 'only a few yards away from the well', and were formerly marked with a piece of inscribed whalebone (Hassell n.d: 310). Hassell also states that there were meant to be trypots near the well 'years ago' (Hassell n.d: 310).

EAST COAST

MIDDLE ISLAND

Date Range: 1862+

Location: Eastern end Archipelago of the Recherché,

1:100,000 AMG Reference: 3529 Cape Arid 182–273 (station) 169–287 (Goose Island look–out)

History

Middle Island was occupied as a semi–permanent base by Eastern Australian sealing gangs from the early 1820s onwards (Lockyer 1826; Rintoul 1964; Cumpston 1970). The sealers were still active on the island during the 1840s (Nairn–Clarke 1842; Inq 5/1/1848) and sealing may have continued intermittently into the second half of the 19th Century (Inq 17/4/1850; BB 1872; BB 1880). Sale (1936), who was a whaler during the 1860s, recalled a story that a group of whalers who had worked at Kangaroo Island and Holdfast (Glenelg) Bay had arrived at Middle Island and set up a station in the mid–1840s. He continues that the station was very successful for a time, but that the 'whaling leaders', led by John Thomas, had then moved to Albany. There is some evidence that Sale is referring to John William Andrews who had previously used the island as a sealing base, and is known to have wrecked his schooner *Vulcan* on Flinders Island while en–route to Middle Island for the whaling season (deLeiuen 1998). It is possible that he had also there prior to this.

The first confirmed colonial whaling station on Middle Island was established in 1862 by John Thomas, manager of Cheyne Beach (GG 29/7/62). The Blue Book (1862) report of the catch from Middle Island was of only eight tuns of oil, (possibly one or two whales) and 750 pounds of bone. This was not a poor return, but by this stage the south coast stations were taking less than 15 tuns each per year. There are no other specific references to whaling activity on Middle Island, although it is highly probable that other colonial whaling parties were to use this location as activity on the east coast increased during the late 1860s and 1870s.

Site Description

Middle Island is located at the eastern end of the Archipelago of the Recherché, approximately 120 km east of Esperance and nine km offshore from Cape Arid. Distance and difficulty of access excluded the possibility of visiting Middle Island as part of this survey, although previous surveys by Pearson (1988) gave particular attention to evidence of whaling and sealing activity. Pearson (1988) located the remains of two stone chimneys, a stone floor, a hut base, and a stone–lined well situated behind the sand dunes next to the granite headland at the east end of Goose Island Bay, on the north side of the island. Further survey work was undertaken by the Western Australian Maritime

Museums in 2001 (Green *et al.* 2001). These remains have not been identified or dated, although Andrews (1959) notes they were there in the late 19th century.

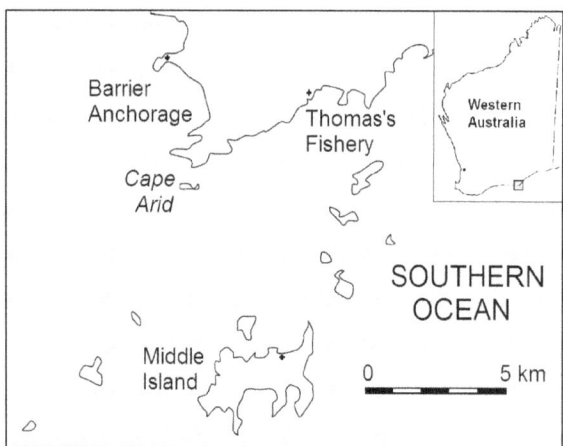

Figure A15 East Coast Stations.

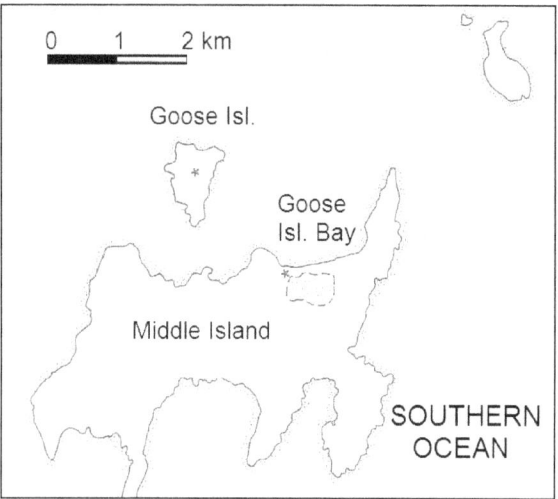

Figure A16 Middle Island.

Pearson (1988) also located a stone cairn and two possible look–outs on Goose Island, north of Goose Island Bay. Of these latter features, the first is a semi-circular dry–stone wall of about 2 m long by 1 m high, with an associated freshwater pool which may have been artificially enlarged. The second is a rectangular dry–stone wall of 2.6 m long, 2.5 m wide and standing 60 cm high. No surface artefacts were located. Pearson suggests that the orientation of the structures would make them ideal look–outs for a whaling station on Middle Island.

BARRIER ANCHORAGE

Date range 1871+

Location: 4 kilometres north of Cape Arid.

1:100,000 AMG Reference: 3530 Sandy Bight 139–405 (station), 138–404 (look–out)

History

In 1871 Thomas Sherratt registered a party of 11 men for the 'east coast' (GG 11/7/1871). Despite poor success (Inq 15/11/1871), in the following year Sherratt renewed his Barker Bay lease and was granted the use of fifty acres at 'a small bay situated about three miles westward from Cape Arid' for the sum of £1 (BL Acc. 346, 8/5/1872). Sherratt's use of his leases to exclude other whalers from these bays was challenged during the next season by rival operator Hugh McKenzie, resulting in all south coast whaling leases being cancelled (BL Acc.346: 16/1/1873; 12/2/1873).

Even without a formal lease, it is probable that Sherratt continued to occupy the Barrier Anchorage station until his last recorded whaling party in 1879. For at least two or more years he also undertook to freight goods to and from the Dempster's Esperance Station, possibly as a means of offsetting the costs of transporting his whaling crews (Erikson 1978).

Site Description

Barrier Anchorage is located on the west side of Cape Arid. In 1988 Pearson identified a tryworks and a look–out at the northern end of the bay (Pearson 1988). In 1993 these features were re–inspected and recorded, but no further evidence for whaling activity was located.

The tryworks is situated above a sloping granite slab approximately 100 m west of a commercial fisherman's camp (Cahill's camp) which is in the northeast corner of the bay. There appear to be several lines of stone over a 6 m stretch of shore, suggesting there may have been more than one trypot position. However, only one hearth, dug out by fishermen some years previously, can be clearly identified. The interior of this hearth yielded a sample of the black consolidated organic matter characteristic of tryworks.

On top of the headland, which rises at least 40 m above the beach, are two semicircular dry–stone structures, each of several meters length and forming an enclosed area of several meters (Figures 4.7 and 4.8). These walls are only 70 cm in height, although if loose rubble was replaced on the eastern wall it might increase to as much as one meter. The orientation of these shelters would provide protection from southerly and south–easterly winds, while the position provides views of the bays along the western side of Cape Arid, as well as the adjacent ocean out towards Middle Island. The 1988 survey found fragments of bottle glass and clay tobacco pipes scattered about the structure, although these were not seen by the 1993 survey.

Information from a local fisherman suggests that a similar look-out feature is located on the island immediately south of Barrier Anchorage and on the high ground behind Cape Arid (Pearson 1988). A look-out at the former location would provide no advantage over the headland position and seems unlikely. Fishermen staying at the nearby commercial fishing camp in 1993 confirmed that there are small sandy bays closer to Cape Arid which might be used as anchorages and therefore may have served as whaling stations. However, they did not recall seeing any structure on Cape Arid itself. The whaling camp was probably situated in the position of the modern fishing camp, a low dune ridge protected by the headland and higher surrounding dunes, and above a sandy, shallow beach.

THOMAS'S FISHERY

Date Range: 1862+

Location: 7 kilometres northeast of Cape Arid

1:100,000 AMG Reference: 3530 Sandy Bight 204–384

History

Although John Thomas of Cheyne Beach registered his 1862 whaling party as operating on Middle Island, another report from that season described his group as being 'at Cape Arid' (Inq 12/11/1862). There is no information on the precise location of this station, although it is not unreasonable to suppose it was Thomas's Fishery. Oral history from the late Mrs. Amy Croker, formerly of Hill Springs station, suggested that Thomas's Fishery was named after Thomas Sherratt, whom she thought operated from there from the 1860s until 1872 (MacIlroy 1987). However, as the historical evidence shows Sherratt's party was situated in Barrier Anchorage, it appears more reasonable that this cove on the east side of Cape Arid was actually named after John Thomas.

Thomas appears to have continued to visit the 'east coast' as his late season station throughout the 1860s (Sale 1936). In 1865 he arranged for the Dempsters of Esperance Station to supply the party with beef for the season (Erikson 1978). Although Thomas was last involved in whaling in 1867, the 1870s saw a resurgence of south coast activity focused on the 'east coast'. It is highly probable that one or more of these later parties, often containing former employees of Thomas, would take advantage of a proven location and existing improvements. For this reason the last use of the bay may well have been in 1879, with the last recorded activity of the Albany whaling parties.

Site Description

Thomas's Fishery is a small sandy cove located 6.5 kilometres northeast of Cape Arid. Mrs. Croker's information included that in the 1920s there had been a stone fireplace which held the tryworks, while across the bay on the southern point there was another fireplace for domestic cooking (MacIlroy 1987). Her suggestion that the camp had been placed upwind to avoid the smell is consistent with the position of habitation areas seen at other sites. She recalled that the trypot had remained in place until the early years of this century, when it was removed to Lynburn (Moonginettee) station. Fishermen had also told her that the floor of the bay was 'covered in whalebones' and that these frequently washed up on the beach MacIlroy 1987: 55).

The 1993 survey of Thomas fishery failed to locate any structural remains of the whaling station, although the topography would confirm Mrs. Croker's description of the possible layout. On the sheltered south side of the bay is a flat area above the dune ridge which would be suitable for the station camp. This is heavily overgrown with vegetation to a height of 3 m. On the north side of the bay are granite sheets which could serve as the processing area, although there appears to have been some storm damage to bordering dunes which may have removed the tryworks. The trypot from Thomas's Fishery was still at the now abandoned Moonginettee station.

ADDITIONAL SITES

Colonial Stations

There are several instances where the stations used by shore whaling parties, usually of a short term nature, have not been identified, some of which have been noted above:

- *Dampier Archipelago:* Although John Bateman later adopted Malus Island as his northwest station, during the 1872 season Pearse and Marmion still occupied the island, raising the question of where Bateman was based. While he may have had a station elsewhere on the island, there still remains the possibility that Rosemary Island was used (Inq 12/6/1872), despite no physical remains having been discovered there (MacIlroy 1987). Bateman may have kept his crew and tryworks aboard his schooner, without recourse to a land station.

- *Fremantle/North Fremantle*: The location(s) of the Fremantle area stations of the 1860s–70s remain uncertain.

- *Vasse:* Hurford and Penney's 1846 party is described as being in Geographe Bay (Inq 26/8/1846). Seymour's diary (n.d.) and other contextual information they must have been situated relatively close to the Castle Rock station.

- *King George Sound:* Prior to James Daniells obtaining the lease of Barker Bay in September 1849 there is evidence that he was already whaling in the area. It is possible that he was using the Barker Bay site without a lease, although he may have been at some other location in King George Sound. After the close of commercial whaling there are various accounts of informal whaling and trying out of oil close to Albany (Wolfe 2003).

- *Mistaken Island*: As noted in the Barker Bay entry, there are several references to whaling activity around Mistaken (Rabbit) Island in Frenchman's Bay.
- *'East Coast'*: Due to the cancellation of station leases the locations of the late period stations on the south and east coast are uncertain.

There are also situations where multiple stations are known to have operated either concurrently in the same bay or location (e.g. Malus Island, Port Gregory, Carnac Island, Bunbury, Torbay, and Doubtful Island Bay). There is limited historical and archaeological evidence for rebuilding or re–use of earlier facilities.

Single–Use sites

The impromptu use of locations for processing whales falls into two categories. The first is the opportunistic stripping of whales which were stranded, or carcasses washed up after either natural death or being lost by shore or pelagic whalers. There are various accounts of Aboriginal groups gathering to exploit such situations (see Chapter Two), while European settlers would also attempt to try out oil as best they could as a way of obtaining free oil (PG 17/8/1833; PG 14/1/1837). Whalers out of season would also chase and kill whales, processing them on the spot, or removing the blubber back to the nearest station tryworks (PG 10/2/1852).

The second category is where whaling parties were unable to return a carcass to the station and instead beached the animal to take the blubber. McKail (1927) provides an anecdote where gale winds and high seas forced the Cheyne Beach party to take its catch into Waychinicup Inlet. While some of the crew stayed with the carcass the rest walked overland to the station, returning the next day with the rest of the boats and the flensing equipment. Presumably the blubber was taken back to the station, rather than attempting to move the trypot to Waychinicup.

Foreign shore stations

As whaling vessels were fully equipped and efficient mobile stations for either pelagic or bay whaling, there was little value in their crews attempting to establish land–based operations. Only three examples which suggest these sorts of shore activity have been located.

The first and only unquestioned account of an American shore station in Western Australian dates to September 1837, when the American whaler *America* left two boats and their crews at Flinders Bay while the vessel cruised the coast. This party constructed a tryworks, which was used on at least one occasion, and probably used tents as their quarters (Turner 1969; 138). The *America*, which was a regular visitor to Augusta,

returned after a month and removed the crew, with no evidence that the exercise was ever repeated. A monument has been erected adjacent to the beach thought to have been the location of this camp.

Another case of foreign shore whaling, but under exceptional circumstances, occurred following the wreck of the American whalers *North America*, *Governor Endicott* and *Samuel Wright* at Bunbury. At least one of the ships crews is known to have salvaged their equipment from the wrecks and spent the rest of the season bay–whaling at Port Leschenault (PG 1/8/1840). This was a temporary situation and apparently allowed by the local authorities because there was no colonial party in the region.

In 1857 a group of Aboriginal people arrived at the Geraldine Lead Mine on the lower Murchison River with the report that at Shark Bay

> There are plenty of white men who live on shore, catch whales and boil oil, all same as at Port Gregory. (PG 20/11/1857)

The *Perth Gazette* suggested that this was probably a party of Americans bay whaling. The comparison to the colonial whaling station at Port Gregory suggests that this group was familiar with whaling, and had not confused it some other European activity.

One way in which foreign vessels bay–whaling along the Western Australian coast could enhance their performance was to increase the range of their look–outs by placing on high points on islands or headlands. An 1850 survey of Cape Riche (Gregory 1850) records a 'whaler's lookout' located on Cheyne Island, although there is no evidence that the bay was used by colonial whalers. Whitecar (1860) describes the *Pacific* erecting look–outs on one or more of the islands of the Abrolhos Archipelago and leaving men to watch for whales while the ship itself cruised.

Most other historical accounts of land activity by foreign whalers relate to the collection of wood, water or other provisions. On both the south and west coasts there were well known watering places which were regularly visited by whaling vessels. The diaries of Haley (1948) and Whitecar (1860) describe the process of rafting the casks to and from the wells. Less commonly, foreign whalers were also known to have established vegetable gardens on both the mainland and offshore islands, sometimes also leaving animals on the islands to feed or breed. The best known of these is the French vessel *Mississippi* which assisted Eyre on his trek across the Nullarbor (Eyre 1845). Another well known incident dates to 1840, when an American crew raised the ire of the colonial government by attempting to clear land in Castle Bay.

> The land which your Governor is anxious to know about is situated 1 short mile from Castle Rock in Geographe Bay being in extent say 1/4

acre of an area for vegetables for our table. (CSR 85/82: 24/1/1840)

The American captain agreed to quit the venture, but also sent the Government resident an account "for work and labor done in clearing Her Majesty's ground" (PG 30/1/1841). The newspaper report of this incident also states that there had been one or two similar instances of the Americans cultivating vegetables, in preference to resorting to the ports.

Sealers Camps

Sealing is often seen as an industry closely allied to whaling, and archaeological surveys in both Victoria and South Australia have dealt with both groups of sites concurrently. There are several ways in which the archaeological signature of sealing camps can closely resemble that of whaling stations. Both are found in coastal contexts (although sealers tended to stay on offshore islands) requiring a sandy beach on which to pull up and maintain their boats. At a base camp the sealers might have one or several small huts for living, storage, and the like, while contemporaneity of use and access to similar sources of supply would produce a similar occupation deposit (although possibly with a higher seal bone content). Finally, in addition to the skinning which was the mainstay of sealing, tryworks were also sometimes used to obtain seal oil.

In 1858, William Whitecar of the American whaler *Pacific* noted in his journal that on Middle Island in the Abrolhos group 'there is a rough house erected, which has remained there for many years, as also the ruins of a tryworks, monuments of a whaling party' (Whitecar 1860: 265). While Whitecar is unlikely to have mistaken the nature of the tryworks, this was probably the remains of the camp of the Pelsart Fishing Company which briefly operated a sealing and fishing venture in the islands during the 1840s (PG 30/3/1844).

APPENDIX B
SELECTED HISTORICAL DATA

B.1 Whaling Stations, Owners, Boats & Men in Western Australia (Blue Books, Perth Gazette, Inquirer)

Year	Station	Coast	Owner or Manager	Boats	Men
1836	DIB	s	Sherratt, T.B. & Lovett, W.	-	-
1837	DIB	s	Cheyne, G	-	-
1837	DIB	s	Sherratt, T.B. & Lovett, W.	-	-
1837	Bathers Bch	w	Fremantle Whaling Co.	3	16
1837	Carnac Isl	w	Northern Whaling Co.	3	20
1838	Fremantle	w	Fremantle Whaling Co.	-	-
1838	Safety B.	w	Duffield, Hunt & Davies	-	-
1838	Bunbury	w	Bull, H	-	-
1838	-	s	-	-	-
1839	Bathers Bch	w	Scott, D & Curtis, Capt. A.	-	-
1839	Bunbury	w		-	-
1840	Bathers Bch	w	Samson, L	-	-
1841	Bathers Bch	w	-		
1842	Two Pple B.	s	Andrews, J	-	-
1843	Bathers Bch	w	-	-	-
1843	Bunbury	w	Child, J.K.	-	-
1843	Two Pple B.	s	Andrews, J	4	30
1844	Bunbury	w	Koombana B. Wh. Co.	-	-
1844	Bunbury	w	Child, J.K.	-	-
1844	Bathers Bch	w	Frem Wh. C	-	-
1844	Torbay	s	Andrews J.	2	-
1845	Bathers Bch	w	Scott, D	-	-
1845	Carnac Isl	w	Curtis, A	-	-
1845	Torbay	s	Sinclair, J	-	-
1846	Castle Rock	w	Habgood & Viveash	-	-
1846	Geographe B.	w	Hurford & Penny	-	-
1846	Bunbury	w	Stafford	-	-
1846	Bathers Bch	w	Frem Wh C	-	-
1846	Torbay	s	Morton	-	-
1846	Cheyne Bch	s	Cook, Craigie & Thomas	-	-
1847	Bathers Bch	w	Scott, D	-	-
1847	Castle Rock	w	Heppingstone, R	3	-
1847	Toby Inlet	w	Ker H.T.	1	-
1847	Cheyne Bch	s	Thomas, J	2	-
1848	Bathers Bch	w	Marmion, P	4	-
1848	Castle Rock	w	Heppingstone, R	-	-
1848	Cheyne Bch	s	Thomas, J	2	-
1849	Bathers Bch	w	Scott, D.	4	-
1849	Marmion	w	Marmion, P	3	-
1849	Bunbury	w		-	-
1849	Castle Rock	w	Chapman, G	2	16
1849	Barker B.	s	Daniels, J	1	-
1849	Cheyne Bch	s	Thomas, J	-	-
1850	Bathers Bch	w	Marmion, P	4	-
1850	Rottnest	w	Dempster, J	-	-
1850	Castle Rock	w	Chapman, G	2	14
1850	Bunbury	w	Onslow & Sillifant	2	-
1850	Barker B.	s	Daniels, J	2	-
1850	Cheyne Bch	s	Thomas, J	2	-
1851	Bathers Bch	w	Bateman, J?	3	-
1851	Bunbury	w	-	2	-
1851	Castle Rock	w	Heppingstone, R	2	13
1851	Barker B.	s	-	2	-
1851	Cheyne Bch	s	Thomas, J	2	-
1852	Bunbury	w	-	2	-
1852	Castle Rock	w	Heppingstone, R	3	-
1852	Barker B.	s	Sherratt, T	1	-
1852	Cheyne Bch	s	Thomas, J	2	-
1853	Bathers Bch	w	-	2	-
1853	Carnac Isl	w	Harwood, J	2	-
1853	Bunbury	w	-	2	-
1853	Castle Rock	w	Heppingstone, R	3	-
1853	Cheyne Bch	s	Thomas, J	2	-
1854	Pt Gregory	w	Sanford, H	4	-
1854	Bathers Bch	w	Bateman, J	3	-
1854	Carnac Isl	w	Harwood, J	3	-
1854	Castle Rock	w	Heppingstone, R	5?	-
1854	Cheyne Bch	s	Thomas, J	2	-
1855	Pt Gregory	w	Sanford, H	4	-
1855	Bathers Bch	w	Bateman, J	3	-
1855	Carnac Isl	w	Harwood, J	3	-
1855	Bunbury	w	-	4	-
1855	Castle Rock	w	Heppingstone, R	4	-
1855	Cheyne Bch	s	Thomas, J	2	-
1856	Pt Gregory	w	Sanford & Harwood	3	22
1856	Pt Gregory	w	Bateman, J	3	-
1856	Bunbury	w	Bateman, J	4	23
1856	Bathers Bch	w	Bateman, J	4	-
1856	Carnac Isl	w	Harwood, J	2?	10
1856	North Fremantle	w	-	2?	-
1856	Castle Rock	w	Heppingstone, R	3	-
1856	Barker B.	s	-	-	-
1856	Cheyne Bch	s	Thomas, J	2	-
1857	Pt Gregory	w	Harwood, J	3	24
1857	Pt Gregory	w	Bateman, J	3	20
1857	Bunbury	w	Bateman, J	3	17
1857	Bathers Bch	w	Bateman, J	-	-
1857	Carnac Isl	w	Harwood, J	-	-
1857	Castle Rock	w	Heppingstone, R	4	-
1857	Barker B.	s	Sherratt, T	2	-
1857	Cheyne Bch	s	Thomas, J	2	-
1858	Pt Gregory	w	Harwood, J	3	23
1858	Pt Gregory	w	Bateman, J	2	-
1858	Bunbury	w	Bateman, J	2	12
1858	Carnac Isl	w	Harwood, J	-	-
1858	Bathers Bch	w	Bateman, J	-	-
1858	Castle Rock	w	Heppingstone, R	-	-
1858	Cheyne Bch	s	Thomas, J	-	-

Year	Station	Coast	Owner or Manager	Boats	Men
1859	Pt Gregory	w	Harwood, J	3	23
1859	Pt Gregory	w	Bateman, J	2	-
	Bunbury	w	Bateman, J	-	-
1859	Bathers Bch	w	Bateman, J	3	-
1859	Carnac Isl	w	Harwood, J	-	-
1859	Bunbury	w	Butty	-	-
1859	Castle Rock	w	Layman, G	-	-
1859	Barker B.	s	Sherratt, T	2	-
1859	Cheyne Bch	s	Thomas, J	2	-
1860	Pt Gregory	w	Harwood, J	-	18
1860	Pt Gregory	w	Bateman, J	2	-
	Bunbury	w	Bateman, J	-	-
1860	Bathers Bch	w	Bateman, J	2	-
1860	Carnac Isl	w	Harwood, J	-	-
1860	Bunbury	w	Butty	-	-
1860	Castle Rock	w	Layman, G	3	-
1860	Barker B.	s	Sherratt, T	-	-
1860	Cheyne Bch	s	Thomas, J	2	-
1861	Pt Gregory	w	Bateman, J	-	-
	Bunbury	w	Bateman, J	-	-
1861	Bathers Bch	w	Bateman, J	-	-
1861	Bunbury	w	Butty	4	27
1861	Castle Rock	w	Butty & Bridges	-	-
1861	Torbay	s	-	2	15
1861	Barker B.	s	Sherratt, T	2	12
1861	Cheyne Bch	s	Thomas	2	14
1862	Pt Gregory	w	Bateman, J	3	22
1862	Bunbury	w	Bateman, J	3	-
1862	Bunb./Min.up	w	Buswell	2	15
1862	Barker B.	s	Sherratt, T	2	12
1862	Cheyne Bch	s	McKenzie, H	2	13
1862	Middle Isl	s	Thomas	2	10
1863	Pt Gregory	w	Bateman, J -		
1863	Carnac Isl?	w	-	(6)	-
1863	Bunbury	w	Bateman, J	3	-
1863	Bunb./Min.up	w	Buswell, J	2	14
1863	Torb./Dbtfl Isl	s	McKenzie, H	2	13
1863	Barker B.	s	-	2	11
1863	Cheyne Bch	s	Thomas, J	2	14
1864	Pt Gregory	w	Bateman, J?	2	-
1864	Bunbury	w	Bateman, J	2	-
1864	Torbay	s	McKenzie	2	-
1864	Barker B.	s	Sherratt, T	2	-
1864	Cheyne Bch	s	Thomas, J	2	-
1865	Pt Gregory	w	Bateman, J	3	20
1865	Carnac Isl?	w	-	3	-
1865	Bunbury	w	Bateman, J	3	-
1865	Barker B.	s	Sherratt, T	2	13
1865	Cheyne Bch	s	Thomas, J	2	13
	Thomas Fshy	s	Thomas, J?	-	-
1865	Doubtful Isl B.	s	McKenzie, H	2	15
1866	Pt Gregory	w	Bateman, J	4	22
1866	Castle Rock	w	Bateman, J	4	-
1866	Cheyne Bch	s	Thomas, J	2	13
1866	Doubtful Isl B.	s	McKenzie, C	2	13
1867	Pt Gregory	w	Bateman, J	4	-
1867	Carnac Isl?	w	-	3	-
1867	Bunbury	w	Bateman, J?	4	-
1867	Cheyne Bch	s	Thomas, J	2	13
1867	Doubtful Isl B.	s	McKenzie, C	2	13
1868	Pt Gregory	w	Bateman, J?	3	15
1868	Carnac Isl?	w	-	2	-
1868	Barker B.	s	Sherratt, T	2	-
1868	Cheyne Bch	s	Thomas, J	2	-
1868	-	s	-	2	-
1869	Carnac Isl?	w	-	3	-
1869	-	s	-	2	-
1870	Malus Isl	w	Pearse & Marmion	2?	21
1870	Pt Gregory	w	Bateman, J	3	29
1870	Carnac Isl?	w	-	3	-
1870	Cheyne Bch	s	Sherratt, T	2	13
1870	Cape Riche	s	McKenzie, J	2	12
1871	Malus Isl	w	Pearse & Marmion	2?	-
1871	Pt Gregory	w	Bateman, J	4	-
	Castle Rock	w	Bateman, J	-	-
1871	Carnac Isl?	w	-	-	-
1871	Cheyne Bch	s	Fisher, N	2	-
1871	Barker B.	s	Sherratt, T	2	-
	Barrier Anch.	s	Sherratt, T	-	-
1872	Malus Isl	w	Pearse & Marmion	3	2
1872	Malus Isl	w	Bateman, J	3	20
1872	Pt Gregory	w	Bateman, J	-	22
	Castle Rock	w	Bateman, J	-	-
1872	Carnac Isl?	w	-	-	-
1872	Cheyne Bch	s	Fisher	2	11
1872	Barker B.	s	Sherratt, T	2	14
	Barrier Anch	s	Sherratt, T	-	-
1872	Cape Riche	s	McKenzie	2	13
	Cape Arid	s	-	-	-
1873	Pt Gregory	w	Bateman, J, J	2?	14
1873	Pt Gregory	w	Pearse & Marmion?	-	12
1873	Carnac Isl?	w	-	-	-
1873	Barker B.	s	Sherratt, T	2	-
	Barrier Anch	s	Sherratt, T	-	-
1873	-	s	McKenzie	2	-
1874	Carnac Isl?	w	-	3	-
1874	East Coast	s	Green, J	2	13
1875	Carnac Isl?	w	-	2	-
1875	Cheyne Bch	s	-	2+	-
1875	East Coast	s	Green, J	2	15
1875	-	s	McKenzie, C	1?	9
1876	-	s	-	2	-
1876	-	s	-	2	-
1877	Malus Isl	w	Bateman, J	-	19
1877	Cheyne Bch	s	Bruce, J & Bruce, J	2	14
1878	East Coast	s	Green, J. & Cooper W.	2	14
1879	East Coast	s	Cowden, J & Breece, J	1	11
1879	East Coast	s	Green, J & Cooper, W	2	13
1879	Barrier Anch.	s	Sherratt, T	2	13

B.2 Number of whaling parties, boats, oil return per boat and number of whalers.

Year	No. of Whaling parties			Estimated No. of whaleboats & productivity						Estimated No. of whalers		
	West	Sth	Tot.	Blue Book	West (est.)	Sth (est.)	Tot (est.)	Oil (tuns)	Oil per boat (tuns) (est.)	West	Sth	Tot.
1836	0	1	1		0	2	2	13	6	0	13	13
1837	2	2	4	10	6	4	10	116	12	42	26	68
1838	3	1	4	10	2	9	11	105	10	61	13	74
1839	2	0	2		6	0	6	-	-	40	0	40
1840	1	0	1		4	0	4	-	-	27	0	27
1841	1	0	1		4	0	4	-	-	27	0	27
1842	0	1	1		0	4	4	-	-	0	27	27
1843	2	1	3		4	4	8	-	-	48	30	78
1844	3	1	4		10	2	12	107	9	69	13	82
1845	2	1	3		7	2	9	100	11	48	13	61
1846	4	2	6		13	4	17	175	10	90	26	116
1847	3	1	4	23	8	2	10	196	20	55	21	76
1848	2	1	3	8	6	2	8	118	15	40	13	53
1849	4	2	6	9	12	3	15	90	6	85	20	105
1850	4	2	6	12	10	4	14	102	7	67	26	93
1851	3	2	5	11	7	4	11	101	9	47	26	73
1852	2	2	4	8	5	3	8	68	8	34	20	54
1853	4	1	5	15	7	4	11	64	6	60	13	73
1854	4	1	5	17	13	2	15	76	5	96	13	109
1855	5	1	6	20	18	2	20	131	7	114	13	127
1856	6	2	8	21	21	4	25	104	4	114	26	140
1857	5	2	7	19	19	4	23	94	4	113	26	139
1858	5	1	6	26	14	2	16			99	13	112
1859	6	2	8	18	14	4	18	115	6	128	26	154
1860	6	2	8	11	16	4	20	41	2	115	26	141
1861	4	3	7	17	13	6	19	54	3	90	41	131
1862	3	3	6	14	5	6	11	60	5	58	38	96
1863	4	3	7	21	11	6	17	42	2	77	38	115
1864	2	3	5	10	4	6	10	80	8	26	39	65
1865	3	3	6	13	9	6	15	130	9	62	41	103
1866	2	2	4	16	8	6	14	75	5	54	26	80
1867	3	2	5	15	11	4	15	43	3	75	26	101
1868	2	3	5	11	5	6	11	34	3	34	39	73
1869	1	1	2	5	3	2	5	50	10	21	13	34
1870	3	2	5	26	8	4	12	109	9	71	26	97
1871	3	3	6	16	12	4	16	119	7	75	15	90
1872	4	3	7	14	12	6	18	84	5	83	38	121
1873	3	3	6	13	9	4	13	52	4	56	26	82
1874	1	1	2	5	3	2	5	10	2	21	13	34
1875	1	3	4	17	3	6	9	45	5	21	41	62
1876	0	2	2	4	0	4	4	14	4	0	26	26
1877	1	1	2	2	3	2	5	32	6	19	14	33
1878	0	1	1		0	2	2			0	14	14
1879	0	3	3		0	6	6			0	40	40

B.3 Summary of Biographical and Ownership Data (After Gibbs 2006 Appendix E).

Recorded span of working career (Years)	West	South	Total	Headsmen
1	260	180	440	23
2	34	27	61	4
3	18	12	30	2
4	1	2	3	1
5	3	4	7	0
6	3	8	11	2
7	3	1	4	2
8	3	4	7	2
9	0	2	2	0
10	0	3	3	0
11	0	0	0	1
12	1	1	2	5
13	1	1	2	1
14	0	0	0	0
15	0	3	3	2
16	1	2	3	
17	3	2	5	
18	0	1	1	
19	0	0	0	
20	0	0	0	
21	0	0	0	
22	0	1	1	
23	0	0	0	
24	1	0	1	
25	0	1	1	
26	0	0	0	
27	0	0	0	
28	0	0	0	
29	0	0	0	
30	0	0	0	
31	0	0	0	
32	0	0	0	
33	0	0	0	
34	0	0	0	
35	1	0	1	

Age at time of first employment (years)	Total (not including headsmen)	Headsmen
17	3	0
18	3	0
19	2	0
20	0	2
21	3	0
22	2	2
23	4	1
24	2	1
25	0	2
26	2	0
27	0	2
28	2	1
29	2	0
30	3	1
31	2	2
32	1	0
33	2	0
34	2	0
35	0	0
36	0	1
37	1	0
38	1	0
39	1	1
40	2	0
40+	0	2

No. of years of ownership of whaling party	West coast	South coast
1	18	13
2	7	5
3	5	1
4	0	1
5	0	0
6	0	1
7	0	1
8	1	0
9	0	0
10	0	0
11-15	1	0
16-20	0	0
21-25	0	2
26-30	1	0

First year of ownership of whaling party	West coast	South coast
1836-40	4	4
1841-45	5	4
1846-50	11	6
1851-55	3	1
1856-60	2	1
1861-65	3	1
1866-70	2	1
1871-75	2	3
1876-80	0	4

B.4 Reported Oil and Bone Production (Blue Books)

Year	Oil				Bone				TOTAL
	West (tuns)	South (tuns)	oil (tuns)	value (£)	West (tons)	South (tons)	Total (tons)	value (£)	value (£)
1836		13	13	520		7	7	630	1150
1837	71	45	116	0	4	2	7	540	-
1838	57	48	105	0	0	0	0	0	-
1839	-		0	0	0		0	0	-
1840	-		0	0	-		0	0	-
1841	-		0	0	-		0	0	-
1842		-	0	0		0	0	0	-
1843	-	-	90	0	-	0	0	0	-
1844	94	13	107	0	0	0	5	800	-
1845	-	-	100	2	-	0	7	910	2935
1846	98	77	163	3871	0	0	4	848	4719
1847	141	55	196	2972	1	1	2	300	3272
1848	46	71	118	1820	0	6	6	570	2390
1849	-	-	90	1450	-	-	2	290	1740
1850	42	60	102	2119	2	2	3	209	2328
1851	38	63	101	2660	2	2	4	735	3395
1852	20	47	68	2501	0	2	2	222	2723
1853	39	25	64	3038	1	1	3	345	3383
1854	46	30	76	2940	1	0	1	206	3146
1855	113	18	131	4983	0	0	0	30	5013
1856	104	0	104	3962	2	0	2	560	4274
1857	53	41	94	3438	0	0	0	0	3439
1858	-	-	40	-	0	0	0	0	-
1859	60	55	115	2364	1	1	2	637	3001
1860	20	21	41	1408	1	1	1	276	1684
1861	31	22	54	1940	1	0	1	138	2078
1862	25	35	60	2060	0	0	1	140	2200
1863	20	21	42	1770	1	0	1	110	1870
1864	40	40	80	4180	1	1	2	397	4827
1865	84	46	130	5424	1	0	2	250	5674
1866	49	26	75	3025	1	3	4	154	3179
1867	39	4	43	1070	0	0	0	0	1070
1868	32	1	34	1340	0	0	0	0	1340
1869	43	6	50	1725	0	0	0	0	1725
1870	96	13	109	3620	0	0	0	0	4370
1871	100	19	119	6867	0	0	0	38	6905
1872	61	24	84	2754	1	0	1	54	2809
1873	45	7	52	1733	0	0	0	52	1785
1874	0	10	10	312	0	0	0	0	312
1875	5	40	45	1350	0	0	0	0	1350
1876		14	14	397		0	0	0	397
1877	21	12	32	402	0	0	0	0	402
1878		-	-	-		-	-	-	-
1879		-	-	185		-	-	-	-

B.5 Exports of oil and bone, and whale products as a percentage of total Western Australian exports.

Year	Oil (£)	Bone (£)	Total (£)	West. Aust. Total exports (£)	Whale products as % of Total exports (%)	Oil exports (tuns)
1836	520	630	1150	5440	21.1	13
1837	2320	540	2860	6906	41.4	106
1838	2780	600	3380	6840	49.4	105
1839	2730	440	3170	-	-	105
1840	-	-	-	-	-	
1841	-	-	-	-	-	
1842	-	-	-	-	-	
1843	300	150	450	7089	6.3	
1844	4514	800	5314	13363	39.8	107
1845	3415	815	4228	13354	31.7	109
1846	3141	1197	3338	20223	16.5	161
1847	3835	455	4288	24535	17.5	120
1848	-	-	4377	34324	12.8	220
1849	1202	284	1486	31558	4.7	81
1850	-	-	2305	29857	7.7	
1851	1404	362	1766	26870	6.6	61
1852	887	229	1116	24181	4.6	29
1853	1470	350	1820	31645	5.8	49
1854	592	239	829	34109	2.4	11
1855	2530	350	2880	46314	6.2	55
1856	2926	532	3452	44740	7.7	78
1857	2520	971	3491	59947	5.8	70
1858	3474	1487	4961	78649	6.3	96
1859	607	1538	2144	93037	2.3	20
1860	1717	560	2277	89247	2.6	50
1861	443	496	939	95789	1.0	13
1862	1219	339	1558	119313	1.3	34
1863	810	297	1107	143106	0.8	18
1864	300	71	371	111902	0.3	6
1865	2950	637	3587	179148	2.0	59
1866	1980	480	2460	152240	1.6	39
1867	1710	337	2047	174080	1.2	34
1868	733	100	833	192636	0.4	14
1869	495	0	495	205502	0.2	10
1870	3142	455	3597	200985	1.8	70
1871	3480	391	4231	199281	2.1	110
1872	1407	162	1562	209197	0.7	40
1873	1650	409	2059	265217	0.8	54
1874	128	130	258	428837	0.1	4
1875	347	10	357	391217	0.1	12
1876	648*	25	673	397293	0.2	22#
1877	884*	244	1128	373351	0.3	25#
1878	1962*	100	2062	428491	0.5	
1879	185*	0	185	494883	0.0	
1880	318*	0	588	499183	0.1	

* - Does not include returns of oil from the *Islander* (exported to Tasmania).
\# - Volume calculated on the basis of reported value of oil per tun.

B.6 Destinations of Oil and Bone Exports (Blue Books)

Year	Oil export (£)			Bone export (£)			TOTAL (£)	Total Export (£) direction	
	Great Britain	Br. Colonies	Total	Great Britain	Br. Colonies	Total		Great Britain	Br. Colonies
1836	520	630	520	-	-	630	1150	1150	0
1837	2320	540	2320	-	-	540	2860	2860	0
1838	2780	600	2780	-	-	600	3380	3380	0
1839	2730	440	2730	-	-	440	3170	3170	0
1840	-	-	-	-	-	-	-	-	-
1841	-	-	-	-	-	-	-	-	-
1842	-	-	-	-	-	-	-	-	-
1843	300	150	300	0	0	150	0	450	0
1844	4514	800	4514	0	0	800	5314	5314	0
1845	3250	700	3415	165	35	735	4228	3950	200
1846	1255	874	3141	1886	323	1197	3338	2129	2209
1847	3425	325	3835	410	130	455	4288	3750	540
1848	2381	573	3570	1189	233	806	4377	2954	1422
1849	679	284	1202	523	0	284	1486	963	523
1850	-	-	-	-	-		2305		2305
1851	846	283	1404	558	79	362	1766	1129	637
1852	0	229	887	887	0	229	1116	229	882
1853	0	239	1470	1470	7	246	1820	239	1477
1854	0	239	592	592	0	239	829	239	592
1855	0	350	2530	2530	0	350	2880	350	2530
1856	2040	502	2926	886	30	532	3452	2542	916
1857	612	971	2520	1908	0	971	3491	1583	1908
1858	0	1487	3474	3474	0	1487	4961	1487	3474
1859	0	979	607	607	594	1573	2144	979	1201
1860	0	320	1717	1717	240	560	2277	320	1957
1861	0	496	442	442	0	496	939	496	442
1862	0	155	1139	1139	184	339	1558	155	1323
1863	0	210	810	810	87	297	1107	210	897
1864	0	36	300	300	35	71	371	36	335
1865	0	637	2958	2958	0	637	3587	637	2958
1866	0	480	1980	1980	0	480	2460	480	1980
1867	300	300	1710	1410	37	337	2047	600	1447
1868	0	100	733	733	0	100	833	100	733
1869	0	0	495	495	0	0	495	0	495
1870	0	405	3142	3142	50	455	3597	405	3192
1871	1374	300	3841	2644	91	391	4231	1674	2735
1872	408	162	1407	999	0	162	1569	570	999
1873	367	42	1872	1505	145	187	2059	409	1650
1874	0	130	128	128	0	130	258	130	128
1875	0	0	347	347	10	10	357	0	357
1876	0	25	648	648	0	25	673	25	648
1877	0	44	884	884	200	244	1128	44	1084
1878	0	0	1962	1962	100	100	2062	0	2062
1879	0	0	185	185	0	0	185	0	185
1880	0	0	588	588	0	0	588	0	588

B.7 Comparison of oil returns from Cheyne Beach and Castle Rock, 1846-1866 (Blue Books).

Year	Cheyne Beach (tuns)	Castle Rock (tuns)	Cheyne Beach (£)	Castle Rock (£)
1846	55	41	1306	
1847	52	27	732	432
1848	71	35	920	
1849	27		432	
1850	35	3	600	60
1851	50	24	1160	720
1852	47	11	1435	495
1853	25		750	180
1854	30		1050	
1855	18	38	455	1520
1856	0	19	0	760
1857	25	18	858	320
1858				
1859				
1860	4	0	135	0
1861	7		210	
1862	2		360	
1863	10		420	
1864	17		680	
1865	26		1120	
1866		9		369

B.8 Reported oil yields (tuns) from individual whales [8(2) represents a report of 8 tuns from 2 whales].

Perth Gazette	Years	Humpback	mean	Right	mean
	1836-40	-	-	-	-
	1841-45	-	-	-	-
	1846-50	2, 3	2.5	8, 8(2), 6	5.5
	1851-55	-	-	12	12
	1856-60	3, 8(2), 10(3), 17.5(4)	3.2	3	3
	1861-65	-	-	-	-
	1866-70	-	-	-	-
			2.85		6.83

Inquirer	Years	Humpback	mean	Right	mean
	1836-40	-	-	-	-
	1841-45	-	-	-	-
	1846-50	4, 3, 4(2), 2, 2	2.5	5, 6, 8, 7, 1, 8(2), 8, 4	5.2
	1851-55	-	-	5, 8, 8	7
	1856-60	3, 1.75, 4, 8(2), 5, 10.5(3)	4.25	10, 8.75, 12	10.25
	1861-65	-	-	10	10
	1866-70	-	-	-	-
			3.38		8.11

Blue Books	Years	Humpback	mean	Right	mean
	1853	4	4	24(3), 5.5	7.37
	1854	-	-	14(4)	3.5
	1860	20(6)	3.3	-	-
	1862	24(6), 1	2.5	-	-

BIBLIOGRAPHY

ABBREVIATIONS

AA	*Albany Advertiser* (1888-), Albany
AM	*Albany Mail* (1883–1889), Albany
AN	Archive Notes. (Battye Library, Perth)
BB	Western Australian Blue Books, Government Printer, Perth
BL	Battye Library of Western Australian History, Perth (may also cite accession as BL Acc. #).
BPP	*British Parliamentary Papers: Colonies - Australia* Irish University Press, Shannon, Ireland.
CoN	*Commercial News and Shipping List* (1855), Perth.
CN	Cartographic Notes. (Battye Library, Perth)
CO	Colonial Office Records, Original Correspondence, Western Australia. Referenced in text as [Series/Volume: Folio, Date]. Public Record Office, London. (Battye Library, C.O. 18).
CSR	Colonial Secretary's Office, correspondence received. (Battye Library, Acc. 36). Referenced in text by [Volume/Folio: Date].
CSF	Colonial Secretary's Office; correspondence forwarded (Battye Library, Acc. 49). Referenced in text by [Volume/Folio: Date].
GG	*Western Australian Government Gazette*, Government Printer, Perth.
Her	*The Herald* (1867–1886), Perth
HRA	*Historical Records of Australia.* Series I and Series III. Watson, F. (ed.), Government Printer, Sydney, 1914/1923. Referenced in text by [Series: Volume: Page, Date].
HTC	*Hobart Town Courier*
Inq	*The Inquirer* (1840–1855), later *The Inquirer and Commercial News* (1855–1890), Perth.
L&S.	Lands and Surveys Department of Western Australia Records (Battye Library, Perth).
PG	*Perth Gazette and Western Australian Journal* (1833–1864), later *Perth Gazette and W.A. Times* (1864–1874)
PR	Printed Reference Collection (Battye Library, Perth).
RN	Research Notes (Battye Library, Perth).
SAA	*South Australian Advertiser.*
SAN	*South Australian News*
SAR	*South Australian Register*
SDUR	Lands and Surveys Department of Western Australia Records (Battye Library, Perth).
SRG	*Swan River Guardian* (1836–1838), Perth
WA	*The West Australian* (1879–), Perth
WAA	Western Australian Archives Card Index of shipping. (Battye Library, Perth).
WAMM	Department of Maritime Archaeology, Western Australian Museum, Fremantle.
WAM	Western Australian Museum, Perth.
WAT	*Western Australian Times* (1863–64), Perth *Western Australian Times* (1874–1879), Perth
WM	*Western Mail* (1897–1955), Perth

PERSONAL COMMUNICATIONS
(affiliations as at time of consultation)

E. Bradshaw	Elizabeth Bradshaw, postgraduate student, Centre for Archaeology, University of W.A.
G. Brown	George Brown, amateur fisherman, Little Grove.
D. Gojak	Denis Gojak, archaeologist, National Parks & Wildlife Service, N.S.W.
K. Kennedy	Mr Kris Kennedy, planning consultant, Subiaco.
J. Lord	Mr J. Lord, Busselton Museum.
M. McCarthy	Mike McCarthy, curator, Dept. of Maritime Archaeology, W.A. Museum.
S. McGann	Sally McGann, M.A. student, Centre for Archaeology, University of W.A.
S. Wallis	Stan Wallis, professional fisherman, Cheyne Beach.
C. Westerberg	Charles 'Snapper' Westerberg, farmer, Cheyne Beach

PUBLISHED & UNPUBLISHED SOURCES

Allen, J. 2008 *Port Essington: The historical archaeology of a north Australian nineteenth–century military outpost.* Australasian Society for Historical Archaeology. Sydney University Press, Sydney.

Allen, J. and R. Jones 1980 Oyster Cove: archaeological traces of the last Tasmanians and notes on the criteria for the authentification of flaked glass. *Papers and Proceedings of the Royal Society of Tasmania* 114: 225–233.

Andrews, A. n.d. *A Sketch of the Colony of Western Australia.* Edward Collyer, London.

Anon 1836 *First Report of the Western Australian Association.* John Cross, London.

Anon 1842 *A Short Account of the Settlement of Swan River, Western Australia, from the years 1834–41. By an Emigrant.* J. Cross, London.

Anon 1843 *A Sketch of Western Australia: The Western Australia Company at Australind.* W. Jeffery, London.

Anon 1936 *Bunbury Centenary Souvenir 1836–1936.* Bunbury Shire Council.

Anon 1977 *Whaling in Geographe Bay; with special reference to the Castle Bay Company.* Busselton Historical Society information pamphlet, Busselton.

Ansel, W. 1978 *The Whaleboat: A study of design, construction and use from 1850 to 1970.* Mystic Seaport Museum.

Appleyard, R. 1981 Western Australia: Economic and Demographic Growth, 1850–1914. In T. Stannage (ed) *A New History of Western Australia.* University of Western Australia Press, Nedlands, pp. 211–236.

Arctic Centre 1981 *Early European Exploitation of the Northern Atlantic 800–1700.* Arctic Centre, University of Groningen, Netherlands.

Atkinson, A. 1988 *Asian Immigrants to Western Australia 1829–1901. The Bicentennial Dictionary of Western Australians Volume V,* University of Western Australia Press, Nedlands.

Backhouse, J. 1843 *A Narrative of a visit to the Australian Colonies.* Hamilton, Adams & Co., London.

Bain, M. 1975 *Ancient Landmarks; A Social and Economic History of the Victoria District of Western Australia, 1839–1894.* University of Western Australia Press, Nedlands.

Bain, M. 1982 *Full Fathom Five.* Artlook Books, Perth, Western Australia.

Bairstow, D. 1984a The Swiss Family Robinson Model: a comment and appraisal. *Australian Journal of Historical Archaeology* 2:3–6.

Bairstow, D. 1984b Historical Archaeology at the Crossroads. *Australian Archaeology* 18: 32–39.

Baker, A. 1990 *Whales and Dolphins of Australia and New Zealand, An Identification Guide.* Allen and Unwin, Sydney.

Bankoff, H. and F. Winter 1979 A House–Burning in Serbia. *Archaeology* 32(5): 8–14.

Bannister, J. 1986 Notes on Nineteenth Century catches of Southern Right Whales (Eubalaena australis) off the Southern Coasts of Western Australia. *Report of the International Whaling Commission* Special Issue 10: 255–259.

Bannister, J, Taylor, S. and H. Sutherland 1981 Logbook records of 19th Century American Sperm Whaling. *Report of the International Whaling Commission* 31: 821–833.

Barker, P. 1982 *Techniques of Archaeological Excavation.* Batsford, London.

Barker, A. and M. Laurie 1992 *Excellent Connections: A History of Bunbury, Western Australia, 1836–1990.* City of Bunbury, Bunbury.

Barnes, P. 2001 *Marlston Hill and All That.* Bunbury Historical Society, Bunbury.

Bates D. 1910 Native Shepherding: An experience of the Perth Carnival. *Western Mail* 12/2/1910.

Bates, D. 1985 *The Native Tribes of Western Australia.* White, I. (ed), National Library of Australia, Canberra.

Bates, D. n.d. Manuscript notes and typescripts. BL. Acc. 1212A.

Battye, J. 1912–13 *Cyclopaedia of Western Australia.* Cyclopaedia Company, Perth

Battye, J. 1924 *Western Australia; A History from its Discovery to the Inauguration of the Commonwealth.* Oxford University Press, Oxford.

Bavin, L. and M. Gibbs 1988 *Report on the Historical and Archaeological Potential of Arthur Head and Directions for Future Management and Research.* Centre for Prehistory, University of Western Australia for the Fremantle City Council.

Beard, J. 1981 *The Vegetation of the Albany & Mt. Barker Areas, Western Australia.* Vegmap Publications, Perth.

Beaudry, M. (ed) 1988 *Documentary Archaeology in the New World.* Cambridge University Press, Cambridge.

Beaudry, M., L. Cook, and S. Mrozowski 1991 Artefacts and Active Voices: Material Culture as Social Discourse. In McGuire and Paynter (eds) *The Archaeology of Inequality.* Blackwell, Oxford, pp. 150–191.

Bechervaise, J. 1954 General History of the Recherche Archipelago. In Willis, J. (ed) *The Archipelago of the Recherche Report.1.* Australian Geographic Society, Melbourne, pp. 3–7.

Beeton, I. 1861 *Beeton's Book of Household Management.* Reprinted 1982 by Chancellor Press, London.

Bell, P. n.d. *Research and Management Issues arising from Sites associated with the South Australian Bay Whaling and Sealing Industry.* Paper presented to the tenth annual conference of the Australian Institute for Maritime Archaeology, Adelaide, 27 September, 1991.

Berndt, R. and C. Berndt (Eds). 1980 *Aborigines of the West: Their Past and Their Present.* University of Western Australia Press, Perth

Bickford, A., Blair, S, and Freeman, P. 1988 *Ben Boyd National Park Bicentennial Project: Davidson Whaling Station, Boyd's Tower, Bittangabee Ruins.* National Parks and Wildlife Service, Sydney.

Billington, R. 1967 The American Frontier. In P. Bohannon and F. Plog (Eds) *Beyond the Frontier: Social Process and Cultural Change.* The Natural History Press, New York, pp. 3–24.

Birmingham, J. 1992 *Wybalenna: The Archaeology of Cultural Accommodation in Nineteenth Century Tasmania.* The Australian Society for Historical Archaeology, Sydney.

Birmingham, J. and D. Jeans 1983 The Swiss Family Robinson and the archaeology of colonisations. *Australasian Journal of Historical Archaeology* 1: 3–14.

Birmingham, J., Bairstow, D. and A. Wilson (Eds) 1988 *Archaeology and Colonisation: Australia in the World Context.* Australasian Society for Historical Archaeology, Sydney.

Birmingham, J., I. Jack, and D. Jeans 1979 *Australian Pioneer Technology: Sites and Relics.* Richmond, Heinemann Educational Australia.

Birmingham, J., I. Jack, and D. Jeans 1983 *Industrial archaeology in Australia: Rural Industry Australian Pioneer Technology: Sites and Relics.* Richmond, Heinemann Educational Australia.

Blainey, G. 1966 *The Tyranny of Distance.* Sun Books, Melbourne.

Boow, J. 1991 *Early Australian Commercial Glass: Manufacturing Processes.* Edited by J. Byrne for The Heritage Council of New South Wales.

Bowdler, S. 1977 The coastal colonisation of Australia. In J. Allen, J. Golson and R. Jones (Eds) *Sunda and Sahul: Prehistoric Studies in Southeast Asia, Melanesia and Australia.* Academic Press, London, pp. 205–246.

Brewer, D.J. 1992 Zooarchaeology: Method, Theory, Goals. *Archaeological Method and Theory* 4: 195–244.

Broeze, F. and Henderson, G. 1986 *Western Australians and the Sea: Our Maritime Heritage.* Western Australian Museum, Perth.

Brooks, A. 2005 *An archaeological guide to British ceramics in Australia 1788–1901.* Australasian Society for Historical Archaeology, Sydney.

Buckton, T.J. 1840 *Western Australia, Comprising a Description of the Vicinity of Australind and Port Leschenault.* John Olivier, London.

Bulbeck, D. 1969 The P. & O. Company's Establishment at King George's Sound 1850–1880. *Early Days - Journal and Proceedings of the Royal Western Australian Historical Society* 7 (1): 103–130.

Burgoyne, I. 2000 *Mirning: we are the whales, a Mirning-Kokatha woman recounts life before and after dispossession.* Magabala Books, Broome.

Burton, A. (Ed) 1954 *Wollaston's Picton Journal (1841–56).* Paterson Brokensha, Perth.

Butchart, D. 1933 Old Colonial Days: A Nonagenarian Looks Back. West Australian (Newspaper) 22 July 1933.

Butlin N., Ginswick J. and P. Statham 1987 The Economy before 1850. In W. Vamplew (Ed) *Australians; Historical Statistics.* Fairfax, Syme & Weldon Associates, Sydney, pp 102–125.

Cameron, J. 1974a Information Distortion in Colonial Promotion: The case of the Swan River Colony. *Australian Geographical Studies* 12: 309–327.

Cameron, J. 1974b Distortions in Pre–settlement Land Evaluation: The case of the Swan River, Western Australia. *Professional Geographer* 26(4): 393–398.

Cameron, J. 1977 Coming to Terms: The development of agriculture in pre-convict Western Australia. *Geowest* 11. Department of Geography, University of Western Australia, Nedlands.

Cameron, J. 1981 *Ambition's Fire; The Agricultural Colonization of Pre–Convict Western Australia.* University of Western Australia Press, Nedlands.

Cameron, F. 1985 *An Analysis of Buttons, Clothing Hardware and Textiles of the Nineteenth Century Chinese Goldminers of Central Otago.* B.A. (Hons) thesis, Anthropology Department, University of Otago, Dunedin.

Cammilleri, C. 1963 *Anthony Curtis: his life in Western Australia, 1830–1853.* Unpublished ms, Battye Library, Perth.

Campbell, M. 1992 *A Preliminary Investigation of the Archaeology of Whaling Stations on the Southern Coast.* M.A. thesis, Anthropology Department, University of Otago, Dunedin, New Zealand.

Chamberlain, S. 1988 *The Hobart Whaling Industry 1830 to 1900.* PhD thesis, History Department, LaTrobe University, Melbourne.

Chamberlain, S. 1989 *Sealing, Whaling & Early Settlement of Victoria: An Annotated Bibliography.* Occasional Report No. 29, Victoria Archaeological Survey, Melbourne.

Chatwin, D. 1998 'If the Government think proper to support it': issues of relevance to Australasian whaling in the demise of the British Southern Fishery. In S. Lawrence and M. Staniforth (eds), *The Archaeology of Whaling and Sealing in Southern Australian and New Zealand.* Australasian Society for Historical Archaeology, Canberra, pp. 87–92.

Chester, E. 1927 Old Colonist's Memory, by Polygon. *Western Mail* (newspaper), 27 January, 1927.

Chester, E. 1931 Early Days in Albany. *Early Days - Journal and Proceedings of the Royal Western Australian Historical Society 1* (9): 70–75

Chittleborough, R. 1965 Dynamics of two populations of the humpback whale, Megaptera novaeangliae. *Australian Journal of Marine Freshwater Research* 16: 33–128

Churchward, L. 1949 Notes on American Whaling Activities in Australian Waters, 1800–1850. *Historical Studies, Australia and New Zealand 4*: 59–63.

Churchward, L. 1979 *Australia and America 1788–1972: An alternative history.* Alternative Publishing Cooperative Limited, Sydney.

Clark, C.M. (ed) 1950 *Select Documents in Australian History, 1788–1850.* Angus and Robertson, Sydney.

Clifton, M. 1841 *First Report to the Western Australia Company*, 30 March, 1841. Battye Library.

Collier, J. 1993 *Tale of the Whale: Watching whales off Western Australia.* Bushtell Enterprises, Perth.

Colwell, M. 1969 *Whaling Around Australia.* Rigby, Adelaide.

Connah, G. 1988 *Of the Hut I Built: The archaeology of Australia's History.* Cambridge University Press, Sydney.

Connah, G., M. Rowlands and J. Oppenheimer 1978 *Captain Richards' House at Winterbourne.* Department of Prehistory and Archaeology, University of New England.

Cousteau, J. and Y. Paccalet 1988 *Whales.* Harry N. Abrams Inc. Publishers, New York.

Coutts, P. 1976 An approach to the Investigation of colonial settlement patterns: whaling in southern New Zealand. *World Archaeology* 7 (3); 291–305.

Coutts, P. 1984 *Captain Mills Cottage, Port Fairy, Victoria.* Records of the Victorian Archaeological Survey Number 17, Ministry of Planning and Environment, Victoria.

Coutts, P. 1985 Towards the development of colonial archaeology in New Zealand. Part 2: Early settlement patterns in New Zealand. *Australian Journal of Historical Archaeology* 3:31–42.

Coutts, P. 1985b *Report on Archaeological Investigations at the 1826 Settlement Site, Corinella.* Records of the Victorian Archaeological Survey No. 18, Ministry of Planning, Victoria.

Crammond, A. 1935 *The Early History and Whaling Days of Fremantle, and Early Settlers.* Fremantle.

Cressey, P., J. Stephens, S. Shephard and B. Magid 1982 The Core–Periphery Relationship and the Archaeological Record in Alexandria, Virginia. In R. Dickens (ed) *Archaeology of Urban America: The Search for Pattern and Process*. Academic Press, New York, pp. 143–173.

Cresswell, O. 1979 *Chinese Cash*. Spink & Sons, London.

Crook, P. 2005 Quality, Cost and Value: Key Concepts for an Interpretive Assemblage Analysis. *Australian Journal of Historical Archaeology* 23:15–24.

Crowley, F. 1953 Master and Servant in Western Australia. *Early Days* 4 (5): 94–113 and 4 (6): 15–32.

Crowley, F. 1960 *Australia's Western Third*. Macmillan, London.

Cuffley. P. 1984 *Chandeliers and Billy Tea: A catalogue of Australian life, 1880–1940*. Five Mile Press, Victoria.

Cummings, W. 1985 Right Whales. In Ridgeway and Harrison (Eds) *Handbook of Marine Mammals Volume 4; River Dolphins and the Larger Toothed Whales*. Academic Press, Sydney, pp. 275–304.

Cumpston, J. 1970 *Kangaroo Island, 1800–1836*. Roebuck Society, Canberra.

Dakin, W.J. 1938 *Whaleman Adventurers*. Angus & Robertson, Sydney.

Dane, A. and R. Morrison 1979 *Clay Pipes from Port Arthur 1830–1877*. Technical Bulletin No. 2, Department of Prehistory, Australian National University, Canberra.

Daniel, G. and M. Cockman 1979 *Wanneroo*. Shire of Wanneroo, Wanneroo.

Davidson, R. 1988 *Whalemen of Twofold Bay*. R. Davidson, Eden, New South Wales.

Davies, P. 2001 A cure for all seasons: health and medicine in a bush community *Journal of Australian Studies* 70: 63–72,159–161.

Davies, P. 2005 Writing Slates and Schooling. *Australasian Historical Archaeology* 23:63–69.

Deagan, K. 1982 Avenues of Inquiry in Historical Archaeology. *Advances in Archaeological Method and Theory* 5: 151–177.

Deagan, K. 1988 Neither History nor Prehistory: the Questions that Count in Historical Archaeology. *Historical Archaeology* 22(1): 7–12.

Decker, R. 1973 *Whaling Industry of New London*. Liberty Cap Books, Pennsylvania.

Delano, A. 1817 *A Narrative of Voyages and Travels in the Southern and Northern Hemispheres*. E.G. House, Boston, Massachusetts.

De Leiuen, C. 1998. *The Power of Gender*. Unpublished Honours Thesis, Flinders University of South Australia.

deMarly, D. 1986 *Working Dress: A history of occupational clothing*. Holmes and Meier Publishers, New York.

Dening, G. 1980 *Islands and Beaches: Discourse on a Silent Land*. University of Hawaii Press, Honolulu.

Dickens, R. (ed) 1982 *Archaeology of Urban America: The Search for Pattern and Process*. Academic Press, New York.

Drake–Brockman, H 1949 The Americans Came. *American Quarterly 1*,(1), Spring 1949

Dunbabin, T. 1925 Whalers, Sealers and Buccaneers. *Royal Australian Historical Society Journal* 11(1): 1–32.

Dunbabin, T 1950 New Light on the Earliest American Voyages to Australia. *American Neptune* 10: 52–64.

Durdik, J., Mudra, M. and M. Sada 1981 *Firearms: A collectors guide 1836–1900*. Hamlyn, Sydney.

Egerton–Warburton, G. 1883 *Albany Past and Present*. Typescript, Battye Library.

Egloff, B. 1994 From Swiss Family Robinson to Sir Russell Drysdale: Towards changing the tone of historical archaeology in Australia. *Australian Archaeology* 39: 1-9.

Enderby, C. 1847 *Proposal for Re–establishing the British Southern Whale Fishery*. Wilson, London.

English, A. 1990 Salted meats from the wreck of the *William Salthouse*: archaeological analysis of 19th century butchering patterns. *Australian Journal of Historical Archaeology* 8: 63–69.

Epstein, D and M. Safro 1991 *Buttons*. Thames and Hudson, London.

Erikson, R. 1974 *Old Toodyay and Newcastle*. Toodyay Shire Council.

Erikson, R. 1978 *The Dempsters*. University of Western Australia Press, Perth, Western Australia.

Erikson, R. (ed) 1988 *The Bicentennial Dictionary of Western Australians pre–1829–1888*. (4 Volumes). University of Western Australia Press, Nedlands, Western Australia.

Evans, K. 1993 *Shore–based Whaling in Tasmania: Historical Research Project*. Unpublished report to the Tasmanian Parks and Wildlife Service, Hobart.

Ewers, J. 1971 *The Western Gateway; A History of Fremantle*. University of Western Australia Press, Nedlands, Western Australia.

Eyre, E. 1845 *Journals of expeditions of discovery into Central Australia and overland from Adelaide into King George's Sound*. T&W Boone, London. (Facsimile edition published South Australian State Library 1962).

Fanning, E. 1832 *Voyages and Discoveries in the South Seas 1788–1832*. Marine Research Society, Salem, Mass. (reprinted 1924).

Ferguson, R. 1986 *Rottnest Island History and Architecture*. University of Western Australia Press, Nedlands, Western Australia.

Ferguson, W. 1987 Mokare's Domain. In J. Mulvaney and J.P. White (eds) *Australians to 1788*. Fairfax, Syme & Weldon Associates, Sydney, pp. 120–142

Flinders, M. 1814 *A Voyage to Terra Australis... Prosecuted in the years 1801, 1802 and 1803*. G&W Nicols, London.

Flint, C. and F. Shelley 1990 Structure, Agency, and Context: The Contributions of Geography to World–Systems Analysis. *Sociological Inquiry* 60: 496–508.

Forster, H. 1985 *The South Sea Whaler; An Annotated Bibliography.* Kendall Whaling Museum, Massachusetts

Gara, T. 1983 The Flying Foam Massacre: An incident on the northwest frontier, Western Australia. In M. Smith (ed) *Archaeology at ANZAAS 1983.* Western Australian Museum, Perth. pp 86–94

Garden, D. 1977 *Albany; A Panorama of the Sound from 1827.* Thomas Nelson, Melbourne.

Garden, D. 1978 *Southern Haven; Port of Albany.* Albany Port Authority.

Gardos, A. 2004 *The Historical Archaeology of the Old Farm Strawberry Hill: A rural estate 1827–1889, Albany, Western Australia.* MA Thesis, Dept of Archaeology, University of Western Australia.

Garrett, D. n.d. *Listing of American whalers in W.A. Waters.* Unpublished ms. Department of Maritime Archaeology, Western Australian Museum.

Gatchell, J. 1844 *The Disenthralled; being reminiscences in the life of the author; his fall from respectability by intemperance - and rescue by the Washingtonian Society; containing also his life as a sailor, shipwreck, and residence among the savage tribes in New Holland.* Troy: N. Tuttle.

Gentilli, J. (ed.) 1979 *Western Landscapes.* University of Western Australia Press, Nedlands, Western Australia.

Gibbs, M. 1994 *An Archaeological Conservation and Management Study of 19th Century Shore–Based Whaling Stations in Western Australia.* Unpublished report for the National Trust of Australia, W.A.

Gibbs, M. 1996 *The Historical Archaeology of Shore–Based Whaling in Western Australia 1836–1879.* Unpublished PhD Thesis, University of Western Australia.

Gibbs, M. 1998 Colonial Boats and Foreign Ships: The Historical Archaeology of Shore–Based Whaling in Western Australia 1836–1879. In M. Staniforth and S. Lawrence (eds) *The Archaeology of Whaling and Sealing in Southern Australian and New Zealand.* The Australasian Society for Historical Archaeology, Canberra, pp. 36–47.

Gibbs, M. 2000 Conflict and Commerce – American Whalers and the Western Australian Colonies 1836–1888. *The Great Circle* 22: 3–23

Gibbs, M. 2001 The Archaeology of the Convict System in Western Australia. *Australasian Historical Archaeology* 19: 60–72.

Gibbs, M. 2002 Behavioral models of crisis response as a tool for archaeological interpretation – A case study of the 1629 wreck of the V.O.C. Ship Batavia on the Houtman Abrolhos Islands, Western Australia. In J. Grattan and R. Torrence (Eds) *Natural Disasters, Catastrophism and Cultural Change.* Routledge: New York, pp. 66–86

Gibbs, M. 2002 The Enigma of William Jackman 'The Australian Captive'- Fictional character or shipwreck survivor? *The Great Circle* 24(2):3–21.

Gibbs, M. 2003a Nebinyan's Song – the Aboriginal whalers of South–Western Australia. *Aboriginal History* 27:11–20.

Gibbs, M. 2003b The Archaeology of Crisis: Shipwreck Survivor Camps in Australasia. *Historical Archaeology* 37(1):128–145.

Gibbs, M. 2005 The Archaeology of Subsistence on the Maritime frontier. *Australasian Historical Archaeology* 23:115–122.

Gibbs, M. 2004 Maritime Archaeology in Australia. In T. Murray (Ed), *Archaeology in Australia.* Australian Scholarly Press, Melbourne, pp. 36–54.

Gibson, A. and J. Whitehead 1993 *Yankees in paradise: the Pacific Basin frontier.* University of New Mexico Press.

Gill, J. 1966 Genesis of the Australian Whaling Industry: its development up to 1850. *Royal Historical Society of Queensland* 8 (1): 111–36

Gill, J. 1967 Notes on the sealing industry of early Australia. *Royal Historical Society of Queensland* 8 (2): 218–45.

Glover, R. 1952 *Captain Symers, Trader.* M.A. thesis, University of Western Australia.

Glover, R. 1979 *Plantagenet 'Rich and Beautiful'; A History of the Shire of Plantagenet, Western Australia.* University of Western Australia Press, Nedlands, Western Australia.

Godden, G. 1964 *Encyclopaedia of British Pottery and Porcelain Marks.* Jenkins, London.

Gojak, D. 1998 An historical and archaeological overview of the whaling industry in New South Wales and Norfolk Island. In S. Lawrence and M. Staniforth (eds) *The Archaeology of Whaling and Sealing in Southern Australian and New Zealand.* The Australasian Society for Historical Archaeology, Canberra, pp. 11–20.

Green, J., C. Souter and P. Baker 2001 *Department of Maritime Archaeology Visit to Middle Island, Recherche Archipelago, Esperance, 29 April–4May 2001.* Report–Department of Maritime Archaeology Western Australian Maritime Museum No. 154.

Green, N. 1983 King George Sound: The friendly frontier. In M. Smith (ed) *Archaeology at ANZAAS.* Western Australian Museum, Perth. pp. 68–74.

Green, N. 1984 *Broken Spears: Aboriginals and Europeans in the southwest of Western Australia.* Focus Education Services, Perth.

Green, N. 1989 *The Aborigines of the Albany Region: The Bicentennial Dictionary of Western Australians, Volume 6.* University of Western Australia Press, Nedlands, Western Australia.

Green, S. and S. Perlman (eds) 1985a *The Archaeology of Frontiers and Boundaries.* Academic Press, Sydney.

Green, S. and S. Perlman 1985b Frontiers, Boundaries and Open Social Systems. In S. Green and S. Perlman (eds) *The Archaeology of Frontiers and Boundaries.* Academic Press, Sydney, pp.3–13

Gregory, F. 1850 Survey notebook No. 4. Battye Library, Perth.

Grey, G. 1841 *Journals of Expeditions of Discovery in North–west and Western Australia during the years 1837, 38 and 39.* T & W Boone, London.

Guinness, C. n.d. *All and About Dunsborough*. Dunsborough.

Gurke, K. 1987 *Bricks and Brick making: A handbook for the historical archaeologist*. The University of Idaho Press, Moscow, Idaho.

Hacquebord, L. 1981 The rise and fall of a Dutch whaling settlement on the west coast of Spitsbergen. Pp. 79–132 in Arctic Centre (1981).

Hainsworth, D. 1967a Exploiting the Pacific Frontier: the New South Wales Sealing Industry, 1800–1821. *Journal of Pacific History* 2: 59–75

Hainsworth, D. 1967b Iron Men in Wooden Ships: The Sydney Sealers. *Labour History* 13:19–25.

Haley, N. 1948 *Whalehunt. The Narrative of a Voyage by Nelson Cole Haley, Harpooner in the Ship* Charles W. Morgan, *1849–1853*. Washburn, New York.

Hall, T. 1990 The World–System Perspective: A Small Sample from a Large Universe. *Sociological Inquiry* 60: 440–454.

Halls, C. 1970 Bunbury's Buried Ships. *Port of Fremantle Quarterly* 3 (9): 24–27.

Halls, C. 1974 *Guns in Australia*. Hamlyn, Sydney.

Hardesty, D. 1985 Evolution on the Industrial Frontier. In S. Green and S. Perlman (eds) *The Archaeology of Frontiers and Boundaries*. Academic Press, Sydney, pp. 213–229.

Harris, E. 1979 *The Principles of Archaeological Stratigraphy*. Academic Press. London.

Harris, M. 1983 *Cultural Anthropology*. Harper & Row, Sydney.

Harrison, R. 2002 Archaeology and the colonial encounter: Kimberley spear points, cultural identity and masculinity in the north of Australia. *Journal of Social Archaeology* 2(3): 352–377.

Harrison, R. 2003 *Ngarranggani ngamungamu jalanijarra [Dream time, old time, this time]: 'lost places', recursiveness and hybridity at Old Lamboo pastoral station, southeast Kimberley, Western Australia*. Unpublished PhD thesis, University of Western Australia, Perth.

Hasluck, A. 1955 *Portrait with Background: A Life of Georgiana Molloy*. Melbourne University Press, Melbourne.

Hasluck, A. 1965 *Thomas Peel of Swan River*. Oxford University Press, Melbourne.

Hassell, A.Y. n.d.a *Early Memories of Albany*. Advertiser Print, Albany.

Hassell, C. n.d.b The Hassells of Albany. Unpublished ms. Battye Library.

Heberle, G. 1985 *Heberle Family Salmon Fishing, Doubtful Island Bay 1946–1961*. Online: http://freepages.genealogy.rootsweb.ancestry.com/~gregheberle/AdobePDF/FishVol1/vol1text.pdf. Accessed 25 January 2009.

Hegarty, R. 1964 *Addendum to "Starbuck" and "Whaling Masters"* Free Public Library, New Bedford.

Henderson, D. 1975 Whalers on the coasts of Baja California: Opening the peninsula to the outside world. *Geoscience and Man*. 12:49–56.

Henderson, G 1980 *Unfinished Voyages -Volume 1:1622 –1850*. University of Western Australia Press, Perth.

Henderson, G. 1989 *Unfinished Voyages -Volume 2: 1851–1880*. University of Western Australia Press, Nedlands.

Heppingstone, I. 1966 Bay Whaling in Western Australia *Early Days* 6 (5): 29-41

Heppingstone, I. 1969 American Whalers in Western Australian Waters *Early Days - Journal and Proceedings of the Royal Western Australian Historical Society*. 7 (1) 35–53

Heppingstone, I. 1973 Whaling in Cockburn Sound and Thereabouts. *Early Days* 7 (5): 91–103

Heppingstone, I. n.d.a. Whaling at Port Gregory. Unpublished ms. Battye Library PR7666.

Heppingstone, I. n.d.b. Whaling at Torbay. Unpublished ms, Royal Western Australian Historical Society.

Hicks, D. and M. Beaudry 2006 *The Cambridge Companion to Historical Archaeology* Cambridge University Press, Cambridge.

Hicks, B. 1966 *History of the Americans at Albany*. Unpublished ms. Battye Library.

Higginbotham, E. 1985 Excavation Techniques in Historical Archaeology. *Australasian Journal of Historical Archaeology* 3: 8–14.

Hope, J. 1929 Early Perth: First Town Plan, Former Draftsman's story. *Western Mail* 15 November 1929.

Hunt, W. 1993 Ethnicity and firearms in the Upper Missouri bison–robe trade. *Historical Archaeology* 27(3): 74–101.

Hutchins, B. 1994 *A Survey of the Near shore Reef Fish Fauna of Western Australia's West and South Coasts - The Leeuwin Province*. Records of the Western Australian Museum, Supplement No. 46. Western Australian Museum, Perth.

Hutchins, B. and M. Thompson. 1983 *The Marine and Estuarine Fishes of South–western Australia: A Field Guide for Anglers and Divers*. Western Australian Museum, Perth.

Irwin, F.C. 1835 *The State and Position of Western Australia, Commonly Called the Swan River Settlement*. Simpkin, Marshall & Co., London

Jacomb, C. 1998 Shore whaling sites of Bans Peninsula. In S. Lawrence and M. Staniforth (eds), *The Archaeology of Whaling and Sealing in Southern Australian and New Zealand*. Australasian Society for Historical Archaeology, Sydney, pp. 68–75.

Jarvis, N. 1979 *Western Australia: An atlas of human endeavour 1829–1979*. Govt Printing Office, Perth.

Jeans, D. 1988 World Systems Theory: A theoretical context for Australian Historical Archaeology. In J. Birmingham, D. Bairstow and A. Wilson (eds), *Archaeology and Colonisation: Australia in the World Context*. Australasian Society for Historical Archaeology, Sydney. pp 57–64

Jenner, K., M. Jenner and K. McCabe 2001 Geographical and temporal movements of Humpback whales in Western Australia. *APPEA Journal* 749–765.

Johnson, J. 1979 *Albany and the Whalers*. Albany Tourist Centre, Albany.

Johnson, M. 1996 *An Archaeology of Capitalism*. Blackwell, London.

Jones, A.G.E. 1981 The British Southern Whale and Seal Fisheries. *The Great Circle* 3(1): 20–29 and 3(2): 90–102.

Jones, O. 1989 *The Parks Canada Glass Glossary for the Description of Containers, Tableware, Flat Glass, and Closures.* Studies in Archaeology, Architecture and History. Canadian Parks Service, Quebec.

Kaberry, P. 1939 *Aboriginal woman: sacred and profane.* Routledge, London.

Kelly, D. and V. Richards 1987 Gas chromatographic analysis of fatty material extracted from suspected tryworks samples. In J. MacIlroy *Nineteenth Century Bay Whaling Stations in Western Australia.* Unpublished report for the National Trust of Australia, W.A., pp. 121–126.

Kelly, G. 1958 *A History of the Champion Bay District.* Unpublished M.A. thesis, University of Western Australia.

Kent, S. 1987 *Method and Theory for Activity Area Research.* Columbia University Press, New York.

Keyser E. 1929 Typescripts of reminiscences and cuttings of author's articles in the Albany Advertiser and other newspapers c1929 (newspaper reports of known date referred to as such in text). Battye Library PR 562.

King, J. 2006 Household Archaeology, identity and biographies. In D. Hicks and M. Beaudry (eds) *The Cambridge Companion to Historical Archaeology.* Cambridge University Press, Cambridge. pp. 293–312.

King P. 1827 *Narrative of a Survey of the Intertropical and Western Coasts of Australia performed between the years 1818 and 1822.* John Murray, London.

Kirch, P. 1980 The Archaeological Study of Adaptation: Theoretical and Methodological Issues. *Advances in Archaeological Method and Theory* 3: 101–156.

Klein, T. 1991 Nineteenth Century Ceramics and Models of Consumer Behavior. *Historical Archaeology* 21: 77–91.

Knight, W. 1870 *Census of the Colony of Western Australia, taken on the 31st March, 1870.* W. Knight, Perth, Western Australia.

Kostoglou, P. and J. McCarthy 1991 *Whaling and Sealing Sites in South Australia.* Australian Institute for Maritime Archaeology Special Publication No. 6. Western Australian Museum, Perth.

Krause, C. and C. Mishler 1988 *Standard Catalogue of World Coins.* Krause Publications, Wisconsin.

Langdon, R. (ed.) 1978 *American Whalers and Traders in the Pacific; A Guide to Records on Microfilm.* Pacific Manuscripts Bureau. Research School of Pacific Studies, Canberra.

Lally, J. n.d. *Development of the Port of Bunbury.* Unpublished Thesis, Claremont Teachers College.

Lawrence, S. (ed.) 2003a *Archaeologies of the British: Explorations of identity in Great Britain and its colonies 1600–1945.* Routledge, London.

Lawrence, S. 2003b At home in the bush: Material culture and Australian nationalism. In Lawrence, S. (ed) *Archaeologies of the British: Explorations of identity in Great Britain and its colonies 1600–1945.* Routledge, London, pp. 212–223.

Lawrence, S. 2006 *Whalers and Free Men: Life on Tasmania's colonial whaling stations.* Australian Scholarly Press, Melbourne.

Lawrence, S. and N. Shepherd 2006 Historical Archaeology and Colonialism. In D. Hicks and M. Beaudry (eds) *The Cambridge Companion to Historical Archaeology.* Cambridge University Press, Cambridge, pp. 69–86.

Lawrence, S. and M. Staniforth (eds) 1998 *The Archaeology of Whaling and Sealing in Southern Australian and New Zealand.* The Australasian Society for Historical Archaeology and The Australasian Institute for Maritime Archaeology Special Publication No. 10, Canberra.

Lefroy, G. 1978 *The Shark Bay Story.* Nanga Museum, Shark Bay.

Lennon, J. 1998 Whaling at Wilson's Promontory, Victoria in the 1840s. In S. Lawrence and M. Staniforth (eds), *The Archaeology of Whaling and Sealing in Southern Australian and New Zealand.* The Australasian Society for Historical Archaeology, Canberra, pp. 64–68.

Leone, M. 1988 The Relationship Between Data and the Archaeological Record: 18th–century gardens in Annapolis, Maryland. *Historical Archaeology* 22(1): 29–35.

Leone, M. and C. Crosby 1987 Middle–Range Theory in Historical Archaeology. In Spencer–Wood, S.M (Ed) *Consumer Choice in Historical Archaeology.* Plenum Press, London, pp. 397–410.

Leone, M. and P. Potter (eds) 1988a *The Recovery of Meaning. Historical Archaeology in the Eastern United States.* Smithsonian Institution Press, London.

Leone, M. and P. Potter 1988b Introduction: Issues in Historical Archaeology. In Leone, M. and P. Potter, (eds) *The Recovery of Meaning. Historical Archaeology in the Eastern United States.* Smithsonian Institution Press, London, pp. 1–22

Levitt, S. 1986 *Victorians Unbuttoned: Registered designs for clothing, their makers and manufacturers 1839–1900.* Allen and Unwin, Sydney.

Levy, W. 1947 *American–Australian Relations.* University of Minnesota Press.

Lewis, M. 1945 Naval Buttons Parts 1 and 2. *Mariners Mirror* 31: 56–83, 114–143.

Linge, G.J.R. 1979 *Industrial Awakening: A geography of Australian manufacturing 1788 to 1890.* Australian National University Press, Canberra.

Lilley, I. and M. Gibbs 1993 *An Archaeological Conservation and Management Plan for the Lynton Convict Hiring Depot, Western Australia.* National Trust of Australia (W.A.) for the Australian Heritage Commission.

Little, B. 1969 The sealing and whaling industries in Australia before 1850. *Australian Economic History Review* 9 (2): 109–27

Little, B.J. (ed) 1992 *Text–Aided Archaeology*. CRC Press, London.

Little, B.J. 1994 People with history: An update on historical archaeology in the United States. *Journal of Archaeological Method and Theory* 1: 5–40.

Lockyer, E 1826 *Journal at King George Sound*. ms. Mitchell Library, Sydney.

Lyman, R. 1977 Analysis of historic faunal remains. *Historical Archaeology* 11:67–83

Lyman, R. 1994 Quantitative units and terminology in zooarchaeology. *American Antiquity* 59(1):36–71.

MacIlroy, J 1979 *Dampier Archipelago Historic Sites Survey*. Unpublished report for the Australian Heritage Commission, Canberra.

MacIlroy, J. 1986 Bathers Beach Whaling Station, Fremantle, Western Australia. *Australian Journal of Historical Archaeology* 4: 43–50.

MacIlroy, J 1987 *Nineteenth Century Bay Whaling Stations in Western Australia*. Unpublished report for the National Trust of Australia, W.A.

MacIlroy, J. 1990 *The Excavation and Conservation of a 19th Century Retaining Wall at Bathers Beach, Fremantle, Western Australia*. Unpublished report for the Fremantle City Council, Fremantle.

MacIlroy, J. and S. Kee. 1986 *Bathers Bay Whaling Station, Fremantle: Excavation Report*. Unpublished report for the Fremantle City Council.

MacIlroy, J. and D. Meredith 1984 *Bathers Bay 1984: Report for the Heritage Commission*. Unpublished report for the Fremantle City Council, Fremantle.

Majewski, T and M. O'Brien 1987 The Use and Misuse of Nineteenth Century English and American Ceramics in Archaeological Analysis. *Advances in Archaeological Method and Theory* 11: 97–209.

Maury, J. 1851 *Whale Chart by M.F. Maury, A.M. Lieut. U.S. Navy*. Published at the National Observatory, U.S. Naval Oceanographic Office, (reproduced in colour in Whipple 1979).

Mawer, G. 2000 *Ahab's Trade: The saga of South Seas whaling*. Allen & Unwin, St Leonards.

McBryde, I. 1979 Ethnohistory in the Australian context: Independent discipline or convenient data quarry? *Aboriginal History* 3: 128–151.

McCarthy, J. 1993 *Thistle Island Whaling Station Excavation Report*. Unpublished report by Austral Archaeology for the Department of Environment and Land Management, South Australia.

McCarthy, M. 1983 Ships Fastenings; A preliminary study. *The Bulletin of the Institute for Maritime Archaeology* 7(1): 1–24.

McCarthy, M. 2008 Boundaries and the archaeology of frontier zones. In B. David and J. Thomas (eds) *Handbook of Landscape Archaeology*. California: Left Coast Press, pp. 202–209.

McGaughan, E. 1916 South Coast memories: Voyages of the Grace Darling. *Albany Advertiser* 11/12/1916.

McGowan, A.1985 *Excavations at Lithend, Port Arthur Historic Site*. Port Arthur Conservation and Development Project, National Parks and Wildlife Service, Tasmania.

McKail, N.W. 1927 Walks with Yesterday: Albany Reminiscences No. 1–16. *Western Mail,* 27 January to 21 April, 1927. MS at BL 1393A (c. 1923).

McNab, R. 1913 *The Old Whaling Days: A history of Southern New Zealand from 1830–1840*. Whitcombe and Tombs, Christchurch.

McNiven I. 2001 Torres Strait Islanders and the maritime frontier in early colonial Australia. In L. Russell (ed.) *Colonial Frontiers: Indigenous-European Encounters in Settler Societies*, Studies in Imperialism Series, Manchester University Press, Manchester, pp.175-97.

McVicar, A. 1993 *Home Butchery in Australia: A guide to butchering, processing and preserving*. Gary Allen Pty Ltd, Smithfield, NS.W.

Mead, T. 1961 *Killers of Eden: The killer whales of Twofold Bay*. Angus & Robertson, Sydney.

Meagher, S.J. 1973 *A Reconstruction of the Traditional Life of the Aborigines of the Southwest of Western Australia, being a study of their material culture and the manner in which they utilised their physical environment*. Unpublished M.A. thesis, University of Western Australia.

Melville, H. 1851 *Moby Dick; or, The Whale*. Reprinted 1967 by W.W. Norton and Company, New York.

Merrilees, D. and J. Porter 1979 *Guide to the Identification of Teeth and Some Bones of Native Land Mammals Occurring in the Extreme South West of Western Australia*. Western Australian Museum, Perth.

Micco, H.B. 1971 *King Island and the Sealing Trade, 1802*. Roebuck Society, Canberra.

Miles, P. 1998 Whales and whaling at the Australian National Maritime Museum. In S. Lawrence and M. Staniforth (eds), *The Archaeology of Whaling and Sealing in Southern Australian and New Zealand*. The Australasian Society for Historical Archaeology, Canberra, pp. 79–86.

Miller, G.M. 1980 Classification and Economic Scaling of 19th Century Ceramics. *Historical Archaeology* 14: 1–41.

Miller, G.M. 1991 A Revised Set of CC Index Values for Classification and Economic Scaling of English Ceramics from 1787 to 1880. *Historical Archaeology* 25(1): 1–25.

Mitchell, A. 1927 Years Ago in Bunbury: The whaling days. *Western Mail* 24 March, 1927.

Molloy, J. 1830–40 Typescript of Official letters. Battye Library, Perth.

Moore, G.F. 1884 *Diary of Ten Years of an Early Settler in Western Australia*. M. Walbrook, London. Facsimile Edition, University of Western Australia Press, Nedlands, W.A. (1978).

Moore, J. 1985 Forager/farmer Interactions: Information, Social Organisation and the Frontier. In S. Green and S. Perlman (eds) *The Archaeology of Frontiers and Boundaries*. Academic Press, Sydney, pp. 93–112.

Morison, M. and J. White (eds) 1979 *Western Towns and Buildings*. University of Western Australia Press, Nedlands, W.A.

Morton, H. 1982 *The Whale's Wake.* University of Otago Press, Dunedin.

Moynihan, J. 1988 *All The News In A Flash: Rottnest Communications 1829–1979.* Institution of Engineers Australia, University of Western Australia Press, Nedlands.

Müller, H. 1980 *Guns, Pistols, Revolvers. Hand-firearms from the 14th to the 19th centuries.* Orbis Publishing, London.

Mulvaney, J. and J. White (eds) 1987 *Australians to 1788.* Fairfax, Syme & Weldon Associates, Sydney.

Murray, T. 1985 Historical Archaeology Losing Its Way? Bairstow at the theoretical crossroads. *Australian Archaeology* 20: 121–131.

Murray, T. (ed) 2004 The Archaeology of Contact in Settler Societies. Cambridge University Press, Cambridge.

Murray, T. and Allen, J. 1986 Theory and the Development of Historical Archaeology in Australia. *Archaeology in Oceania* 21:85–93.

Nairn–Clarke, W. 1842 Remarks respecting the islands on the coast of S.W. Australia. *Inquirer* 10/9/1842, 8/10/1842.

Nash, M. 2003 *The Bay Whalers: Tasmania's shore-based whaling industry.* Navarine Publishing, Hobart.

Nolan, J. 1992 *Locating and Digging Antique Bottles in Australia..* Crown Castleton, Victoria.

O'Connor R, Quartermaine G. and C. Bodney. 1989 *Report on an Investigation into Aboriginal Significance of Wetlands and River in the Perth–Bunbury Region.* Western Australian Water Resources Council.

Ogle, N. 1839 *The Colony of Western Australia; A manual for Emigrants 1839.* James Fraser, Regent Street, London.

Oldham, R and J. 1968 *Western Heritage: A study of the colonial architecture of Perth, W.A.* Lamb printing, Perth.

O'May, H. 1957 *Wooden Hookers of Hobart Town and Whalers out of Van Diemen's Land.* Government Printers, Hobart.

Orser, C. 1988 *The Material Basis of the Postbellum Tenant Plantation; Historical archaeology in the South Carolina Piedmont.* University of Georgia Press, London.

Orser, C. 1996 *A Historical Archaeology of the Modern World.* Plenum Press, New York.

Oswald, A. 1975 *Clay Pipes for the Archaeologist.* British Archaeological Reports Number 14, Oxford.

Paynter, R. 1988 Steps to an Archaeology of Capitalism: Material change and class analysis. In Leone, M. and P. Potter, (eds) *The Recovery of Meaning. Historical Archaeology in the Eastern United States.* Smithsonian Institution Press, London, pp. 407–433.

Pearson, M. 1981 *Seen Through Different Eyes: Changing land use and settlement patterns in the Macquarie River region of New South Wales, from prehistoric times to 1860.* Unpublished Ph.D. thesis, Dept. of Prehistory, Australian National University.

Pearson, M. 1983 The Technology of Whaling in Australian Waters in the 19th Century. *Australian Journal of Historical Archaeology* 1: 40–54.

Pearson, M. 1984 *Report on the Historical Archaeological Resource of the Arthur Head area.* Unpublished report to the City of Fremantle. Centre for Prehistory, University of Western Australia.

Pearson, M. 1985 Shore–based Whaling at Twofold Bay: One Hundred Years of Enterprise. *Journal of the Royal Australian Historical Society* 71: 3–27.

Pearson, M. 1988 *The Archipelago of the Recherche; Historical and Archaeological Reconnaissance.* Unpublished report to the Dept. of Conservation and Land Management, Perth.

Pearson, S. 1988 *Building Materials Analysis, First Government House, Sydney.* Heritage Resource Services, ANUtech, for Dept of Planning , N.S.W.

Peregrine, P. N. 1990 Archaeology and World–Systems Theory *Sociological Inquiry* 60: 486–495.

Piper, A. 1990 Can taphonomy aid in the analysis of faunal material from historic archaeological sites? In S. Solomon, Davidson, I and D. Watson (eds) *Tempus 2: Problem Solving in Taphonomy:* University of New England, Armidale, N.S.W., pp. 149–157.

Potter, P. 1992 Middle–Range Theory, Ceramics and Capitalism in 19th Century Rockbridge County, Virginia. In B. Little (ed) *Text–Aided Archaeology.* CRC Press, London, pp. 9–23.

Prickett, N. 1981 *The Archaeology of a Military Frontier, Taranaki, New Zealand, 1860–1881.* Unpublished Ph.D. thesis, University of Auckland, New Zealand.

Prickett, N. 1983 An Archaeological Reconnaissance of the Shore Whaling Industry on Kapiti Island, New Zealand. *Records of the Auckland Institute and Museum* 20: 41–63.

Prickett, N. 1993 The Tasmanian Origins of New Zealand Shore Whaling. *Archaeology in New Zealand* 36(4): 190–204.

Prickett, N. 1998 The New Zealand Shore Whaling Industry. In M. Staniforth and S. Lawrence (eds) *The Archaeology of Whaling and Sealing in Southern Australian and New Zealand.* The Australasian Society for Historical Archaeology, Canberra, pp. 48–54.

Prickett, N. 2002 *The Archaeology of New Zealand Shore Whaling.* Wellington: New Zealand Department of Conservation.

Quinlan, M. 1992 Making Labour Laws Fit for the Colonies: The introduction of laws regulating whalers in three Australian colonies 1835–1855. *Labour History* 62: 19–37

Quinlan, M., M. Gardner, and P. Akers 2003 Reconsidering the collective impulse: formal organization and informal associations among workers in the Australian colonies, 1795–1850. *Labour/Le Travail* 52 (Sept 2003). Online journal [http://www.historycooperative.org/journals/llt/52/quinlan.html] Accessed 12 Dec. 2007.

Quirk, K. 2007 The Victorians in 'Paradise': Gentility as social strategy in the archaeology of colonial Australia. PhD thesis, University of Queensland.

Raab, L.M. and A.C. Goodyear. 1984 Middle–Range Theory in Archaeology: A critical review of origins and application. *American Antiquity* 49(2): 255–268)

Reece R. and R. Pascoe 1983 *A Place of Consequence: A pictorial history of Fremantle.* Fremantle Arts Centre Press, Fremantle.

Reitz, E. and C. Scarry 1985 *Reconstructing Historic Subsistence With An Example From Sixteenth–Century Spanish Florida.* Special Publication Series No. 3, Society for Historical Archaeology.

Reynolds, H. 1982 *The Other Side of the Frontier.* Penguin Books, Victoria.

Richards, R. 1991 The Cruise of the *Kingston* and *Elligood* in 1800 and the Wreck Found On King Island in 1802. *The Great Circle* 13 (1): 35–53.

Ridgeway, S. and R. Harrison 1985a *Handbook of Marine Mammals. Volume 3: The Sirenians and Baleen Whales.* Academic Press, Sydney.

Ridgeway, S. and R. Harrison 1985b *Handbook of Marine Mammals Volume 4: River Dolphins and the Larger Toothed Whales.* Academic Press, Sydney.

Rintoul, J. 1964 *Esperance Yesterday and Today.* Service Printing Company, Perth.

Ritchie, N. 1986 *Archaeology and the History of the Chinese in Southern New Zealand during the Nineteenth Century: A study of acculturation, adaptation and change.* Ph.D. thesis, Anthropology Department, University of Otago, New Zealand.

Ritchie, N. 1987 Chinese Coins Down Under: Their role on the New Zealand goldfields. *Australian Journal of Historical Archaeology* 5:41–48.

Rockman, M. 2003 Knowledge and Learning in the Archaeology of Colonization. In Rockman M. and J. Steele (eds) *Colonization of Unfamiliar Landscapes: The archaeology of adaptation.* Routledge, London, pp. 3–24.

Rodrigues J. and R. Anderson 2006 *Pakington Whaling Station.* Dept. of Maritime Archaeology, Western Australian Museum, Report No. 214.

Roe, J. 1854 Port Gregory – Surveyed by Lieutenant Roe, R.N. 1854. Battye Library, Perth.

Roycroft, R. and C. Roycroft 1976 *Australian Bottle Price Guide.* Reliance Printing, Deniliquin.

Roycroft, R. and C. Roycroft 1977 *Australian Bottle Price Guide - Volume 2.* Reliance Press, Deniliquin.

Russell, L. 2007 'Dirty Domestics and Worse Cooks': Aboriginal women's agency and domestic frontiers, Southern Australia, 1800–1850. *Frontiers* 28: 18–46.

Sale, Capt. J. 1936 'Albany Memories' *West Australian* 7/3/1936. Manuscript at BL Acc. 2301A.

Schiffer, M. 1972 Archaeological context and systemic context. *American Antiquity* 37:156–165.

Schiffer, M. 1977 Toward a unified science of the cultural past. In South (ed) 1977b *Research Strategies in Historical Archaeology.* Academic Press, London, pp 13–40.

Schmid, E. 1972 *Atlas of Animal Bones.* Elsevier Publishing Company, London.

Schmidt, P. and S. Mrozowski 1988 Documentary insights into the archaeology of smuggling. In M. Beaudry *Documentary Archaeology in the New World.* Cambridge University Press, Cambridge., pp.32–42.

Schuyler, R. 1977 The Spoken Word, the Written Word, Observed Behaviour and Preserved Behaviour: the Contexts Available to the Archaeologist. *The Conference on Historic Site Archaeology Papers 1975* 10:99–120.

Schuyler, R. (ed) 1978 *Historical Archaeology: A Guide to Substantive and Theoretical Contributions.* Baywood Publishing, New York.

Scott, D. and Fox, R. 1987 *Archaeological Insights into the Custer Battle: An assessment of the 1984 field season.* University of Oklahoma Press, London.

Sears 1906 *The Great Price Maker: Sears, Roebuck & Co. Catalogue No. 116, 1906.* Reprinted by Castle Books, New Jersey (n.d.).

Serventy, V. 1953 The Archipelago of the Recherche, part 4: Mammals. *Australian Geographical Society.* Report no.1 (4).

Seymour, F. n.d. Castle Rock diary of Frederick William Seymour. Unpublished manuscript, Battye Library Acc. 2838A/2.

Shann, E. 1926 *Cattle Chosen: The story of the first group settlement in Western Australia 1829–1841.* Oxford University Press.

Sharp, L. 1952 Steel axes for stone age Australians. In Spicer, E. (ed.), *Human problems in technological change: A casebook.* Russell Sage Foundation, New York, pp. 69–90.

Shaw, B. 1979 The Evolution of Fremantle. In J. Gentilli (ed) *Western Landscapes.* University of Western Australia Press, Nedlands, pp. 329–345.

Shaw, L. 1991 Gunning for whales: A brief outline of the development of harpoon guns. *The Great Circle* 13 (2): 111–118.

Sherratt, T.B. 1836 *Ledger kept by Thomas Brooker Sherratt 1835–1836.* Draft typescript by A. Wolfe, 1997. Albany Public History Collection Acc. 10M.

Shoemaker, N. 2005 Whale Meat in American History. *Environmental History* 10(2): 269–294.

Sichel, M. 1978 *Costume Reference 6 - The Victorians.* Batsford, London.

Sinclair, K. and W. Harrex 1978 *Looking Back; A Photographic History of New Zealand.* Oxford University Press, Wellington.

Smith, C. (Ed) 1993 *A Collectors Guide to Popular Antiques.* Colour Library Books, Surrey.

Smith, G. 1973 *A Guide to the Coastal Flora of South–Western Australia.* Handbook No. 10, Western Australian Naturalists' Club, Perth.

Smith, G.T. 1977 The Birds of Bald Island. *Western Australian Naturalist* 14(1): 17–19.

Solomon, S., Davidson, I and D. Watson (eds) 1990 *Tempus 2: Problem Solving in Taphonomy.* University of New England, Armidale, N.S.W.

South, S. 1977a *Method and Theory in Historical Archaeology.* Academic Press, London.

South, S. (Ed) 1977b *Research Strategies in Historical Archaeology.* Academic Press, London.

South, S. 1988 Whither Pattern? *Historical Archaeology* 22(1): 25–28.

Spencer, R. n.d. The Letters of Sir Richard Spencer (1833–40). Typescript held by Albany Historical Society

Spencer–Wood, S. and S. Heberling 1987 Consumer Choices in White Ceramics: A comparison of eleven early nineteenth century sites. In Spencer–Wood, S. (Ed) *Consumer Choice in Historical Archaeology.* Plenum Press, London, pp. 55–84.

Stackpole, E.A. 1953 *The Sea Hunters: New England Whalemen.* Greenwood Press, Westpoint.

Staniforth, M. 1987 The casks from the wreck of the *William Salthouse*. *The Australian Journal of Historical Archaeology* 5: 21–28.

Staniforth, M., S. Briggs, & C. Lewczak 2001 Archaeology unearthing the invisible people: European women and children and Aboriginal people at South Australian shore–based whaling stations. *Mains'l Haul* 36 (3): 12–19.

Stannage, T. (ed.) 1981a *A New History of Western Australia.* University of Western Australia Press, Nedlands, Western Australia.

Stannage, T. (ed) 1981b *Convictism in Western Australia. Studies in Western Australian History IV.* University of Western Australia Press, Nedlands.

Starbuck, A 1878 *History of the American Whale Fishery from its earliest inception to the year 1876.* (2 Volumes) U.S. Fish and Wildlife Service, Govt. Printer, Washington.

Statham, P. 1980 *Economic Development of the Swan River Colony; 1829–1850.* Unpublished Ph.D. thesis, University of Western Australia.

Statham, P. 1981a Swan River Colony 1829–1850. In T. Stannage (ed) *A New History of Western Australia.* University of Western Australia Press, Nedlands. pp. 181–210.

Statham, P. 1981b Why Convicts I & II. In T. Stannage (ed) *Convictism in Western Australia. Studies in Western Australian History IV.* University of Western Australia Press, Nedlands, pp. 1–18.

Statham–Drew, P. 2003 *James Stirling: Admiral and Founding Governor of Western Australia.* Nedlands: University of Western Australia Press.

Steffen, J. 1980 *Comparative Frontiers.* University of Oklahoma Press, Norman.

Stelle, L.J. 2001 *An Archaeological Guide to the Historic Artefacts of the Upper Sangamon Basin.* Parkland College, Illinois. (http://virtual.parkland.edu/lstelle1/len/archguide/documents/arcguide.htm) accessed 6 March 2009.

Stephens, R. 1951 Builders of Albany: George McCartney Cheyne. *Early Days - Journal and Proceedings of the Royal Western Australian Historical Society* 4 (3): 38–51.

Stephens, R. 1963 Thomas Booker Sherratt: Albany merchant, bay–whaler, ship–owner and self-appointed builder and lay reader of Albany's Octagon Church. *Early Days: Journal and Proceedings of the Royal Western Australian Historical Society* 6 (2): 49–67.

Stirling, J. 1827 Captain James Stirling to Governor Darling. Report on a visit to West Australia, 18/4/1827. HRA Series 1, Volume XII: 551–584.

Stirling, J. 1837a 'Extract of a Despatch from Governor James Stirling to Lord Glenelg, dated Western Australia, Perth, 15 October 1837, enclosing Statistical Report upon the colony of Western Australia'. BPP Colonies - Australia 5:233–256.

Stirling, J. 1837b Copy of a despatch from the Governor of Western Australia to Lord Glenelg, 3 December 1837. BPP Colonies-Australia 5: 257–267.

Stirling, J. 1837c Copy of a statistical report which accompanied Sir James Stirling's Despatch of 15 October 1837. BPP Colonies - Australia 5: 268–284.

Stirling J. 1838 J. Stirling to Right Honourable Lord Glenelg. C.O. 20/317: 3/12/1838, #41.

Stodart, E. and I. Parer 1988 *Colonisation of Australia by the Rabbit.* Project Report No. 6. C.S.I.R.O. Australia, Canberra.

Storr, G.M. 1965 Notes on Bald Island and the adjacent Mainland. *Western Australian Naturalist* 9(3): 187–196.

Suckling, A.J. n.d. *The History of the Northampton District.* Teachers Higher Certificate Thesis, Claremont Teachers College (copy held in Battye Library, Perth).

Torrence R. & A. Clarke 2000a Negotiating Difference.. In Torrence R. & A. Clarke (eds) *The Archaeology of Difference: Negotiating cross–cultural engagements in Oceania,* One World Archaeology 38, Routledge, London, pp. 1–31.

Tower, W.S. 1907 *A History of the American Whale Fishery University of Pennsylvania.* Series in political economy and public Law, No. 20. University of Pennsylvania, Pennsylvania.

Townrow, K. n.d. *An Archaeological Survey of Sealing and Whaling Sites in Victoria.* Unpublished manuscript, Victoria Archaeological Survey, Victoria.

Townsend, C.E. 1935 The Distribution of certain whales as shown by log book records of American whaleships. *Zoologica* 19 (1): 3–50.

Trotter, M. and B. McCulloch 1989 *Unearthing New Zealand.* G.P. Rooke, Wellington.

Tuck, J.A. and Grenier, R. 1981 A sixteenth–century Basque whaling station in Labrador. *Scientific American* 245: 125–136.

Turner, T. 1956 *The Turners of Augusta.* Paterson Brokensha, Perth.

Uren, M. 1948 *Land Looking West; The Story of James Stirling in Western Australia.* Oxford University Press, London.

Vamplew W. (ed) 1987 *Australians; Historical Statistics.* Fairfax, Syme & Weldon Associates, Sydney.

Vancouver, G. 1798 *Voyage of Discovery in the North Pacific Ocean...* Robinson, London.

Vinnicombe, P. 1987 *Dampier Archipelago Project. Resource document, survey and salvage of Aboriginal sites, Burrup Peninsula.* Report for Woodside Offshore Petroleum Pty Ltd., Western Australian Museum, Perth.

Wace, N. and B. Lovett, 1973 *Yankee Maritime Activities and the Early History of Australia.* Research School of Pacific Studies, Australian National University, Canberra.

Wallerstein, I. 1974 *The Modern World–System.* Academic Press, New York.

Walters, I. 1984 Gone to the Dogs: A study of bone attrition at a central Australian campsite. *Mankind* 14(5): 389–400.

Webb, E. 1963 *An Outline of the History of Two People's Bay.* Unpublished ms. (AHS/74m/3), Albany Historical Society, Albany

Weeks, W. 2006 American Expansion 1815–60. In R. Schulzinger (Ed) *A Companion to American Foreign Relations.* Wiley–Blackwell, pp. 64–78.

Weld, F. 1872 Visit to the Northwest coast in HMS Cossack. *Votes and Proceedings of the Legislative Council of Western Australia, 1872*; Paper no. 13. Western Australian Government Printers, Perth.

Wells, F. and C. Bryce 1985 *Seashells of Western Australia.* Western Australian Museum, Perth.

Wesley, C. 1979 A survey of the W.L. Crowther Library. *The Great Circle* 1 (2): 44–59.

Whipple, A. (ed) 1979 *The Whalers.* Time–Life Books, Amsterdam.

White, I. 1980 The Birth and Death of a Ceremony. *Aboriginal History* 4: 33–42.

White, J. 1979 Buildings in Western Australia 1829–1850. In Morison, M. and J. White (eds), *Western Towns and Buildings.* University of Western Australia Press, Nedlands, W.A., pp. 74–89

Whitecar, W. 1860 *Four Years Aboard the Whaleship embracing cruises in the Pacific, Atlantic, Indian and Antarctic Oceans in the Years 1855, '6, '7, '8, '9.* J & B Lippincott & Co. Philadelphia.

Whittemore, J. 1992 *The Book of Buttons.* Houghton Mifflin, New York.

Wilkie, L. 2006 Documentary Archaeology. In D. Hicks and M. Beaudry (eds) *The Cambridge Companion to Historical Archaeology.* Cambridge University Press, Cambridge, pp.13–33.

Williams–Mitchell, C. 1982 *Dressed for the Job: The story of occupational costume.* Blandford Press, Poole.

Wilson G. and A. Kelly 1987 *Preliminary Analysis of Clay Tobacco pipes for the First Government House Site, Sydney.* Report to the Department of Planning, N.S.W..

Winn, H. and N. Reichly, 1985 Humpback Whale. In S. Ridgway and R. Harrison (eds) *Handbook of Marine Mammals. Volume 3: The Sirenians and Baleen Whales.* Academic Press, Sydney, pp. 241–273.

Wolfe, A. 1994 *The Albany Maritime Heritage Survey 1627–1994*, Report to the Heritage Council of Western Australia, Albany Port Authority & Albany Maritime Heritage Association.

Wolfe, A. 2003 *A Cruel Business: A history of the whaling industry at Albany, Western Australia.* M.A. Thesis, University of Western Australia.

Wollaston, J.R. 1991 *The Wollaston Journals: Volume One, 1840–1842.* G. Bolton and H. Vose (Eds), University of Western Australia Press, Nedlands, Western Australia.

Wood, W. 1990 Ethnohistory and Historical Method. *Archaeological Method and Theory* 2:81–109

Woods, P. 1980 *Coastal Management in Western Australia.* Dept of Conservation and Environment Bulletin No. 49, Perth.

Wurst, L. 2006 A class all its own: Explorations of class formation and conflict. In M. Hall and S. Silliman (eds) *Historical Archaeology.* Blackwell, Oxford, pp. 191–206.

Yarrow, S. and L. Batchelor 1979 *Every Name Tells a Story: The origins of major town names in Western Australia.* Regency Publications, Perth.

Yentsch, A. 1991 The Symbolic Divisions of Pottery: Sex–related attributes of English and Anglo–American household pots. In R. McGuire and R. Paynter (eds) *The Archaeology of Inequality.* Blackwell, Oxford, pp. 192–230.

VanderVeen, J. 2007 People, pots, and prosperity: the ceramic value index and an assumption of economic class. Proc. Indiana Academy of Science, Dec.2007.Online at:
[http://www.thefreelibrary.com/Proceedings+of+the+Indiana+Academy+of+Science-p2254] Accessed 21 April 2009.

www.ingramcontent.com/pod-product-compliance
Lightning Source LLC
Chambersburg PA
CBHW040508240426
43662CB00051B/2467